Social Episodes

the study of interaction routines

European Monographs in Social Psychology

Series Editor: HENRI TAJFEL

In preparation

EUROPEAN MONOGRAPHS IN SOCIAL PSYCHOLOGY 17
Series Editor: HENRI TAJFEL

Social Episodes

the study of interaction routines

JOSEPH P. FORGAS
*University of Oxford
and University of New South Wales*

1979

Published in cooperation with
EUROPEAN ASSOCIATION OF EXPERIMENTAL
SOCIAL PSYCHOLOGY
by
ACADEMIC PRESS
London   New York   Toronto   Sydney   San Francisco
A Subsidiary of Harcourt Brace Jovanovich, Publishers

ACADEMIC PRESS INC. (LONDON) LTD.
24/28 Oval Road
London NW1

United States Edition published by
ACADEMIC PRESS INC.
111 Fifth Avenue
New York, New York 10003

British Library Cataloguing in Publication Data
Forgas, Joseph P
  Social episodes.
  1. Social interaction—Research
  I. Title
  301.11'07'2   HM291   79–40925

  ISBN 0–12–263550 7

PRINTED AND BOUND IN ENGLAND BY
W & J MACKAY LIMITED
CHATHAM

Preface

Preface-writing is a most satisfying, yet anxious task in the course of producing a book. Satisfying, since it is usually the last job to be done, and anxious because it is the first section encountered by the reader, which often determines whether he/she will want to go any further.

The topic of this book is the emerging interest of social psychologists in the study of natural interaction sequences, or social episodes. Social episodes are typical, recurring interaction routines within a cultural milieu which we perform with automatic skill many times in our lives: going to see a doctor, a dinner party, academic colloquia, an intimate conversation with your spouse or lectures are examples of such routine episodes. Much of everyday interaction consists of the cooperative acting-out of such episode scripts—yet, surprisingly, social psychologists have shown little interest in the study of such interaction routines until recently. While analyses of interaction situations can be found throughout history, from the writings of Plato through Macchiavelli to Goffman, it is only in the past few years that the tools of *empirical* social psychology have been brought to bear on this problem. For too long, social psychologists have shied away from the study of complex interaction episodes, firstly, because no adequate descriptive methods to study them were available, and secondly, because too much of their interest was taken up with the study of one single episode, that which was created in the laboratory by themselves.

The ferment that characterized social psychology in the seventies, as evidenced by notable contributions in the present series, was a necessary prerequisite for the empirical study of social episodes to become possible. I have tried in this book to merge the unique methodological and statistical sophistication that social psychologists have achieved in the past decades with the freshness of some of the recent ideas affecting the discipline, to try to propose a new approach to the study of natural interaction episodes. In doing so, I have attempted to draw on both lines of social psychology's dual heritage: psychology and sociology. In both of these disciplines, interest in the study of natural interaction episodes has a long and distinguished history. I feel that it is absolutely essential that we anchor the concept of social episodes in that history, in order to establish the continuity between the present approach and that of numerous foregoing contributions. The first few chapters are thus devoted to discussing the background and origins of the study of social episodes.

The book also contains a methodological chapter, describing four influential research strategies which are applicable to the study of social episodes. New techniques, such as multidimensional scaling (MDS) have a particularly important role to play in such research. Scientific methodology and research on everyday interaction routines are by no means antithetical as commonly assumed, and it is of major importance that the applicability of well-tried empirical techniques to the study of social episodes should be established right from the start.

Numerous empirical studies on how social episodes are cognitively represented, identified and performed are summarized in the second half of the book, many of them original studies carried out by us. This material has implications far beyond the boundaries of social psychology proper. Personality theorists, clinical psychologists and other applied psychologists routinely deal with cognitive representations of social episodes, without having a reliable means of quantifying such episode domains. Many clinical techniques are also based on the manipulation of episode-definition competencies, something which is done without the benefit of relevant quantitative measures. The applicability of some of the techniques described here to areas of applied psychology are considered in some detail in Chapter 9.

The book was in fact completed in two different countries, more than ten thousand miles apart. About half of the manuscript was prepared while I was at the University of Oxford, England, and I must acknowledge my deep gratitude to many people there who have played an essential part in the generation of the ideas presented here. Michael Argyle and Rom Harre are the two foremost. My contacts and numerous discussions with Michael were a great help, and his advice and comments were always appreciated. Rom Harre has probably had a greater influence on me than he ever realized. His book with Paul Secord played the role of a catalyst in the generation of some of my ideas, and his seminars and talks during 1975 and 1976 were a further important influence, although I disagree with some of his propositions, as will transpire later. Peter Warr, of the University of Sheffield has seen some of the studies presented in Chapters 7 and 8 in their early stages, and his comments were most helpful. Gerry Ginsburg, on sabbatical at Oxford from the University of Nevada, Reno, was a most helpful and friendly influence during his stay in 1976.

The second part of the manuscript was completed in Sydney, Australia, at the University of New South Wales. It was not easy to work on the book and to keep up with my teaching commitments at a new institution. It was made much easier by understanding, help and suggestions from Laurie Brown, and by the resources made available by the Australian Research Grants Commission towards the later parts of the project. Financial assistance from the Light Foundation, St. Catherine's College, Oxford, and the German Academic Exchange Service (DAAD) at earlier stages were also most important. Louise Kahabka has typed the manuscript with great skill and speed and her contribution went well beyond that, to include grammatical as well as stylistic corrections. Susan Morris helped with the proofs and the subject index.

By the curious logic of preface writing, one always mentions the most important, and intimate, helpers last. I could not begin to enumerate the ways in which my wife Letitia has helped me. Besides moral support, understanding and love, which one all too easily takes for granted, she has done an immense amount of work on proof reading the manuscript several times over, correcting my clumsy sentences (but don't blame her if there are still such to be found on these pages), and collating and organizing the references. My gratitude is also due to my parents. I should acknowledge their gentle (and not so gentle) prodding when I didn't do as well in primary school as they thought I should. Perhaps I should also mention the role of our cat, Pudernyak, who kept me amused during the inevitable breaks in writing on long, sunny Sydney mornings.

Needless to say, none of the above mentioned persons or institutions are in any way responsible for the content or the form of this book, except, perhaps, the cat.

Sydney
August, 1979   JOSEPH FORGAS

To Teeshie

Contents

1

Introduction

Much of our normal everyday behaviour is neatly organized into recurring routines. Getting up in the morning, having breakfast, chatting with an acquaintance on the street or going to see a doctor are all episodes which occur with predictable regularity in our lives. Episodes such as these are so typical that little more than a summary label is needed to recall and define the kinds of behaviours which they entail. Some of these episodes are pleasant ones, others are not; some we look forward to with expectation, others with anxiety. The way we perceive and cognitively represent these episodes says something interesting about us as individuals and the values and customs of our social environment. Yet you would search in vain in textbooks of social psychology for research on the perception of these simple everyday routines: quantitative research into social episodes was practically non-existent until a very few years ago.

In recent years, critics of the variable-manipulating type of experimental social psychology have become increasingly vocal, demanding that more attention be paid to social behaviour as it occurs in everyday life, as against the sometimes absurd manipulations introduced in the laboratory. Many of these critics have provided well-argued and convincing reasons why naturalistic social behaviour, occurring within the framework of routines such as the ones mentioned above, should take pride of place in research. Yet these exhortations have, on the whole, resulted in little change in the kind of work that is carried out in social psychology laboratories, and is published by social psychology journals. Is this reluctance to change due to the academic community's alleged conservatism, or is it caused by some other reason? It seems likely that studies of social episodes have been relatively rare because of the lack of acceptable empirical methodologies.

The aim of this book is to propose a new definition of social episodes as cognitive representations of typical interaction sequences, and to present a first survey and synthesis of this increasingly important area in social psychology. In particular, recent innovative applications of multidimensional scaling (MDS) techniques to the study of social episodes opened up new possibilities for empirical research, and will be discussed in some detail here (Forgas, 1976a, 1978a,b, 1979a,b).

Interest in naturalistic interaction sequences is thus one of the major themes of social psychology in the seventies. Numerous criticisms of laboratory social psychology in the past decade resulted in the emergence of half a dozen or so new orientations. Some of these relied on research strategies borrowed from other disciplines, such as linguistics, social anthropology and ethology; the methodologies used were also widely different and eclectic. It is argued here that the single common denominator of these new strategies is their shared concern with everyday interactions, or "episodes". The best of this work has managed to merge the methodological sophistication of traditional social psychology with the conceptual originality and freshness of the new ideas affecting the discipline. Another noticeable trend in social psychology in recent years has been the growing interest in problems of social cognition (Carroll and Payne, 1976), and in particular, the study of cognitive representations of everyday social reality. The emerging study of social episodes is closely related to these developments. This book seeks to fill a gap in the academic textbooks of social psychology available today, by presenting a summary and synthesis of the background, theories and recent research conceived within the framework of this new area of social psychology. Social episodes as a term is central to this orientation, and will be used as a basic integrative concept in the book.

The psychological and sociological traditions in social psychology

The study of social episodes can also be viewed as an important development in the recent rapprochement of those two alternative branches of social psychology, the psychological and the social. This bifurcation of the discipline has deep historical roots. McDougall's textbook published in 1908 is the first example of an explicitly psychological approach to social behaviour, even though many of his propositions are long forgotten today. His basic approach, which centres on the individual, and seeks to explain his social behaviour in terms of individual characteristics, is still with us today. Allport's influential definition of social psychology as the study of how the feelings, thoughts and behaviour of the individual are influenced by the actual, imagined or implied presence of others (Allport, 1924) has further helped to enshrine the principle that social psychology is the study of the individual's behaviour as it is affected by others. More recent textbooks can be even more categorical in this respect. Thus, Berkowitz (1975) simply states that social psychology is a study of individuals' reactions to social stimuli. By focusing on the individual, to the relative exclusion of broader and more general social and group forces, psychological social psychology has been notably successful in adapting the quantitative, experimental method of psychology to the study of social behaviour. The price of this achievement has been a sacrifice of social relevance, and a relative ignorance of more complex and general social processes which are not easily recreated in the laboratory.

Yet the sociological approach to social psychology is at least as old as the psychological. The early works of Le Bon and Tarde, and Ross's textbook of social psychology which appeared in the same year as McDougall's, are excellent examples of this sociological approach. Instead of focusing on the individual and his characteristics, sociologically-oriented social psychology sought to understand how external, societal forces come to influence social behaviour. In a sense, the roots of sociological social psychology go even deeper than that, and reach back to the cultural sociology of Max Weber, who, more than any of the other grand theorists in the 19th century, was interested in how an individual's attitudes, beliefs and motivations come to determine his society, and how, in turn, ideologies and beliefs in a culture shape individual behaviour. The work of W. I. Thomas and his famous dictum that if people define situations as real they are real in their consequences further illustrates the sociological perspective on social psychology, with its emphasis on the individual's experience of society as an important determinant of social behaviour. More recently, writers such as Goffman, Lyman and Scott, and Garfinkel have contributed to the development of a social psychology which has more in common with the methods and traditions of sociology than with that of psychology.

For too long, these two traditions have evolved in isolation, without much contact and interpenetration, even though the subject matter they sought to study was the same. One of the most promising developments in the seventies is that this bifurcation of the discipline has finally been recognized, and increasing numbers of social psychologists on both sides of the fence seek to learn about the achievements of the other side. Although the divide is not just one of approach, but more fundamentally, one of methodology, there have been some fruitful attempts to fuse the perspective offered by sociological social psychology with the more developed methodological armoury of psychological social psychology. It is in this area that social episodes and their study are of interest, since they offer a unique opportunity for applying quantitative, empirical methodology to the study of phenomena hitherto only subjected to descriptive, journalistic analysis.

But there is another way in which the psychological and the sociological approaches to the study of social behaviour can meet halfway in the analysis of social episodes. As mentioned before, the psychological tradition is characterized, above all, by its emphasis on the individual as the focus of analysis. The sociological approach, in contrast, seeks to understand processes which may be broadly described as situational and external to the acting individual. The concept of social episodes straddles this divide. On the one hand, social episodes are socio-cultural units, already established and existing social routines within a defined milieu, and in this sense, they are situational, external to the individual and most appropriately studied using an essentially sociological approach. On the other hand, social episodes are predictors of behaviour only to the extent that individuals are aware of them, and consensual episode definitions will inevitably be modified as a function of the idiosyncratic characteristics of the individuals enacting them. In this sense, a psychological approach, concentrating on individual perceptions, interpretations and performance of social episodes would appear to be the most promising strategy. In either case, the concept of social episodes calls for an integrated, socio-psychological perspective on social behaviour, incorporating both individual and situational variables and both the psychological and the sociological traditions in social psychology.

Situationism in the social sciences

Concern with situations and episodes as valid objects of study has been evident in many areas of social science in recent years, such as personality theory, sociology and social psychology. The emerging research on social episodes is also rooted in recent developments in these disciplines.

In personality theory, the shortcomings of purely trait-based conceptualizations of human behaviour (Vernon, 1964) have resulted first in a renewed interest in situations as determinants of behaviour (Mischel, 1968), and more recently in the development of interactionist models of the person–situation relationship (Mischel, 1973; Ekehammar, 1974). Although individual characteristics in such models can be represented by a wide array of already existing tests measuring personality variables, comparable measures of situational features are not yet available. There is a growing consensus in personality theory, maintaining that the lack of progress in the discipline is caused by the fact that "we lack a satisfactory classification of situations. We need a systematic way of conceptualizing the domain of situations and situational variables before we can make rapid progress in studying the role of situations in determining behaviour" (Frederiksen, 1972, p. 115). Several studies of social episodes to be described here demonstrate that social situations and episodes can be reliably quantified and represented in terms of how individuals perceive them. This approach could be directly relevant to the development of taxonomic systems of situations, currently lacking in personality research.

In social psychology, there is an increasing recognition that many studies of social behaviour and perception may lack external validity because the situational context in which such behaviour or perception normally occurs has been ignored in laboratory research. Traditionally, researchers in social psychology have assumed that the situation and the episode are merely vehicles for the manipulation of independent variables. With the recognition that the laboratory experiment as an episode has its own rules and requirements (Rosenthal, 1966; Wuebben et al., 1974) it became evident that the context provided by the cultural definition of the episode has to be taken into consideration if the external validity of much of the laboratory research in social psychology is to be improved. Studies described in Chapter 8 show that the context provided by the appropriate episode has indeed an important and significant effect on social perception.

Finally, situations and episodes have also been in the forefront of interest in sociology, where Thomas's (1928) original interest in the "definition of the situation" has gained a new lease of life with the spreading influence of such new schools as dramaturgical models, ethnomethodology, and other microsociological approaches (Lyman and Scott, 1972). These schools, although widely differing in their approaches (for a more detailed review see Chapter 4), are all interested in the cues used in the definition and identification of a given episode, and the strategies used to enact social episodes. An empirical approach to some of these problems is also an important characteristic of the research on social episodes.

Before a detailed consideration of the conceptual background to the study of social episodes can be undertaken, it will be necessary to outline in a preliminary form (a) the general approach adopted here as related to current methodological controversies in social psychology; (b) to present a rationale for studying social episodes, and (c) to clarify some of the terminology to be used throughout this book.

The general approach

In recent years, criticisms of "traditional" experimental social psychology in the positivist mould have become particularly widespread, and suggestions for alternative approaches are becoming more and more numerous (Argyle, 1969, 1976; Armistead, 1974; Gergen, 1973; Harre and Secord, 1972; McGuire, 1973; Warr, 1973a, 1977). These arguments will be considered in more detail in the following chapter. It is such criticisms of experimentation for its own sake which have led to an increasing interest in naturalistic units of social behaviour, such as social episodes, as legitimate objects of study. Critics of laboratory social psychology argue that the objects of study presently dominating research are often of no intrinsic interest, and are studied simply because they are relevant to some previously established paradigm (e.g. McGuire, 1973). More radical critics also maintain that the empirical methodology developed in social psychology, based on a model borrowed from the natural sciences, is itself mistaken, and not appropriate to the study of social behaviour (e.g. Harre and Secord, 1972; Levine, 1974). The alternatives offered, such as Gergen's (1973) historical approach, Levine's (1974) "adversary" model, or Harre and Secord's (1972) espousal of subjective accounts as sources of data, although intuitively appealing, do not yield the kind of objective data on which the establishment of scientific facts could be based.

In the context of present day social psychology, it seems necessary to state at the outset the position taken in relation to these issues. It is accepted here that the first criticism, pointing out the irrelevance of many traditional areas of investigation, is substantially valid. The interest in social episodes as a topic for investigation reflects an agreement with this criticism. The second, and more extreme criticism, implying the rejection of a whole methodological armoury in favour of a vaguely stated descriptive or journalistic approach to social psychology, on the other hand, does not appear to be a promising alternative.

A good example of the suggested radical departure from established methods is the way in which social episodes were proposed to be studied. Harre, one of the most influential theorists advocating a "new" approach, argues for example:

"Scientists need not produce laws as a result of their studies. They might, instead, in some fields, be the entrepreneurs of understanding. The upshot of an investigation might be a set of concepts with which episodes can be understood. The use of the concepts may provide no general knowledge, no expectation of future behaviour. But it may make each episode intelligible in itself. Perhaps the creation of such a conceptual scheme is the proper ambition of the social sciences." (1970, p. viii)

Although the heuristic value of this approach in producing new insights is unquestionable, its impact on social psychological research (as distinct from theorizing) has been limited. The effectiveness of this and many other stimulating criticisms of established social psychology has unfortunately been reduced by an inability to propose acceptable alternative methodologies. In effect, in the past few years the curious situation has arisen in which hardly anyone disagreed with the exhortations to study relevant, naturalistic social phenomena, while very few people were actually doing so; many social psychologists, although increasingly convinced of the failure of traditional research areas, nevertheless continued to carry out studies in that framework, because of the lack of acceptable alternatives.

The concept of social episodes was one of those terms injected into current usage by reformists. While the term has found nearly instant acceptance, and considerable lip service has been paid to the necessity of studying natural units of social behaviour such as social episodes, very little in the way of empirical research has been forthcoming. This was probably due to (a) the lack of an adequate conceptualization of the term, (b) the absence of an operationalization, and of quantitative methods for studying episodes, and (c) the lack of a taxonomy which would have enabled investigators to classify different social episodes, at least in a preliminary form. One of the purposes of this book is to propose a definition of social episodes, rooted in the historical evolution of the concept, and to suggest quantitative methods which are applicable to its study.

The general approach adopted here can thus be summarized as one strongly influenced by recent criticisms of the irrelevance of many research topics in contemporary social psychology; hence the choice of social episodes as the central topic for this book. At the same time, it will be maintained here that the use of empirical methods, resulting in quantified and objective representations of how social episodes are performed, perceived, and cognitively represented, is the most promising strategy for a social psychological approach to the study of social episodes.

The rationale for studying social episodes

The ultimate justification for studying social episodes is that this understanding may help to explain naturalistic, everyday social behaviour. Traditional social psychology, in its pursuit of manipulating one or a few variables at a time, was firmly committed to studying the esoteric and unrepresentative social situation most characteristically created in the laboratory (Brunswik, 1956; Pervin, 1975a). Social psychologists have only recently developed an interest in the study of everyday social interaction and routines, a topic of much interest to sociologically oriented investigators (Douglas, 1970). Of the wide array of naturally occurring social behaviours, only some will be explicable in terms of cultural notions of the episode being enacted. A useful step in delimiting the usefulness of the concept of episode is to identify the kinds of actions and behaviours which it can potentially explain, and the kinds of actions which it cannot. Clearly, social episodes may be useful in illuminating regularities in rather complex interactive routines, yet say little about simpler, operant behaviours.

Even Skinner (1971) has found it necessary to distinguish between two kinds of behaviour, "rule-governed" and "contingency-governed". Most social behaviour can be best understood as the performance of acts which are governed by the rules and roles of the immediate cultural milieu, and where such rules are cognitively represented by the actor (Collett, 1977; Harre and Secord, 1972). The distinction between different kinds of actions is thus crucial for delimiting the usefulness of a concept such as "social episode".

Typologies of action are still overwhelmingly speculative. One such typology, by Porter (unpublished data, 1975), described in Pearce (1976, p. 3) appears to be particularly useful in the present context. According to this typology, action can be (a) "controlled", e.g. reactive, determined or caused in the Humean sense; this kind of action can be explained by identifying its causal antecedents, i.e. the sufficient and necessary conditions for its occurrence, (b) "Influenced" action is "structured by socialization and is approximately explained by describing the rules a person follows as he conducts purposive action" (Pearce, 1976, p. 4). Influenced actions are typical of social episodes which are implicitly regulated by cultural expectations and norms. It is this type of action which is most likely to be explicable in terms of a probabilistic relationship between the actor's perception of the social episode, and his behaviour. Finally, (c) "creative" action refers to behaviours which deviate from the ordinary, expected sequence of events. It may involve "following the rules in a novel way or acting independently of the rules" (Pearce, 1976, p. 4).

The study of social episodes may thus have a role to play in explaining "influenced" action, that is social behaviour which is culture specific, norm-bound, and is governed by a set of implicit rules. Indeed, Harre and Secord (1972) chose to define episodes at one point as "any part of human life, involving one or more people, in which some internal structure can be determined" (1972, p. 153). The operational definition of an episode in this sense would be a set of rules specifying the appropriate and expected behaviours which can be legitimately performed in that episode. This operationalization is only one of several alternative possibilities in social psychology. Its shortcoming is that rules and rule structures are notoriously elusive, it is difficult to demonstrate cultural, let alone individual agreement about them, and the context-dependence and complexity of these rules make any exhaustive representation impossible (Robinson, 1977). Rather than explicitly representing rules, the alternative strategy most favoured here is to think of social episodes as global cultural and cognitive units of which individuals have an implicit understanding.

It will perhaps be useful at this point to elaborate the concept of episodes even further. Just as roles describe expected and sanctioned ways for individuals to behave, episodes describe expected and sanctioned ways of interaction. In an analogy borrowed from role theory, three aspects of episodes will be identified for further discussion: (a) episode expectations; (b) episode definition; and (c) episode performance.

On the one hand, there exists a set of cultural expectations of patterns of action appropriate for a given episode, which could be called episode expectations, a term analogous to role expectations in role theory. From the available cultural episode repertoire, the individual will select the episode which he wishes to enact. This selection will obviously be influenced by the cues already available to him, such as the behaviour setting (Barker and Wright, 1955), and the proposed definition of the episode advanced by the partner(s). This second aspect of social episodes may be referred to as the definition of the episode, a process whereby the cultural repertoire is adapted/adjusted to the unique interaction situation. Sociologists in particular have considered the definition of the episode an important concept in understanding social behaviour (Thomas 1928b). The final aspect of the term "episode" is the actual unique sequence of behaviour which will make up any particular interaction. This may be called episode performance, a term again related to role theory, where the enactment of a particular role is called role performance. In the most active research areas concerned with the perception of episodes, social episodes are understood in the first sense, as cultural units or representations of stereotypical, and not necessarily actual, sequences of interaction. This orientation appears to be dictated by the available methodology as well as by the current state of research in this area. Studies of how typical social episodes are perceived will have to come first, before the study of the complex negotiating process involved in the definition of the episode, or the study of actual behaviour sequences making up an episode performance, become feasible.

In summary, the present book is concerned with the study of social episodes, most commonly defined as the cultural and cognitive representation of an interaction which determines *episode expectations*. The study of social episodes should facilitate the understanding and explanation of a particular class of actions and behaviours, which can be called "influenced" behaviours. This approach is also supported by the evolution of the concepts of situation and episode to be reviewed later.

Terminology

The term "social episode" is at present used in a number of different senses in many areas of social science, such as sociology, social psychology and even linguistics. The communality between these different uses is that "episode" always refers to a unit of social interaction. In the past, very similar concepts of interaction units were called a "situation", an "encounter" or even a "performance". In the review of the background of the study of social episodes that follows, these alternative terms will frequently emerge. The purpose of this section is to offer a preliminary statement regarding the relationship between these terms.

The extensive literature on "situations" is clearly the precursor of the more current interest in episodes. Historically, the term situation was used as an extension of the concept of stimulus, referring to more complex stimulus configurations as determinants of behaviour. Social situation, in the widest sense, means all the potential and actual stimuli which are capable of influencing social behaviour in a given setting. Parallel to this S–R theoretical concept of situations, evolved a sociological conceptualization, originated by Thomas (1928b). In the sociological sense, a social situation is a unit of social interaction, defined and regulated by the culture, and it is maintained that interactants will have to come to some implicit agreement about the definition of the situation before interaction becomes possible. These two historical approaches to situations may be thought of as the two sides of the same coin, defining the external (given), and internal (perceived) characteristics of a unit of social interaction.

"Social episode" as a term on the other hand is used in extremely diverse senses. According to one approach, episodes are the smaller units, building blocks as it were, of larger and more complex social situations. A dinner party (a social situation) is thus constituted by a number of social episodes, such as (1) arrival and greetings, (2) pre-dinner drink and chat, (3) dinner proper etc. (Argyle, 1976). The problem with this approach is that the boundaries between the units are difficult to establish objectively, and situations and episodes cannot be clearly distinguished. Another orientation (Harre and Secord, 1972) uses the term episode as a generic label of stereotypic, goal-directed recurring interaction sequences with a culturally determined meaning. According to these authors, the study of formal (explicitly regulated) episodes may provide the clue to the understanding of naturalistic enigmatic (unique) episodes.

It would be well beyond the scope of this work to disentangle all the definitional ambiguities surrounding these terms; this brief resumé is intended simply to illustrate that situations and episodes can both refer to units of social interaction. In view of the general confusion, any attempt at a consistent separation of these terms here would be fraught with difficulties. For one thing, many researchers and theorists use the terms nearly interchangeably. In addition, although "episode" is the newer term, its conceptual roots are to be found in the evolution of the concept of situations, as will be argued later. For these reasons, and for the purposes of the present discussion, no systematic distinction between the terms "social situations" and "social episodes" will be made. These terms will be thought of here as referring to units of social interaction, with temporal and often physical boundaries, and with a culturally known and accepted scheme of appropriate behaviours (a "script"—Abelson, 1976). Since these interaction units are cognitive as well as cultural objects, members of a given cultural background should usually have a shared representation of the sequence of events they entail. Social episodes are thus not only cultural objects, but also cognitive objects, units of knowledge and expectations that an individual has about a specified sequence of interaction. This approach is most clearly related to the symbolic interactionist conceptualization of situations, as culturally given "objects" which are perceived by individuals with a significant degree of consensual agreement, and which are continuously moulded and redefined through social interaction.

However, symbolic interactionism is not the only theory which has implications for the study of social episodes. Scattered throughout the social psychological literature, one may come across many and diverse attempts to propose a definition and operationalization of a natural unit of interaction. Perhaps we should briefly look at these attempts before embarking on the task of defining social episodes.

Towards a definition of social episodes

Early conceptualizations of the situation in social psychology were predominantly ecological and external, while more recent approaches tend to emphasize the cognitive and perceived situation. The external, ecological approach to social situations is based on the theoretical stands taken by authors such as Chein (1954), Gibson (1959) and the environmental psychologists (e.g. Craik, 1971) who prefer to think of situations as physical, potential rather than actual, and therefore objectively determinable stimulus configurations. A second important influence was learning theory, and social learning theory in particular. Rotter (1954, 1955), for example, while recognizing that situations have subjective meanings, remained within the learning theoretical tradition in defining situations externally: "Behaviours, reinforcements and situations may be defined in objective terms, although their significance and systematic formulae are concerned with constructs relating to personal or acquired meaning" (Rotter, 1955, p. 260).

Sherif and Sherif (1956, 1963, 1969) also stressed the importance of the objective social environment as the most relevant determinant of behaviour, an approach which has stimulated the development of classificatory systems of objective situations by Sells (1963) and by Arnault (1963).

In contrast, concern with the internal, subjective situation has its roots in the phenomenologist tradition of Koffka (1935), and Lewin's (1951) field theory, in which the life space, or psychological environment, rather than the objective environment is emphasized. Murray (1951) also argues: "in most cases it is impossible to describe, formulate and classify the situational processes in terms of their physical properties" (p. 458). There is also a distinct tradition in the psychology of perception which maintains that only the actively perceiving organism taking contextual factors into account gives objectively existing stimuli a potential to influence behaviour (Avant and Helson, 1973; Helson, 1959, 1964). Thus, the interaction situation or the environment can only be defined with reference to the individual (Klausner, 1971), and perception and reactions to situational stimuli involve the whole organism, with all its central processes, values and traditions as it interacts with the environment (Ittelson, 1973).

There are many theorists who suggested that such internal, cognitive representations of situations should occupy pride of place in psychological research. Thus, Snygg's (1941) phenomenal field, Lewin's (1951) life space, Piaget's (1952) schemata, Kelly's (1955) personal constructs, Herbst's (1970) behavioural world, Merleau-Ponty's (1962) perceived situation or phenomenal field, and Bieri's (1971) cognitive structure are all terms used to describe such internal representations of situational variables.

Perhaps Lewin's field theory has been the most influential in this respect. Roger Barker's understanding of the behaviour setting, influenced by field theory, is an example of how the objective, measurable physical environment, and an individual's behaviour within it, can be welded into a unitary system: individuals "construct their own private worlds within the setting" (Barker, 1960, p. 18), and idiosyncratic perceptions result in different individual behaviours. The setting itself can be defined in terms of its objective ecological characteristics and in terms of communalities of individual behaviours, which occur within it. Although Barker's taxonomy of behaviour settings is in physical terms, it is clear that without the individual's awareness of the social meaning of these settings the scheme would be meaningless. In other words, interactive behaviour in a given environment depends on how individuals perceive that environment (Insel and Moos, 1974, p. 127). In the same vein, objective dimensions characterizing situations provide information congruent with but not identical to information obtained from studies of perceived situations (Moos, 1974).

It seems, then, that social psychological conceptualizations of situations or episodes are increasingly reliant on internal, cognitive representations of interactive settings. Thus, "situation definition is a subjective analysis of what a situation calls for, and its demands, and an internalized plan of behaviour (not necessarily of an aware nature)" (Altman, 1968, p. 25). On the other hand, the cultural, stereotypical, recurrent nature of situations is also emphasized. In these terms, a situation is "a set of circumstances that is likely to influence the behaviour of at least some individuals, and that is likely to recur repeatedly in the same form" (Frederiksen *et al.*, 1973, p. 22). More phenomenologically oriented definitions also suggest that episodes have to be seen as not only recurring, but in some sense "natural" units of interaction (Harre and Secord, 1972).

This brief sample of different definitions of situations and episodes indicates an apparent shift from the ecological and external situation to the *cognitive*, perceived situation on the one hand, and from situations as unique environmental contingencies to episodes as *cultural*, recurring stereotypical interactions on the other. Other, and more complete reviews tend to arrive at a similar conclusion: "the situation is a function of the observer, in the sense that the observer's cognitive schemas filter and organize the environment in a fashion that makes it impossible ever to completely separate the environment from the person observing it" (Bowers, 1973, p. 328). At the end of his review, Ekehammar (1974) also concludes that it is the perceived, subjective situation which is most relevant to the understanding of situational or episodic regularities in behaviour. Endler and Magnusson (1974) emphasize a similar point: "It seems reasonable to assume that it is the meaning which an individual assigns to a situation which is the most important situational factor affecting his behaviour" (p. 15). Even Mischel, best known for his social learning theoretical formulations, has increasingly moved towards a cognitive-perceptual conceptualization of the relevant situation: "assessing the acquired meaning of stimuli is the core of social behaviour assessment" (Mischel, 1968, p. 190).

Our definition of social episodes needs to take into account these changes towards a cognitive-cultural conceptualization of situations, and at the same time, ensure that the proposed definition allows the quantification and measurement of social episodes, using social psychological techniques.

Social episodes will be defined here as cognitive representations of stereotypical interaction sequences, which are representative of a given cultural environment. Such interaction sequences constitute natural units in the stream of behaviour (Dickman, 1963; Harre and Secord, 1972), distinguishable on the basis of symbolic, temporal, and often physical boundaries. More importantly, however, there is a shared, consensual representation in the given culture about what constitutes an episode, and which are the norms, rules and expectations that apply. This definition of episodes as cultural objects implies that individual members of a specified culture should have an implicit cognitive knowledge and understanding of the episodes practised in their environment. The major task of the proposed study of social episodes is thus to empirically represent at least some aspects of this implicit knowledge.

This definition of episodes as cultural objects is indebted to the symbolic interactionist tradition (Stone and Farberman, 1970). It is also closely related to some other definitions of interaction units, such as Goffman's "focussed interaction" (1963), Watson and Potter's "episode" (1962), Barker and Wright's "behaviour units" (1955), Bjerg's "agons" (1968), and Scheflen's idea of a "presentation" (1964). At the same time, this definition is also similar to the pursuits and interests of empirical social psychology. The perception and cognitive representation of social episodes may be studied by essentially the same methods as the perception of any other category of social objects. The major purpose of this book is to develop this conceptualization of social episodes, and to explore the way in which empirical social psychological techniques may be applied to their study. Other, anthropological, linguistic or sociological methods recently proposed for the study of social episodes will also be considered as complementary to this effort.

Plan of the book

Having thus introduced the concept of social episodes, and made the first hesitant steps towards defining and operationalizing this elusive term, it may be in order to say a few words about how the book is to be organized to fulfil the aims outlined above. Because of the very mixed parentage of the concept of social episodes, and because of the fairly sketchy research in this area to date, this book will have to be two things at once. Firstly, it will be necessary to review and summarize theories and approaches both in psychology and in sociology which are the precursors of the more recent interest in social episodes. Secondly, the existing empirical research will have to be summarized and evaluated, and future prospects for the study of social episodes mapped out. In both of these tasks, we will have to be extremely selective, otherwise we might lose from sight the main reason for this book in the first place: to establish the study of social episodes as a respectable branch of empirical, academic social psychology.

The next chapter aims to set the scene for the book, by outlining the place for the study of social episodes in the context of present-day social psychology. Social psychology in the seventies is characterized by a great deal of soul-searching, and in this chapter we shall seek to summarize the most salient issues which have emerged from the controversies of the seventies. These centre on the question of the kind of paradigm social psychology ought to follow, and in particular, the scientific ideal as it has been represented in social psychological research to date. Criticisms of the laboratory experiment are at the heart of this issue, and will be described in some detail. A related problem concerns the argument about the importance of prediction as against description as the most promising objectives in the present stage of development in social psychology. The question of social relevance, and more generally, of a social psychology built on commonsense understanding will also be discussed here, as an issue frequently raised by recent critics of the discipline. In the final part of the chapter, the merits and problems of some of the alternative methodologies recently advanced by critics of social psychology will be critically evaluated. By the end of this chapter, we should see how the study of social episodes is rooted in the particular controversies and discussions which have characterized the seventies, and how the proposed study of social episodes is built on, and is in a sense a synthesis of, these criticisms.

Chapter 3 is a review of different approaches to the study of situations and episodes in psychology. The aim of this chapter is to establish the proposition that the study of social episodes, although apparently a completely new approach in social psychology, has in fact important conceptual roots in psychological theory. It is necessary that the concept of social episodes should be anchored unambiguously in psychological theory, if we want to benefit from the accumulated insights of decades of foregoing research. These are identified by reviewing the major theoretical schools of thought in psychology, and the conceptual relationship between terms such as "situation" and "episode" is further analysed. The survey of relevant psychological theories encompasses three major schools: traditional learning theory, cognitive phenomenological theories, and symbolic interactionism and social learning theory. In the next part of the chapter the main changes in psychological approaches to episodes and situations are summarized, suggesting that conceptualizations have changed along four dimensions: from atomism to holism, from physical to social, from actual to potential, and from the objective to the subjective situation. Empirical research, demonstrating situational regularities in behaviour is discussed, suggesting the important role situations and episodes play in social behaviour.

Just as in psychology, the concept of social episodes has important roots in sociology. Current concern with social episodes, and the intricate processes of interpersonal behaviour in social psychology were historically preceded by a similar interest in the "situation" in sociology. Furthermore, the "new" social psychology is indebted for many of its ideas to social anthropological and microsociological schools, such as the dramaturgical model of Goffman, ethnomethodology, or the sociology of the "absurd". Chapter 4 is intended as a survey of interest in episodes in these disciplines, with a view towards identifying those approaches which are most promising in their social psychological implications. The survey begins with a consideration of the positivist approach to sociology, and Max Weber's cultural sociology as a major alternative is discussed. Based on Weber's interpretative sociology and symbolic interactionism, W. I. Thomas's work is a significant step towards establishing situational analysis as a major theme in sociology. The phenomenological sociology of Alfred Schutz is also considered, as a major influence on contemporary microsociological schools, such as ethnomethodology, or Goffman's dramaturgical model. The concluding section of this chapter identifies the main threads of thought common to these orientations, and the implications of the sociological approach for the study of social episodes are evaluated.

Having thus identified the conceptual roots of social episodes in psychology and sociology, in Chapter 5 we turn our attention to the methodologies which are applicable to the study of social episodes. Four main contemporary research strategies are identified. Perhaps the best established techniques concentrate on the ecological component of interaction episodes. This strategy concentrates on the symbolic role and function of the environment in the definition of social episodes (Barker, 1968). The methods used are most distinctly related to those of environmental psychology, and include a wide range of techniques, from participant observation to laboratory experiments. The second strategy is the perceptual approach, aiming to study social episodes as they are perceived, or cognitively represented by individuals, groups, or subcultures. The methodologies most frequently used in this research are factor analysis, multidimensional scaling (MDS), and the different social psychological rating techniques. These are surveyed in some detail, and examples of their applications are offered. This strategy appears to be most closely related to the traditional methods and concerns of social psychology, and it represents the most active research orientation over the past few years. The third, structuralist strategy derives from linguistics, and its aim is to understand and represent the structural rules of behaviour followed within specified episodes. Qualitative linguistic methods predominate, although some statistical methods, such as subjective probabilities, transitional probability tables and hierarchical clustering techniques are also used occasionally. Finally, the roles–rules strategy seeks to study social episodes in terms of the implicit rules and roles that social actors can be shown to follow. The methods of this approach are relatively less developed, and extensive use is made of open-ended paper-and-pencil techniques, as well as intensive interviews. The chapter ends with a comparison of the main characteristics of each of these strategies, and it is concluded that the ecological and perceptual strategies appear most promising for the social psychological study of social episodes.

The ecological approach to the study of social episodes represents perhaps the earliest attempt to study naturalistic social interaction by empirical means. Chapter 6 is concerned with the background and prospects of this strategy. The first part of the chapter describes attempts to construct ecological taxonomies of interaction episodes, based on behaviour setting surveys. The importance of ecological variables and "environmental props" in interaction episodes is discussed, with special reference to the implications of ecological analysis to clinical settings.

In Chapter 7 one of the major topics of the book is introduced, the study of the perception and cognitive representation of social episodes. Numerous *ad hoc* studies of situation perception were the precursors of the recent systematic attempts to analyse episode perception. Three empirical studies carried out by us are described, seeking to quantify and evaluate differences in episode perception as a function of the general subculture, the immediate group milieu and individual differences in social position, respectively. These studies convincingly show that it is quite feasible to construct reliable and meaningful models of how episode domains are cognitively represented using multidimensional scaling techniques.

This theme is further developed in Chapter 8, in which research on the different factors affecting episode perception is considered. Idiosyncratic differences between judges, the cultural constraint embodied in different episodes, the role-relationship between the interactants, and the physical environment or behaviour setting are some of the variables which influence how we perceive social episodes, and which have been studied by empirical means to date. As well as studying the components of social episodes, it can also be shown that global episodes have an important influence on other areas of perception, such as interpersonal perception. Evidence from three studies by us suggest that the perception of familiar others, as well as interpersonal judgements by members of a permanent small group are not consistent across situations, but are strongly dependent on the episode context. Even perceptions of observed behaviours in an interaction are dependent on the definition of the episode. It is concluded that episodic requirements are important components of the social perception process, and should be explicitly taken into account in studies of social judgement.

However, the study of social episodes has even more far-reaching implications for personality theory, clinical psychology, and social psychology, the three areas of social science where interest in episodic regularities in behaviour has been most acute in recent years (Chapter

9). Personality theorists are showing a growing interest in methods of classifying situations, and the techniques proposed here for analysing episode perception would be readily suited to such a task. Clinical psychology has been revolutionalized by the advent of the situationalist behaviour therapies, as an alternative to intrapsychic models of mental illness. Even though these therapies typically rely on manipulating a client's perception of the episode confronting him, there are no systematic methods for describing and quantifying such episodes. The methods proposed here could play an important part in such an endeavour. Last, but not least, social psychologists have also tended to operate on the implicit assumption of cross-situational consistency in social perception and behaviour. Much criticism of social psychology could be pre-empted if episodic changes in social acts were explicitly taken into account in research. This chapter contains some specific proposals for implementing the study of social episodes in each of these areas.

Finally, in the last chapter, Chapter 10, we shall once again go over the ground covered, and the main themes of the study of social episodes will be drawn together. In the first part of the chapter the three major trends which precipitated the study of social episodes are summarized: (a) cognitivism, or a growing interest in internal, cognitive representations of the social world; (b) situationism, or the increasing awareness of situational and episodic, as against intrapsychic regularities in social behaviour. Finally, (c) after the criticisms of the last decade, recent changes in social psychology resulted in the greater eclecticism and methodological sophistication of the discipline. These developments are jointly responsible for the emerging interest in the study of social episodes. The already substantial body of research on social episodes, including many of the studies carried out by us and described here, is summarized in the next part of this chapter. The theoretical and practical implications of this research are considered next. Interest in social episodes is increasingly present in personality and social psychology, while the clinical applications of the research are likely to be of increasing importance in the future. The development of diagnostic tools, which can be used to identify social episodes which are sources of difficulty, or to establish the characteristics of pathogenic episodes and situations in a given cultural environment, is a promising possibility. In the last quarter of this chapter, a number of potentially interesting research projects, relying on the conceptualization and methodology developed for the study of social episodes, are outlined.

2

Social Episodes and the Current State of Social Psychology

There can be little doubt that social psychology in the seventies is characterized by more soul-searching and self-doubt than at any other time in the brief history of the discipline. Since the beginning of this century, the time to which empirical social psychology traces its origins, there was no period when the search for new approaches and methods was quite as intense as it is today. The time from the initial definition of the field by McDougall (1908) and Ross (1908) to Allport's (1924) first survey of social psychological research was a period characterized by the first uncertain but promising steps of a newly defined field of enquiry. The thirties saw the publication of classical works by Lewin, Sherif and others, which defined areas of research which were to remain influential for decades. The forties and fifties reflected the impact of the war on the direction of social psychological research, and the establishment of such classic models with applied implications as authoritarianism, achievement motivation and cognitive dissonance. Finally, the sixties saw the explosive multiplication of social psychological research in innumerable new areas. McGuire (1973) described this age in nearly poetic terms: "It was a prestigious and productive area in which droves of bright young people, a sufficiency of middle-aged colonels, and a few grand old men were pursuing their research with the confidence and energy that is found in those who know where they are going. Any moments of doubt we experienced involved anxiety as to whether we were doing our thing well, rather than uncertainty as to whether it needed to be done at all" (p. 146). Certainly, concern with methodological rigour and sophistication received more emphasis than more general questions pertaining to the external validity, social relevance and even intrinsic interest of social pyschological research. Perhaps we should have been openminded enough to anticipate Hebb's (1974) dictum that research that is not worth doing at all is not worth doing well.

As it turned out, the vigorous expansion of social psychology in the sixties was also the harbinger of the reappraisal that is now taking place. As the research effort expanded, expectations of relevant and practically useful findings, and the development of more and more powerful explanatory theories of social behaviour grew with it. Somehow, these expectations were left largely unsatisfied. We might get some insight into the roots of the current malaise by considering the kind of research that characterized the "exuberant sixties". Christie (1965), after surveying research in the period 1949–59, predicted a trend by suggesting that "within a few years the number of published articles in the *Journal of Abnormal and Social Psychology* should reach an asymptote with all articles reporting experiments on college students using analysis of variance designs" (p. 151). This prediction very nearly came true, as Higbee and Wells (1972) found in their review of research trends in the sixties. "In the 1969 *Journal of Personality and Social Psychology*, 9 out of 10 articles involved experimental manipulation, 3 out of 4 involved college students as subjects, and 4 out of 5 used an analysis of variance design" (p. 966). Clearly, the growing methodological dominance of the laboratory experiment was intimately related to the developing dissatisfaction with social psychology on the part of both outsiders and its practitioners. Many of the criticisms of the discipline to be considered in this chapter centre around the laboratory experiment in particular, and the theoretical and philosophical underpinning of this methodology in general. Even in the heyday of laboratory studies, there were already a few isolated voices calling for a more eclectic and open approach to the study of social behaviour (McGuire, 1967; Sargent, 1965; Ring, 1967; Kelman, 1967). Although these calls have radically multiplied in the past ten years, and even the most ardent supporters of the experimental method admit the desirability of a more eclectic armoury of methodologies (Schlenker, 1974), the "shift" from laboratory experiments has been largely an illusory one to date.

The frustrations implied by this situation are never very far from the surface. One social psychologist described his personal disenchantment with the discipline in these terms: "what seemed to be involved was my participation in a big intellectual and academic game, in which, because of the 'name of the game', problems were being manufactured rather than formulated; methodological tools were being used because they had the 'good scientific stamp of approval' rather than because they had been logically and theoretically derived from a problem; quantification was to be achieved at any cost rather than arriving at the definition and understanding of given social phenomena; and finally, the search for, and development of problems were to be determined by the model of the physical and biological sciences rather than looking for or developing models that might fit existing complex human social psychological problems" (Proshansky, 1976, p. 304).

The main reason for this reluctance to implement many of the "new" methodologies suggested in the past few years is mainly that they are seen by many psychologists as unacceptably "soft", anecdotal, journalistic and unreliable. Therefore it is necessary to recognize that for any proposed change in social psychology to become effective, the first requirement is that methodologies should be at least as robust and reliable as the laboratory experiment is claimed to be. One of the major aims of this book is to argue that phenomena such as social episodes, hitherto assumed to be too vague or badly defined to be worthy of serious study, can in fact be researched using quantitative, descriptive methodologies which are no less "objective" than those commonly used in experiments. The present chapter in particular will review the most important points of criticisms of social psychology currently voiced, and the remedies offered, with a view to outlining the place the study of social episodes should take in the current flux of ideas.

The question of paradigms

Many criticisms, in one way or another, maintain that social psychology must undergo a profound "paradigmatic shift" if its difficulties are to be resolved. In contrast, our approach is based on the realization that social psychology is not in a state of "paradigmatic crisis" in Kuhn's terms, and that what is required is not so much the emergence of a completely new paradigm, but a more tolerant attitude towards the development of alternative topics of research and methodologies. Even though such highly regarded social psychologists as Berkowitz (1976), Smith (1972), McGuire (1973) and Bruner (1976) hint at the possibility of an imminent paradigmatic shift, the present crisis can just as well be described as a crisis of confidence as a paradigmatic crisis. As Elms (1975) thoughtfully points out, to have a paradigmatic crisis, one must first have a paradigm; it is doubtful that the "experimental method" as used in social psychology would qualify, even in Kuhn's extremely loose definition of the term. Rather, after the heady days of the fifties and sixties, the real difficulty and complexity of doing research in social psychology is becoming apparent. New and more complex techniques, and more importantly, more and more flexible approaches to problem selection are needed. This book seeks to contribute to both of these areas, by pointing to the study of social episodes as a promising, and indeed already established area of research, and by suggesting a number of new, eclectic methodologies which are applicable to the study of such naturalistic interaction sequences. Techniques advocated here, such as multidimensional scaling, are already widely used in a number of areas of social psychology. As the review of recent criticisms of social psychology indicates, the use of such descriptive methodologies is advocated in many of them.

The scientific method in social psychology

As Bruner asserted in his Herbert Spencer Lecture in Oxford, the scientific method as applied in psychology implies an essentially nineteenth century, mechanistic view of man: "in the later nineteenth century, psychology modelled itself on those natural science neighbours in whose district it has decided to build its mansion, and had suffered the consequences thereafter" (1976, p. 1589). The varieties of social psychological research may be characterized in terms of three major divisions: mechanistic v. holistic, individual v. social, and pure v. applied (Warr, 1973). It is quite clear that contemporary academic social psychology is mainly mechanistic, individual and pure, an imbalance which gives "excessive weight to only a small part of our subject matter. A more human psychology might be attained by shifts along each of the three principal dimensions" (Warr, 1977, p. 2).

The most common conception of scientific method relies on analogies drawn from the methods and procedures applied in the natural sciences in the last century. This entails a cluster of beliefs concerned with the inductive method, the verification of hypotheses, and the gradual accumulation of scientific facts, leading to the eventual emergence of ever more general theories of increasing explanatory and predictive power. Although this view may seem naïve today, especially in the light of the epistemological revolution brought about by Popper's

(1959) and later Kuhn's (1962) work, it is nevertheless quite obvious that much research in social psychology in the most productive part of the fifties and sixties was based on an implicit epistemology not unlike the one just described. There can be little doubt that the overwhelming majority of research published in social psychology over the past few decades is concerned with the demonstration of hypotheses derived from existing theories, that there is general reluctance to change those theories in the face of disconfirmatory, or even contradictory findings, and that this adherence to established theories, and the reluctance to postulate new hypotheses and definitions is justified by an implicit belief in the methods and procedures of 19th century natural science. As McGuire (1973) writes, "we social psychologists have tended to use the manipulational laboratory experiment not to test our hypotheses but to demonstrate their obvious truth. We tend to start off with an hypothesis which we have no intention of rejecting . . . if the experiment does not come out 'right', then the researcher does not say that the hypothesis is wrong, but rather, that something was wrong with the experiment" (pp. 448–449). In other words research in social psychology was, and is, largely based on a philosophy of science seeking to verify hypotheses by demonstrating their validity, rather than by seeking to falsify them, as Popper suggested.

Popper's (1959) devastating criticism of this particular interpretation of the scientific method has somehow failed to make a profound impact on the methods of social psychologists. His suggestion that scientific theories should be stated in the most unambiguous terms possible, that hypotheses derived from such theories should be formulated in a way which allows refutation by experience, and that contradictory empirical results should not be explained away by recourse to *post hoc* hypotheses and explanation, have not been followed. Much of the scientific activity in social psychology today bears the characteristics of Kuhn's (1962) "normal science"—as if Kuhn's description of this state of affairs would somehow legitimize the activity itself. Popper (1970) has this to say about normal science: "Normal science . . . is the activity of the non-revolutionary, or more precisely, the not too critical professional: of the science student who accepts the ruling dogma of the day; who does not wish to challenge it; and who accepts a new revolutionary theory only if everybody else is ready to accept it—if it becomes fashionable by a kind of bandwagon effect" (p. 52).

One of the most ubiquitous hallmarks of our "normal" social psychology is the nearly universal reliance on the laboratory experiment.

The laboratory experiment in social psychology

There are three main stages in scientific research: the creative, or hypothesis-generating phase in which a few elements or variables are selected from an infinite pool of potentially relevant variables, to suggest a particular relationship or causal link. The second stage, or "critical stage", involves the testing and evaluation of these hypotheses by routine and well-rehearsed procedures. Finally, the research efforts culminate in the third phase, when the results of the second, critical phase are ploughed back into the construction of theoretical models, capable of predicting and explaining the much wider range of phenomena surveyed in the first stage. Perhaps the most general theme echoed in recent years is that social psychological research has for too long been locked into the procedural niceties of the second stage, with the increasing neglect of the first and the third stages. In other words, there has been a preponderance of studies evaluating hypotheses based on already existing models, and a marked lack of both descriptive-analytic studies which could have led to the emergence of new sets of hypotheses and integrative efforts of theory construction which summarize empirical findings within an established paradigm. As a result, a situation has been created in which these failures of relevance and integration could be interpreted by many as failures of the scientific method *per se*.

The laboratory experiment tends to be criticized on at least three counts. Firstly, there are very serious methodological problems involved in experimentation with human subjects which are ultimately caused by the fact that subjects possess insight and intelligence, and will seek to understand the requirements of the experimental situation and behave accordingly. Their understanding is often at variance with what the experimenter seeks to convey, and given the complexity of the cognitive processes involved, the scope for misunderstanding is likely to remain great. The complexities of the interface between experimenter and subject are now well recognized, and numerous methodological refinements seek to overcome these difficulties (Rosnow *et al.*, 1973, Orne, 1962). One way of looking at demand characteristics and experimenter effects is in terms of conceptualizing the social psychological experiment as an episode, with its own rules, expectations and internal structure. Some of the methods suggested in this book could be eminently applicable to the quantification of the experimental episode. As Brunswik (1956) suggested, we should spend at least as much time and effort on sampling situations as we spend on sampling subjects; with a feasible method of quantifying episodes, it should be possible to sample them, and to exactly define the range of episodes for which the findings of a laboratory "episode" can be expected to hold.

A second problem of social psychological experiments is ethical: under what circumstances is it justifiable to cause anxiety to, lie to, or deceive subjects? The current rules leave quite a lot to the conscience of the experimenter, and some researchers suggest that deception, for example, cannot be justified either on ethical or on methodological grounds.

The third issue is that laboratory experiments tended to foster an attitude to social psychology which increasingly relies on the study of esoteric, even absurd situations as a means of understanding everyday reality. It may be argued that (a) the creative phase of such research is aborted, insofar as hypotheses are not generated in terms of their potential relevance to existing issues in society, but are derived from already existing theories; and (b) the evaluation ("critical" stage) of those hypotheses should rely on descriptive, correlational or field methods instead of the ubiquitous laboratory experiment, by definition far removed from the realities of everyday social life. As a result of these criticisms, the late sixties and early seventies saw the emergence of a new movement which "has as its creative aspect the derivation of new hypotheses for their *ad hoc* interest and social value. And in its critical aspect, this new paradigm involves testing these hypotheses by field experiments, and where necessary, by correlational analysis of naturalistic data" (McGuire, 1973, p. 447).

However, even these remedies are suspect in several respects. Firstly, even though one may use "social relevance" as the criterion for the construction of hypotheses, the underlying deeper assumption often remains the same i.e. that simple linear cause–effect relationships exist, and can be demonstrated between the variables studied. After decades of experimentation, it may be that the time has arrived for social psychologists to pay more attention to the complex interactive and multiple-determined aspects of social behaviour. The main argument for this comes not so much from philosophical considerations, but simply because statistical quantitative techniques capable of coping with data of this kind are now becoming widely available.

McGuire, one of the most influential "inside" critics of established social psychology suggests that a "new paradigm" envisaged but not yet developed in any detail would have two hallmarks: "On the creative side it will involve theoretical models of the cognitive and social systems in their true multivariate complexity. . . . Correspondingly, the critical aspect of this new paradigm involves hypothesis testing by multivariate time series designs" (p. 450). In essence, the new model proposed has thus the distinguishing marks of relying on (a) cognitive models of information storage and processing as the relevant variables for under-standing social behaviour, and (b) by necessity, it implies the use of multidimensional techniques of description (such as multidimensional scaling) and hypothesis testing (multivariate analysis of variance) as its main research methods. As will be seen later, these two themes are central to most of the criticisms of established social psychology, and in some ways, they constitute the starting point of the approach to be outlined here. Our definition of social episodes is a cognitive one, emphasizing an individual's perception of stereotypical interaction sequences. The methods of study proposed are multidimensional, with special emphasis on the description of these cognitive structures. This is consonant with growing demands for more emphasis on the explora-tory descriptive stage of research in the discipline.

Description versus prediction

In the stages of scientific research mentioned earlier, the description of the phenomena to be studied logically precedes the evaluation of exact hypotheses. However, in the dominant research mode of the day, the laboratory experiment, description is simply bypassed, or replaced by the researcher's intuitive understanding of the topic under study. The absence of descriptive studies from social psychology is all the more noticeable, since many of the more profound influences on the discipline in the last few years originate from descriptive, journalistic studies of naturally occurring phenomena. Thus, Goffman's works, using a journalistic-interpretative method, or the ethological approach to animal behaviour now adapted to study phenomena such as non-verbal communication, rely on the observation and scientific interpretation of naturally occurring events. Such giants of psychology as Piaget have relied on similar methods to construct elaborate theoretical schemes. Clearly, social psychology is in need of incorporating such techniques in its methodological repertoire.

But there are also other reasons for taking the problem of description seriously. There is an emerging consensus that the past few decades were characterized by too much attention being paid to the procedural minutiae of the "critical" hypothesis-testing phase, without commensurate attention to the much more crucial process of hypothesis generation. There is a growing agreement that we should emphasize more the creative, hypothesis-formation stage relative to the critical, hypothesis-testing stage in social psychological research. It is finally becoming accepted that it is relatively useless to amass methodological sophistication in testing hypotheses which are trivial, without intrinsic interest, or even untestable.

Exactly what implications does this have for the use of descriptive techniques in research? Contrary to popular conception, hypothesis formation is not quite the mystical, creative process that it is often made out to be. There are many descriptive research techniques which can make hypothesis formation a lot easier. The recent history of social psychology, especially since the search for relevance became so prominent in the late sixties, is full of cases of research into new, and hitherto unstudied areas. Only infrequently was the hypothesis-testing stage preceded by a thorough survey and description of the range of applicable phenomena. As a result, the emerging theoretical models all too often concentrated on narrow, unrepresentative and specific cases, while the more general nature of the relationships studied was ignored, in the absence of a proper initial descriptive study. Research on risky shift, which turned out to be a sub-case of general group polarization (Moscovici and Zavalloni, 1969), or obedience under laboratory conditions (Milgram, 1963; Mixon, 1974) are examples of such a hit-and-miss approach to selecting phenomena for study, without the benefit of a thorough survey and description of the whole range of relevant variables. Social psychology as a field of study is still full of unexplored phenomena waiting to be studied. It is to be hoped that as new research areas emerge, the hypothesis-testing phase will not precede, and often pre-empt the descriptive phase as frequently happened in the past. It should be recognized that the thorough description of a new range of phenomena, as a pre-requisite to hypothesis generation, is an important stage in the scientfic process.

As the variables of concern to social psychologists will inevitably become more cognitive and complex, it also follows that techniques of description will have to become more sophisticated, capable of handling complex, multidimensional data. Fortunately, it appears that such excellent multidimensional techniques of description as the family of multidimensional scaling methods have arrived just in time to satisfy this growing need. Description thus does not have to be open-ended, journalistic and unquantifiable. McGuire (1973) argues that "Our students should also be acquainted with the newer analytic methods that make more possible the reduction of the complex natural field to a more manageable number of underlying variables whose interrelations can be determined. To this end, we and our students must have the opportunity to master new techniques for scaling qualitative data, new methods of multivariate analysis, such as those devised by Shepard and others" (p. 454). A substantial part of this book is based on the quantitative, descriptive analysis of social episodes by methods such as the ones proposed here.

Social episodes and the question of social relevance

The remoteness of the modal social psychological experiment from everyday life and behaviour is thus well recognized. The reduction necessary to select and control variables by studying something as complex as social behaviour in the laboratory is most visible in social psychological research. Other branches of psychology routinely use even more extreme reductions without incurring the same criticism, simply because their subject matter is beyond the commonsense nature of everyday life. Since social psychology deals with phenomena which are open to instant intuitive, commonsense understanding and evaluation, it is obviously of great importance to clarify the relationship between everyday reality and science here.

Traditionally, social psychological experiments seem to be based on a researcher's intuitive, commonsense understanding of some aspect of naturally occurring social behaviour, which is then demonstrated under much reduced and controlled conditions in the laboratory: "because of inadequate conceptual frameworks the individual experimenter uses uncritical common sense to connect theory and empirical procedures" (Harre and Secord, 1972, p. 79). To a significant extent, this involves the demonstration of specific instances of obviously true statements, and not the critical evaluation of hypotheses as such, as we have seen earlier. The staging of the conditions for an expected outcome to occur is the main skill involved, and not the critical consideration of an as yet unsubstantiated relationship. Thus it can be seen that even traditional, laboratory psychology is intimately interwoven with the commonsense understanding of everyday behaviour by its authors. Commonsense impinges on social psychological research in yet another way; for the manipulations and staging involved in illustrating laboratory instances of a common occurrence are such that it is obvious both to the layman and the critic that what is being demonstrated is no longer the familiar phenomenon of their everyday experience. Laboratory conformity has thus little to do with "real life" conformity; the risky shift effect is not likely to influence group decisions about nuclear war, as was once suggested, and processes of attraction between quasi-strangers are unlikely to ever explain the natural processes of intimacy and attraction (Levinger and Snoek, 1972). Yet each one of these research areas was conceived with an eye on the everyday, natural instances of the behaviours concerned.

The relationship between everyday reality and social psychological research is an even more intimate one. In order to increase "relevance", it is not sufficient to simply turn our attention to phenomena judged to be "relevant" at a given time. We must also recognize that our commonsense understanding of the social world, and the processes of scientific enquiry are mutually complementary, rather than conflicting avenues to increasing understanding, as Heider's (1958) oft-quoted, but little followed "naïve psychology" so potently demonstrated. The study of social episodes is envisaged as a study which should explicitly capitalize on our commonsense understanding of the social world, very much in the spirit of Heider's naïve psychology. Our competence, often implicit and not verbalized, to recognize and interpret a wide range of extremely complex social situations thus becomes a prime object of study. Such a close relationship between "scientific" and "commonsense" knowledge is increasingly recognized by social psychologists today.

Scientific, as well as everyday knowledge depends on a great number of unstated presumptions. "Single presumptions or small subsets can

in turn be probed, but the total set of presumptions is not of demonstrable validity, is radically underjustified. Such are the pessimistic
conclusions of the most modern developments in the philosophy of
science" (Campbell, 1974, p. 3). Commonsense and science are thus
not necessarily opposing extremes, as often suggested; rather, they
constitute different stages along an evolutionary continuum of knowing. Commonsense knowledge incorporates a highly selected set of
explanations, "based upon presumptions built into the sensory/ner-
vous system and into ordinary language, presumptions which have
been well-winnowed, highly edited and thus indirectly confirmed
through the natural selection of biological and social evolution. For
scientific theories, still more presumptive, the natural selection process
is continued through the competitive selection from among existing
theories (Popper, 1959, 1963, 1972; Quine, 1969)" (Campbell, 1974,
p. 3). Science thus does not replace commonsense knowing; instead,
it is based on it, and furthers it.

    How can we view social psychological research in this context? In
the first place, the oft-emphasized dichotomy beween the scientific
experiment and the commonsense world should be finally discarded.
The intuitive, commonsense roots of even the best controlled and
executed laboratory study should be clearly recognized: science should
elaborate and further our everyday understanding of such phenomena.
The problem with many existing studies is that they implicitly assume
that such furthering of our knowledge can only be achieved via the
reduction and breaking up of the phenomena into its minute, control-
lable elements. A complementary way, already suggested on the previous
pages, is to attempt to describe and quantify commonsense phenomena
in their entire complexity, and to use this data as the base from which
scientific hypotheses, and ultimately, higher-level explanations may
be derived. In terms of the main concern of this book, the study of
social episodes is a good example of such an approach. Clearly, social
episodes, and perceptions of social episodes, are exceedingly complex
phenomena—at the same time, they are part of the commonsense
knowledge of every member of a given culture and are routinely used
and referred to in everyday social life. The first task in studying
episodes is thus to represent, and if possible, quantify, this knowledge.
As will be shown in Chapter 5, this can be readily accomplished,
admittedly at the cost of losing some of the intrinsic richness of the
commonsense knowledge of our informants. Once this elusive data

base is recorded and quantified, in other words, once the stage of quantitative descriptions has been reached, it is possible to evaluate a number of hypotheses about this data base. These hypotheses can elaborate, specify, and quantify the commonsense knowledge on which they are based, and at their best, can in fact provide new insights about social episodes. For example, it can be shown that a judge's status and position in his group is related to his perception of social episodes, and it can also be shown that social status and episode perception are quantifiably related (Chapter 7). One of the most important points to emerge from the current soul-searching in social psychology pertains to the issue of the relationship between everyday behaviour and science. The approach to the study of social episodes suggested here will hopefully contribute to the development of a social psychology in which scientific research, and commonsense everyday knowing will be seen as complementary rather than antagonistic, based on principles such as the ones proposed by Heider (1958) in his "naïve psychology".

Models of man and the study of social episodes

The second main theme running through many of the contemporary criticisms of social psychology focuses on our conception of human beings as passive "subjects", rather than as active, intelligent and creative individuals. This issue is the underlying common denominator between such widely different recent approaches to social psychology as Harre and Secord's (1972) call for studies of "accounts", the "adversary model" proposed by Levine (1974), or the advocation of role-playing as an alternative to experiments by Mixon (1974) and Ginsburg (1979).

What sort of a "model of man" is implied by our concern with the study of social episodes? And what are the implications of some of these recent criticisms for the kind of conceptualization and methodology we should seek to develop to study social episodes effectively? These are some of the questions we shall discuss in the following pages.

Harre and Secord (1972) suggest that the dominant model of psychology (and not only social psychology) includes three sets of assumptions. First, a mechanistic model of man implies that behaviour should be explained in terms of external stimuli, that the same causes should consistently result in the same effects, and that intervening, organismic variables should be minimized. This set of assumptions is perhaps the least tenable, and most frequently criticized. The history of learning theories itself demonstrates the impossibility of persevering with a purely external variable approach (Hilgard and Bower, 1966), and the lack of uniform reactions to the same stimuli even within the same organism are well demonstrated.

The second set of assumptions pertains to a Humean conception of efficient causes. This implies that psychologists seek to establish invariable causal relationships between stimulus and response, that external stimuli are seen as "approaching the status of efficient causes" (Harre and Secord, 1972, p. 27), and that internal, organismic factors are considered only as conditions for the primary cause–effect relationships studied. This is a much more difficult point to argue, since there can be little doubt that for many behaviours external variables can be regarded as the efficient causes, a point which was repeatedly made by radical learning theorists, such as Skinner. It is the overgeneralization of these findings to much more complex behaviours which is objectionable in this context.

The third set of assumptions relates to the belief that the logical positivist methodology is the best scientific approach to behaviour, implying a "verificationist theory of meaning, . . . an operationist theory of definition, . . ." and the view that "the role of theory is restricted to providing a logical organisation of the given facts" (p. 28).

These three sets of beliefs add up to a conception of man as "subject", a reactor rather than an actor, and implies that the ideal methodology for study is the controlled experiment, with its independent and dependent variables. The main objection against this view comes from the humanistic-phenomenologist stream in psychology, who argue that "human beings must be treated as agents acting according to rule, and it must be realized that it is unscientific to treat them as anything else" (Harre and Secord, 1972, p. 29). What Harre and Secord (1972) propose is in fact the replacement of the Humean, mechanistic and logical positivist view of science with a rational, realistic conception of science. This would imply an anthropomorphic conception of human beings as rational, thinking and feeling individuals. Their personal reports and accounts of their behaviour are proposed as the new raw data for behavioural science. This would place the emphasis on the study of reasons, rather than causes, as explanations of behaviour, and on the intensive study of the social contexts and rules which individuals perceive as relevant to their behaviour.

Harre and Secord (1972) further expand the notion of social rules by suggesting that social psychologists should turn more of their attention to the study of life situations. "Central to all analysis of social life is the concept of episode . . . An episode is any sequence of happenings in which human beings engage which has some principle of unity" (p. 10). This approach has a close affinity with the phenomenologist tradition in psychology on the one hand, insofar as it places emphasis on an individual's understanding and perception of his environment and actions within it. On the other hand, Harre's views are also related to the symbolic interactionist theory of G. H. Mead, which emphasizes the dialectic interdependence between the individualistic, creative, and the socially "given" elements in social behaviour. Both of these approaches will be considered in more detail later.

The main methodological tool suggested by Harre and Secord (1972) to implement their ambitious programme of reforming social psychology is based on the systematic collection and interpretation of explanatory accounts by social actors. Since similar propositions for an increased reliance on subjective verbal statements as data have been advanced by others, it may be appropriate to consider the collection of accounts as a methodology in some detail here. The present approach to the study of social episodes clearly implies that we study how individuals and social groups come to construct and cognitively represent the interaction situations in their environment. A consideration of subjective accounts as data is thus particularly relevant to this task.

The collection of subjective accounts

It is received wisdom by many today that science is, by its very nature, non-normative. In other words, subjective values, norms, or preferences have no role to play in the methods of science, and correspondingly, science cannot resolve issues which are normative or subjective in their substance. Insofar as human beings, as the custodians and perpetrators of science are themselves subject to values or even prejudices, these must be minimized as far as possible in the interest of good science.

One of the major implications of this view can be found in psychology. Apart from the early flowering of introspectionism, and interest in consciousness which ended with Titchener's death in 1927, subjectivity has been banished from psychology, and topics such as insight, consciousness or phantasy were not considered to be fit subjects for study. As a corollary to the banishment of consciousness from psychology, verbal, open-ended or introspective evidence was also considered to be unacceptable as the basis upon which scientific knowledge could be developed. This objection is based on two arguments. Firstly, reports of an introspective nature refer to events which are by definition private and impossible to substantiate. Secondly, introspective reports can be subject to a wide range of uncontrollable distortions and unforeseen modifications. These prohibitions are seldom applied consistently, however. Much of social psychological, as well as human experimental research relies on subjects' self-reports of internal events (admittedly, simple and easily interpretable events) as their measures of variables. Even as staunch an anti-introspectionist as Watson recognized that "given an identifiable external stimulus accessible to independent observers, the verbal report of inner experience could be used as an index, or as a form of response amenable to reliability checks and to systematic study" (Levine, 1974, p. 666). Could verbal reports be used perhaps as sources of scientific data even in situations where the external stimulus is not readily identifiable? To some extent, this issue has a foregone conclusion; verbal self-report data are already used in a wide range of situations, particularly in personality and social psychology. To the extent that this is the case, suggestions made by Harre and Secord (1972), Levine (1974), Gergen (1973) and others to rely on verbal accounts are not radically new.

However, it is important to remember that the use of verbal accounts is still restricted by an important limiting consideration: even though the "external stimulus" may no longer be directly observable, it is important that there should be some means for establishing the reliability of such verbal accounts. One possibility for demonstrating reliability is to use several intersecting measures of the same phenomenon. When dealing with phenomena which are essentially consensual, or cultural in nature, such as the concept of social episodes, the degree of consensual agreement between different informants about an episode is an important indicator of the reliability of the measurement technique, as well as the cultural generality or salience of the object studied.

In the approach to the study of social episodes advocated here, open ended, or structured verbal materials are one of the most important sources of data. This approach is similar to the procedure recommended by Harre and Secord (1972), the collection of accounts of act–action structures. However, it does represent a development of that technique insofar as questions of reliability and validity are explicitly considered, and consensual agreement within a given culture regarding their episodes is taken as an important indicator of the validity of the technique itself.

The emphasis on subjective reports, that is, "using the human observer as the basic research instrument in human science" (Levine, 1974, p. 667) is an idea common to many of the recent critics of social psychology. The use of subjective accounts in the study of social episodes as proposed here must, however, be tempered by acknowledging the necessity for these reports to be reliable and valid in order for them to be of any use at all. Once again, the approach taken here is a synthesis of old and new methods, rather than a radically new departure.

The issue of the scientific status of subjective reports and observations emerges in yet another context. Should the psychologist, as an experimenter and a student of social behaviour, be able to use his observations, his understanding of the situation as "data"? Rigid adherence to an illusory "objective" model of science in psychology has meant that, all too often, researchers were not given any scope to communicate their unquantifiable observations within the accepted framework of scientific communication. The banishment of insight and subjective interpretation in order to maintain the inviolable subject–object, observer–observed stance has some curious consequences: ". . . I feel that in our determination to maintain this difference we have gone too far . . . All too often the scientific psychologist is observing not mind or behaviour but summed data and computer printout. He is thus a self-incarcerated prisoner in a platonic cave, where he has placed himself with his back to the outside world, watching its shadows on the walls" (McGuire, 1973, p. 453). Lately, many social psychologists have become fed up with this restriction, and began to eye with increasing envy the freedom to comment of researchers such as Goffman, Garfinkel or Lyman, who have come to the study of social behaviour not from a psychological, but from a sociological background, free from the above restrictions of mechanistic science.

Warr, a psychologist deeply concerned with the application of social psychology to real-life problems, echoes this sentiment: "The observations made by a trained and skilled psychologist as he takes part in a field experiment are themselves valid scientific data. They assist him in his understanding and they should be acceptable as evidence in his scientific publications. A detailed account rather than a brief summary is essential so that other researchers can evaluate his conclusions" (Warr, 1977, p. 6). Interest in social episodes is partly attributable to the impact of such detailed observations of social behaviour as those offered by Goffman, Matzo, Garfinkel and others. The present approach again is one which seeks to fuse the intuitive, journalistic methodologies predominantly used by these authors with the more quantitative methods commonly used in social psychology. The two methodologies are clearly complementary rather than mutually exclusive: the subjective interpretations support and elaborate the numerical findings of the quantitative analyses. The interdependence of these two approaches will be highlighted in some of the studies described later in the book while the exact nature of the methodologies suggested will be developed in Chapter 5.

In summarizing Harre and Secord's (1972) work, it must be said that their impact on the practice of social psychological research has been greater on both sides of the Atlantic than that of most other critics. Their criticism of the rather narrow conception of what is scientific in social psychology is powerful, and their suggestions to study units of social behaviour such as social episodes is also of great importance. Unfortunately, the methodologies suggested to achieve this in the latter parts of their book leave a lot to be desired, and this might explain why the proposed study of episodes has not progressed very far. Their reliance on the journalistic, anecdotal method as nearly the sole source of information about episodes is difficult to reconcile with the need for replicable and, preferably, quantifiable data which lies at the heart of scientific endeavour. One of the most important influences on the writing in this book, and for some of the studies presented herein can undoubtedly be traced to the arguments of Harre and Secord (1972). It is equally important to note, however, that the approach suggested here is substantially different from that offered by these authors.

Subject versus confederate—role-playing as a source of data

One of the general themes voiced by Harre and Secord (1972) and by many critics of experimental psychology concerns the widespread practice of treating human subjects as something less than fully conscious, perceptive and intelligent beings: the individual's interpretation and understanding of the events studied is intentionally ignored.

The remedies suggested are commonly based on a strategy which seeks to obtain the full and conscious cooperation of the subject in the scientific enterprise. This can be in the form of the collection of unstructured accounts (Harre and Secord, 1972), or in the form of obtaining the cooperation of the subject to enact (role-play) specified social situations. Role-playing as an alternative methodology has received increasing attention in the past few years. It is a strategy which promises to utilize the subject's cognitive and social skills to the full, without deceiving him, at the same time providing data which is claimed to be no less valid than data obtained in controlled experiments.

It is interesting that role-playing as a methodology is intricately interwoven with conceptions of the "social episode" as the relevant framework within which role-play takes place. The definition of the subject in role-play as a conscious, intelligent and consequently *rule-following* agent (Harre and Secord, 1972; Mixon, 1972) implies that the social context within which he acts is an integral part of the study. "Social episode" is a term most frequently used by role-play theorists to denote this "context" (Mixon, 1974; Forward *et al.*, 1976; Harre, 1970). "Role playing can then be used to further understanding by exploring social episodes; interpretations based on the exploration can be tested by another form of role-playing" (Mixon, 1974, p. 81). This approach is radically different from the "received wisdom" in experimental studies.

The necessity to deceive subjects was long taken for granted in social psychology. As Forward *et al.* (1976) point out, there are at least two major theoretical traditions which are used to justify deception. The first one is "the strict behaviouristic position that regards human cognitive factors . . . as being epiphenomenal . . . In this tradition, deception is believed to be an appropriate control for such irrelevant cognitive activities in the study of 'real' behaviour" (p. 596). The second theoretical tradition accepts that the subjects' cognitive interpretation of the situation can affect his behaviour, but since the situation, typically a laboratory experiment, is by definition an artificial one, deception as to the real object of the study is used in order to obtain "natural" behaviour in a contrived situation (Rosenthal and Rosnow, 1969). In terms of this argument, the subjects' cognitive capacities are seen as a threat, rather than as an aid to the efficacy of the experiment. The use of deception techniques has been criticized not only on ethical grounds, but also on the grounds that (i) they make no use of the full range of information that can be provided by the subject and (ii) they seek to "divert or misdirect the intentional strategies of subjects away from the behaviour to be investigated" (Forward *et al.*, 1976, p. 597). In other words, the behaviour studied will be peripheral to the subject, not fully in the centre of his intentional strategies, as a result of the deceptive cover-story; and (iii) typically, subjects used in social psychology experiments are not "naïve", and are unlikely to behave naturally in deceptive experiments.

The role-playing model, in contrast, seeks to co-opt the subject as a partner in the scientific enterprise, to use him as a partial collaborator and informant on an explicit, contractual basis which does not involve deception (Kelman, 1967, 1972). It is based on "eliciting the subject's positive motivations to contribute to the experimental enterprise . . . by conscientiously taking the roles and carrying out the tasks that the experimenter assigns to him" (Kelman, 1967, p. 9). In practice, role-enactment methodologies include a fairly heterogenous, and often *ad hoc* range of procedures, which characteristically involve asking the subjects to behave, or verbalize intentions to behave, in a range of "as if" type situations. The independent variables are commonly manipulated by varying the verbal description or definition of the hypothetical situation provided by the experimenter. Thus, Mixon (1972, 1974) used the role-playing method to analyse how subjects in Milgram's classic obedience study understood and interpreted the episode. He argued that given that the psychological experiment is, by definition, "a situation of almost unrivalled compliance . . . Milgram's situation was one that could be defined either as an experiment where expected safeguards had broken down, or as an experiment where expected safeguards only appeared to have broken down" (1974, p. 74). In Milgram's study, the experimenter's behaviour was matter-of-fact, indicating no alarm at the apparent suffering of the subject. This defined the situation as "being under control" to the subjects, who were prepared to continue administering electric shocks. By changing the experimental scenario in such a way that it "became perfectly clear that the experimenter believed the 'victim' was being seriously harmed all actors indicated defiance to experimental commands" (Mixon, 1974, p. 80).

Role-playing techniques can be further used in simulation studies, asking groups to enact certain episodes (Kelman, 1967). Studies of juries, or negotiating groups often use this simulation procedure. Another alternative is to ask subjects to enact specified social episodes in terms of "scripts" provided by the experimenter, which contain predetermined variations of theoretical interest to the experimenter (Ginsburg, 1979). This approach comes close to demonstrating cause–effect relationships typically obtained in laboratory studies. A variant of this technique relies on asking subjects to indicate under what circumstances, or as a result of which kinds of instruction they would act in a given way, for example, in a hypothetical experimental situation (Mixon, 1972). It should be noted however that role-playing is a technique to explore conscious, rule-governed acts, and not merely behaviours; thus, role-play always involves, and implies the presence of a social episode, a term used by those advocating role-playing methodologies as a summary term to denote the social context of the behaviour.

Role-play as a tool of exploration involves the elaboration of common, typical social episodes. "Exploration involves extending common knowledge. Much of social behaviour, no matter how well observed and reported, is not well understood. Suppose an investigator is simply puzzled by a social scene or episode and wonders why people in particular roles in a particular context do what they do. A scenario can be drawn up, and actors can repeat the puzzling scene as many times and with as many modifications as are necessary to understand the scene. The scenario method is a way of tinkering with what might be called a working model of a social episode" (Mixon, 1974, pp. 78–79). In this exploratory stage, role-play can be used to (i) represent the whole range of feasible, or acceptable behaviours within a given social context (taxonomic function); (ii) the most frequently occurring, or most typical acts given the social episode can then be identified (stereotyping function); and finally (iii) the sequential rules governing the flow of events within a given episode can be subjected to study using the role-play method (time-sequencing function). These three functions are in effect different facets of the systematic description of an episode which should precede the hypothesis testing stage in research.

But role-play can also be used in a quasi-experimental fashion, to evaluate experimental hypotheses; ". . . role-enactment experiments may incorporate many standard features of experiments, such as constructing experimental conditions across 'factors' of interest (i.e. providing 'scripts' that vary the states of given rule/role contexts), randomly assigning actors to conditions . . . , using repeated measures designs, and standardizing scripts and procedures so that studies may be replicated by others" (Forward *et al.*, 1976, p. 601).

However, some of the more unbridled claims made for role-play by its advocates should be taken with a pinch of salt. Role-playing is not likely to completely replace experimentation in the near future, neither is it probable that deception as a standard methodological procedure will disappear. There are several critics who have commented on the shortcomings of the method. Since in role-play subjects know that the situation is not real, their responses, in effect cognitive estimates as to their likely behaviour, will also be one step removed from reality. As a result, even if motivated to be honest, subjects (i) may not know with any certainty how they would actually behave in a real situation; (ii) their responses can be affected by a variety of unintended distortions, such as social desirability, demand characteristics etc. Bearing these shortcomings in mind, Freedman (1969) suggests that "the use of role-playing under most circumstances constitutes a return to the pre-scientific days, when intuition and consensus took the place of data" (p. 108).

How does role-play fit into the current theme of social episodes? Role enactment can be seen as one of several methodologies, all characterized by a desire to use not just the observable behaviours, but also the whole conscious, interpretative capabilities of subjects as sources of data. This may take the form of collecting unstructured accounts (Harre and Secord, 1972), simulation, role-play or adversary argumentation (Levine, 1974). Surprisingly, all discussions of role-playing as a methodology are based on the implicit assumption that it is used as a nomothetic rather than as an idiographic method: to study groups, populations or cultures, and not individuals. In a sense, this is indeed "science by consensus", as alleged by Freedman (1969), insofar as consensuality in role-playing studies indicates the existence of a shared, cultural pattern of responding in a given episode. It is in this context that role-play is an important tool in the research into social episodes: it can tell us how, all things being equal, individuals from a given cultural background are likely to behave in a specified episode. These are indeed important data, and a necessary prerequisite for more sophisticated experimental studies. Again, Mixon's (1972) study is a good example. Logically, and in accordance with accepted tenets of how science should proceed, Mixon's study should have preceded Milgram's. Mixon described a wide range of circumstances and conditions which may lead to obedience or to its absence. It is essentially a study which explores the range of potentially important variables, but does not establish any causal link between a set of circumstances and obedience, mainly because the episode studied lacks reality. Milgram's study on the other hand can be seen as one concentrating on one specific constellation of circumstances, one specific episode (an unconcerned experimenter in an experimental setting), and establishes that this set of circumstances is sufficient to induce obedience. To the extent that the episode is similar to those it seeks to simulate in real life, the experiment has external validity. And indeed, an episode where inhumane orders are given by an individual who is (i) apparently unconcerned with the fate of the victim, and (ii) has authority and is in complete charge of the situation is not a bad approximation of the episodes Milgram sought to simulate. The point is that role-play is a more open and flexible technique than experimentation, and in this case more appropriate in the preliminary, hypothesis-generating, descriptive stage of research. The study of social episodes is one of those fields where role-playing techniques hold some promise of relevance, both as tools of description for charting culturally accepted scenarios for given social episodes, and as tools of hypothesis testing, for establishing the causal functions of specific events within the context of a particular episode.

Social episodes and applied social psychology

Since our conceptualization of social episodes and indeed, the whole approach underlying the study of naturalistic interaction sequences has a close affinity with applied social psychology, it may be of interest to consider briefly some recent research strategies proposed by researchers concerned with applied problems.

The motivation to seek new alternatives is rooted in the intrinsic inapplicability of the experimental method to many important areas of industrial, community and clinical psychology.

One of the interesting new models for the scientific study of social behaviour was modelled on the legal system for establishing the truth, and is labelled the "adversary model" (Levine, 1974). The model has certain key assumptions. The first one is that "important problems of psychology involve whole human events that always take place in a historical and social context. Whole human events cannot be properly treated or understood when divorced from a total social and historical context" (Levine, 1974, p. 665). Indeed, the study of social episodes is motivated by exactly the same, seemingly obvious yet often ignored assumption. Social episodes are meaningful, total units of social inter-action, and their study is a necessary step for placing social behaviour into its relevant socio-cultural context.

The adversary model takes the legal analogy further, however. Courts through the ages were engaged in looking at whole human events, using the tool of human intelligence, seeking the consensus of the relevant community and using a code of proceedings in their deliberations. Rules of evidence are particularly important as com-ponents of this system, since they regulate what is acceptable and what is not in the adversary proceedings. Rules of evidence regulate (a) the presentation and evaluation of materials, (b) ensure the efficiency of the proceedings, (c) safeguard higher principles deemed to be import-ant, i.e. the ethics of obtaining information, and (d) limit the inferences that can be made from evidence presented. There are some important analogies between these functions, and the processes involved in scien-tific research. Does this analogy extend so far that the legalistic model can in fact be substituted for the existing model, in order to arrive at scientific truth? As a general remedy for the shortcomings of the lab-oratory experiment, this is surely too exaggerated a reaction. But in specific instances of applied research, mainly clinical and community studies, the use of quasi-adversary procedures may be a salutary innovation.

In contrast to Levine's (1974) rather drastic proposal, another emi-nent applied social psychologist, Peter Warr, seeks to reform rather than to abandon the experimental method. Warr's contribution to the current argument about the method of social psychology is the advo-cation of "aided experiments" in field settings. Aided experiments are different from traditional experiments to the extent that the role of the experimenter is different. He is much more involved with the experiment, instead of attempting to minimize his effects, he is an active agent of change during the experiment, and acts as an observer and as an interpreter after the experiment. A second feature of aided experiments is that the researcher has more freedom, indeed an obligation, to use his intelligence, training and insight to comment on, and to interpret the experiment, both to the participants, and to the scientific community at large.

Perhaps these examples are sufficient to illustrate the point that the proposed study of social episodes is not of purely academic interest. Social psychologists working in applied areas have for long recognized the limitations of traditional methods, and recent proposals have included many of the points that we are also concerned with. This includes arguments for studying social episodes in their natural complexity, to regard subjects or clients and their accounts as reliable sources of data rather than objects to be manipulated, and a renewed interest in cultural conventions or rules which apparently regulate much of social behaviour. An empirical method for studying and quantifying social episodes would have important implications for clinical, industrial and community psychology, and some of these possibilities will be further developed in Chapters 9 and 10.

Summary

In this chapter we have considered many of the issues which underlie the debate concerning the nature, objectives and methods of social psychology in the seventies. Since this debate is far from finished, and its ultimate results will not be known for some time, it may be that this summary has not been quite correct in its emphasis on the various issues. Nevertheless, it is of undeniable importance to interpret and come to terms with the *Zeitgeist* of the discipline, particularly in a work which seeks to advocate new concepts and approaches. What can we distil from the current confusion, the multitude of arguments and counter-arguments regarding the most fundamental assumptions and research methods in social psychology?

Firstly, it is unlikely that a profound paradigmatic shift, as advocated by some critics is the answer. Rather, the gradual evolution of a broader range of research topics, and a more eclectic set of methodologies appears to be the most promising path. Social episodes may be one of these new areas of research, and a rich choice of new research strategies is also in the process of emerging (Ginsburg, 1979).

Much of the recent dissatisfaction can be traced to a particularly restrictive combination of experimental orthodoxy and theoretical parochialism during the past few decades, which has resulted in social psychology being seen by many as increasingly scholastic and far removed from the rich interest of everyday social behaviour. Among the broad spectrum of critics it is possible to discern a number of shared concerns, which hold important implications for the study of social episodes. There is a broad agreement that the social psychologist's idea of what constitutes acceptable scientific method has been unnecessarily restrictive, closer in emphasis to the now discarded assumptions of 19th century natural science than contemporary epistemological ideas. As a result the dominant mechanistic model of man and atomistic conceptions of the relationship between variables is being replaced by theories emphasizing the cognitive-phenomenological aspects of social actors, and the interactive relationship between the variables influencing social behaviour. Another point of agreement is the strong emphasis that many critics place on the importance of the descriptive stage of research as a necessary prerequisite to the critical phase. Calls for greater social relevance are also generally characteristic of recent comments on the state of social psychology. Finally, a renewed emphasis of the cooperative rather than manipulative relationship between experimenter and subject is another point of agreement.

The study of social episodes incorporates each one of these consensual points recently made about social psychology. Indeed, we may look at social episodes as a term which most appropriately embodies the communalities between critics. Episodes are natural units of interaction which focus on the cognitive competencies of social actors and the interactive relationship between the individual and his culture; descriptive techniques are eminently applicable to the study of interaction episodes, as are recently developed role-playing and other quasi-experimental techniques. Most importantly, however, the study of social episodes is of undoubted social relevance, with potentially very important practical applications in applied areas. In a very real sense, then, we might say that the study of social episodes was born of the recent malaise of social psychology, and it may represent an answer to at least some of the problems which were commonly identified.

3

Episodes and Situations in Psychology: A Historical Review

The concept of social episodes is not a neologism in social psychology, without conceptual roots; in fact, something akin to the present concern with how episodes, or more generally situational factors, influence social behaviour has been very much in the forefront of psychological thinking for many years. The basic aim of the present chapter is to trace the conceptual evolution of the term "episode" in psychology, with a view towards establishing the most important trends in this evolution.

Much of what follows will concentrate on psychological thinking about "situations" rather that "episodes" as understood here. As suggested earlier, the two terms have much in common, and a consistent separation would be not only difficult but also futile. The concept of "situations" is the more general and earlier one, and if we want to discover the conceptual roots of episodes, this is where we must begin. This is to some extent inevitable. The history of psychology, with its early insistence on the physical, objective and quantifiable situationthe only legitimate object of study, means that we first have to look at situations, if we want to discover the conceptual roots of the term episode.

The concept of situation, while a central construct in psychology, has suffered from a lack of clear definition to the extent that it has become nearly meaningless in modern usage: "often the concept of situation is left undefined, and frequently it is used interchangeably with the concepts of stimulus and environment" (Pervin, 1975c, p. 8). Some theorists despair of the term even more: Cottrell (1970), for example, writes: "I sometimes suspect that the utility (of this term) is quite as great in preserving an illusion of understanding as it is in conveying genuine comprehension" (p. 68). The general confusion about what a situation or an episode should really mean makes a historical review particularly difficult, since one can never be sure whether two authors use the terms in an even approximately comparable sense.

The existence of a number of further alternative terms, used interchangeably with situations, such as social encounters (Goffman, 1963), presentations (Scheflen, 1964) and behaviour settings (Barker and Wright, 1955) suggests that a historical review of the terminology with a view towards extracting areas of agreement among different authors, is long overdue. Such attempts are not necessarily successful, and intuitively meaningful terms are often made irreversibly ambiguous for scientific use (Glass, 1968; Hillery, 1955). Nevertheless, it is the aim of the present chapter to selectively review some of the most important theoretical contributions which include a situational component in their models of behaviour. In the second part of the chapter, empirical evidence demonstrating situational and episodic regularities in social behaviour will be considered.

For the present purposes, three large groups of theories will be distinguished:

(1) Early S–R theory in the radical behaviourist tradition, emphasizing a physicalistic, atomistic and objectively measurable concept of situation.

(2) In contrast, cognitive-phenomenological theorists such as Lewin, Koffka and Murray, have concentrated on molar situations as perceived and interpreted by the actor.

(3) Finally, social learning theoretical and symbolic interactionist approaches in some ways represent an attempt to reconcile the contradictions of the former two schools.

Learning theory

In a sense the first scientific attempt to understand how the environment, both physical and social, affects behaviour began with the advent of behaviourism. Watson's (1913) radical behaviourism, as well as Guthrie's (1952) later contiguity theory were more concerned with atomistic stimulus-response chains than with the behavioural effects of more complex situations: "Watsonian behaviourism has fragmented the physical environment into discrete quantifiable stimuli in order to study precisely their effect on the human organism" (Tuan, 1972, p. 250). In early learning theory there was no place for anything but an atomistic, physical and objectively measurable concept of the stimulus.

The first sense in which the term "situation" is used is thus to refer to more complex, molar, stimulus configurations (Pervin, 1975c). The initial conception of the stimulus as objective and external, with potential rather than actual effect on the organism (Gibson, 1960; Chein, 1954) gradually gave way to a more sophisticated, interactive view which in effect reflects the evolution of learning theory itself. Thus Thorndike's theory, although radically different from Watson and Guthrie in that it explicitly recognizes the "satisfying" and "annoying" effects of environmental stimuli, and thus introduces the reinforcement principle, is still based on a conceptualization of the situation which is objective and atomistic. Tolman's (1935) behaviouristic theory postulated a model in which environmental stimuli, heredity, past experience and physiological state jointly determine behaviour. Tolman regarded the situation as physical rather than phenomenological, and non-interactive with either the actor or other components in his model. However, in his later works (Tolman, 1948; 1949) the beginnings of a cognitive conceptualization of the situation are apparent: instead of direct S–R links, something like a cognitive map within the "black box" is now postulated. Tolman has not only recognized the role of motivations and goals as important intervening variables in the learning process; he has also shifted from atomistic to molar learning situations, thus paving the way for the emergence of later, more comprehensive conceptualizations of the situation.

Perhaps the first psychologist to emphasize the interactive nature of the organism–situation relationship was Kantor (1924, 1926). His conception of situations as "stimulus conditions" was strongly interactionist: the individual should be studied "as he interacts with all the various types of situations which constitute his behaviour circumstances" (Kantor, 1924, p.92). This exhortation seems especially relevant today, when it is becoming clear that research in learning theory is increasingly fragmented, especially because it failed to pay due attention to the natural behaviour circumstances of the organisms it studied (Seligman, 1970). Kantor's early work is also important in another respect: he has made the elementary distinction between the ecological, or physical environment and its internal representation from the actor's point of view. While Kantor's work is essentially behaviouristic in orientation, his conception of the individual is not that of a "reactor" to situational changes, but an "interactor". In his later theory, labelled "interbehaviourism" (Kantor, 1969), while firmly interactionist, he again discards all considerations of an unobservable, phenomenological "situation".

Kantor's interactionist formulations were the precursors of the more sophisticated and influential models of theorists such as Helson (1959, 1964). In his adaptation-level theory Helson pays particular attention to contextual and situational factors in perception and behaviour, differentiating between "focal" and "contextual" stimuli. Helson also argues that person variables "can be studied and understood only as they interact with concrete situations, and operationally such concepts have no meaning apart from situational factors" (Helson, 1959, p. 610).

The further development of learning theoretical formulations (Hilgard and Bower, 1966) has led to increasing reliance on cognitive intervening variables, and more and more elaborate empirical predictions (Hull, 1943, 1951). In a sense this development culminated in the social learning theories, where social and cultural factors were first accorded the status of a stimulus, and where internal processes are most widely invoked. However, it is important to note that it was early learning theory, itself a reaction to Wundtian introspectionism, which first focused attention on situational variables as relevant determinants of behaviour. While these early conceptualizations were often somewhat simplistic, they laid the groundwork for later more elaborate models of situational differences in behaviour. Perhaps more surprising is the fact that while early learning theorists repeatedly emphasized the importance of environmental and situational variables in human behaviour, a systematic study of the characteristics and attributes of these variables was never carried out. Instead, the effects of a selection of *ad hoc* stimuli on behaviour were studied, without any attempt to establish the representativeness of those stimuli used as independent variables, and the relationship between the stimuli studied and other, neglected, situational variables. A taxonomy of situations, which would have been crucial for specifying the stimulus side of the S–R formula, was never constructed. By insisting that all stimuli were in essence alike, learning theorists have managed to ignore that which should have been the focus of their attention. The current malaise of researchers in areas of fundamental learning processes, in some ways similar to the doubts haunting social psychologists, is the price paid for ignoring the "situation" for so long. Yet, as numerous recent reviews (Ekehammar, 1974; Bowers, 1973; Endler and Magnusson,

1974) point out, a systematic study of situational factors as co-determinants of behaviour has not been carried out to date.

Cognitive-phenomenological theories

While Watsonian behaviourism was an extreme reaction against Wundt's psychology of consciousness, Wertheimer originated a movement which, while still concerned with human experience, aimed at studying it as an indivisible whole. *Gestalt* psychology, insisting on the unity of human experience, had two important effects on the conceptual status of situations; first, the distinction between physical and psychological, or objective and subjective environments was finally explicitly stated. Second, the idea of the insightful, understanding individual allowed for an interactive rather than a unidirectional relationship between person and situation. The *Gestalt* psychology of Koffka (1935) is an excellent illustration of this new conceptualization. Koffka has explicitly recognized the difference between the "geographical", or objective situation and the "behavioural", or subjective situation. In his system, the behavioural environment is a derivative of the geographical environment, as a result of the interaction between the person and the objective situation: "*G* is the geographical environment. It produces *BE*, the behavioural environment; in this, and regulated by it, *RB*, real behaviour, takes place, and parts of it are revealed in *PHB*, phenomenal behaviour" (Koffka, 1935, p. 40).

It is important to note that in Koffka's system it is the behavioural environment, *BE*, rather than the geographical environment, *GE*, which ultimately determines behaviour—a position which is very much in agreement with some of the most recent cognitive formulations (Mischel, 1973).

Kurt Lewin's extremely influential "field theory" (1935, 1936, 1938, 1951) was the first comprehensive model of human behaviour in which situational variables were accorded a central place. As Mischel (1975) recently stated, "although Lewin told us about the environment's role long ago, his impact seems to have been more on textbooks . . . than on personality theorists" (p. 8). There are three central propositions in Lewin's theory which have greatly affected later conceptualizations of situational effects on behaviour.

The first important contribution of Lewin's theory is implicit in the famous $B = f(p,e)$ formula: behaviour is a function of both the person and the environment. However, the immense experimental work directly stimulated by Lewin's formulation has largely bypassed the evaluation of the effects of given situations on behaviour. A systematic study of situational characteristics was again not undertaken, even though this would have followed directly from the postulates of the theory.

The second main contribution of Lewinian theory was its emphasis on the psychological, subjective, as against the objective environment as a determinant of behaviour. Both "life space", containing all determinants of behaviour, and the phenomenal field, or psychological situation, are subjective concepts, defined as seen by the actor, rather than in terms of objective, physical qualities: "the situation must be represented in the way in which it is "real" for the individual in question, that is, as it affects him" (1936, p. 25). The similarity between this assertion, and the famous "Thomas theorem" (Merton, 1957) so influential in sociology, is striking: "if men define situations as real they are real in their consequences" (Thomas, 1928, p. 522). It is all the more surprising therefore that psychologists and sociologists arrived at this insight independently, that there was very little cross-fertilization of ideas, and that in both these disciplines, the concern with the phenomenological situation has remained a minority preoccupation to date. Only very recently, in the works of Goffman and Garfinkel, has the fusion of psychological and sociological traditions become a reality.

Thirdly, Lewin's conception of the situation, or the phenomenal field, is essentially holistic: the actor's perception of the situation, including his own role and function within it, is indivisible. As will be argued later, any meaningful definition of social episodes will also have to rely on such a holistic orientation.

Although perhaps less influential than Lewin's classic theory, Murray (1938, 1951) devoted more attention to the interactive relationship between the person and his environment than any other psychologist. Strongly influenced by the holistic orientation of the *Gestalt* psychologists, and the geographical-behavioural environment distinction of Koffka in particular, Murray argued that "the conduct of an individual cannot be formulated without a characterization of each confronting situation, physical and social . . . the organism and its milieu must be considered together, a single creature-environment interaction being a convenient short unit for psychology" (Murray, 1938, pp. 39–40).

The clue to the person–situation interaction in Murray's theory is the need-satisfying or frustrating potential of the environment (press), and its relation to the individual's needs. Murray has also proposed an explicit distinction between the objective, physical, and the subjective, psychological aspects of the situation: he coined the much quoted terms of "alpha press" and "beta press" to denote these two respective aspects of the situation.

In describing individuals in terms of needs, and situations in terms of need-satisfying potential (press), Murray created a conceptual system in which both individuals and situations could be described in terms of a common dimensional framework of classification. Murray's awareness of the importance of a descriptive taxonomic system of both persons and situations led him to propose an initial two-dimensional system of positive–negative and mobile–immobile press (Murray, 1938, p. 120). These two dimensions bear a surprising resemblance to the universal evaluative and activity dimensions first proposed by Osgood et al., (1957) (cf. Ekehammar, 1974). Murray's interest in a taxonomy of different situations, however, was not followed up until very recently.

Influenced by the *Gestalt* psychologists and Lewin, several other psychologists proposed theories essentially cognitive-phenomenological in orientation. Angyal (1941), in his quest for a unified science of man, emphasized the inseparability of organism and environment, and the essentially subjective nature of different situations: "every person has his own personal world consisting of objects, the content of which is highly individualistic and not comparable with the content they have for another person" (1941, p. 160). Murphy's (1947) eclectic "biosocial" theory of personality clearly recognizes the effects of socio-cultural situations on the individual, yet he fails to make a clear distinction between objective and subjective situations.

Perhaps the ultimate development in the phenomenologist tradition is Rogers' (1951, 1959) humanistic theory of the self. The episode or situation in this theory becomes an aspect of the phenomenal field of the individual, which cannot be genuinely known or experienced by anyone else to the same extent. According to this theory, the person is the best and most valid source of information not only about himself, but also about his meaningful environment: "the organism reacts to the field as it is experienced and perceived. This perceptual field is, for the individual, reality" (1951, p. 484). External stimuli and the "objective situation" are in themselves meaningless in this system—it is only the subjective situation which matters. Rogers' theory is in a sense the end of the road: in contrast with the behaviourist concept of the situation as strictly physical and external to the organism, in self theory the situation becomes predominantly socio-cultural and internal.

Social learning theory and symbolic interactionism

The theoretical orientations discussed in this section are related in the sense that both social learning theory and symbolic interactionism developed as a reaction to some of the more manifest rigidities of learning theory, attempting to incorporate a wider range of cognitive and phenomenological variables in their models of behaviour. While in social learning theory this was accomplished by the incorporation of a large number of social and cognitive variables within an essentially learning theoretical framework and terminology, symbolic interactionism represents a wholly new departure, which provides a most promising theoretical framework for the study of social episodes.

Social learning theory in particular has stimulated continuing interest in the role of situations in human behaviour—after all, it was the traditional S–R paradigm which first suggested the immense significance of environmental and situational contingencies. Most current concern with situational differences in behaviour in psychology is kept alive by social learning theorists, such as Mischel's (1968, 1973) arguments for taking situational factors into account in personality theory. One of the more influential definitions of situations was offered by Rotter (1954, 1955) who, while recognizing that situations have subjective meanings, remained within the learning theoretical tradition by defining situations objectively: "Behaviours, reinforcements and situations may be defined in objective terms, although their significance and systematic formulae are concerned with constructs relating to personal or acquired meaning" (Rotter, 1955, p. 260). The ambivalence reflected in this statement is characteristic of learning theoretical approaches to situations: while recognizing that the perceived, phenomenological episode or "situation" is the most relevant influence on actual behaviour, the definition is nevertheless couched in objective terms in order to fulfil the essential axioms of learning theory. A similar ambivalence is also detectable in Mischel's (1968) earlier argument for a situational theory of behaviour. Rotter's contribution to the study of situations was important in another respect: he was among the first to realize that the persistent failure of psychological research to come to grips with the problem of describing and classifying situations would have to be rectified if social behaviour is to be understood. However, his proposition for a classification of situations in terms of need concepts was again not followed up by empirical research.

The lack of research on episodes and situations, both objective and subjective, and on situational effects on behaviour was increasingly emphasized by later theorists. Jessor (1956), in arguing for phenomenological theories of personality, pointed out that one of the most important tasks facing psychology in the future "is the development of an adequate psychological data language to describe the environment" (p. 178).

The contribution of Egon Brunswik to an adequate conceptualization of the social situation is perhaps the most important such development in the past few decades. Brunswik (1956) went a step further than most theorists before him in claiming a central place for the study of situations in psychology. In proposing a "representative design" in psychology, he suggested that "proper sampling of situations and problems may in the end be more important than proper sampling of subjects, considering the fact that individuals are probably on the whole much more alike than are situations" (p. 39). Brunswik's propositions have highlighted the difference between traditional "systematic" design where a few arbitrarily selected variables, unrepresentative of the organism and its normal environment, are studied in an *ad hoc* situation, and what Brunswik called "representative" design, based on the representative sampling of the life situations relevant to the oraganism's everyday functioning. In emphasizing the unrepesentatives of many of the episodes and situations normally studied in laboratory experiments, he foreshadowed the much more recent concern with the unique characteristics of the laboratory episode by Orne (1962), Rosenthal (1966) and others. Brunswik was thus the first psychologist for whom the sampling of situations was of greater importance than the sampling of individuals. He has also proposed an influential taxonomy of different situational events in terms of (a) their relation to the actor (distal–promimal–central), and (b) in terms of their objective observability (e.g. overt v. covert distal variables). While he was most interested in the effects of overt distal variables (the objective situation) on distal responses, he acknowledged the existence of other kinds of relationships.

Some more recent social learning conceptualizations of situation are strongly reminiscent of ideas first developed by the symbolic interactionists. Spielberger (1975), for example, strongly emphasizes the effects of previous experience on the perception and interpretation of situations: "the greater the periodic occurrence of a particular type of situation, the higher the probability that an individual will develop consistent or coherent patterns of behaviour to cope with the situation" (p. 2). This proposition is very similar to the symbolic interactionist argument maintaining that the cultural definition of the situation, emerging in the course of social interaction, will come to determine subsequent behaviour in that situation.

Symbolic interactionism

The symbolic interactionist theory of social behaviour represents in many respects the most sophisticated and acceptable conceptualization of social episodes and situations. Symbolic interactionism is in a sense the ultimate attempt to create a theory of social behaviour which would synthesize the behaviourist and phenomenologist, the environmentalist and mentalistic approaches to human behaviour: Mead's social behaviourism "was an attempt to correct many of the crudities of early behaviouristic psychology . . . /he/ believed that the scope of behaviourism could be extended to include the neglected introspective phenomena . . ." (Desmonde, 1970, p. 57). For these reasons, symbolic interactionism is a particularly important theory to consider in relation to the study of social episodes.

As a theory, it is truly social psychological, taking the process of social interaction as its starting point and aiming to bridge the traditional individual-society split in psychology—yet its impact has been more marked in sociology than in psychology. Symbolic interactionism may be defined as a theory which focuses on the process of social interaction (rather than on the individual, as psychology does, or on social systems, as sociologists do), emphasizing the symbolic, cognitive nature of human social interaction as distinct from processes of animal behaviour. Mead's social psychology is neither totally positivistic nor totally subjective—"it is the only truly social psychology, opting neither for the primacy of the individual nor for that of society"

(Kando, 1977, p. 108). By concentrating on the *process* of interaction, the theory does not reify either the isolated individual, or the social system as most other theories do, and consequently it escapes many of the criticisms of other social psychological models, outlined in the previous chapter. The essence of the theory is that it focuses on the dynamic, dialectic and ever-changing process of interaction to explain both the individual and the social system he creates. In terms of its institutional impact, symbolic interactionism is a coherent school of thought, which constitutes the humanistic alternative, the so-called "loyal opposition" in social psychology and sociology (Mullins, 1973).

Mead's "social behaviourism" (which was only later re-named symbolic interactionism (Blumer, 1969, p. 1)) had as its main objective the reconciliation of behaviourist and phenomenologist formulations, and he was equally critical of Watson and Wundt for presenting a one-sided, biased view of man. According to some critics, this attempt at a reconciliation also constitutes the greatest weakness of symbolic interactionism: "Mead's works pose a problem for any analyst, for the simple reason that they incorporate a fundamental conflict in Mead's thought between social behaviourism and more phenomenologically oriented ideas"(Douglas, 1973, p. 16). Ultimately, this ambiguity boils down to the dual image of man implied by symbolic interactionism, that of the independent, creative, insightful individual, Mead's "I", and that of the thoroughly socialized "Me". The distinction between the "I" and the "Me" as two aspects of the self was first proposed by William James (1892). The "Me" refers to the self as object, which incorporates the social self, as seen and reacted to by others, and changing in the light of feedback received in the course of social interaction. The "I" on the other hand is the subjective self, the reflexive self, the initiator of creative, independent action which defines the situation (Thomas, 1928b)—the "I" is the choosing and reviewing aspect of the self. Another way of viewing the difference between the "I" and the "Me" is in terms of determinancy; while the "Me" is wholly socialized and externally determined, the "I" is indeterminate. Most of the criticism of symbolic interactionism centre around the ambiguous relationship between these two aspects of self. Kuhn (1970) suggests that "Much of this confusion and contradiction in symbolic interactionism may be summed up . . . as a contradiction between determinancy and interdeterminancy in Mead's overall point of view" (p. 72). The concept of situations, and social situations in particular, has a crucial part in bridging the gap between the "I" and the "Me".

Situations in symbolic interactionist theory are social objects, created and continuously redefined in social interaction: "in each episode or encounter that we engage in we find that the situation is partially structured by past definitions, it has already been defined in terms of role scripts and normative expectations. At the same time, the episode is always open, it is subject to re-interpretation, and the attendant possibility of the creation of new accounts and meanings" (Brittan, 1973, p. 84). It is the human capacity for symbolic processes, the capacity to assign meaning to, and to distil consensual elements from unique situations which is crucial to this definition. But the essential contradiction of symbolic interactionism is also reflected in its approach to situations: are situations and episodes cultural "givens", embedded in culture and influencing behaviour, or do they represent the outcome of creative insightful individual behaviour? In fact the link between the "external" and the "internal" situation or episode is the experience of the individual himself: "the internalization in our experience of the external conversation . . . which we carry on with other individuals . . . is the essence of thinking; and the gestures thus internalized are significant symbols because they have the same meanings for all individual members of given society . . . (Mead, 1956, p. 159). By internalizing and symbolically representing the social episodes he participates in, the individual acquires social expertise, which is the essence of "Me". Yet episodes are not acted out in a repetitive, stereotypical fashion in real life—it is the role of the "I" to continuously re-assess, monitor, and re-define the social episodes the individual engages in.

There are thus two distinct aspects to the symbolic interactionist concept of situations and episodes: episodes are *structural* units, sociocultural objects, which are perceived by individuals with a degree of consensual agreement; and they are also *processes*, the continuous creation and re-creation of meanings through social interaction by creative individuals. It is interesting to note that in areas of social science where the impact of symbolic interactionism was most profound, such as sociology, this unity of external and internal social situations is rarely appreciated. Usually one or the other aspect of this dualistic definition of situations is emphasized, but rarely both. For example, researches in the tradition of Znaniecki and Wolff tend to emphasize the "culturally given" nature of social situations, while the followers of Thomas, together with most ethnomethodologists, place more emphasis on the creative process situations entail. The choice of emphasis appears to be primarily a function of the particular research orientation of the author: an analysis of culture implies a definition of situations as cultural objects, and the study of idiosyncratic human behaviour calls for an emphasis on the creative aspect of situation definition.

The influence of symbolic interactionism has been immense in the social sciences, stimulating new directions in sociology, such as most of the microsociological orientations, and providing new impetus to many of the phenomenologically orientated social psychologists. The current popularity of symbolic interactionism is largely due to its central assertion: "Symbolic interactionists repudiate the notion that man is a passive neutral agent . . . Man is both actor (the 'I') and acted upon (the 'Me'), both subject and object (Stone and Farberman, 1970, p. 9). Considering the criticisms of social psychology outlined in the previous chapter, this emphasis should recommend symbolic interactionism as a theory with an unrealized potential to influence social psychology. As we have seen earlier the approach to social situations proposed by the symbolic interactionists has strongly influenced the definition of social episodes adopted in this book. The impact of symbolic interactionism on sociology, especially ethnomethodology and dramaturgical theories, will be discussed in more depth in the following chapter.

Since symbolic interactionism is primarily a social psychological, and not a sociological theory, it is surprising that its effect on social psychologists has been so negligible. This is largely due to the fact the "social" has been consistently ignored in social psychology, ever since the discipline chose to define itself as a sub-area of psychology (Kando, 1977; Lindesmith and Strauss, 1956), with its attendant emphasis on quantification, prediction and the easy control and operationalization of variables. Symbolic interactionism is not a simple, linear, cause–effect model of human behaviour as are most other psychological theories. Rather, it empahsizes the ongoing, dialectic, fluctuating nature of social interaction processes. As we have seen in the previous chapter, the nearly universal reliance on one-directional, linear, cause–effect models is perhaps the most potent source of criticisms of the social psychology of the seventies (McGuire, 1973; Harre and Secord, 1972). Surely symbolic interactionism represents a more plausible and realistic model of social behaviour? More plausible it may be, but it was found to be extremely difficult to translate its theoretical predictions into empirical research.

The main source of difficulty is the ambiguity of many of Mead's concepts. Many critics suggest that Mead, rather than eliminating has simply re-labelled the duality of individual and society in the form of the "I" and the "Me". Certainly, the "I" and the "Me" are not empirically distinguishable, and indeed, the "I" can be regarded as a general residual category, where everything that cannot be explained by socialization is lumped (Meltzer and Petras, 1972; Kolb, 1944). Yet the concept of the "I" is the most important aspect of the theory, which distinguishes it from simpler social learning conceptualizations. Mead was also criticized on the ground that his image of man is that of purely rational, reasoned being—there is no place for emotions or irrational impulses in his model (Blumer, 1969) unless these are also lumped together with the "I". Cooley, the other main exponent of symbolic interactionism, who has strongly influenced Mead, on the other hand takes feelings and emotions about the self explicitly into account (Cooley, 1966). Taking symbolic interactionism as a school of thought rather than as the theory strictly speaking developed by Mead, there is clearly the possibility of taking emotions into account.

The charge of untestability is a more difficult one to contend with, and this is clearly the reason for the limited effect symbolic interactionism had on social psychology. Symbolic interactionism is about processes rather than objectively existing entities, and consequently, it is content-less, atheoretical and is subject to conflicting interpretations. In order to evaluate it, one must first specify its content. The study of the relationship between social structure and the perception of social episodes, described in Chapter 7 (Forgas, 1978 a) is an example of exactly such a study. Numerous empirical investigations (cf. Kando, 1977) using methods such as the Twenty Statements Test (TST) have shown that predictions derived from symbolic interactionism can in fact be evaluated empirically. Clearly, it is difficult to construct simple, linear, cause–effect hypotheses from Meadian theory, simply because the whole concept of such relationships is itself a violation of one of the most important tenets of the theory. But this does not have to mean that the theory is untestable; rather, it may reflect the limited conception of what is considered scientific method in social psychology.

What can we learn about social episodes from symbolic interactionism? Mead has highlighted most clearly the dual, yet indivisible nature of social situations; they are consensually defined, and to that extent, external, and objectively existing entities, embodying the rules, roles, norms and expectations of a proper sequence of behaviours as developed in a cultural milieu. At the same time, episodes are unique, internal and volatile, and subject to redefinition and alteration at a moment's notice—this is the "I" in action. In attempting to study social episodes, we can concentrate either on the consensual, or on the unique element. Most research stimulated by symbolic interactionism to date has tended to emphasize the typical, socially given nature of social episodes (Garfinkel, 1967; Goffman, 1964; Lyman and Scott, 1972; Stone and Farbermann, 1970). The scope for analysing and explaining unique, non-typical episodes is there, however, and some of Goffman's penetrating analyses have highlighted the unique rather than the typical in what goes on in social interaction.

So far, only a brief outline of the tenets of symbolic interactionism has been given. The considerable empirical and theoretical work directly stimulated by this school largely falls within the domain of sociology, and as such, it will be considered in more detail in the following chapter. At the end of this section it may be in order to quote Stone and Farberman's (1970) optimistic claim for the theory just discussed: "Symbolic interactionism will emerge as the dominant perspective of the future. Psychoanalysis, learning theory and field theory will ultimately be laid to rest in the vast graveyard of social science theory" (pp. 19–20). While it would be difficult to unreservedly share this optimism it is certainly true that symbolic interactionist theory, with all its ambiguities and contradictions, offers one of the most appropriate conceptual frameworks for studying social episodes.

This brief outline of the different theoretical approaches to the concept of situations was included for two purposes: to demonstrate the range of options available for definition, and to trace the historical evolution of the concept through the different theories. Both of these objectives are important in demonstrating that concepts such as situation and episode are deeply rooted in psychological theory, and their development indicates a clear line of conceptual evolution. With the advent of new, catchy phrases, it is often implied that radically new alternatives are being offered; as Robinson (1972) argues: "Instead of carefully and studiously inspecting our past, and sifting it in the light of such new enthusiasms as we have, . . . we dispense with it and leap on to some new bandwagon" (p. 51). Perhaps this brief review has helped to better anchor "episodes" in psychological theory.

In conclusion, the development of the concept "situation" in psychological theory could be summed up in terms of two dimensions of change: (a) early emphasis on the physical or ecological environment has gradually shifted towards emphasis on the social or cultural environment, and (b) early theories of situations as objective, measurable entities have become more cognitively and phenomenologically oriented, with the "situation as perceived" emerging as the main concern.

The evidence for situational consistencies in behaviour

As the theories reviewed in the previous section indicate, concern with situational effects on behaviour is by no means a new phenomenon. Yet empirical research demonstrating situational as against individual consistencies in behaviour was fairly scarce until relatively recently. Much of the work to be reviewed here features prominently in the continuing controversy in personality theory, regarding individual v. situational consistencies in behaviour.

Many of the studies to be cited below show that actual, or reported behaviour varies in different situations, thus tending to disprove the widespread implicit assumption of individual consistency in psychology. Nearly all of these situations are "social" in the sense that the actual or implied influence of others is present (Allport, 1924). In reviewing these studies, we are less interested in taking sides in the debate regarding the role of personal v. situational variables in the determination of behaviour, than in demonstrating the potency of social episodes in accounting for important differences in actual or reported actions.

Studies demonstrating situational consistencies in behaviour can be classified into two groups, in terms of their methodology. The first group includes studies where subjects' *behavioural reactions* to different situations have been evaluated, while the second method relies on *self-report reactions* to a range of situations, collected via questionnaires. In another sense, the first group may be regarded as being based on reactions to objective, actual situations, and the second on reactions to cognitive representations of actual situations, or subjective situations.

Studies of objective situations

Perhaps the earliest study explicitly concerned with situational consistency was Hartshorne and May's (1928) study of "deceit", a trait widely assumed to be person-specific, and not greatly affected by social and situational factors. A large number of children were placed in a series of staged episodes which were more or less conducive to cheating behaviour, and their reactions ("honesty") were scored and correlated across episodes. These authors found that contrary to popular contempory belief, "honesty" was not completely constant within individuals, but varied widely across situations, although a residual, individual-specific factor was also demonstrated. The authors argue, however, that even this intra-individual consistency "is a function of the situation, in the sense that an individual behaves similarly in different situations in proportion as these situations are alike" (p. 385). It should be remembered though, that in this study the similarity of two episodes was defined simply by the existence of similar levels of pressure to cheat. Already in this early study, the necessity to have some measure of situational perception is explicitly recognized. Hartshorne and May have also emphasized that the individual's understanding and representation of the situation is often more relevant to understanding his behaviour than objective and readily identifiable situational features.

Hartshorne and May's (1928) work on "honesty" has stimulated continued interest. For example, Burton (1963) applied factor-analysis to their original data, with essentially comparable results. A new study, designed along the lines of the original Hartshorne and May experiment, was carried out by Nelson et al., (1969), who concluded from their factor-analysis that situational factors, as well as the interaction of the person and the situation, indeed play an important part in "temptation behaviour".

A more sophisticated series of studies we carried out by Raush and his co-workers (Raush, 1965, 1972; Raush et al., 1959a,b; Raush et al., 1960), who observed samples of aggressive and normal boys in six different situations or life settings, and recorded their interpersonal behaviours. This was the first study where the total variance in different behaviour categories was partitioned into components attributable to situations, individuals, and interactions. These studies demonstrated for the first time that the interaction factor is more important than either situations or individuals alone. However, the theoretical implications of these findings were not explored until much more recently (Bowers, 1973).

Moos and his co-workers (Moos, 1968, 1969, 1970, 1972, 1973; Moos and Clemes, 1967; and Daniels, 1967) studied patients and staff in different situations in a psychiatric ward, and collected their data either by self-report, or through observer ratings. In an important study Moos (1968) asked psychiatric patients and staff members to indicate their feelings in a range of interaction situations. For the patients individual differences turned out to be more important than situational factors, whereas for staff members situational factors were relatively more important. It appears that in normal social interaction the cultural expectations embodied in the definition of the situation or episode are of prime importance, while for psychiatric patients idiosyncratic behaviour which is not contingent on socially defined norms may be more typical. In a follow-up study, which at the same time managed to break away from the usual self-report technique, Moos (1969) observed psychiatric patients behaving in a number of situations, and recorded eight indices of actual behaviour, including both verbal and non-verbal measures. He reports that non-verbal behaviours and smoking were person-specific, while other behaviours, such as talking and nodding for "yes" were more situation-specific.

Altman and his co-workers (Altman, 1968; Altman and Haythorn, 1965, 1967a,b; Altman and Lett, 1970; Haythorn and Altman, 1967) studied Navy conscripts' reactions to such situational variables such as isolation, degree of environmental stimulation, and personal compatibility or incompatibility with their partners. In this series of studies it was found that interactive behaviours, the use of space, and stress reactions were all strongly affected by situational variables. Mutual self-disclosure, for example, one of the dependent variables, was found to vary with situation rather than personal compatibility. The authors suggest that "interpersonal relations are not only *affected* by environmental milieus such as isolation, but also . . . the physical environment is actively used to manage social relationships in accordance with interpersonal compatibility" (Altman, 1968, p. 7), for example, by the way subjects use furniture and props, and by the territorial subdivision of available space.

It was also suggested that verbal behaviour, and different speech forms are often subject to strong situational specificity (Hymes, 1967).

In an interesting study Staples and Robinson (1973) studied different address forms used by staff in a department store as a function to the setting and the status relationship. They found strong situational differences in the use of address forms by staff, suggesting that status relationships between the employees implied by the address forms were not constant but fluctuated across situations. Clearly, the definition of an interaction episode always includes the specification of the status relationship between the interactants, and behaviours, such as address forms, vary as a function of such episode definition cues. A similar relationship was shown in a study by Forgas *et al.*, (1979a), summarized in Chapter 8.

Still using objective situations as independent, and observed behaviours as dependent variables, Magnusson and his co-workers (Magnusson *et al.*, 1968a; Magnusson and Heffler, 1969; Magnusson *et al.*, 1968b) reported a series of studies in which the objective difference between situations was manipulated by selectively controlling situational features such as group task or group composition. While this manipulation of situational similarity is obviously rather unrefined, these authors were nevertheless able to show that observers' personality ratings of the actors were highly correlated across "similar" episodes, and non-significantly correlated across dissimilar episodes. The apparent lack of intra-individual constancy in behaviours across different situations was thus again demonstrated.

Perhaps the most striking demonstration of situational effects on behaviour is the recent prison simulation study reported by Zimbardo (1973). In this experiment, college students selected by tests and interviews for the absence of any antisocial tendencies or other personality disturbances, were placed in a simulated prison setting. These authors report that after less than a week, otherwise normal subjects performing the role of prison guards display extreme instances of aggression, cruelty, sadism and other antisocial behaviours. The authors argue that these extreme reactions, which completely disappear once the prison episode is terminated, are the result of the "inherently pathological characteristics of the realistically simulated prison situation itself". This experiment was since successfully replicated at the University of New South Wales, Australia.

All of the studies outlined above used either self-ratings or observed ratings of actual behaviours in "real" situations as criteria for situational consistency. On the whole, the evidence is in support of a situation-specific element in social behaviour which apparently functions in interaction with person-specific factors. Studies of subjective, perceived situations yielded essentially similar results.

Studies of subjective situations

The most influential questionnaire study of reactions to different situations was Endler and Hunt's (1966) S–R inventory of anxiousness. In this instrument, subjects were asked to indicate the relevance of 14 possible responses to a range of anxiety-evoking situations. The results showed the apparent importance of situations in determining responses. This apparent situation-dominance was found to be misleading in their reanalysis of the original data (Endler *et al.*, 1966), when with a more sophisticated method they were able to compare the contributions of different sources to the total variance. Persons and situations were negligible in comparison with the size of the interaction effect, a finding supporting the interactionist point of view (Bowers, 1973). Follow-up studies by the above authors (Endler and Hunt, 1969; Endler, 1973) have yielded similar results, suggesting the generality of their findings. In the latter study, psychiatric patients were found to be relatively more "idiosyncratic" than normals in their behaviour across different situations, supporting Moos's (1968) results based on a rather different methodology. In another study, Endler and Hunt (1968) studied reactions to hostility-evoking situations—again, the interaction of individuals with situations explained the largest proportion of the variance.

Similar self-report inventories of different behaviours in different situations were used by Sandell (1968) to study elementary choice behaviours, and by Bishop and Witt (1970) to study leisure activities. Triandis's (1972) "behaviour differential" scales are also concerned with the assessment of self-report behaviours in hypothetical situations involving different categories of partners.

An interesting innovation in this line of research was Argyle and Little's (1972) study, in which situations were defined in terms of interpersonal relationships. These authors asked students to rate how they would behave in situations involving 12 hypothetical others, on 18 dimensions—once again, situational and interaction factors proved to be more important than personal factors in accounting for the variance.

Ekehammar *et al.*, (1974), following Endler and Hunt's (1962) earlier work argued that "individuals differ not mainly with regard to certain stable traits of behaviour, but . . . regarding their specific ways of adjusting . . . to situations" (p. 4). They asked 128 students to indicate their behaviours in reaction to 17 situations, and found that an overwhelming proportion of the variance was explained by person/situation interaction. Magnusson and Ekehammar (1975) have further developed this line of research, attempting to develop a technique for classifying individuals into homogeneous groups on the basis of their having similar profiles of reactions to similar situations.

An innovative use of the questionnaire method was initiated by Pervin (1975a,b, 1976) who, on the basis of Brunswik's arguments for a representative design in psychology, asked small samples of subjects (N=1, N=5) to produce a representative sample of their recurring interaction situations, and then analysed descriptions, behaviours and feelings about these situations. This approach overcomes the objection of using extreme, unrepresentative situations by asking subjects to describe only situations personally experienced by them. A significant variation in feelings and behaviours across situations was found by Pervin (1976) using this superior method. This study, as it is more concerned with the perception of episodes will be discussed in Chapter 7 in more detail. Questionnaire studies by Price and Bouffard (1974), Werdelin (1975), and Magnusson and his co-workers (Magnusson, 1971; Ekehammar and Magnusson, 1973; Magnusson and Ekehammar, 1973) also fall within this category. These latter authors in particular have explicitly argued that in studying situational effects on behaviour, the individual's subjective, cognitive representation of the "psychological environment" is of the greatest relevance.

Episodes and situations in psychology: a summary

As this brief review of the career of terms such as "episode" and "situation" in psychology indicates, concern with situational consistencies, as against individual differences in behaviour is as old as the discipline itself. Having said that, it is also beyond dispute that interest in, and the study of, situations and episodes as against individuals has remained a minority preoccupation, while the main thrust of research has concentrated on the study of individuals and groups, based on the implicit assumption of cross-situational consistency in behaviour. Even such explicitly "situational" theories as learning theory have in fact neglected to undertake a serious study of the situation and the episode, allegedly the major determinants of human behaviour. The dissatisfaction with the one-sidedness of most psychological theories has again and again manifested itself in recurring criticisms of the individual-consistency model by the most far-sighted psychologists. Thus, as long ago as 1956 Brunswik proposed that the representative sampling of situations is as important as the sampling of subjects for psychology. Cattel (1963) suggested that the study of how situations are perceived by individuals should be of central interest for psychologists, and Cronbach (1957, 1975) has repeatedly pointed out the dangers inherent in the bifurcation of psychology into two disciplines, concerned with the variation due to individuals and the variation due to situations in behaviour respectively. Thus, the first thing that this review indicates is that interest in episodes and situations was always there in psychology, and it would be misleading therefore to suggest that the study of social episodes proposed in this book is something radically new. While the study of social situations has not been regarded as a central issue for social psychology to date, there are important precedents and foundations upon which such an approach to social behaviour can be built. All too often, social psychology has been characterized by the rise and fall of different areas of investigation prompted more by a change in fashion than by anything else. Hopefully, by linking the proposed study of social episodes with pre-existing theories in psychology, it will be possible to transcend the ebb and flow of fashion, and make a plausible case for the permanent incorporation of this area of research into the discipline.

The second substantive reason for reviewing the evolution of situational concepts in psychology was to chart the main transformations in conceptualizations over the years. There are several very clear lines of evolution which can be discerned. The concept of situation emerged from the concept of stimulus in psychology, with a gradual shift from the atomistic to the holistic, from the physical to the social, and from the objective (external) to the subjective (perceived) situation. Gibson (1960) in his influential discussion of the concept of stimulus in psychology has suggested that there are at least eight dimensions along which conceptualizations of the stimulus differ. Most of these dimensions of disagreement may equally well be applied to the concept of episode or situation. In his recent review of the concept of stimulus and situation, Pervin (1975c) pointed out some of the possible areas of disagreement: "are situations to be defined objectively, or by the perceiver, are they potential or actual, and do they motivate the organism broadly, or trigger specific responses?" (p. 8). Some of the most important dimensions of disagreement, and an indication as to where the concept of "social episodes" might be positioned along them, are summarized below.

HOLISM V. ATOMISM

This distinction is mainly an historical one. The concept of a holistic, complex "situation" evolved from the early behaviourists' atomistic definition of the stimulus, to include a broader and more general set of environmental variables. A parallel distinction between the "molar" and the "molecular" environment was made by Gibson (1960), and Wohlwill and Carson (1972). This same terminology is used in a somewhat different sense by Postman and Tolman (1959), who define the molar environment as including all the situations an individual is likely to encounter in the course of his daily activities. As far as the study of social episodes is concerned, we are clearly more concerned with the complex, holistic situation as it affects the individual than with single, atomistic situational variables. If we are to maintain and enhance the real-life relevance of our investigations, as nearly all recent critics of social psychology urge us to do, we shall have to study social episodes in their natural complexity, as whole units of behaviour and experience.

PHYSICAL V. SOCIAL SITUATIONS

The initial definition of situations, first in purely physical terms, has gradually evolved towards a more cognitive, and also more social conceptualization. The distinction between the "physical" and the "social" situation is becoming increasingly blurred and untenable as the arbitrariness of separating physical from social variables is recognized. Thus, purely physical "behaviour settings" were shown to affect behaviour not so much by virtue of the physical restrictions they impose on behaviour, but because they are seen by social actors as symbolizing and representing the social norms and conventions of their culture (Barker, 1968). Even purely physical microenvironments,

such as architectural spaces, rooms etc. are not devoid of social content
(Craik, 1971; Laumann and House, 1970). The delicate interchange
between physical and social factors in the definition of an interaction
episode is explicitly recognized by many psychologists (cf. Altman and
Lett, 1967; Argyle, 1976). Recently, Mehrabrian and Russell (1974)
suggested that both physical and social environments could be analysed in terms of the same dimensional framework. Social episodes, as
complex units of social interaction, would clearly have a physical as
well as a social component. The separation of these two sets of factors,
for other than analytic reasons, would be counterproductive here, since
their interaction in structuring the social life of individuals is more
important than the study of either physical or social factors in
themselves.

THE POTENTIAL V. THE ACTUAL SITUATION

The theoretical distinction between potential and actual stimuli, the
first capable of affecting behaviour, and the second actually doing so,
is a long debated one in psychology (Chein, 1954; Gibson, 1959, 1960).
A similar distinction has also emerged in animal ethological studies,
where it was found that while the identification of a potential stimulus,
one that can act as a releaser of some fixed action pattern, is relatively
unproblematic, the specification of the contextual information and the
internal states of the organism necessary for such a stimulus to actually
elicit a fixed action pattern can be extremely complex (Tinbergen,
1965). With respect to human behaviour in different interaction episodes a similar distinction can be made. While a stereotypical episode
(e.g. a dinner party) is a potentially important determinant of very
similar behaviours by a large number of people, actual behaviour will
be a function of a large number of additional, contextual, and individual factors as well. Thus, a dinner party as a social episode is *potentially*
the determinant of a specific sequence of behaviours, but whether
those behaviours are going to be performed at any *actual* dinner party
is far from certain. Nearly all studies of social episodes and situations
have concentrated on the stereotypical consensual (i.e. potential) situation, rather than on actual, unique behaviours. Very few researchers
have shown any interest in understanding unique behaviours in unique
situations, probably because consensual agreement about, and similarity of responses to, potential episodes provide more generalizable

insights than would studies of unique, idiosyncratic behaviours. The difference between potential and actual situations is reflected in Sells' recent argument for two kinds of situational effects: "Two general modes of environmental influence on behaviour are assumed . . . (1) developmental programming, . . ./a/life-long set of processes involving internalization of experiences, and (2) contextual influence, in which . . . behavioural choices are affected by the ongoing configuration of circumstances . . ." (1973, p. 2). What this distinction highlights is the difference between generalized, accumulated expectations about a social episode (the "potential" situation), and behavioural reactions to an actual situation. This distinction parallels the formulations of social learning theory and symbolic interactionism, which assume that a set of expectations about social episodes are accumulated as a result of previous experience, leading to the emergence of symbolic representations of stereotypical social episodes. But behaviour in any given real situation will be a function both of these generalized expectations and of the specific qualifying contextual cues present in the actual situation. The study of social episodes should encompass both the potential and the actual episode. Most existing work has concentrated on the characteristics of potential (stereotypical) episodes, and this is discussed in some detail in Chapter 7. Perhaps equal emphasis should be given to the study of unique interaction episodes in order to balance our research. Methods for doing so will be discussed in more detail in Chapter 5.

OBJECTIVE V. SUBJECTIVE SITUATIONS

This is perhaps the most pervasive dimension of disagreement regarding the nature of the situation or episode today. The distinction has a long history, as the foregoing review had indicated, although the most influential statement of the difference between the objective and the subjective situation is still that of Murray (1951): "the situational constituent . . . that . . . can . . . be discriminated objectively . . . I have called the alpha situation. What the situation means to the subject, that is, how he interprets it, is the beta situation" (p. 458). The division between psychologists on this issue is as acute today as it was 20 years ago. Brunswik (1950, 1956) in his well known theoretical model of stimuli proposed a distinction between distal (objective), proximal and central (subjective) stimulus processes, although he preferred to define stimuli in distal (objective) terms. Gibson (1959) also proposed that in the study of environmental determinants of behaviour a clear and explicit distinction should be made between causal factors inside and outside the organism. Several other theorists made the same distinction, e.g. Kantor (1924, 1926) between biological and psychological environment, and Koffka (1935) between the geographical and the behavioural environment. Ekehammar (1974) summarized the difference as follows: "these various terms are used with somewhat different meanings, but the essential conceptual distinction is between the objective, outer world, as it affects the individual, and the subjective world, the environment as the individual perceives and reacts to it" (p. 13). These alternative definitions have significant implications for empirical research. Researchers who observe actual behaviour in reaction to different situations tend to emphasize the subjective situation as the relevant object of study (Barker, 1968; Moos, 1972; Insel and Moos, 1974), while investigators who study objective characteristics of situations define them in operational terms.

As far as the study of social episodes is concerned, the subjective rather than the objective situation appears to be the most promising focus for research. There are many reasons for this. Some of the factors which make up a social episode are simply not accessible to objective assessment, other than through the judgements and perceptions of the individuals participating in them. The effective episode, that is the episode which is salient to an individual in his normal social routines, may not be the one which can be studied objectively. The only approach likely to reveal the significant characteristics of an episode is one which relies on the cognitive faculties of the individual interpreting them. This does not mean, however, that the study of social episodes is bound to be bogged down in an inevitable quagmire of subjectivity. Both the data collection techniques, and the methods of analysis which can be applied to such accounts are objective in the sense that they yield replicable and quantifiable information. What is meant by the subjective conceptualization of social episodes is simply that they should be studied as they are interpreted and perceived by the social actor, and not in isolation.

The review of approaches to episodes and situations in psychology has thus yielded two important insights. Firstly, it was established that concern with situational differences in behaviour is a well-established part of psychology, and not a neologism. Secondly, it was shown that transformations in the conceptualization of social situations and episodes have tended to move from the physical to the social, the atomistic to the holistic, the actual to the potential, and the objective to the subjective situation.

There is another respect in which the psychological literature can contribute to our understanding of social episodes. Psychologists have not only theorized about the importance of situational factors in behaviour, but they have also carried out empirical studies to show that such differences do indeed exist. These studies showed that the often unstated assumption in social psychology, that the major source of variability in social behaviour is to be sought in the individual, needs to be seriously questioned. Episodes and situational factors clearly play an important and little studied role in the generation of social behaviour, in interaction with individual variables.

If the complex interaction between the person and the situation is to be disentangled, the first logical step is the construction of appropriate techniques for the empirical measurement of situations and episodes: "The establishment of the dimensions of situations which are relevant for social behaviour is in a far more primitive state than the parallel study of personality" (Argyle and Little, 1972, p. 28). The study of social episodes is an important step towards accomplishing this objective.

4

Episodes and Situations in Sociology

Social psychology is a boundary science—it bridges the gap between the study of society, sociology, and the study of individual behaviour, psychology. In most of its history, social psychology was much closer to the methods and interests of psychology than that of sociology. Having borrowed its dominant image of man from psychology, and having faithfully followed the rise and fall of such theoretical movements as introspectionism, behaviourism and phenomenology in psychology, social psychologists have remained strangely impervious to developments in the field of their other neighbour, sociology. One of the recurrent calls in social psychology during the tumultuous seventies is the call for putting the "social" back into social psychology. This call has many variants, some merely referring to social relevance, and others insisting on a much more profound reorientation, towards a genuinely social psychology. Several new textbooks of social psychology, written from a consistent theoretical perspective such as symbolic interactionism (Fernandez, 1977; Kando, 1977) seek to rectify the imbalance by giving such a sociological tint to social psychology. Inevitably, these efforts are limited in their impact, because they are forced to ignore much that has been done under the guise of psychological social psychology during the past five or so decades, research which is close to the heart of social psychologists, and which has been carried out without much reference to sociology. Nevertheless, an increasingly insistent demand for the incorporation of sociological knowledge into social psychology is one indicator of the gradual *rapprochement* between the two disciplines in the seventies.

There is another, and perhaps more important, point of contact. This has been brought about by the impressive success of theorists such as Erving Goffman and Garfinkel in analysing social behaviour in settings which one would have thought were properly the domain of social psychology. Their approach to the study of social behaviour is much closer to the methods of sociology and social anthropology than to the methods of psychology. Significantly, these "microsociological" schools trace their origins to a minority school in sociology, which, as a discipline, was traditionally more interested in macro rather than micro processes. In proposing the study of social episodes as a major new theme in social psychology, it is important that we should not fall into the same trap as many other proponents of new directions before, that of disregarding parallel developments in related disciplines. This caution is particularly warranted when the topic to be proposed is the study of social episodes, and the parallel discipline is sociology. The concept of the social situation has a long and distinguished history in sociology, originating with W. I. Thomas's (1928b) propositions, the "Thomas theorem" (Merton, 1957), and leading to the current position, where it can be asserted that "there is now a general agreement in sociology that definitions of situations are necessary conditions for human conduct" (Stone and Farberman, 1970, p. 147). Thus the approach proposed here is at least as much indebted to sociological theory as to psychology. The aim of this chapter is to review the different sociological and social anthropological approaches to the study of situational components of social behaviour, with a view towards extracting the main lines of development from them, and applying that knowledge to the social psychology of episodes. Microsociologists such as Goffman have had much to contribute to the rejuvenation of social psychological thinking in the past decade. It is only proper that we should pay serious attention to their approach and its precursors in sociological thinking.

Positivist Sociology

Modern sociology traces its origins to Auguste Comte, who endowed the new discipline with two characteristics which are still dominant today. The first one is methodological: sociology was to rely on the same methods of inquiry which proved so successful in natural sciences, namely, observation, experimentation, and above all, quantification. The second characteristic refers to the overall conceptualization of society. Comte, and many others since him, preferred to think about society as an organic, functional system, an approach, incidentally, which can be traced as far back as Plato's "Republic". Functionalism and a systems approach are still in the forefront of sociological thinking today, an orientation which was given new momentum by the impact of the theory of evolution, and social Darwinism in the last century. The hallmark of sociology, as first defined by Comte, is that it is concerned with large-scale, macro phenomena; it has very little to say about social processes on a smaller scale or microsociology. The other definitive figure in the history of sociology is, of course, Emile Durkheim. His main contribution was his insistence that society is more than the sum of its component parts (i.e. individuals), and that the proper task of sociology was to study social facts, which are independent of, and not reducible to, individual variables. "The determining cause of a social fact should be sought among the social facts preceding it and not among the states of individual consciousness" (Durkheim, 1938, p. 110). Society is the determining cause, and not the outcome, of individual behaviour, however esoteric or idiosyncratic that behaviour may appear to be. Durkheim's classic study of suicide is an excellent illustration of this argument. Suicide, perhaps the most individualistic act possible, can be explained in terms of social facts, according to Durkheim. Thus, individuals commit suicide because of particular kinds of relationships to society; this relationship can be anomic, when the individual is not normatively integrated into society; altruistic, when integration is excessive, and the individual chooses to sacrifice himself for society; or egotistic, when the individual is structurally unintegrated. This view accords an all-important role to society, while ignoring to a large extent the role of the individual in society, the effects of his perception and interpretation of the social system on his behaviour, and ultimately on the social system itself. While insisting on the "social facts" approach, Durkheim is nevertheless forced to take into consideration an individual's definition of the situation in his explanation of anomic and egotistic suicide (Ball, 1972; Nisbet, 1965). Functionalism has remained the dominant school of sociology to date, the Grand Old Paradigm (GOP), as Kando (1977) refers to it. More recent theorists, such as Merton and Parsons have essentially remained faithful to Comte's and Durkheim's initial two-fold commitment to a positivistic methodology, and a functionalist view of society. The GOP can be characterized, above all, by the lack of attention it pays to small scale social processes, and by its insistence that such processes can play no part in the creation and definition of large-scale, macrosociological facts. This emphasis on large-scale so-cial processes is also characteristic of contemporary theories (Merton,

1957; Parsons, 1951). Merton's theory of criminal and deviant behaviour (1957) in essence follows the formula used by Durkheim to explain suicide. According to Merton, deviance and criminality can be explained in terms of the lack of legitimate means to achieve culturally valued objectives, such as material success; both "cultural goals" and "institutionalized means" are extra-individual variables, or social facts, to use Durkheim's terminology. Similarly, although Talcott Parsons' early work in the "Structure of Social Action" (1937) suggested a deep awareness of the importance of individual, meaningful acts in the explanation of social behaviour, he tended to adopt a more rigid mechanistic stance in his later work. His emphasis on coercive, mechanistic social norms and values as determinants of behaviour is ultimately in line with the functionalist view of society as a consensual, self-maintaining system.

A slightly different, although still positivistic and functionalist orientation is apparent in George Homans' theory of The Human Group (1950). After decades of dominance by the functionalist, macrosociological schools, interested in "social facts" but not in people, Homans (1964) pleaded to "bring men back" into sociological explantations. He suggested that the ultimate generalizations that sociologists should come up with should be generalizations about how typical people behave in typical situations. This emphasis is very similar to the basic stance adopted by Weber and his followers in their "interpretative" sociologies. Homans, deeply impressed by the achievements of behaviourist psychology, suggested that the task of sociology was to integrate and synthetize these psychological principles of behaviour to account for social phenomena. For him, "The central problem of social science remains the one posed in his own language and in his own area by Hobbes: How does the behaviour of individuals create the characteristics of groups?" (Homans, 1967, p. 106). Homans' theory, while still functional in approach, is the first one in which individual, situational behaviour is accorded some importance in the social system. Homans differentiates between the external (task-oriented, physical survival) system, and the internal (social) system. The elements of the total system are (individual) activity, (social) interaction, sentiment, and norms. Homans' most important contribution lies in his analysis of the interrelationship between these elements of the system, and the internal (social) system in particular. For example, sentiment and activity can be related, in the sense that positive sentiments will be expressed in activity (e.g. giving gifts); activity and interaction are related, insofar as joint activity is likely to lead to interaction, and eventually, sentiment. While these propositions are not particularly surprising, they are important, since they signal the recognition of the contribution of individual behaviours to social systems. The examples Homans uses to illustrate the working of the external and internal systems are especially interesting, since they demonstrate the effects of situational factors on social behaviour. The study of the Bank Wiring Observation Room is an excellent example of the interdependence of the environment (physical, technical and social), the social situation, and the emergent social system created amongst the workers. The evolution of sociology's major theoretical paradigm, functionalism, can thus be characterized by an initial disregard of the social situation, and microprocesses of social behaviour in general. When these are treated at all, for example in Homans' work, they are regarded as secondary to the main concern of the analysis.

Cultural sociology

Dominant as structural-functionalist theories are in sociology, there are several alternative approaches which posit a divergent view of human societies. Foremost among them is the sociological school founded by Max Weber. Although he is still predominantly interested in large-scale, macrosociological phenomena, his theory is more humanistic, interpretative and culture-oriented than functionalist theories. His conception of society, as distinct from Durkheim's, is based on a theory of individual behaviour and cognition. Weber differentiates between simple "behaviour" and subjectively meaningful social action: "Action is social . . . by virtue of the subjective meaning attached to it by the acting individual . . . it takes into account the behaviour of others and is thereby oriented in its course" (Weber, 1968, p. 248). Individual action is thus the smallest building block of society. Social relations are the next step, defined as the probability of social action between individuals. Social order, in turn, can be defined as a set of prescriptively regulated social relations, which in turn, are the building blocks of organizations, and eventually, the state. Weber's theory is thus radically different from Durkheim's, in that he does not reify social systems and social facts as having an existence independent of the individuals who make up the system. Rather, he consistently emphasizes that even very large scale and complex social-historical processes, such as the advent of capitalism, or the workings of bureaucracies, can ultimately be analysed in terms of individual actions, and the subjective meanings attached to them. The first important characteristic of Weber's theory is that it is social psychological in its foundation: meaningful individual behaviour is its basic unit of analysis. The second characteristic which is particularly important for our present discussion of social episodes is its methodology. Weber attempts to synthesize the positivistic, causal methodology of the natural sciences with a culture-oriented, interpretative methodology which seeks to identify meanings as well as causes. Thus, an understanding of a social act requires not only an explication of its causes, but also the coming to terms with its reasons and its meaning. Causes can be determined by the well-known methods of empirical science. The identification of meanings on the other hand requires the use of rationalist rather than empiricist methodology, the use of reason and intuition, seeking to identify the motive or "subjective meaning which seems to the actor himself or to the observer an adequate ground for the conduct in question" (Weber, 1947, pp. 88–100). This hybrid methodology, based on a synthesis of scientific and intuitive processes, is particularly interesting in light of the current debate about the role of intuition and subjective accounting in social psychology (Harre, 1977; Schlenker, 1977). Weber's concern with subjective meaning also paves the way for the different microsociological schools, which focus in on the processes whereby subjective meanings are created, maintained and enacted. The concept of social episode, although not explicitly used by Weber, is implied by his formulations. Social episodes could be regarded as one aspect of the social order, regulating social relations by virtue of the subjective meaning that individuals attach to them.

Other aspects of Weber's theory are also relevant to our consideration of social episodes. His taxonomy of ideal types of action is enlightening. Weber distinguishes between traditional (habitual), affectual (emotion-governed), value-oriented (Wertrational), and goal-oriented (Zweckrational) types of action. These four types of action represent increasing levels of rationality, or meaningfulness, in Weber's terms. It is interesting to note that it is not possible to differentiate these four kinds of action simply by observing behaviour. The differences between them refer to motivational factors in the actors performing the action. This clearly suggests that the study of any social

phenomenon in terms of its empirically observable surface characteristics is likely to yield a limited understanding only. Thus, social
episodes can be described or analysed in terms of what people actually
do in a given episode. This analysis would, however, by definition
ignore the true meaning of those actions.

This categorization of action need not refer to ideal types of individual behaviour only. It is tempting to translate Weber's system into
a taxonomy of different kinds of social episodes. Thus, we could postulate four ideal types of social episode: traditional, affective, value-
oriented and goal-oriented. Indeed some of the a priori taxonomies of
social episodes proposed in the literature (without any reference to
Weber) bear a surprising resemblance to this category system (Bjerg,
1968; see also Chapter 6). Traditional social episodes are similar to
what Goffman calls routines, and Harre and Secord's (1972) formal
episodes. The identification of an episode in terms of its meaning, as
well as its structure and the implied sequence of behaviours is an
important extension of the traditional concerns of social psychology.
Weber's concern with subjective meaning is very similar to many of
the newly-proposed approaches to social psychology, which seek to
study meaningful actions, or accounts thereof, instead of looking at
observable behaviours in isolation. The study of social episodes could
clearly benefit from taking Weber's system seriously.

We have not said very much about Weber's best known work, *The
Protestant Ethic and the Spirit of Capitalism*. Above all, this work is about
the role of ideas in history, and more specifically, the relationship
between ideas and economic systems. While this work is clearly macrosociological and socio-historical in orientation, its basic unit of
analysis is again the individual. It is his actions, motivations and
meaningful construal of the social environment which ultimately provide the possibility for a fusion between protestant ethic, and a particular economic system, early capitalism. The concept of *elective affinity*
is important in this context, since it describes the process whereby
individuals selectively accept and internalize those aspects of an ideational system which is relevant to, and compatible with, their condition. Weber's model is much more complete than Marx's crude economic deterministic ideas about culture and society. Elective affinity is
an important process for social psychology to consider. In our discipline we have paid little attention to the relationship between an
individual's objective, socio-economic circumstances and his selection

of an ideational system to give meaning to his actions. Elective affinity provides us with one possible way of looking at such a relationship between social-structural and cognitive-perceptual variables. In summary, Weber's work is perhaps more relevant to the new-found concerns of contemporary social psychology than the work of any other sociologist. His synthesis of scientific and intuitive methodologies, his concern with reasons as much as causes, with actions rather than behaviours, and with the subjective meanings in particular is echoed by many critics of traditional social psychology. We should be mindful of this tradition when proposing a new field of study, such as the study of social episodes.

From the above discussion of Weber's work, it should be reasonably clear that his ideas have a lot in common with that of the symbolic interactionist school, discussed in the previous chapter. These two theoretical orientations, Weber's interpretative sociology, and symbolic interactionism, lie at the root of the many microsociological theories which, finally, have something explicit to say about social situations and social episodes.

The definition of the situation

W. I. Thomas, and Florian Znaniecki can be regarded as the two forerunners of the many burgeoning microsociological schools today. W. I. Thomas was influenced both by Dewey's pragmatism, and Mead's social behaviourism. Significantly, Thomas's original credo was symbolic interactionism, and Znaniecki's methods bear more than a passing resemblance to Weber's. Thomas and Znaniecki are of course best known for their gigantic joint work, *The Polish Peasant in Europe and America*. This work represents an important milestone in the development of both sociology and social psychology. It is an eminently social psychological work, which seeks to analyse the processes of change and adaptation by Polish peasants to their new social environment in America. It is a study both of personality and individual actions, as well as of social structure and social systems. The units of analysis are mainly social psychological, such as values, attitudes, motivations, and the social situation. Thomas and Znaniecki identify three typical reactions to the new culture: clinging to the values and traditions of the "old country" ("philistine"); readiness to sample, accept and assimilate all new experiences provided by the new culture ("bohemian"), and finally, the rational creative selection of elements of the old and the new culture ("creative"). Thomas and Znaniecki analyse these processes of cultural change using an ingenious and eclectic set of methodologies. In fact, their innovative use of methodologies is as important as their substantive findings about the adaptation processes of Polish peasants. Since they conceptualize social system and structure in terms of individuals' meaningful actions, their analyses centre on evidence which gives them insight into the meanings and interpretations immigrant peasants place on their experiences, instead of just studying their behaviour, or social facts about them. Their methods include extensive case studies, analysis of biographies, study of letters and other written documents by their subjects, and demographic analyses. The result is a rich and complex picture, reflecting the multifaceted adaptation processes that this immigrant group had to undergo. The concept of the "definition of the situation" is central to Thomas and Znaniecki's analysis of this transformation.

In keeping with the general humanistic orientation of their theoretical framework, Thomas and Znaniecki had to confront the problem of how creative and insightful individuals come to understand and interpret the social reality around them, and ultimately, how their actions will act back on that reality. All social psychologies which are intent on not reifying either the individual or society will have to confront this problem, and have to come to some decision regarding the nature of the individual/society interface. The "definition of the situation" is Thomas and Znaniecki's answer to this problem. The definition of the situation is a social process, and not an objectively existing social entity: "Preliminary to any self-determined act of behaviour there is always a stage of examination and deliberation which we may call *the definition of the situation*" (Thomas, 1923, p. 41). The definition of the situation is thus a process of social dialogue and negotiation. The concept is somewhat ambiguous, since it can equally well be applied to large-scale processes, or smaller social units, such as small groups and even dyads. While concern with the definition of the situation, or situational analysis is already present in *The Polish Peasant*, Thomas has further developed this approach in his later works, such as in *The Unadjusted Girl*. The high point of this development is his 1928 address to the American Psychological Association, entitled "The behaviour pattern and the situation". Situational analysis can only be understood in the context of Thomas's overall theoretical view of man and society. Sociology was for him the study of social organization, or more precisely, the study of the socially systematized schemes of behaviour imposed on individuals. The other key concept is social personality, which can be thought of as the pattern of attitudes and dispositions which an individual holds—the subjective reflection of the social order, as it were. Situational analysis is the method whereby we can understand the relationship between social order and social personality, that is, between socially imposed schemes of behaviour and the individual's subjective construal of it. "The individual does not find passively ready situations exactly similar to past situations; he must consciously define every situation . . . The individual, in order to control social reality for his needs, must develop not a series of uniform reactions, but general *schemes* of situations; his life-organization is a set of rules for definite situations, which may even be expressed in abstract formulas" (Thomas, 1966, p. 29). Thomas goes on to suggest that the Philistine, Bohemian and Creative character-types differ in their approaches to the definition of situations. The Philistine may find that "a few narrow schemes are sufficient to lead the individual through life . . . This type of schemes constitutes the common stock of social traditions in which every class of situation is defined in the same way and forever" (op. cit., p. 29). In contrast, inconsistency of situation definition is the hallmark of the Bohemian type, while the Creative "individual searches for new situations to be defined simply in order to widen and to perfect his knowledge or his aesthetic interpretation and appreciation; or his aims may be practical, . . . and then the individual searches for new situations in order to widen his control of the environment" (op. cit., p. 30). In the ongoing relationship between social order and social personality, neither of these two forces is the dominant one. "In the continual interaction between the individual and his environment we can say neither that the individual is the product of his milieu, nor that he produces his milieu; or rather, we can say both. For the individual can indeed develop only under the influence of his environment, but on the other hand during his development he modifies this environment by defining situations and solving them according to his wishes and tendencies. His influence upon the environment may be scarcely noticeable socially, may have little importance for others, but it is important for himself, since as we have said, the world in which he lives is not the world as society or the scientific observer sees it, but as he sees it himself" (p. 32).

These aspects of Thomas's theory foreshadow a much more recent concern with the situation, which has preoccupied personality theorists for some years now (Chapter 9). If it could be shown empirically that there are indeed consistent tendencies for an individual to define the situations he encounters in systematic ways, then this would be a most important, and highly general, personality characteristic to consider. Personality theorists, in seeking to apportion behavioural variance to the person and to the situation, have so far neglected to look for more general schemes of situation definition in individuals. Thomas's propositions of the differences between the Philistine, Bohemian and Creative types is suggestive in that respect. However, his theory was also ahead of his time in another respect: he conceived of the relationship between the social order and the social personality in basically interactionist terms, long before such a formulation was widely accepted in psychology. In doing so, he arrived at essentially the same conclusion as personality theorists involved in the person–situation controversy 50 years later—namely, that the interaction of these two factors is more important than the effects of either one of them in isolation.

The definition of the situation is thus a crucial component in Thomas's system, and one which is of direct relevance to the concerns of social psychology. Not only are the "behaviour patterns and the total personality . . . overwhelmingly conditioned by the types of situations and trains of experience encountered by the individual" (op. cit., p. 154), but the individual as a social agent is himself instrumental in defining the situations making up the social order. The situation is thus the very essence of society: "As long as definitions of situations remain constant and common we may anticipate orderly behaviour reactions. When rival definitions arise . . . we may anticipate social disorganization and personal demoralization" (op. cit., p. 166). Studies of social situations and social episodes can thus highlight the fluidity and changeability of the social order. Thomas's own studies of migrants, unadjusted and marginal groups illustrate how these methods can be used to explicate the social experience of crucial groups. In his 1928 address to the ASA he also foreshadowed another application: "it is desirable to extend our studies of this situational character to the large cultural areas, to the races and nationalities, in order to understand the formation of behaviour patterns comparatively, in their most general and particular expressions" (p. 167). This task has been embraced by social psychologists such as Triandis and others, and their studies of crosscultural differences in social behaviour, using the behaviour episode as the central unit of analysis, have been extremely successful in explicating cultural patterns of behaviour, and in training foreigners to assimilate those patterns.

Thomas is thus the first important figure in sociology to emphasize the importance of immediate, small-scale episodes and situations in making up the social order. His work has important implications for social psychology, since he trod much the same ground as that which constitutes the present domain of social psychology. It is only because of the relative isolation of social psychology from developments in sociological thought that his ideas have not made more of an impact to date in our discipline.

Besides introducing the concept of situational analysis into sociology, an important aspect of Thomas's contribution was his emphasis on the subjective situation as the most important determinant of action. This is most saliently expressed in the so-called "Thomas theorem" (Merton, 1957): "if men define situations as real, they are real in their consequences" (Thomas, 1928, p. 522). Thus Thomas argued that beyond studying "social facts" as proposed by Durkheim (1938), sociologists should also pay serious attention to how social actors come to define and understand social situations: ". . . in order to understand social conduct we must look to existential causality, that is to the meanings of situations and the situated meanings within them as they are phenomenologically experienced by the actors" (Ball, 1972, p. 62).

Situational analysis

This approach focused attention on small-scale microsociological processes, as against the larger social processes which Durkheim and his followers were interested in. Only such a situational analysis, according to Thomas, will reveal the relevant causes of social behaviour: the process of how social actors perceive and construct the social world around them. Ball (1972) suggests reasons why such an approach was never adopted by mainstream sociology: "It is because . . . the logic, both theoretical and methodological, is antithetical to the basic model of conduct applied . . . Both sociology and psychology, in their conventional forms, as does everyday life, operate with what may be called the *personal consistency assumption* . . . situations are taken as given, unproblematic, essentially epiphenomenal to the conduct which is to be explained" (pp. 65–66). Thus the long-standing neglect of situational variance both in personality theory, and in sociology, has become a central issue of contention between the positivist and the phenomenologist camps in these disciplines. Interestingly, while in personality theory "situationism" gained ground mainly as an offspring of learning theory (Mischel, 1968), in sociology it was the phenomenologists who were most interested in situations: interest in situationalism and trans-situationalism is the characteristic that has most distinguished phenomenological sociologists from the absolutist (structural) sociologists (Douglas, 1973).

While Thomas's understanding of the situation is thus essentially phenomenological, his followers often emphasize more culture-specific definitions.

Florian Znaniecki, the co-author of *The Polish Peasant* with W. I. Thomas, has also contributed to the humanist tradition in sociology. Born in Poland, and dividing his academic life between that country and the United States, Znaniecki developed a sociological theory notable for its reliance on culture as a central explanatory concept. In his early, largely philosophical, works he sought to establish the ontological status of culture as an irreducible factor in human affairs. Culture, however, is not disembodied; it can only be studied as it exists for "certain conscious and active historical subjects . . . living in a certain part of the human world during a certain historical period . . . In a word, the data of the cultural student are always 'somebody's', never 'nobody's' data. This essential character of cultural data we call the humanistic coefficient" (Znaniecki, 1969, p. 137), a term which symbolizes Znaniecki's perhaps best-known contribution to sociology. Following Thomas, Znaniecki also considered situational analysis to be an essential aspect of the sociological method. However, his definition relies much more on the "culturally given" nature of situations. Indeed, he saw situations as crucial elements of culture, which determine the subjective experiences of individuals. Thus, "reality is supposed to assume similar aspects in similar situations; and if it has a certain aspect for the given individual at the given moment, it is because it is determined for his actual experience by some actual situation of which it is part. Therefore whenever similar situations are found, we expect similar experiences of given reality . . . (Znaniecki, 1969, p. 8). Thus Znaniecki understood situations to be the stereotypical representations of typical interactions, crystallized in a given culture.

This approach is much nearer to the symbolic interactionist position, as outlined above, and is also related to the contemporary microsociological theories of Garfinkel (1967), Goffman (1963) and others. Similarly, Wolff (1964) argued for a more consensual conceptualization of situations as "culturally formulated, embodied and shared perceptions and interpretations of situations considered identical or similar" (1964, p. 182).

The present definition of the concept of social episodes, as foreshadowed in the first chapter, is very closely related to those sociological formulations of situations which contain a strong cultural, consensual element. Definition of social episodes as cultural units has the great advantage that it allows the operationalization and study of stereotypical, commonly occurring situations, avoiding the problems involved in studying unique and non-recurring actual interactions.

Following Thomas's work, situational analysis acquired a permanent, if restricted, place in sociology. Waller (1961), for example, relied on this technique in his enlightening analyses of family interactions and the social environment and behaviour of such specific occupational groups as teachers or academics (Waller, 1938, 1932, 1937). He tends to emphasize the culturally given aspect of social situations and episodes in his analysis. His definition of "definitions of situations" reflects this view: "Many persons living together . . . have mapped out clearly the limitations of behaviour inherent in the social situations most common in their culture. From their experience has arisen a consensus of what is and what isn't thinkable in those situations. We may refer to these group products as definitions of situations" (Waller, 1970, p. 162).

Waller was also the first to become interested in how actors come to "stage" a particular situation, that is, how they use situational and symbolic props to achieve a desired definition. This conscious manipulation of situational components in the interest of optimal self-presentation later became one of the central elements in Goffman's work.

Following Thomas, sociological thinking about situations has developed in three major directions. On the one hand those most consistently following Weber's, and later, Thomas's sociology became increasingly interested in the processes whereby social actors understand and assign meaning to situations. Phenomenological sociologists, such as Schutz, have developed this line of thinking the furthest.

Secondly, increasing interest in the staging process has developed into a theoretical orientation which can be summarized under the heading "dramaturgical models" of social behaviour. The third influential line of thinking evolved from the notion of implicit cultural knowledge of situational requirements with its chief concern of explicating these implicit rules, either by consciously breaking situational conventions (Garfinkel, 1967) or by studying subjective accounts (Harre and Secord, 1972; Lyman and Scott, 1972). This third orientation can be subsumed under the heading "ethnomethodology". The phenomenological, dramaturgical, and ethnomethodological schools are by no means clearly defined entities. But for the purposes of our discussion, they represent three contemporary approaches to the study of social episodes, and they will be treated from this perspective.

The phenomenological approach

Perhaps the most influential representative of phenomenological sociology is Alfred Schutz. Born in Austria, achieving prominence in the United States, Schutz was one of a whole generation of sociologists who helped to transmit the traditions of the German *Geisteswissenschaften* across the Atlantic. Schutz's contribution to sociology is unique among these theorists however, to the extent that he consistently rejected the premises of the ruling American approach to sociology, based on logical positivism and empiricism. Rather, Schutz was an exponent of the interpretative, cultural sociology practised by Max Weber. To him, the aim of sociology is the exploration and formulation of the laws and principles according to which human social life is organized. As such, sociology must undoubtedly concern itself with the subjective meanings individuals attach to the social world around them.

Besides Max Weber, Schutz was most profoundly influenced by the phenomenological philosophy of Husserl. In essence, Schutz sought to extend Weber's approach to social analysis in a way which would make it possible to construct more accurate models of the phenomenological processes which occur at the level of the individual. A crucial concept in understanding these processes is the concept of the lifeworld, which, according to Husserl, refers to all direct everyday experiences, actions and motivations through which social actors relate to their environment.

Schutz sought to elaborate this concept of the life-world with respect to social behaviour. The "natural attitude" towards the life-world is to take it for granted, to accept it as reality, and to act in a pragmatic, utilitarian fashion towards it. There are important factors which influence and restrict the behaviour of any individual in his life-world: "Man finds himself at any moment of his daily life in a biographically determined situation" (Schutz, 1970, p. 73). Biographically determined situation means that the situation contains not only external constraints, in terms of the social, cultural and habitual limitations which are inherent in it, but also internal constraints. The situation is an episode in the continuing life of an individual, it reflects "the sedimentation of all of man's previous experiences, organized in the habitual possession of his stock of knowledge at hand, and as such is his unique possession, given to him and to him alone" (Schutz, 1970, p. 73). In other words, situations or episodes are biographical, since they are subjective, and no two individuals could experience them in the same way. Thus Schutz, not surprisingly, emphasizes the subjective, internal phenomenological situation to the relative exclusion of the cultural, consensual and given situation.

One of the more interesting and relevant aspects of Schutz's work is his theory as to how the individual makes sense of the situations he encounters. In defining the situation and in making plans for action, the individual has to rely on his "stock of knowledge at hand that serves him as a scheme of interpretation of his past and present experiences" (Schutz, 1970, p. 74). This stock of knowledge is constantly changing as a result of new experiences, and it is created by a process which Husserl called the "sedimentation" of meaning. This stock of knowledge has its own structure, contradictions, and is of differing relevance to the situation at hand.

But the situation is not entirely subjective: although individuals construct their own life-worlds, they use building blocks which are given by their culture and their society. These accepted ways of acting, or "folkways" of a given culture, to use W. G. Sumner's term, will have to be incorporated into the person's life-world: "the system of folkways establishes the standard in terms of which the in-group 'defines the situation'. Even more: originating in previous situations defined by the group, the scheme of interpretation that has stood the test so far becomes an element of the actual situation" (Schutz, 1970, p. 80). The individual's cognitive view of his world thus includes not only his idiosyncratic construction or his life-world, but also knowledge about appropriate ways of acting in specific situations. These recipes for action, which were more recently called "scripts" by Abelson (1976) are in effect the reflections of culture and society in the minds of individuals. Contrary to Durkheim's conception of social facts as external, causal and coercive agents of behaviour, Schutz conceives of culture and society as existing within individuals. Their effectiveness depends on individuals seeking to find their place in their society and to act in a meaningful fashion. For such a system of cultural recipes to be effective, it is not sufficient for isolated individuals to be aware of them; rather, the cultural community, or group, arrives at and maintains a collective interpretation of its customs. This in turn requires individuals to be aware not only of their own life-worlds, but also that other members of their group share elements of that life-world. Intersubjectivity as well as subjectivity is a prerequisite for a phenomenological theory of social action. The taken-for-granted type of social action, based on a "knowledge of trustworthy recipes for interpreting the social world and for handling things and men in order to obtain the best results in every situation with a minimum of effort" (Schutz, 1970, p. 81), is also the essence of what we understand under the concept of social episode. Social episodes are the building blocks of culture to the extent that they embody such taken-for-granted sequences of action. Although Schutz's theory emphasizes the individual, unique and biographical aspects of such episodes, the consensual, shared component of episodes may be of equal interest to social psychologists. Schutz's theory is important in that it provides a model for analysing how such consensual notions of correct behaviour are assimilated by the individual as parts of his life-world, and how ultimately such episodes come to affect his behaviour.

The connection between socially constructed reality, and individual adjustment is perhaps best illustrated in Schutz's best known essay, "The Stranger". This is an analysis of the phenomenological experience of an individual who approaches a new cultural community from the outside. (It is interesting to note that nearly all sociologists who contributed to the development of microsociology did concern themselves at some stage of their career with the problem of the outsider, the migrant, or the stranger. W. I. Thomas's work on the Polish peasant, Willard Waller's interest in the returning soldier and Schutz's more abstract essay on the stranger are examples of this common preoccupation.) The stranger, having acquired the prescriptions and action recipes of his native community, will find that his stock of knowledge is no longer relevant in his new environment. He will have to observe, reconstruct and assimilate the appropriate rules of social conduct in his new community if he is to become an effective member. To him the cultural pattern of the host group does not have the authority of a tested system of recipes, and this, if for no other reason, because he does not partake in the vivid historical tradition by which it has been formed. This is in contrast to a member of the in-group, who "looks in one single glance through the social situations occurring to him and . . . catches immediately the ready-made recipe appropriate to its solution. In these situations his acting shows all the marks of habituality, automatism and half-consciousness. In other words, the cultural pattern of the approached group is to the stranger not a shelter but a field of adventure, not a matter of course but a questionable topic of investigation, not an instrument for disentangling problematic situations but a problematic situation itself and one hard to master" (Schutz, 1970, pp. 87–93). The experience of the stranger is an excellent illustration of how much we rely on the taken-for-granted recipes for social action provided by the group. It also suggests that a study of those recipes, or social episodes, is the best avenue for facilitating assimilation and culture contact. It is not surprising that the most successful such programme to date in social psychology, developed by Triandis (1972) and his co-workers, does in fact rely on the study and interpretation of typical episode scenarios by would-be strangers.

Schutz has devoted considerable effort to the clarification of the cognitive interface between individual and society. His analysis of symbols, signs and markers is enlightening, but only of marginal relevance here. More interesting from our point of view is his later work analysing the different kinds of relationships that might exist between the individual and the situation—the kinds of relevance a situation may have for an individual. Firstly, motivational relevance denotes a relationship in which, in a situation which is well known and taken for granted, the individual seeks to define the situation in light of his motivations and aims at that time. In other words, in completely familiar situations it is possible to infuse individual motivational components into the definition of the situation.

The motivational tendency towards situation definition may be suspended if the situation is not sufficiently well known, or does not contain the elements for a motivational definition. The situation is thus problematic, and it will become relevant to the individual as a topic for investigation, that is, as an object of cognitive effort. This kind of relevance Schutz called thematic relevance. "The unknown or problematic in a situation becomes relevant only insofar as it blocks the forming of a definition of the situation in accordance with the person's present intentions and plans" (Wagner, 1970, p. 22).

Finally, the recognition of such a "problematic" situation necessitates that the situation be defined in some alternative ways before problem solving can begin. Aspects of the situation which are used in arriving at an interpretation of the problem are of interpretational relevance to the actor. Schutz's analysis of different degrees (from peripheral to central) and different kinds (motivational, thematic and interpretative) of relevance is a particularly important contribution to the understanding of how individuals find their way in the complex situations they are presented with, and how they achieve a degree of cognitive control over their life worlds.

The second cognitive process which both Husserl, and in his footsteps, Schutz, were interested in also pertains to the individual's efforts to organize his knowledge. This is the process of typification, or categorization. Both the physical and the social world is experienced in terms of types. Systems of typification are formed, maintained and altered by all members of the culture: the knowledge of these categories and of their appropriate use is an inseparable element of the sociocultural heritage. Typification has a number of important functions in social life. It helps to transform unique individual actions into the performance of typical social roles. "The chances of success of human interaction, that is, the establishment of a congruency between the typified scheme used by the actor as a scheme of orientation and by his fellow men as a scheme of interpretation, is enhanced if the scheme of typification is standardized. . . . The socially approved system of typifications and relevances is the common field within which the private typifications . . . originate. This is so, because the private situation of the individual as defined by him is always the situation within the group" (Schutz, 1970, pp. 120–121). In other words, situations, episodes and scenarios refer to typical, standardized, idealized courses of action, and not to unique sequences which are unlikely to recur in the same form, a distinction very similar to the potential-actual situation distinction described previously (Chapter 3).

Beyond analysing the cognitive aspects of the life-world, Schutz was also interested in the phenomenology of acting within the life-world. He distinguished among three types of action of increasing premeditation: conduct, or meaningful action in general; action, or planned and predesigned conduct; and working, or action planned to bring about specific outcomes. As can be seen, the actor's motivation is a crucial element in differentiating between different types of action.

The first kind of motivation occurs in the ongoing process of carrying out an action, when the actor experiences his actions as oriented towards achieving something in the future. This is an essentially subjective process, which Schutz called the *in-order-to* motivation. Once the action is accomplished, it can be explained in terms of past experiences and occurrences. This *post hoc*, reflective kind of motivation was so called by Schutz "because" motivation, which is objective and is accessible to an observer as well as the actor. Thus, the "in-order-to" motive refers to the attitude of the actor living in the process of his ongoing action. It is ". . . essentially a subjective category . . . The genuine because motive, however, . . . is an objective category accessible to the observer" (Schutz, 1970, p. 128). Schutz also noted that in ordinary language, it is common to mix up these two kinds of motives, since language permits the expression of most of the "in-order-to" motives by "because" sentences, but not the other way around.

This leads us to the next aspect of the life-world, the world of social relationships. The philosophical cornerstone of Schutz's theory of social relationships is intersubjectivity, that is, the phenomenological awareness by actors of the existence and independent subjectivity of others. This is taken to be an unquestionable, fundamental category of human experience: "this world is not only mine, but also my fellow men's environment; moreover, these fellow men are elements of my own situation, as I am of theirs" (1970, p. 164). Direct, immediate experiences of others arise in what Schutz called the "communicative common environment", a situation or episode in which two or more individuals are able to communicate with each other. This situation is simultaneously experienced by both actors and thus has two subjective foci. Intersubjectivity thus involves an element of mutual understanding between the actors involved, an understanding which according to Schutz, must be rooted in the understanding of each other's motives. One way of grasping the essence of social interaction is by analysing the reciprocity of motives. An actor's in-order-to motive is to bring about a given action in the other. If this action occurs, it becomes the "because" motive for the next act, and so on. This understanding of the other is the essence of social interaction: "Suppose you are speaking to me and I am understanding what you are saying, as we have already seen, there are two senses in this understanding. First of all, I grasp the "objective meaning of your words, the meaning which they would have had, had they been spoken by you or anyone else. But second, there is the subjective meaning, namely what is going on in your mind as you speak. In order to get your subjective meaning, I must picture to myself your stream of consciousness as flowing side by side with my own. Within this picture I must interpret and construct your intentional acts as you choose your words. To the extent that you and I can mutually experience this simultaneity, growing older together for a time, to the extent that we can live in it together, to *that* extent we can live in each other's subjective contexts of meaning" (Schutz, 1970, p. 167).

This view of social interaction has a surprising similarity with some of the models suggested as replacements for experimentation by critics of empirical social psychology. It concentrates on the experience and meaning of social acts within interaction episodes, and the contingent sequencing of interactive moves. Both ethologists and linguists have concerned themselves with the sequential structure of social behaviour, and their efforts have influenced social psychologists. However, only in Schutz's work do we find the beginnings of an analysis of the intersubjectivity of such coordinated action, one of the most important features of human social interaction in specific social episodes.

The above categories constitute Schutz's analysis of the cognitive aspects of the life-world. In particular, this analysis demonstrates the way in which Schutz approached the problem of mediating between the sphere of direct human experience, which was for him primary, and cultural and sociological spheres. As this brief summary shows, Schutz relied heavily on Thomas's work on the definition of the situation in his own analyses. His main contribution is the elucidation of motivational and intentional principles which may influence the process of situation definition. His analyses are strongly social psychological in character, and are directly relevant to our concern with the analysis of social episodes. In Schutz's terms, social episodes may be defined as typifications of habitual, prescribed ways of interaction, which constitute parts of the life-worlds of individuals who are members of the culture. In turn, they will contribute a unique, biographical element to the definition of the episode, and will seek to define it in ways which have relevance for them, and which correspond to their motivations. Schutz's system is primarily centred on the individual, and his unique phenomenal world. He has relatively little to say about the process of negotiation whereby individuals seek to make their definitions of the situation socially acceptable. Schutz's concept of the situation clearly lies toward the subjective end of the objective–subjective continuum represented by the different theorists discussed so far. Yet even in his phenomenological theory he acknowledges, and indeed attributes particular importance to the consensual, cultural aspect of episodes which is of concern to social psychologists. Stimulated by Schutz's work, phenomenological sociology is gaining increasing acceptance and popularity nowadays.

Curiously, Schutz's influence extended in two widely differing directions. On the one hand, Berger and Luckman (1967) relied heavily on Schutz's theory in their macroscopic analyses of general, large-scale social processes, reminiscent of Durkheim's scope, although not his orientation. Their analysis of the existence and maintenance of different "symbolic universes" in pluralistic societies via processes of legitimation and objectivation is enlightening, but not particularly relevant to our present concern with social episodes. The other line of influence which can be traced to Schutz's work is much more relevant and leads us to the multitude of microsociological schools, particularly ethnomethodology, currently flourishing in sociology. Cicourel is one of the more influential representatives of this tradition.

Strongly influenced by Schutz's phenomenologist theory, as well as by Garfinkel's ethnomethodology, Cicourel (1964) advanced a radical critique of the methods and theories of conventional, absolutist sociology. The central point raised by Cicourel relates to the confusion of natural, everyday concepts and meanings and derived, second-order theories constructed by social scientists. In accordance with the Sapir–Whorf theory, Cicourel argues that "the clarification of sociological language is important because linguistic structure and use affects the way people interpret and describe the world. Since sociologists have evolved their own theoretical terminologies and frequently discuss, on the one hand, in these often varying terms the language and substance of each other's theories and on the other hand the language of persons in everyday life, . . . it is quite likely that the syntax and

meaning of these languages will become entangled" (p. 1). Such con-
founding of sociological language about theories and social events, and
the language used by subjects under study in field research and other
research methods such as content analysis and laboratory experiments
is a pervasive problem in social science. A further general theme raised
by Cicourel is the problem of correspondence between measurement
categories and the observable social world to which these categories
are applied. He raises the possibility that "because the concepts on
which sociological theories are based have inherently no numerical
properties, we can not know which numerical properties to look for in
the correlative observable . . ." (pp. 2–3). By focusing on the ambiguities inherent in using everyday language for sociological analysis,
and by suggesting that some of the familiar measurement strategies
used by sociologists may be conceptually dubious, Cicourel has deliv-
ered a salutary warning to practitioners. Following Schutz and the
ethnomethodologist school, Cicourel presented the most comprehensive argument yet, pointing out that "to the extent that it draws on
first-order, everyday explanations, sociology is just another life-world,
a 'folk-sociology' created by its members, with no less, but no greater
validity than any other socially constructed reality" (Mennell, 1974,
pp. 55–56). As an alternative, Cicourel espouses the kind of interpretative, cultural sociology developed by Max Weber. "By insisting that
sociologists do not devote enough attention to the study of 'subjective'
variables, especially those which contribute to the contingent character
of everyday life, I hope to stress the importance of constructing models
of social action which specify typical motives, values and course-of-
action types within the context of an environment of objects with
commonsense properties as originated by Weber" (Cicourel, 1964, p. 4).

Cicourel has accomplished much the same task in sociology as Harre
and Secord sought to accomplish in social psychology, namely, to
present a coherent critique of the dominant research methodologies in
their respective fields, a critique which was in each case based on a
single consistent theoretical perspective, that of phenomenology. In
neither case have they completely achieved their objective, although
they have both been successful in contributing to a greater methodological eclecticism and tolerance in their respective disciplines. As far
as the study of social episodes is concerned, much of what has been
said about Harre and Secord's propositions also applies to Cicourel.
Perhaps the main contribution of Cicourel to our endeavour is his

reaffirmation of the open-ended, ever-changing character of social reality. "The recipes of everyday living consist of a set of analogies which are constantly being masked, altered and created during the course of interaction. The study of cultural meanings, with their invariant and innovative properties, remains empirically open" (p. 224). In seeking to understand how individuals come to cognitively represent social episodes and recipes for acting in them, we should never forget that such knowledge is always abstract, and one step removed from the open-ended, primary reality of social interaction.

Current microsociological approaches

In this section of the chapter we finally enter the domain of those sociologists who are most directly responsible for the renewed interest in social episodes in social psychology. Writers such as Goffman, Garfinkel, Matza, Lyman and Scott, Douglas, and Brittan are becoming well known names not only in sociology proper, but also in social psychology. The dramaturgical model developed by Goffman, perhaps more than any other theory, was responsible for the fermenting dissatisfaction with the restrictive and manipulative models employed in social psychology. His work is of particular relevance to our present concern with social episodes as worthwhile objects of empirical study in social psychology.

Looking at these different schools in some detail, it is easy to fall prey to the misapprehension that there are substantial, and even irreconcilable differences between them. While there would undoubtedly be some truth in this conclusion, it is much more important to be aware of the similarities between these theories. The line of evolution in sociological theory traced in this chapter, from Weber through Thomas, Znaniecki, Mead and Waller to Schutz, Goffman and the others describes the common lineage of all current microsociological models. There are some other spiritual ancestors we did not speak about here, mainly social anthropologists. Goffman's initial training and interests owe as much to the methods of social anthropology as to that of sociology, or for that matter, social psychology. But ultimately, contemporary microsociological theories represent only the most recent reincarnation of a long sociological tradition, that of cultural analysis, the study of meanings and reasons for social action as an alternative to the study of social facts.

The dramaturgical model

This approach to social behaviour has evolved very differently from
Thomas's original concern with the situation. While Thomas sought
to understand how individuals come to represent and enact the phenomenal situation, Goffman, the main exponent of the dramaturgical
model, is no longer concerned with how men come to represent situations; to him, it is the situation that defines the actor, and not vice
versa, cultural determinism carried to the extreme. Lyman and Scott
(1972) aptly characterize Goffman's actor as follows:

> "Goffman's social actor, like Machiavelli's prince, lives externally. He
> engages in a daily round of impression management, presenting himself
> to advantage when he is able, rescuing what he can from a bad show
> . . . Machiavelli's Prince and Goffman's social actor have no interior
> specifications. Rather, situations specify them . . . Goffman has also
> adopted the specific unit of investigation derived from Machiavelli's
> conception of social life—the episode. Since the world is created anew
> in each encounter, it is precisely these engagements that form the
> comprehensible units for sociological investigation" (pp. 20, 22).

The dramaturgical model provides perhaps the most widely used
framework within which the concept of episode is invoked. As episodes
inevitably imply some segmentation of social life into more or less
coherent units, the theatre with its condensed presentation of reality
in clearcut sequences provides as obvious analogue. Goffman suggested that the social actor's approach to social events around him can
best be understood in terms of such a theatrical analogy. An individual, encountering the numerous social episodes going on around him,
will seek to assess and understand what is going on within this "strip"
of activity. This endeavour, according to Goffman, is very similar to
a theatre-goer's experience, who, upon viewing the proceedings on
stage, will try to figure out the meaning of the performance. He will
look for a plot which would render the action meaningful, or else, will
impose a plot of his own. The principles employed in staging, and
conveying the plot, such as the different cues and frames used to define
actions, are equally characteristic of everyday social behaviour. Just
as there exist only a limited number of basic plots in the theatre, there
are only a finite number of real-life plots, which Goffman refers to as
"primary frames" (Goffman, 1974). To be able to successfully participate in social interaction, an individual will have to acquire appropriate strategies for performing the roles he seeks to assume. Much of

Goffman's work focuses on the analysis of such interactive strategies as they are employed in natural situations.

While the theatrical analogue has often been recognized by writers in the past, it is only relatively recently that the dramaturgical model was applied to the systematic study of social behaviour. Within this framework, episodes are treated as dramatic performances, the conscious self-monitoring of the actors is always assumed, and the discovery of the script, stage directions and the strategies employed by the actors is the main objective. This model was most extensively developed by Goffman (1959, 1961, 1963, 1964, 1967, 1971, 1972, 1974). His propositions are mainly concerned with the creation of a framework for the explanation of behaviour within such a quasi-dramatical episode.

The analysis of social episodes, stereotyped, and even institutionalized interaction sequences, is central to Goffman's work. Like Schutz, he considers intersubjectivity to be an essential element of interaction: "focused interaction occurs when people effectively agree to sustain for a time a single focus of cognitive and visual attention, as in conversation, a board game or a joint task. . . . I call the natural unit of social organization in which focused interaction occurs a focused gathering, or an encounter, or a situated activity system . . . " (1963, p. 7). Thus, the intersubjectivity of the actors takes place within the context of a socially ordered and predestined episode, since "an encounter exhibits sanctioned orderliness arising from obligations fulfilled and expectations realized" (1963, p. 19). Goffman's analyses concentrate on the subtle and not so subtle rules which thus define and make up social episodes, and not on how individuals construct such episodes. In his analysis of encounters, he suggests that concepts such as "boundary" (between the encounter and the outside world), "transformation rules", or "tension" and tension release in the encounter are important in specifying the approved and normal sequence of events. "The process of mutually sustaining a definition of the situation in face-to-face interaction is socially organized through rules of relevance and irrelevance . . . it is to these flimsy rules, and not to the unshaking character of the external world, that we owe our unshaking sense of realities . . . To be awkward or unkempt, to talk or move wrongly, is to be a dangerous giant, a destroyer of worlds . . . " (1963, p. 81). The analysis of such rules is the recurring theme in Goffman's many penetrating analyses of social behaviour. Such rules are condensed into culturally given "definitions of situations" in Thomas's terminology or frames as Goffman recently referred to them: "I assume that definitions of situations are built up in accordance with principles of organisation which govern events—at least social ones—and our subjective involvement in them; frame is the word I use to refer to such of these basic elements as I am able to identify" (Goffman, 1974, p. 11). This appears to be a *post hoc* and circular definition of frames, however, and it points to the rather controversial methodology on which Goffman's analyses are based.

The methodology implied by the dramaturgical model essentially relies on the use of everyday language and commonsense understanding to give meaning to the social phenomena studied. Douglas (1973) points out some of the shortcomings of this method: "we find the highly detailed accounts and subtle analyses of the social meanings of things . . . by Matza and Goffman with almost no explicit account of the methods involved, and certainly no analysis of the objectivity of such methods . . . Matza and Goffman's research methods then, are apparently more systematic forms of journalistic accounts" (pp. 28–29). Goffman's approach in particular is indebted to G. H. Mead for its theoretical foundations. Goffman, however, tends to emphasize the "culturally given" nature of social situations, and his analysis by definition obscures those creative and innovative aspects of interaction which cannot be subsumed under the heading of stage directions, script, etc. "Ultimately, Goffman, while mapping out the intricacies of 'face work' etc., is committed to a view of action which places the actor very much at the mercy of the script. He cannot get beyond the script because, by definition, the script is the total world—the stage on which his performance is validated" (Brittan, 1973, p. 86). This approach is even manifest in Goffman's latest book: "Presumably, a 'definition of the situation' is almost always to be found, but those who are in the situation ordinarily do not create this definition, even though their society often can be said to do so: ordinarily, all they do is to assess correctly what the situation ought to be for them, and then act accordingly" (Goffman, 1974, pp. 1–2). This statement impressively illustrates the difference between Goffman's and Schutz's understanding of situations and episodes. While for Schutz episodes are by definition biographical, Goffman neglects this subjective element, although he is still concerned with how actors experience and interpret situations—situations which they do not create, but which are "given" to them.

Despite its undoubted popularity, Goffman's work has also received its fair share of criticism. Many of the critics emphasize the methodological ambiguity of Goffman's efforts, and cast doubt on the scientific reliability, and consequently, usefulness of his conclusions. Does social interaction really proceed in the way Goffman suggested, as a Macchiavellian, if co-operative enterprise to "bring off" the show? Much of what Goffman has said is not radically new; exchange theorists (Homans, 1958, 1961; Blau, 1964) symbolic interactionists or indeed, even empirical social psychologists would be able to come to similar conclusions.

A related criticism is the lack of theoretical sophistication in Goffman's work, and the nearly complete absence of abstract and more inclusive theoretical models which would go beyond his immediate observations. This is most obvious in his most recent work (1974), in which repeated apologies in this regard do little to alleviate the reader's fears that there may be little of demonstrable generality in the undoubtedly interesting tales Goffman presents. The orientation of the present work is clearly indebted to Goffman for pointing out the importance of stereotyped, scripted interactions in everyday social life, and for his analyses of such episodes. If we want to go beyond his work, however, we shall be forced to abandon his quasi-literary methods, and rely on the quantitative methods of social psychology. The emerging study of social episodes is based on the conceptual approach of cultural sociologists from Weber to Thomas, a tradition which has been passed on to us in Goffman's works in a most salient form. Social psychological techniques may, in turn, contribute to such sociological models by showing the way to new possibilities for quantifying and analysing such elusive data as social episodes.

In summary, then, the dramaturgical model represents perhaps the strongest and most relevant antecedent of the approach adopted here. Its emphasis on culturally coded episodes as the basic units of analysis, the interest in the social actors' cognitive strategies for enacting an episode, and its reliance on common, everyday encounters as the major source of data are points which are strongly reflected in the proposed social psychological study of social episodes. Two important differences need to be emphasized, however. The dramaturgical approach as applied in microsociology and social anthropology is committed to an anecdotal-journalistic methodology while in the present work quantitative methods of description will be given preference. Secondly,

Goffman and his followers are mainly concerned with strategies of performance within an episode, taking the actors' knowledge of the cultural requirements of the episode as given. In contrast, the main concern in the present studies is the quantitative representation of how actors come to perceive culturally defined stereotypical episodes.

Ethnomethodology

The second important school of microsociology concerned with social episodes is ethnomethodology (Garfinkel, 1967). Although this term does not denote a unified theoretical approach, nor even a clear methodological perspective on the study of social behaviour, it has been adopted by those sociologists who are interested in studying the commonsense everyday knowledge members of a given society have of the affairs of that society. Garfinkel at one point defines ethnomethodology as "an organizational study of a member's knowledge of his ordinary affairs, of his own organized enterprises, where that knowledge is treated by us as part of the same setting that it also makes orderable" (Garfinkel, 1975, p. 18). More generally, ethnomethodology is the study of the cognitive methods we employ in everyday living to construct coherent and meaningful patterns of interaction (Kando, 1977). These native methodologies (hence ethnomethodology) are in fact habitual cognitive strategies for making interaction intelligible. Although these methods are employed by everyone all the time, like grammatical rules of speech, they are not easily articulated. Since practitioners of ethnomethodology (that is, all of us) are not able to rationally articulate their rule-following behaviour, Garfinkel proposes several subterfuges for discovering them. One such method is "Garfinkelling", or the process of deliberately creating a disturbance in the social fabric so that in the resulting confusion and efforts to restitute order, the original rules and conventions of the situation manifest themselves. The second technique is based on the close analysis of persons who are attempting to "pass" in a deliberately chosen role which is not originally part of their repertoire. The rationale here is that someone "passing" will be aware of the conventions that regulate behaviour in the chosen group in a way that those who assume that role naturally wouldn't be. Garfinkel's study of Agnes, a male transsexual who has been passing as a female is an example of this technique.

A further distinguishing mark of ethnomethodology is that it is more concerned with process than with stable facts: "Where others might see 'things', 'givens' or 'facts of life', the ethnomethodologist sees (or attempts to see) *process*: the process through which the perceived stable features of socially organized environments are continually created and sustained" (Pollner, 1975, p. 27). From the ethnomethodological perspective, social episodes are of interest insofar as actors achieve them. The processes used to enact a particular episode, and the tactics used to accomplish its cultural legitimacy are of interest. The cultural definition of the episode is usually accepted as given: the individual members' realization of that episode is the object of study. Thus, ethnomethodological analysis is again based on the assumed knowledge of the cultural definition of an episode. The present approach, concerned with the classification and quantification of perceptions of culturally defined episodes, may be of interest to ethnomethodologists, in that it enables them to transcend the limitations of the descriptive, speculative analysis of episodes used so far.

As a microsociological school, ethnomethodology is perhaps the most extremely situational in its conception of social behaviour. Ethnomethodologists are hesitant to admit cross-situational constancy in meaning—for them, the achievement of communication and social interaction is intrinsically problematic, and is always bound by situational conventions. The process whereby social order is negotiated and achieved is the subject matter of ethnomethodologist research. Thus, in a typical quasi-experiment, the "counselling-study", students were induced to participate in an apparent counselling situation. To their consternation, the counsellor responded to their questions with a randomly determined sequence of yes and no answers. The subjects' attempts to make sense of this inconsistent situation, their efforts to infuse meaning into the meaningless are the raw data the ethnomethodologists are interested in.

Even better known are Garfinkel's efforts to use disruption as a tool for analysing our taken-for-granted routines for achieving meaning in different situations: "Procedurally it is my preference to start with familiar scenes and ask what can be done to make trouble . . . and to produce disorganized interaction/which/should tell us something about how the structures of everyday activities are ordinarily and routinely produced and maintained" (Garfinkel, 1967, p. 37).

Ethnomethodologists have also involved themselves in more linguistically oriented efforts to understand social behaviour. Following

Chomsky's structural linguistics, they sought to study the surface and deep structure of rules which make the infinite variety of "new" social acts possible (Garfinkel and Sacks, 1970). Even the simplest social episode, a dyadic conversation, contains many hidden and implicit elements which are necessary to make communication at all possible. The sentences actually uttered are *indexical*, deriving their meaning from implicit, taken-for-granted information which is specific to the culture, the actors, and to the situation. The participants in any interaction will have to achieve a working understanding of such indexical expressions, "drawing not only on their stock of knowledge, including linguistic knowledge, but also on their exploration of the situation at hand" (Mennell, 1974, p. 53). Ethnomethodology is thus the most "episodic" of the microsociologies, intent on getting inside a given episode as it were to analyse the explicit and hidden processes whereby interaction and the communication of meaning becomes possible. Their stance is very similar to that of social psychology—but their methods are heuristic, intuitive and subjective. As the manifold disagreements between ethnomethodologists and positivist sociologists on the one hand, and amongst ethnomethodologists themselves on the other have demonstrated, these kinds of data make it extremely difficult to arrive at a scientific reconciliation of different interpretations of the same phenomenon.

An assessment of the relevance of ethnomethodology to our interest in social episodes is not an easy task, mainly because of the opaqueness of the theory. Both the substance and the style of Garfinkel's writings is such that it tends to isolate ethnomethodology from other contemporary sociological schools. In addition, as Swanson (1968) pointed out, Garfinkel makes a number of assumptions which are at best unnecessary, and at worst dubious. For example: that everyday life is the only subject matter for ethnomethodology, that there is an irreconcilable difference between the rationalities of science and everyday life, and that ethnomethodologists are unique in studying the latter; that because ensuring the replicability of data is a practical enterprise, there is no necessary gain in applying it, and that the ethnomethodological perspective is that of a stranger or an alienated member of the culture studied. There is little acknowledgement of relevant previous work in Garfinkel's writings, and his selection of topics for investigation and the methods employed in studying them gives the impression of whim and convenience, rather than that of a carefully worked out research strategy. As Swanson (1968) pointed out, in Garfinkel's works we find the near absence of any statement of problems or hypotheses, or of any systematic basis on which his next subject for study is chosen. The absence of a coherent strategy and the natural interaction of observation and inference in Garfinkel's works is also noted by Coleman (1968).

It is paradoxical that ethnomethodology, while it is most explicitly concerned with the study of naturalistic social episodes, has relatively little to contribute to a social psychology of such episodes. The basic assumption, that *all* interaction episodes can be analysed in terms of conventions and rule-following, is arguable (see Chapter 1). Since individuals are not normally in a position to elucidate the rules they follow (Robinson, 1977), and since contrary to Garfinkel's assumptions, observable everyday actions and the rules that produce them are not identical (Wallace, 1968), it appears that ethnomethodology is restricted to ingeniously demonstrating the obvious in everyday social routines. However, there are aspects of the theory which could profitably be incorporated into a social psychology of episodes. As Harre and Secord (1972) note, the study of "passing" is a useful methodological tool, which has some potential particularly in the early, descriptive stages of social psychological research. We are also in sympathy with Garfinkel insofar as he emphasizes implicit cognitive strategies as the subject for analysis. Before more exact functional models of such cognitive processes can be developed, it is necessary to specify and quantify the informational content that goes into rule-following. The perception and cognitive representation of global episodes is one such cognitive domain which is of particular interest here. It may well be that the kind of studies ethnomethodologists carry out may one day be incorporated into quantitative social psychological research, with the native cognitive methodologies used to make interaction intelligible empirically condensed into mathematical formuli. Before that day arrives, however, we shall have to devise means for quantifying and representing a social actor's implicit knowledge about his social milieu. Hopefully, the study of how social episodes are cognitively represented may contribute to the accomplishment of this task.

Summary

In this chapter we have attempted to trace the evolution of the sociological approach to social interaction episodes. Of necessity our review of the literature had to be extremely selective. Nevertheless, it appears from the research surveyed that in sociology, just as in psychology, there exists a veritable tradition of interest in the study of social interaction episodes. While positivistic macrosociology in the mould created by Comte and Durkheim was naturally less interested in small scale interaction processes than in the study of large-scale social facts, the interpretive cultural sociology of Max Weber has exerted a growing influence over the years, stimulating a long tradition of research into social situations. The second major influence on sociological studies of social situations is the symbolic interactionist school, and the writings of G. H. Mead, C. H. Cooley and H. Blumer in particular. These two major sources are fused in the works of W. I. Thomas and F. Znaniecki, the first sociologists who accorded a central place to the study of social situations in their work. Finally, the third major theoretical influence on sociological thinking about social episodes can be identified in the phenomenological philosophy of Husserl, transmitted to mainstream sociology by Alfred Schutz.

Following Schutz's work, phenomenological sociology enjoys something of a boom nowadays. Phenomenological analyses of social behaviour, and collections of microsociological writings in the phenomenological tradition are reaching a wider audience than ever before (see Douglas, 1973 and Brittan, 1973). However, contemporary microsociological schools were not influenced solely by phenomenology. Symbolic interactionists who were particularly interested in the individual's experience, such as Blumer, and cultural sociologists in the tradition of Weber and W. I. Thomas have also strongly contributed to the current burgeoning interest in microsociology. Concern with the social situation or episode and its requirements occupies an important place in all of these theories. Indeed, interest in the social situation can be construed as the single most important differentiating factor between structuralist and humanistic sociological schools, and a hallmark of humanistic orientations: "It is the recognition of the fundamental importance of the question of situationalism and transsituationalism that has most distinguished phenomenological sociologies from absolutist (structural) sociologies" (Douglas, 1973, p. 35). In the diversity of sociological orientations outlined in this chapter, from Weber's interpretative sociology to Schutz's phenomenology, the basic idea running through is that "human events are always to some degree dependent on the situational context in which they occur and can be adequately explained only by taking into consideration that situational context" (Douglas, 1973, p. 37).

While agreement regarding the importance of situations is a common hallmark of all interpretative-phenomenologist sociologies and the most important feature which sets them apart from structuralist functionalist sociologies, there is wide disagreement regarding the exact definition of what is meant by a "situation" or "episode". The possible alternatives range from a construal of situations as culturally given to the subjective, phenomenological definition of Schutz. This dualism is most succinctly reflected in Wolff's dictionary definition of the term. "The phrase *definition of the situation* denotes (a) the individual agent's or actor's perception and interpretation of any situation in which he may find himself (the actor's definition of the situation) or (b) culturally formulated, embodied and shared perceptions and interpretations of situations considered identical or similar (cultural or social definition of the situation). There is a two-fold connection between these two kinds of definitions of the situation. The cultural definition enters and becomes part of the actor's definition through social interaction . . ., primarily socialization . . .; the actor's definition may produce change in the cultural definition. /The term/ . . . quickly became . . . the dominant phrase for denoting two facets of the theory of social acts . . . (a) it pointed to the requirement of determining the meaning of a situation to the actor, thus involving social science in the use of categories of meaning, motive and attitude. (b) It stressed the fact that the dimension of such meaning was cultural in character, i.e. shared, symbolically formulated, and transmitted through the process of socialization; internalized in the personality of the actor, and yet also confronting him as the shared attitudes and beliefs of his fellows" (Wolff, 1964, p. 182).

The dual nature of situation as the term was developed in sociology gave rise to two different orientations in contemporary microsociological analysis. Firstly, normatively oriented models are most interested in the culturally given aspect of episodes. Some dramaturgical analyses of situated behaviour can be regarded as normative in this sense.

In contrast, situations as products of creative, individual action are analysed by microsociologists such as Garfinkel, Cicourel, and Lyman and Scott in *The Sociology of the Absurd* (1972). This approach is ultimately based on Schutz's phenomenological sociology, and its crucial element is that it includes an individual, autobiographical component as part of the situation.

This apparent birfurcation of efforts to implement situational analysis in sociological research is clearly contrary to the intentions of the spiritual founders of the movement. Thus, Mead's symbolic interactionism, Weber's interpretative sociology and Schutz's phenomenological sociology were similar in their efforts to emphasize the interactive, dialectic relationship between socio-cultural and individual aspects of situation definition. To emphasize the primacy of either component is contrary to the spirit in which the current microsociological schools originated. As far as the study of social episodes, as part of the empirical, quantitative discipline of social psychology is concerned, we should also clearly recognize that situation definition is a two-faceted phenomenon. In keeping with the historical tradition in our discipline, it is likely that research into commonalities in the perception of social episodes or situations, that is, socio-cultural situations, will be in the forefront of interest, at least initially. This nomothetic orientation has served social psychology well so far. But we should not forget that there is an equally interesting, and much less researched problem, the problem of how unique individuals come to construct and interpret their social world, and how their actions reflect this interpretation. By proposing a study of social episodes as a new theme in social psychology, we should be in a better position to focus on such idiosyncratic processes, which are as important to our understanding of social behaviour as are the cultural definitions of episodes. It may well be that one of the by-products of concentrating on the study of social episodes will be that the long neglected idiographic methods of analysis will be given an equal place in the discipline.

5

Methods for Studying Social Episodes

The first four chapters of this book surveyed the background of the current interest in social episodes in social psychology. This is a most important task, since without a proper appreciation of the substantial work already carried out in psychology as well as sociology, the concept of episodes may appear but another neologism, and proposals to study episodes could be discounted as yet another fad in a discipline already severely affected by changes in fashion. But now the time has arrived to discuss the future; what kinds of techniques are available for studying social episodes, what further directions can research take, and in which areas of psychology can the study of social episodes be most fruitfully implemented. The remainder of this book is devoted to discussing the range of empirical techniques already established as appropriate to the study of social episodes, and to the discussion of the history and prospects of the four most promising research orientations.

The present chapter seeks to present a methodological summary of the four most common research strategies used to study social episodes. These can be subsumed under four labels, (a) the ecological approach, (b) the perceptual approach, (c) the structural sequencing approach and (d) the roles—rules approach. Since the aim of this book is primarily to offer a synthesis of the new ideas now current in social psychology and the methodological sophistication of traditional social psychological research, it is of particular importance that the credibility of the proposed methodologies be convincingly established. This is the task of this chapter.

The four research strategies

The four research strategies to be discussed here are by no means the only ones which are applicable to the study of social episodes, nor is it certain that they will prove to be the most fruitful ones in the future.

Rather these four approaches appear to be most characteristic of current work on social episodes, with the greatest promise for the immediate future.

There are important differences in emphasis between the four strategies discussed here. Both the perceptual and the ecological approaches seek to study global, complete interaction episodes, or more precisely, the relationship between such self-contained behaviour sequences. In contrast, both the structuralist and the related roles–rules strategies aim to study actions, moves and behaviours that occur within the framework of specified episodes. The objective is to discover the *within-episode* structure of behaviour and the rules that govern it, in contrast to the previously mentioned strategies which concentrate on *between-episode* differences. Both the perceptual and the ecological strategies employ methods which are fairly closely related to techniques already in use in social psychological research. These techniques, on the whole, satisfy the conventional requirements of empirical science, and rely on observable, quantifiable and replicable data as the basis of their analyses. Thus, both perceptions of social episodes and the ecological behaviour settings in which such episodes occur can be studied by social psychological methods, although in both cases, a great deal of ingenuity is required to adapt existing techniques, and in some cases, to invent new ones. In contrast, the research strategies oriented towards discovering the structure and the roles and rules governing behaviour within social episodes owe more to the methods and techniques of linguistics, sociology, and social anthropology than to those of social psychology. The data are essentially judgements by social actors of the appropriateness or otherwise of behaviour structures generated by hypothetical rule systems or "grammars" (a role similar to Chomsky's "native speaker" criterion for evaluating syntactic rules); or else, open-ended, interpretive accounts by actors as to their motives, intentions and perceptions while acting within an episode. The replication and quantification of these data may be problematic at times, and the transplantation of these methodologies from other disciplines poses additional problems. Notwithstanding these differences, the dividing line between these two kinds of research strategies is not a particularly sharp one. The structure and rules within an episode are intimately related to how that episode is globally perceived, and in turn, cognitive representations of global episodes are closely related to actual behaviour within that episode. The contrast in methodological emphasis between these strategies does not imply a conflict in subject matter. Rather, at the current stage in the study of social episodes, we may regard these four research strategies as complementary, each making a unique contribution to our enterprise. It is not accidental, however, that the two "psychological" strategies, the perceptual and the ecological, are the ones which resulted in the most extensive research findings to date. We shall summarize these findings in Chapter 6 (ecological) and Chapters 7 and 8 (perceptual). No such chapters summarizing research can be included for the other two strategies yet, since they both represent relatively new and as yet less productive orientations. Perhaps in a few years, this situation may have changed radically.

The ecological strategy

Unlike the three other methodological orientations discussed here, the interest in the ecological study of behaviour settings has preceded the current interest in social episodes by several decades, resulting in the establishment of a distinct research tradition quite independent from the study of social episodes. With the re-emergence of interest in natural social interaction episodes, the approach to the study of behaviour settings developed by Barker and his co-workers (Barker, 1968; Barker and Wright, 1955; Barker and Schoggen, 1973) gained a new significance.

The kind of ecological psychology practised by these researchers at the Midwest Psychological Research Station in the USA, and intermittently, in Yorkshire, England, is unique in its orientation. The global aim of the programme was to develop concepts and methods applicable to the study of the ecological environment of molar human behaviour. Not surprisingly, this work has received renewed attention from social psychologists in recent years. Barker's methodology is an interesting and ingenious fusion of three research strategies. Firstly, he relies on the kind of microsociological analysis developed by the Chicago school of sociology, based on intensive participant observation of the "culture" of smaller scale social units, such as suburbs, small towns, or even a street corner gang. Secondly, Barker's analyses are also related to social anthropological work, with its open-ended and descriptive analyses of typical behaviour patterns performed in specified settings. Finally, and perhaps most importantly, the method used by Barker has a strong psychological flavour which can ultimately be traced to Lewin's field theory: his understanding of behaviour settings or environments is as elements which are part of the "life space" of individuals, and which influence human behaviour by virtue of their function in the psychological field of social actors.

Behaviour settings can be defined as enduring, standing patterns of behaviour, which are consistently related to specific physical environments (Barker, 1968). There are many identifiable properties of such behaviour settings which are of interest—the list of such properties bears a surprising resemblance to lists of attributes of social episodes proposed in the roles–rules framework, for example by Argyle (1976). Thus, behaviour settings have a geographical locus, a temporal locus, occupancy time, action patterns, behaviour mechanisms, and so on. Studies of behaviour settings employ an eclectic methodology. Some characteristics, such as the physical environment, the behaviour structure (sequence), or the category of participants is directly observable. The effect of behaviour settings as independent variables on behaviour can be studied in a quasi-experimental fashion, observing and recording changes in the behaviour of a selected group of individuals as they pass from one behaviour setting to another.

Before such studies can be embarked upon, the first task is to conduct a behaviour setting survey comprising the listing and recording of all possible behaviour settings in the given community. There are numerous criteria which may be used in eliminating locations which are not uniquely associated with characteristic behaviour patterns. These settings are not genuine behaviour settings in the sense of the definition. The degree of interdependence or overlap between behaviour settings can be empirically established by working out the number of features which are identical across settings. This measure can be used as a criterion for merging behaviour settings, resulting in an eventual sample of physical environments with non-overlapping interaction patterns. In effect, settings with a high index of interdependence are merged into a single setting category. Similarly, quantitative measures are used to rate and compare the occupancy of behaviour settings, the action patterns which occur within them, their local autonomy, etc. For example, distinct action patterns, each describing a particular kind of purposive interaction can be defined, such as business, education, government, aesthetics, nutrition, personal appearance, physical health, professionalism, recreation, religion and social contact, and the degree to which each of these action patterns occurs in each behaviour setting is rated on a set of scales. As this brief summary shows, this apparently vague and description-oriented general approach to the ecological study of interaction episodes is in fact strongly psychological in its emphasis on quantifiable and replicable data bases.

A further interesting aspect of the study of behaviour settings is the emphasis of the method on establishing empirical taxonomies. Barker refers to such taxonomical categories of behaviour settings as behaviour setting genotypes: "Behaviour setting genotypes are empirically determined classes of settings" (1968, p. 88). Such classificatory categories can be arrived at in terms of objective criteria, in terms of the potential interchangeability of the performers, action patterns, behaviour and other features of the situation.

Related to the concept of action patterns is the concept of behaviour mechanisms, of which five are distinguished by Barker: affective behaviour, gross motor activity, manipulation, talking, thinking. As in the analysis of action patterns, the occurrence of behaviour mechanisms in different settings is also rated by independent judges. Barker reports that the reliability of judgements of action patterns, behaviour mechanisms and other behaviour setting attributes is "well above that usually accepted as adequate for studies of distributions of ratings" (p. 90).

The substantive findings of this research strategy will be considered in the next chapter. Presently, only the methodological aspects of the ecological approach to the study of naturally occurring social behaviour are of interest. The study of behaviour settings appears to be one of the first attempts to analyse naturally occurring behaviour, and more exactly, cultural patterns of naturally occurring social behaviour, using empirical methods. The techniques proposed are not in themselves radically new, and are based on fairly straightforward scaling strategies. There may be several potential difficulties which need to be remembered when applying this strategy. Most of the quantified data is based on judgements or ratings, in terms of judgemental criteria or rating scales constructed by the experimenter on a priori grounds. It is important that such judgemental dimensions should reflect the natural perceptions of the judges, otherwise their responses will have only limited validity. In other words, judges should perceive the same action patterns and behaviour mechanisms as those which are identified by Barker. It appears that quite a few of Barker's categories subsumed under labels such as behaviour mechanisms or action patterns, are rather abstract, and thus their meaningfulness to the judges may be open to doubt. The problem of unitization, or the decision as to what exactly is a behaviour setting unit, can also be difficult. Although the use of quantitative indices for sifting out overlapping and redundant behaviour setting labels is undoubtedly a sound one, it is quite possible to think of aspects of behaviour settings which could not be quantified in this way. Overall, it is hard to escape the feeling that Barker's method, by its very reliance on quantitative data, leaves out some unique and fascinating features of naturalistic social behaviour. However, this would not be a wholly fair conclusion. The social anthropological, descriptive-analytic component is at least as strong in this work as the psychological one. On the balance, it appears that Barker's approach deserves more detailed scrutiny and follow-up than is entailed in the frequent lip-service that is being paid to his work. By matching his overall conceptual orientation and interest in studying the natural flow of social behaviour with the more sophisticated and sensitive statistical scaling techniques available today, a very powerful method indeed for studying naturalistic social episodes could be created.

Some more recent, and perhaps less ambitious, research projects have an apparent methodological affinity with Barker's orientation. Price and his co-workers (Price, 1974; Price and Bouffard, 1974) used essentially a behaviour setting approach in their studies of social situations. Rather than seeking to construct an encyclopaedic summary of all important behaviour settings in a given milieu, they were satisfied to study a small selection of *ad hoc* behaviour settings, and a similarly small number of behaviours which could occur in those situations. Their methodology again relied on the ratings technique, asking judges to rate the perceived appropriateness of each of a number of behaviours in each of a number of behaviour settings. By summarizing such judgements across behaviours, an overall index of restrictiveness or constraint for every situation can be calculated, defined in terms of the number of behaviours which are appropriate in that setting. Thus private settings are compatible with a much wider range of permissible behaviours than are public settings. Since some of the behaviours studied were socially sanctioned e.g., belching, this is perhaps not surprising. Similarly, the situational generality of different behaviours was established by measuring the appropriateness of behaviours across diverse situations. Again, some behaviours, such as talking, have a wide situational generality, while others, such as belching, can only be performed in a restricted range of situations. These findings are perhaps not very surprising. Nevertheless, the idea of calculating indices of restrictiveness for different settings is an ingenious one, and with a wider and more representative range of episodes, the findings could be much more interesting.

This brief summary of the kinds of methods which have been used to study behaviour settings will, I hope, suggest an interesting, although perhaps not quite new way of studying social episodes. The building blocks of this method are simple scaling techniques, supplemented by participant observation and intensive interviews as a means of representing uniquely situated interactions within a specified milieu. Taken individually none of these methods is radically new. It is the unique conceptual framework and the ingenious combination of methods produced by Barker for studying behaviour settings which is the most novel aspect of this strategy. The connection between what we understand by social episodes here, and what Barker defines as behaviour settings, is an extremely close one. Both concepts refer to stereotyped, culturally coded sequences of interactive behaviours within a spatially and temporarily defined framework. The indices for studying such encounters developed by Barker are but the first step in explaining the manifold features which characterize situated interactions. The taxonomic studies carried out by his team provide excellent illustrations of the power of such methods, and strongly support the view that mere "description" of such cultural domains is a rewarding and worthwhile task in itself.

The perceptual strategy

The previous survey (Chapter 3) of the historical roots of concepts such as episode and situation clearly indicates a line of development from atomistic to molar, from environmental to cognitive, and from the physical, objective situation to the perceived, subjective situation and episode. It is not particularly surprising, therefore, that the perceptual approach to the study of social episodes has been the dominant one to date. In principle, the many different studies already relying on such an approach share the common assumption that social episodes or situations can be construed as cognitively mediated "mental objects".

Consequently, perceptions of episodes can be studied in exactly the same way as perceptions of other social objects, be they other people, role relationships, or political doctrines. (Strictly speaking, we should be talking about the cognitive representation rather than the perception of social episodes, since we are interested in representing already existing cognitive structures, and not in studying the process of how they are perceived. However, the bastardization of the term "perception" is so deeply entrenched in social psychology that it would seem futile to insist on terminological pedantry here.)

The typical research strategy in studies of perceptions of social episodes or situations involves the following major stages:

(a) The collection, elicitation or sampling of the episodes or situations to be studied.

(b) The construction and administration of some judgemental task to subjects, which requires them to indicate their explicit or implicit perception of the group of episodes selected for study.

(c) Judgements are typically analysed with the help of statistical methods which reduce the complexity of the initial judgements, and if possible, reveal the underlying structure in the discriminations judges make. Normally, techniques such as cluster-analysis, factor-analysis or multidimensional scaling are employed.

(d) Interpretation of the factors, clusters, dimensions or categories derived using the statistical techniques mentioned before. Investigators may be interested in the clustering of the attribute dimensions used, or in the clustering of the episodes studied. Often, interpretations are based on intuition, although objective procedures now exist for the empirical interpretation of both cluster-analytic (Rosenberg and Sedlak, 1972) and factor-analytic solutions. Multidimensional scaling results, for example, are nearly always interpreted with the help of empirical techniques.

(e) Finally, once internal representations of social episodes are quantified, it is possible to formulate and evaluate hypotheses about the variables that affect episode perception, the extent of differences between different *a priori* clusters of episodes in cognitive space, individual and group differences in episode perception, etc. In the following pages the steps involved in each stage of the perceptual research strategy in the study of social episodes will be discussed in some detail.

SAMPLING AND SELECTION OF EPISODES

The kind of sampling procedure used depends largely on the aims of the study. These can be of two major types. The first one is taxonomic-descriptive, that is, the study seeks to establish the perceived relationship between a set of social episodes or situations which were not previously subjected to empirical study. In this case, it is of particular importance that the episodes studied should be broadly representative of the normal interaction patterns of the subjects, and be characteristic of their subcultural milieu. The second possible aim of perceptual studies of social episodes is to assess the perceived differences between episodes representing a subcategory of the subcultural milieu, episodes which are of some particular interest to the investigator on *a priori* grounds. For example, anxiety-evoking episodes and situations have been extensively studied because of their obvious relevance to clinical psychology. In this case, the representative sampling of social episodes is not so crucial, although it is still important that the episodes used as stimuli should be meaningful and personally experienced by the judges.

In either case, the need to sample social episodes within a given subject group or subcultural milieu often arises. The methods applicable to such a task are fairly limited, and require some ingenuity on the part of the researcher. Ever since Brunswik's (1956) advocation of the representative design in psychology the need for a technique for sampling situations and episodes has been recognized, yet no clear-cut solutions have emerged. The statistical procedures for drawing a representative sample of individuals from a known subject population are difficult to apply, mainly for two reasons. First, the total population of episodes to be sampled is hardly ever known, nor is it feasible to construct a listing of all possible episodes which might occur within a subcultural domain. Secondly, the unitization of episodes is often problematic. In the case of sampling subjects, we always know what constitutes a unit in the population to be sampled. In sampling episodes, deciding what constitutes a unit is always a problem, mainly because of the ongoing, flowing nature of social behaviour (Barker, 1968). Although some attempts have been made to unitize empirically the "stream of behaviour" (Dickman, 1963; Newtson, 1973) these efforts have not yet resulted in commonly accepted and empirically established categories of episodes.

The only alternative left to derive a representative sample of social episodes is to rely on some form of self-report by the subjects regarding their typical and recurring activities. Using this approach, the task of unitization is simply left to the implicit judgements of subjects, which is probably the most sensible solution, since they are likely to know much better than the investigator which sequences of their social activities can be regarded as episodic units. The extent of agreement between subjects from a particular milieu in identifying an episode is an important index of the cultural salience of that episode. The techniques which can be used for collecting representative samples of episodes range from participant observation to paper-and-pencil techniques. Thus in a study of a small academic group (Forgas, 1978a), participant observation was used to ascertain the range of most frequently practised and typical episodes. This method was feasible in this context because the group was small, familiar to the investigator, and a wide range of group activities could be surveyed by participant observation. In other studies, paper-and-pencil techniques are more promising. The most frequently used such technique is the diary-method. This consists of the provision of a more-or-less prestructured diary form to subjects, who are then required to record all of their social activities over a specified period, normally 24 hours. The form can be constructed in such a way that information about the time, place, setting, participants, purpose and outcome, as well as the subject's feelings, interpretation and evaluation of the episode can be obtained. Occasionally, subjects are also asked to list a series of descriptive adjectives relevant to their perception of each episode. These additional categories of information are necessary in later stages of the study. For example, the adjectives describing episodes provided by subjects can be used in the construction of bipolar judgemental scales in a later, more quantitative stage of the study (Beach and Wertheimer, 1961; Fuchs and Schafer, 1972). The diary method is best employed when a larger, less familiar social milieu is studied. For example, in a study of perceptions of social episodes by housewives (Forgas, 1976a) or by a larger group of students (Price and Bouffard, 1974), the diary method was used to obtain a representative sample of episodes and situations.

Perhaps the most important message about the sampling of social episodes is that it is an essential part of any research project. Far too many studies of perceptions of social situations have relied on an *ad hoc*, intuitive collection of episodes as their stimulus material. The perceptual dimensions derived from such studies lack face validity, simply because we do not know whether the judges think in terms of the same episodes as the investigators do. Even in studies seeking to study the perception of fairly well-circumscribed episode domains, such as the numerous studies of perceptions of anxiety-arousing episodes, there may still be doubt about the results, caused by the fact that we do not know how relevant or meaningful the selected episodes were to the subjects. To use Kelly's (1955) terminology, the stimulus materials used, as well as the constructs on which they are to be judged must, by necessity, lie within the "range of convenience", or experience of the subjects. Otherwise, the quality of those judgements is open to question.

THE JUDGEMENTAL TASK

Once a representative sample of social episodes is obtained, the next step is to obtain some quantifiable judgemental data indicative of the perceived differences between the episodes sampled. The task that will be used is largely a function of the planned data analytic procedure. Two major classes of judgemental tasks can be distinguished, those using preselected scales or dimensions, and those allowing subjects to make unstructured judgements, thus allowing them to express the implicit cognitive distinctions they make between the different episodes. The former procedure is mainly used when a factor-analytic evaluation of the results is contemplated, while unstructured similarity-rating tasks are often used as input to multidimensional scaling (MDS) analyses, although the distinction is not an absolute one.

When structured judgements are desired, this nearly always means that a selection of bipolar semantic differential type scales are provided to the subjects. Since there is already a burgeoning literature on the uses and abuses of such scales (Warr and Knapper, 1968; Osgood *et al.*, 1957), it should not be necessary to go into much detail here. Perhaps the most important point that needs to be made is that whenever bipolar scales are provided to the subjects, it is of crucial importance that those scales should be relevant and meaningful to them. This is particularly so in the case of judgements of social episodes, since episodes are an extremely complex, elusive and even ambiguous stimulus domain, and are not customarily judged in terms of preselected scales. Add to the cognitive difficulty of judging such a complex group of stimuli the added handicap that the bipolar scales used are not relevant, and the result may well be a relatively meaningless set of judgements. The validation of the scales used for every study is thus a necessity. Often, descriptive adjectives relevant to the perception of the episodes studied can be collected in the pilot study stage, and there are quantitative procedures which can be used for constructing bipolar scales from such free-response description data (Beach and Wertheimer, 1961; Fuchs and Schafer, 1972).

A more satisfactory, but also more demanding method of collecting judgements is the use of non-structured tasks. The different multidimensional scaling methods which have become widely used in social psychology since the early seventies have revolutionalized the methodology of social perception research. The main advantage of these techniques from a social psychological point of view is that they no longer require subjects to make judgements in terms of preselected scales, a weakness which dogged descriptive social perception studies from the beginning. For MDS techniques, a matrix of some measure of psychological distance or similarity between the elements to be scaled is sufficient input. (The psychological definition of similarity may be in itself problematic, however, see Tversky, 1977). For the various non-metric scaling techniques (e.g. Kruskal's (1964) TORSCA 9), categorical or ordinal judgements are sufficient as input, yet output configurations are on an interval scale. This seemingly unreasonable transformation of data is achieved by using the non-ordinal information implicit in a complete matrix of judgements. The advantages of this data collection procedure are obvious, particularly when the objects to be scaled are complex and abstract social stimuli, such as social episodes.

There are several ways of obtaining psychological distance measures between elements. Psychological distance can be operationalized as (a) similarity or (b) co-occurrence between the elements to be scaled; "experimental measurements may. . ./also/be. . . similarities, confusion probabilities, interaction rates between groups, correlation coefficients or other measures of proximity or dissociation of the most diverse kind" (Kruskal, 1964a, p. 1). This broad definition of similarity allows the experimenter a considerable latitude in deciding which kind of judgemental task is most appropriate for his purpose. Three of the more frequently used methods, all designed to deal with judgemental data in social psychology, are (a) direct similarity ratings, (b) the multiple groupings technique, and (c) similarity measures derived from judgements on objective scales (Forgas, 1979a).

The first method, direct similarity ratings, is the most straightforward technique, which simply requires subjects to indicate the perceived similarity of the stimuli on a predetermined numerical scale. The stimuli can be presented either in pairs, in the form of a list of all possible combinations, or in the form of a cross-tabulated matrix. This method yields fully metric judgemental data which can be used as input to metric MDS techniques. Since subjects are merely asked to indicate the perceived similarity of the stimuli, in terms of whatever explicit or implicit criteria they consider relevant, judgements should reflect the cognitive distinctions subjects naturally make, unadulterated by the imposition of preselected scales. This method is most appropriate when the stimuli are readily representable and fairly tangible, and when it is reasonable to assume that subjects are capable of making similarity judgements on an interval scale. Thus, MDS studies of perceived group structure, where the stimuli are other people well known to the judges, often use this method (Jones and Young, 1973; Davison and Jones, 1976; Forgas, 1978a).

The multiple groupings technique simply requires subjects to make categorical judgements about the stimuli. In this method, subjects are provided with a set of cards, or with a list of the stimuli, and are asked to sort or allocate the cards into separate affinity groups, in terms of perceived similarity, association, contiguity and any other criteria considered relevant. This method is appropriate when the stimuli are highly complex and abstract. Its main disadvantage is that it only yields categorical data for each individual subject. It is possible, however, to aggregate data over subjects, by constructing "group" similarity matrices. The data in such a matrix indicates how many judges from the group have placed any two stimuli into the same category. This data collection method has the advantage of allowing a clear, unambiguous presentation of the stimuli, and requires only a fairly straightforward and tangible response from the subjects. Some studies of social episodes (Forgas, 1976a) have relied on this technique.

Measures of similarity between the elements may also be obtained indirectly from judgements of the stimuli on bipolar or Likert-type scales. In some instances the use of preselected bipolar scales as a means of obtaining measures of similarity is not only a permissible, but a preferable method of data collection (Wish *et al.*, 1976). Since such ratings are not used directly as input to MDS, as is the case, for example, with factor analysis, but are first converted into similarities, the usual objections against the use of preselected scales can be mollified. Since calculated similarities are constructed on the basis of judgements on several scales, it is not necessary to assume that all scales used will be equally relevant, as long as at least some of them will be. The usual data collection procedure thus involves:

(1) The rating of all stimuli on a number (normally at least 10) of bipolar scales, which are hypothesized to be related to the cognitive dimensions underlying the stimulus space.

(2) Similarity measures are extracted from these judgements by aggregating judgements over scales or over individuals. This can be accomplished by using a profile distance formula, such as the one proposed by Osgood and Suci (1952), Cronbach and Gleser (1953) and Wish *et al.* (1976). In this formula, the dissimilarity $\delta_{jk(s)}$ between elements j and k on scale s is expressed as

$$\delta_{jk(s)} = \sqrt{\frac{1}{N} \sum_{i=1}^{N} (X_{ij(s)} - X_{ik(s)})^2}$$

where N is the total number of subjects, and $X_{ij(s)}$ and $X_{ik(s)}$ stand for subject i's rating of elements j and k on scale s. This method of collecting judgements has been used in several studies of perceptions of social episodes, which will be further discussed in Chapter 7.

This is far from being an exhaustive list of the different judgemental tasks which can be constructed. Particularly with MDS methods, where the input required is some measure of psychological distance or similarity, there is considerable scope for the experimenter to design new and relevant data collection procedures to suit the subject, the occasion and the type of episodes studied.

ANALYSIS

As was suggested previously, the analytic procedure used is usually designed to reduce the complexity of the original judgemental data, by extracting communalities in the measurement dimensions or the episodes studied (e.g. by factor-analysis), by categorizing the episodes (cluster-analysis), or by seeking to explicate the cognitive dimensions implicit in similarity judgements (MDS).

The choice of the method of analysis also depends on whether the perceptual space for episodes is assumed to be categorical (groups of episodes clustered together) or dimensional (differences between the perception of different episodes measurable on an interval scale). There is some evidence from studies using both categorical and dimensional methods (Forgas, 1976a) that the dimensional solutions are preferable, and are likely to include a sufficient reflection of any categorical clustering of the episodes in perceptual space.

Factor-analytic studies of episode perception (Magnusson, 1971; Ekehammar and Magnusson, 1973) tended to yield intuitively meaningful groupings of episodes, perhaps because the factors are typically interpreted intuitively. A further limitation is that the solutions are often in effect categorical rather than dimensional. That is clusters of episodes loading on a particular factor are lumped together and labelled, but only rarely are dimensional differences within this cluster analysed.

Cluster-analytic methods, particularly hierarchical clustering, can provide a clear and concise representation of the perceived relationship between a group of episodes. Unfortunately, this method is not used as frequently as it could be. Cluster-analytic solutions can also be helpful in aiding the interpretation of multidimensional scaling solutions. Multidimensional scaling is, on the whole, the most satisfactory method of analysis, not only because of the lack of limitations on the data collection procedures used, as suggested earlier, but also because it is the method most suitable for the objective interpretation of the output. Contrary to popular misconceptions, MDS methods are not more complicated or difficult to use and interpret than factor-analysis, and have several advantages in comparison. Two kinds of MDS programmes have been most widely used in the analysis of perceptions of social episodes. Non-metric MDS programmes, such as Kruskal's (1964) TORSCA 9 are most suitable when (a) the input data are non-metric and (b) the investigator is not particularly concerned with perceptual differences between individuals. Thus, representations of the perception of a sample of social episodes within a defined subcultural group or milieu can be adequately analysed by this technique.

More recent MDS programmes are capable of taking individual differences between judges into account. Tucker and Messick's (1963) "points of view" analysis assumes that in the perception of any group of stimuli, a limited number of "points of view", or typical perceptual styles exist. The analysis relies on a two-step procedure; first a factor-analysis of intersubject correlations is used to identify "hypothetical" representative subjects, each one representing the centroid of a cluster of real subjects. In the second step, for each such "hypothetical" subject similarity judgements are subjected to MDS analysis, resulting in different solutions for each "point of view". Critics of this method point out that it accomplishes little more than a series of separate MDS analyses would have done.

A different model was developed by Carrol and Chang (1970), who in their INDSCAL (Individual Differences Multidimensional Scaling) model assume that the same dimensions underlie the judgements of all subjects, but that these dimensions have different salience for different individuals. The INDSCAL model constructs a stimulus space representing the perception of the stimuli by a hypothetical average judge. In addition, it also constructs a subject space, where the positioning of individual judges reflects the relative salience of each stimulus dimension for that particular judge. The subject's coordinates (subjects weights) can then be used to stretch or contract the group stimulus dimensions in order to arrive at the stimulus space as perceived by that particular individual (see Fig. 1). This model has the added advantage that the stimulus dimensions are not arbitrary (as, for example in the case of TORSCA 9), and need not be further rotated. Since the stimulus space is constructed on the basis of the extraction of the most "common" implicit dimensions from similarity matrices representing a number of judges, the resulting stimulus dimensions "should correspond to meaningful psychological dimensions in a very strong sense" (Carrol and Chang, 1970, p. 286). The INDSCAL model has frequently been used to study perceptions of social episodes (Forgas, 1978a, 1979a) or interpersonal relationships (Wish et al., 1976). It allows empirical comparisons to be made between the perceptual styles of individual judges, or subgroups of judges. Perhaps the one shortcoming of the INDSCAL method is that it is a metric scaling technique, that is, it is assumed that the input data are on an interval scale.

This problem has been eliminated by a more recent and versatile individual differences MDS programme, that of Young et al. (1978): ALSCAL. This programme allows both metric and non-metric data inputs, and appears to be promising as an omnibus programme for analysing perceptions of social episodes.

The most recent innovations in MDS techniques are oriented towards a further extension of the flexibility of the method, whilst at the

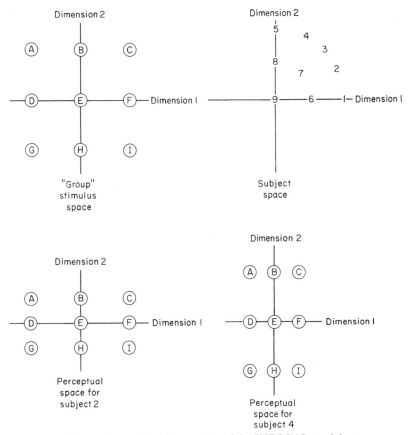

Fig. 1. A graphical illustration of the INDSCAL model.

same time reducing the complexity of the judgemental tasks required for assembling similarity matrices, particularly if a large sample of stimuli are to be scaled. Since MDS methods require a complete matrix of $N(N-1)/2$ judgements from each subject as input, such a matrix is difficult to assemble with more than about 25 episodes, and the time and concentration involved in making such a large number of complex judgements can be tedious and time consuming for subjects. Several authors (Young and Cliff, 1972; Spence and Domoney, 1974; Baker and Young, 1975; Girard and Cliff, 1976) have contributed to the development of MDS methods which require only a subset of all possible judgements as data. Thus, Young and Cliff's (1972) ISIS (Interactive Scaling with Individual Subjects) procedure involves subjects in real-time interaction with the computer, which requires judges to make similarity judgements only until a satisfactory representation of the stimulus structure is achieved. This method "allows the generalization of current MDS systems in two directions: (a) a very large number of stimuli may be scaled, and (b) the scaling is performed with individual subjects facilitating the investigation of individual as well as group processes" (Young and Cliff, 1972, p. 385). This method, although not yet widely available at the time of writing, is particularly promising for the study of perceptions of social episodes. The effective lifting of the limitation of 25–30 episodes as the maximum number that can be scaled in one analysis is obviously an important improvement. Even more significant is, however, the possibility of studying individual subjects as well as larger groups. The shifting emphasis in social psychology towards the increased importance of idiographic methods (Pervin, 1976) promises to create important new applications for such a method. Studies of perceptions of social episodes in individuals of differing social skills, backgrounds or cultures would be an important development, with potentially far-reaching practical applications in clinical and social psychology.

In this review of the different analytic techniques available for evaluating perceptions of social episodes, more space and time has been spent discussing MDS techniques than other methods. This is no coincidence. MDS is perhaps the best example of a methodological development which could potentially open up new avenues of research. This is particularly so in social psychology, where many of the current criticisms and propositions for alternative methods can only become feasible if methods capable of the empirical representation of complex, internal cognitive domains, such as MDS, are applied. Perceptual studies of social episodes using the different MDS techniques are thus perhaps the single most promising development in the "new" social psychology so widely advocated. It is for this reason that MDS techniques are described in relative detail here. For any researcher interested in implementing these methods, much more adequate and detailed summaries of the uses of MDS methods exist (Forgas, 1979a; Shepard *et al.*, 1972).

INTERPRETATION

This is the ultimate and perhaps most important stage in analysing perceptions of social episodes. Depending on the particular aims of the study, it is at this stage that substantive insights regarding the perceived structure of episodes can be gained.

As mentioned previously, factor-analytic and cluster-analytic techniques are typically associated with the intuitive interpretation of the results. Studies using factor-analysis (Magnusson, 1971) or cluster-analysis (Forgas, 1976a; Price, 1974) base the interpretation of the emerging episode structure on the intuitively discovered similarities between episodes having related factor loadings, or being assigned into the same cluster. This procedure is often sufficient to enable the investigator to make meaningful statements regarding the relationship between the episodes, even though the labelling of clusters or factors was not based on empirical evidence.

Multidimensional scaling studies tend to use a more complex, but perhaps also more reliable procedure for interpreting stimulus configurations. Interpretation essentially consists of the identification or labelling of the stimulus dimensions defining the perceptual space for episodes. This can be accomplished intuitively, by identifying the episodes at the extremes of a particular dimension and labelling the dimension accordingly, or empirically, by fitting separately scaled bipolar dimensions to the stimulus space constructed by multidimensional scaling. The latter method is based on regression analyses, whereby the coordinates or stimulus episodes in the MDS space are used to predict their mean ratings on a series of independently obtained bipolar scales.

HYPOTHESIS TESTING

It has often been argued that descriptive techniques such as factor-analysis or multidimensional scaling are self-serving, insofar as it is nearly always possible to construct some sort of a simplified representation of the objects studied, but that such representations are rarely of intrinsic interest unless the variables thus identified are used in subsequent experimental studies. It is quite true that the advance of factor-analysis, and more recently multidimensional scaling has resulted in a period of extensive "dustbowl empiricism", manifest in the indiscriminate factor-analysis or scaling of any and every stimulus domain just in order to obtain more or less elegant, and more or less intuitively appealing representations.

Such excesses notwithstanding, it is important to note that the simplified representation of complex stimulus fields can be an important achievement in itself, a significant aid to creativity and ingenuity, and a useful contribution to the process of hypothesis generation, much neglected in social psychology (McGuire, 1973). However, what is done after such a representation is achieved is equally important. By allowing the investigator to quantify otherwise unquantifiable cognitive objects, such as social episodes, techniques such as MDS make it possible to actually statistically test hypotheses about such internal structures. Once again, it is in studies based on MDS procedures that such quasi-experimental analyses have most frequently been carried out, perhaps because of the relative novelty of the method.

Once a satisfactory representation of an episode domain is achieved, we can quantify each episode in terms of its dimensional coordinates in multidimensional space. Similarly, assuming that an individual differences MDS model, such as INDSCAL is used, we can quantify each individual judge's perceptual style in judging social episodes in terms of his/her subject coordinates within the same multidimensional space. Thus, it becomes possible to statistically evaluate hypotheses about expected differences between groups or clusters of episodes and groups or clusters of judges. By definition, it is necessary to use multivariate techniques if such hypotheses are to be evaluated since both episodes and subjects are defined in terms of multiple dimensions. Canonical correlation, multiple discriminant analysis and multivariate analysis of variance are examples of such frequently used statistics.

The range and variety of questions that can be asked from such data is nearly infinite. Perhaps a few examples may illustrate the possibilities. Will two similar, but unrelated sports teams perceive the social episodes occurring within their milieu in the same way? Are sport-related as against purely social episodes significantly differentiated in the episode space? Is there a significant relationship between an individual's status and perceived position in his immediate reference group, and his style of judging the group and its social episodes? Should a change in the episode have a significant effect on the way members of a small group perceive each other? Is a judge's age, sex, attitude and personality related to how he perceives aggressive or violent episodes? Each one of these questions has in fact served as the basis for empirical studies, which resulted in satisfactory tests of the relationships mentioned.

A further possibility for carrying out quasi-experiments with social episodes is to select the stimulus sample to be judged in such a way that it already represents the manipulation of some independent variable. For example, if one seeks to assess the respective influence of the behaviour setting and the interaction partner on perceptions of global episodes containing both of these components, a factorial combination of these two variables resulting in a number of composite episode labels may be used as stimuli. Once the cognitive representation of these episodes is quantified with the help of MDS, the dimensional coordinates of the episodes may be regarded as multiple dependent variables, and a multivariate analysis of variance may be carried out to evaluate the respective contribution and interaction of the original independent variables, behaviour setting and interaction partner.

Although these techniques for testing hypotheses about social episodes are clearly most promising, only the first uncertain steps have been taken to explore the full potential of these methods. All the same, the very possibility of such studies convincingly illustrates the point that a pairing of conventional experimental methodology and the study of complex, naturalistic social situations is indeed possible.

As the foregoing outline of the methodology used in studying perceptions of social episodes suggests, the possibilities for putting these methods to ingenious new uses are far from exhausted. To date, most of the relatively few studies in existence addressed themselves to the taxonomic question, that is, they sought to identify differences in the perception of a sample of social episodes (Chapters 7 and 8). They treated episodes as holistic, global units. This method can obviously be extended in several other directions. The internal structure of particular episodes could be studied using the perceptual strategy. For example, what is the perceived appropriate behaviour structure within such stereotypical episodes as leave-taking, dinner parties, or research seminars? The units of analysis in such studies would be the behaviours, moves or acts that make up an episode. To some extent, research in this vein has already been carried out by Barker and his associates, within an ecological frame of reference. The application of the methods outlined here, particularly multidimensional scaling, to the discovery of the internal structures of social episodes is a most promising avenue for further research.

Structuralist sequencing strategies

One of the strongest influences in the social sciences in recent years originates in structuralist theories both in linguistics (Chomsky) and in social anthropology (Levi-Strauss). In particular, largely as a result of the increasing popularity of the kind of structural linguistic models developed by de Saussure (1974), Jakobson (1972), Chomsky (1965) and others, social psychologists, too, have become interested in the structural aspects of social behaviour. Whereas traditional models in social psychology are based on an essentially mechanistic conceptualization of human interaction, linguistic theory emphasizes the importance of rules, meanings and "grammars" as the most important explanatory concepts in understanding social episodes. The general assumption of such structuralist approaches is that social movements, acts and episodes are organized in a hierarchical structure, and that there exists a grammar or syntax for social behaviour just as there is one for language. A corollary assumption, first proposed by de Saussure (1974), is that properties and characteristics of the units that make up social behaviour are defined by their position in the structure of events. According to the model, social interaction can thus be viewed as a highly structured series of communications, both verbal and non-verbal. The task of the social psychologist in these terms is the discovery of the surface and deep-structure of the communicative chain, and the formulation of rules, ultimately leading to the development of a rule system or grammar to describe that interaction. (It is interesting to note that structuralist theories of behaviour, or rather, consciousness, have a long and distinguished history in psychology reaching back to Wundt, and before him, to the British associationist philosophers of the 18th and 19th centuries. The relative lack of success of these early structuralist strategies may hold out a warning for the current structuralist theories of social behaviour as will be discussed in more detail later.)

The analogy between the structure of literary sentences and the structure of social behaviour at first sight appears a convincing one. In both cases, clearly identifiable units or "moves" are apparent, and the relationship between these units is seemingly regulated by some invariant rules. The methodological problems in attempting to extend the linguistic method to social behaviour can be daunting, however. The discovery of unvarying "units" in social behaviour, analogous to morphemes in linguistics, can be as problematic as the empirical validation of hypothesized rules by reference to that ubiquitous linguistic authority, Chomsky's native speaker.

The first methodological task facing all structuralist theories is thus the problem of unitization—that is, the determination of which behaviours are the basic "units" in an episode, the units which make up its structure. This is an extremely serious problem, since unlike the situation in linguistics, where the smallest meaningful unit in language is unequivocally given in the form of a morpheme, there is no comparable universal smallest meaningful unit in social behaviour. Typically, there are two methodological solutions to the problem of unitization.

Those interested in discovering the structural properties of linguistic aspects of social behaviour, studying conversational episodes only, can to some extent rely on linguistic units in their analysis. Thus, the most frequently invoked unit is a speech act (Austin, 1962), typically a single utterance or sentence expressing one "move" on the part of the communicator (Clarke, 1977). Such a unit is most frequently identified intuitively, by the investigator, who relies on the structural properties of language in his decision as to what constitutes a speech act. Clearly, from the point of view of empirical social psychology this method can be highly unsatisfactory. Different investigators may identify speech acts differently, and the unit of meaning expressed by the same utterance may be different, depending on the situational or episodic context in which it is uttered. Finally, the communicative intention of the speaker is not taken into account; what the investigator identifies as one "unit" may in fact be part of a larger scheme put together by the speaker to express a single meaning or message.

The alternative to intuitively identified speech acts is the empirical determination of behaviour units which are consensually perceived by judges as constituting one meaningful act. One of the earliest methods of this kind was developed by Dickman (1963), who was concerned with the question "to what extent does the human 'stream of behaviour' attain structure and orderliness in the eyes of other human beings?" (p. 23). Everyday experience tells us that we do in fact recognize units of behaviour, and readily label them in terms such as "eating breakfast", "driving to work" or "reading mail". Dickman's procedure consisted of showing the subjects a short, 8-minute film sequence showing a fairly continuous sequence of action, and then asking them to sort 144 cards, each describing one phase or action in the movie, into groups such that "each group represents one happening in the movie" (p. 26). Results showed that there was 75% or better agreement between subjects identifying rough transition points in the movie. There were important differences between the subjects, however, in the number of units they identified. On the basis of his results, Dickman concludes: "The 'stream of behaviour' attains orderliness in the eyes of other humans to the extent that goals and motives are imputed to the behaviour" (p. 40). It is thus clear from Dickman's analysis that behaviour units are not objective entities, rather, they are to some extent "created" by the judges, on the basis of their attribution of intentions and motives to the actors. Nevertheless, the perception of behaviour units shows a considerable degree of similarity across individuals, and the degree of consensus between judges can be used as a criterion for establishing the existence of reliable units of behaviour. However, Dickman's procedure also has its shortcomings. Firstly, the smaller units, written on cards, which make up the "stream of behaviour", are themselves somewhat ambiguously defined. They are called "phases" by Barker and Wright (1955), and are defined as the smallest segments in an action hierarchy, which cannot be further broken down, except into "actones", which are muscular movements and adjustments which do not imply goal-oriented behaviour in themselves. In a sense then, the validity of Dickman's behaviour units hinges on the validity of their constituent elements, phases, which are in turn, intuitively constructed. The second methodological problem is that subjects are asked to make their judgements after they have seen the film, and are thus required to rely on their memory for their judgement of continuities or discontinuities in action. The card labels only provide a very restricted range of information, and the phrasing of the different phases written on cards can itself influence choice. Apart from these problems, Dickman's work was important as one of the first attempts to apply quantitative, experimental methodology to the establishment of behaviour units. As he pointed out, there is little doubt that we automatically think in terms of discrete units rather than an ongoing stream of behaviour. Dickman's method has provided the first objective measure regarding the "communality of agreement among independent observers relative to the units of behaviour contained in a given sequence" (p. 23).

A different procedure for measuring the perceptual organization of behaviour was developed by Newtson and his co-workers (Newtson, 1973, 1974; Newtson et al., 1977). Newtson's work is based on the same premises as Dickman's: "our experience of behaviour is discrete, or structured, rather than undifferentiated and continuous . . . we see persons doing this and then that, and then something else, performing a series of discrete describable actions. To measure this 'parsing' of the stream of stimulus information presented by behaviour, we provide subjects with a button operating a continuous event recorder, and instruct them to press the button when, in their judgement, one meaningful action ends and a different one begins" (Newtson, 1976, p. 2). These data are then analysed by selecting an (arbitrary) time interval, which may be 2, 5, or 10 seconds, and counting the number of subjects who recorded a transition point within that interval. Results of empirical studies show that while there is a highly significant agreement among judges in segmenting a sequence of behaviour into units, there are also very important individual differences in the level of perceptual organization employed by judges. Thus, the same two-minute sequence of interaction may be fragmented into six units by one judge, and two units by another—even though both judges correctly identify the transition point separating the two "major" units. Beyond such naturally existing individual differences, instructional set can also have an important effect on the size of the units reported. Further, the social context in which the judgements are made can also influence the size of the units reported. Thus, in a situation in which the interactants had unequal power, the low-power individual tended to fragment the behaviour of the high-power partner into finer units than vice versa (Frey and Newtson, 1973). More will be said about the substantive findings of this line of research later—at the moment we are only concerned with the methodological significance of this approach in the construction of empirical behaviour units for structuralist analysis. It appears that the approach taken by Dickman (1963) and later Newtson (1973) may eventually provide a feasible empirical basis for constructing behavioural units. The reliability of these measures has been found satisfactory, and the communality between judges in identifying a transition point is an important index of the validity of the unit thus established.

Having thus gone some way towards settling the issue of unitization, either by using *ad hoc* speech acts, or empirically established behaviour units, the proper task of structural analysis can begin. In essence, the task of the investigator is to establish sequential rules regulating the flow of behaviour—in other words, he has to discern rules and regularities, or a "grammar", apparently governing the generation of natural social behaviour. Again, a number of research strategies can be distinguished.

Strategies aiming to discover the structural properties of social behaviour in episodes can be classified into two large groups. The classical method is perhaps best illustrated by Chomsky, who relies on the
construction of abstract and elaborate models of rule systems which
could generate the sentences that the ubiquitous "native speaker" of
the language would deem to be appropriate. This is a "from the top
down" procedure, in which the construction of the models is based on
intuition or rational considerations, and only in their evaluation
against observable behaviour do empirical criteria play a role. While
this strategy appears to have all the desirable characteristics of falsi-
fiability as suggested by Popper (1959), it suffers from the shortcoming
that there appears to be no limit to the number of acceptable *ad hoc*
rule systems that can be proposed. Nevertheless, this linguistic strategy
appears to be the most frequently used in structuralist research. Underlying the linguistic strategy is the assumption that human social behaviour is not governed by the kind of causal laws which characterize
natural science, but rather that the source of regularity in social behaviour is to be found in conventions, rules, or "grammars".

There are a number of specialized "from the top" methodologies in
social psychology which can be used to construct models of such rule
systems, to be later evaluated against everyday practice. Such generative models of interaction can be based on computer simulation, or the
construction of symbolic mathematical or logical models representing
the rules hypothesized. Needless to say, the resulting rule systems have
to be extremely complex in order to approximate anything like the
complexity of natural social episodes. A further problem is that social
rules or conventions have no logical truth values (Collett, 1977), and
consequently the formulation and evaluation of hypothetical generative rule systems in probabilistic terms can be a daunting task.

The second major approach to the study of the structure of social
behaviour relies on an inductive, "from the bottom up" procedure.
The methodology involves the collection of a body of raw data, representing empirical observations as to the structure of natural social
behaviour. These data are then analysed in order to explicate and
quantify the underlying regularities, and on the basis of such analyses,
generative rules are developed.

There are numerous methodological problems at each stage of this
process. The collection of naturally occurring social behaviour can be
problematic, not only due to the serious problems of unitization, but

also because of the extreme variability and richness of permissible behaviour sequences in any one episode. The most important consideration is the extremely large number of different contexts or episodes within which any social move can be enacted, and which tend to influence the meaning of a given social act. Since there are no acceptable taxonomies of social contexts or social episodes available, the many meanings of even such a stereotyped move as saying "Good morning" are nearly impossible to chart. As a social move, "Good morning" may be a greeting, a reproach (i.e. to an employee late for work), a joke (e.g. when uttered at night), or a question (with appropriate intonation). Indeed, just as the construction of a structural theory of language without regard to semantics and pragmatics (Morris, 1946) may be problematic, the context and intended meaning of speech acts and social moves is intimately tied to their sequential structure. Most existing studies tended to bypass the issue of context, and proceeded on the implicit assumption that it is possible to develop generative rules of sufficient power which would not be context-dependent. These rules would postulate that, for example, "questions are followed by answers", or "threats are followed by counter-threats", etc. On the whole, such inductive methodologies which disregard contextual variations have so far yielded little more knowledge than the formalistic statements of obviously true relationships, such as the ones just quoted.

The statistical methods used in analysing sequences of social acts have as their raw data the transitional frequencies of given pairs of social acts. The aim of the analysis is typically the construction of some kind of hierarchical clustering scheme, which would show the available alternative moves at each turn of the interaction, with a quantitative estimate of the probability of occurrence of each alternative. Even for fairly simple and restricted interactions, such elementary "grammars" can be exceedingly complex (Clarke, 1978, report to the SSRC, unpublished). More sophisticated techniques for analysing behaviour sequences have been developed by ethologists (Hinde, 1970), primarily for the detection of transition points or choice points in elementary behaviour sequences, such as fixed action patterns in animals. Although the applicability of such methods to the analysis of molar behaviour units in human social interaction is not without its problems, the ethological approach provides one of the more promising contexts for structuralist research. Taken in its totality however, structuralist-oriented research has not contributed much to our understanding of social episodes. The main reason for this is that most of the existing work seeking to construct structuralist models of social behaviour has barely got beyond the initial stage of determining the units to be studied. Perhaps the only branch of this work which has apparently yielded tangible and replicable results is, paradoxically, the rather atheoretical research by Newtson and his co-workers who sought to study sequences in the stream of behaviour. Only very recently did these workers attempt to interpret their findings within a unique theoretical framework, and this framework turned out to be more concerned with social perception and attribution theory than with the structural properties of the behaviour units they studied (Newtson et al., 1977).

In this brief methodological review we have tried to chart the techniques and strategies used in one of the most popular branches of research into naturalistic interaction, the structuralist approach. If this review suggests that the initial promise of structuralist theories has been rather difficult to translate into acceptable methodologies, this is not unintended. Indeed, it often seems that the apparent conceptual sophistication of structuralism may well be impossible to translate into actual research work. Such reservations notwithstanding, it appears that a number of these research techniques, such as the analysis of transitional probabilities, or the ethological study of behaviour sequences can be fruitfully applied to studying social behaviour in different episodes. The relatively meagre results produced by such techniques so far, perhaps appear meagre only in comparison with the grandiose promises of structuralist theorists. More atheoretical and open-minded applications of very similar methods by ethologists, for example, have yielded important new insights. Rather than seeking to dismiss these methods therefore, I hope this survey has been successful in suggesting their potential, which is certainly not restricted to structuralist research.

The other area where these methods have considerable promise is in the area of analysing behaviour units, rather than whole episodes. The work originated by Dickman, and further developed by Newtson is important in its own right and not just as an adjunct to structuralist research. By focusing on the process of how information about social events is acquired rather than on already existing knowledge, Newtson's approach is one of the few studies in social psychology which is truly perceptual rather than cognitive in emphasis. Furthermore, the implicit units used by different cultures, groups and individuals to identify meaningful chunks of behaviour is of obvious heuristic interest.

The roles–rules approach

There are important similarities between the structuralist approach just discussed and the roles–rules approach. Both orientations aim to discover the conventions and regularities governing social behaviour within social episodes. The main difference is in the methods chosen to achieve this end. Structuralist theorists rely either on model building and evaluation, or on the inductive construction of such rule systems from observed behaviour. In either case, the social actors' knowledge of the rules is only indirectly studied. The roles–rules approach on the other hand is traditionally associated with a methodology which relies on the social actors' direct testimony of their understanding of the conventions regulating their behaviour as its main source of data.

The concept of roles and rules is obviously central to such an approach. Both roles and rules refer to expected, and often sanctioned regularities in behaviour, viewed from the perspective of the individual or the group, respectively. Roles can be understood as collections of rules which regulate the behaviour of a specified category of individuals, and conversely, rules specify expected behaviours in specific situations from occupiers of given role categories. The conceptual foundations of such a rules-based approach to the study of social behaviour reach back a long way in social psychology. Interest in roles, norms and the sanctions that go with them is perhaps as old as the discipline itself (Ross, 1908; Sherif, 1935; Newcomb, 1943). The major difference between these traditional approaches and the contemporary roles–rules model is that whilst the former defined social norms as extra-individual constructs, the latter conceives of rules as subjective, perceived expectations, realized in the phenomenological field of the individual.

There are two main variants within the roles–rules strategy. The first one is represented by Harre's proposals for an ethogenic approach to social psychology. This strategy is closely related to the phenomenologist tradition in sociology in general, and the contemporary micro-sociological schools of Goffman and Garfinkel in particular. The methods suggested are descriptive and analytic in orientation, relying on an open-ended accounting process as the primary source of data.

A somewhat different approach is being developed by Argyle (1977), who appears to be in fundamental agreement with Harre regarding the necessity to study the roles, rules, customs and conventions which regulate social behaviour. He is also interested, however, in numerous other aspects of social situations such as the use of props, specific terminologies and motivational themes, and the social skills involved in performing social episodes. More importantly, Argyle's approach is based on social psychological techniques, and is closely related to his previous model of social skills.

The basic methodology for establishing roles–rules systems thus rests on the "Why not ask them" principle, first proposed by Allport (1924), and recently expounded in Harre and Secord's (1972) influential book. They argue that the methods of mainstream psychology failed to establish causal mechanisms of social behaviour because of their adherence to an outdated, superseded concept of causality, a mechanistic model of man and a rigid reliance on logical positivist methodologies. According to this view, people behave the way they do not because they react to external causes, but because of the meanings they assign to situations and the rules and conventions they follow; in other words, because of their understanding of the requirements of the social world around them. It follows therefore that the best method of discovering the causes of social behaviour is not one which concentrates on external, environmental contingencies but one which seeks to obtain information about how actors perceive situations, and how they understand and interpret the rules and conventions which regulate behaviours in such situations. In such a methodology, the accuracy of measurement problem, so important in traditional social psychology, is replaced by concern with the precision of meaning of the accounts collected (Harre and Secord, 1972, p. 126). In other words, the investigator is now mainly concerned with establishing the precise meaning of the account given by his informant regarding the reasons he assigned to his actions. This methodology is deeply rooted in cultural, interpretative sociology as well as in some current linguistic methodologies. It is intrinsically unquantifiable, and descriptive rather than predictive in its orientation. The collection of accounts is perhaps the most radically new methodology to arise from the numerous criticisms of social psychology in the seventies. There can be no doubt that it highlights a most important, and often inexcusably neglected stage in research, that of the naturalistic description of the phenomena to be studied. As an all-encompassing methodology, however, it leaves a lot to be desired. It is inexact, heavily influenced by the subjectivity of both the researcher and his subject, and non-quantifiable. It may be that this approach to the study of rules and roles has more affinity with the domain of anthropology or even journalism than with that of psychology. This is not meant as a derogatory statement, but rather as a boundary-defining one. There are important and essential kinds of information that can only be collected by way of the kind of descriptive methodologies advanced by Harre and Secord (1972). It is even important to emphasize that such an exploratory, descriptive stage is a crucial part of the research process in social psychology. But it is not the only feasible and truly scientific method in social psychology, as its proposers assert (Schlenter, 1977). Thus the "why not ask them" principle has important limitations. Is there a more acceptable way of ascertaining roles–rules structures in social episodes?

The answer is clearly yes. Using accepted techniques in social psychology, any subjective descriptive data can be quantified and subjected to objective analyses. Accounts of behaviour sequences, perceptions of acceptable and non-acceptable kinds of behaviours, interpretations of others' performances are all sources of data for such analyses. In fact, more quantitative approaches (such as these) strongly rely on the direction established by Harre and Secord and others. The main difference is that the subject of analysis is no longer the unique individual in his unique life-situation, but a specified cultural group or milieu. This is a rather fundamental deviation from the original aims of the rules approach, but it is also an inevitable one. The study of roles, rules and conventions inevitably implies that the object of study is a more or less clearly defined cultural group rather than a unique individual: roles, rules and conventions are inalienably cultural products. By concentrating on the individual as the basic unit of analysis, we place a strong restriction on what is considered as an acceptable datum, without a commensurate gain in the conceptual validity of the eventual findings.

The methods used to "objectify" judgemental and free-response data are fairly traditional, and need no detailed elaboration here. The main characteristic of such methods, as Harre and Secord assert, is that they filter out individual differences. While this can be regarded as a shortcoming, due to the essentially social nature of the objects studied, it is unlikely to be a serious one.

There are a number of developments in the study of roles and rules which can only be touched upon here. For example, Argyle has further developed Harre and Secord's original model to take into account a number of further episodic variables besides roles and rules. Argyle's (1975, 1976) eclectic approach to the study of social situations emphasizes the importance of ecological props as well as the role and rule structures in defining an episode. This "rules–games model" (Argyle, 1976, p. 174) assumes that "social situations are akin to chemical compounds, in being discrete, not continuous entities. Each situation . . . is a structured system of interdependent parts . . . the interactors must master the basic components of these situations" (pp. 175–176), which include a set of behaviours, motivational themes, rules, roles, pieces (or props), concepts (or terminology) and traits. In other words, the successful performance of an episode depends on the interactants having adequate knowledge of the categories described. This approach seems to be clearly related to the earlier social skills model (Argyle, 1969), and appears to be particularly promising in its clinical applications. This is a logical development, and furthermore, it extends the rather restrictive conceptual scheme proposed by Harre and Secord in directions which have been of traditional interest to social psychologists. In particular, the fusion of the behaviour setting approach and the roles–rules approach implied by this scheme is promising.

In summary, the roles–rules approach to the study of social episodes appears to be a hybrid one, with an eclectic and rather unspecific set of methodologies. Perhaps the single core component of these methods is that they all rely on informants or the social actors themselves for their data regarding the roles and rules they follow. The methods can be completely open and descriptive, or more objective and quantifiable depending on the predilections of the investigator. Although this particular approach has been most influential conceptually, it has yielded only limited research results so far.

Some recent studies which claim to implement Harre and Secord's (1972) "ethogenic" methodology in practice, fall short of providing a convincing demonstration of the capabilities of the method. For example, in their study of classroom aggression and violence on the football terraces, Marsh et al. (1978) claim to have collected scientific evidence supporting their highly unusual interpretation of these behaviours. Others may not, and indeed, did not, agree with the theories presented. Unfortunately, since the evidence in such ethogenic analyses is little more than selected, interpreted and annotated quotes from social actors (i.e. school children and football fans), it is unlikely that the controversy created by this study will be scientifically resolved, and thus advance our understanding of these undoubtedly important matters. The research programme developed by Argyle appears more promising, and some of the studies to be described later (Chapters 7 and 8) could be just as easily credited to the roles–rules approach as to the perceptual strategy. Perhaps the inevitable fate of the roles–rules approach to the study of social episodes is that it will be absorbed by other, more practical methodologies. The perceptual approach, the structuralist approach and the behaviour setting approach all have important affinities with the roles–rules model, and their gradual merger seems a distinct possibility.

Summary

As this brief survey of the wide range of methods applicable to the study of social episodes indicates, there is no shortage of available techniques. Furthermore, this being a relatively new field of investigation, the researcher's ingenuity in devising new *ad hoc* methods, or applying techniques developed in other areas of social psychology, is not limited by too many established precedents.

These four research strategies can be compared in terms of a number of features (Table 1). In terms of their unit of study, both the ecological and the perceptual strategy seek to represent whole global episodes, while the structural and the roles–rules strategy complement them by focusing on intra-episodic regularities in behaviour. These differences in the unit of study may be viewed as complementary rather than conflicting. The discovery of the internal synchronic and diachronic structure of specific episodes may contribute to our understanding of how the episode as a global unit is cognitively represented, and in turn studies of global episodes will probably reflect differences in the internal structure of the episodes studied.

The aims of these four strategies are also somewhat different. The ecological strategy to date has been most closely interested in constructing taxonomies of interactions in terms of their physical settings (Chapter 6). The perceptual approach, while still taxonomic and descriptive in its main emphasis, no longer anchors social episodes to the physical setting, and has also developed methods for critically

TABLE 1

Some characteristics of the four research strategies applicable to the study of social episodes

	Ecological	Perceptual	Structural	Roles–Rules
Unit of study	Global episode	Global episode	Behaviour sequences within episode	Roles and rules within episode
Aims	Ecological taxonomy of interaction settings	Perceptual taxonomy of interaction episodes, and study of variables affecting episode perception	Construction of rule system or grammar generating behaviour sequences	Description of roles and rules specifying behaviours
Methods	Observation Descriptive statistics	Observation, interviews and questionnaires. Dimensional or categorical analysis of episode domain, followed by critical evaluation of hypotheses	Observation followed by inductive model construction, or, construction of hypothetical models (simulation) followed by deduction and testing via observation	Interviews and open-ended collection of accounts and explanations
Empirical research to date	Numerous "behaviour setting surveys", extensive studies of small-scale behaviour settings	Some empirical research representing the perception of social episodes in given subcultural milieus (taxonomic-descriptive) and several studies evaluating differences between episodes and/or judges	Some preliminary studies. No definitive "grammar" for any one episode yet	Some empirical studies, concerned with the analysis of specific episodes, e.g., football terraces, classroom interaction, etc.

evaluating hypotheses about the factors affecting episode perception. The structuralist sequencing approach ultimately aims at the construction of complete rule systems or grammars, which would be capable of generating acceptable sequences of interactive moves within specific episodes. The aims of the roles–rules model are similar, although the derivation of complete rule systems is not necessarily implied.

However, it is in the area of methodologies and the actual research output generated that the four strategies differ most. The behaviour setting surveys and the ecological analyses of interaction settings carried out within the framework of the first strategy are based on psychological scaling methods on the one hand and on anthropological description on the other. Perceptual studies of social episodes, in turn, capitalize on the most up-to-date statistical scaling techniques, such as MDS, paired with multivariate statistical techniques for hypothesis testing. In both of these areas a substantial research literature exists. Studies of behaviour settings have been carried out for some decades now while increasing research activity in the seventies has contributed to the growing literature on the perception of social episodes. It is probably not coincidental that research activity is most lively in these two areas, which also rely most heavily on conventional social psychological methods in their approach.

In contrast, both the structural and the roles–rules strategies borrow more heavily from linguistics and anthropology than from social psychology for their methods. This is particularly true for the structuralist strategy, where linguistic methods predominate. The last strategy, the roles–rules model, is much more heterogeneous. On the one extreme, we find the kind of purely descriptive and analytic studies advocated by Harre and Secord (1972), and represented by works such as *The Rules of Disorder* by Marsh *et al.* (1978), and studies by Harre (1977) and Harre and DeWaele (1976). Relying exclusively on the collection of accounts, these studies provide interesting and stimulating descriptions of rich segments of social life—the data collected are not, however, sufficient to establish the validity of the theories proposed, or to explain these phenomena.

On the other extreme of the roles–rules model we find a much more eclectic methodology as advocated, for example, by Argyle (1977). While he is still primarily interested in explicating the taken-for-granted rules and customs that govern social interaction, the techniques constructed for achieving this end rely heavily on conventional social psychological methods. Basically, these are still judgemental techniques: subjects are asked to judge the appropriateness of different actions, to identify the critical, defining features of interaction episodes, or to report on their own behaviours in different episodes. The main difference between this and the perceptual strategy is that Argyle is most interested in studying the behaviour routines within episodes, whereas the perceptual strategy attempts to evaluate between-episode differences as a preliminary to later micro-analyses of within-episode sequences.

There are a few studies directly stimulated by the structuralist-sequencing strategy (Clarke, 1977), but the difficulties of implementing this method in practice are clearly reflected in the relative scarcity of empirical studies to date. The roles–rules model has been more successful in generating research. The studies carried out by Harre and his associates have already been mentioned. Argyle and his group is also engaged in an intensive research programme, and several studies oriented towards discovering the roles and rules regulating interaction within episodes are already under way (Argyle *et al.*, 1979).

In summary, the four research strategies applicable to the study of social episodes discussed here offer a rich variety of approaches and techniques. The ecological approach is perhaps the best established such model, and it will no doubt continue to generate research. The perceptual strategy is currently the most fertile area, and in some ways, it represents an ideal fusion of the cognitive-phenomenological orientation of many contemporary ideas in social psychology and the most modern and powerful statistical methods of description available today. The structuralist approach as a research strategy is still relatively isolated from mainstream social psychology, perhaps because of its strong reliance on linguistic models, and the rather obscure and grandiose conceptual schemes which are advocated to justify its applicability to the study of social behaviour. Perhaps a gradual dilution of such conceptual orthodoxy, and a greater openness to psychological techniques will help to reintegrate this research strategy into mainstream social psychology. Finally, the roles–rules strategy is perhaps the vaguest and most general of those discussed here, having ties with both the structuralist and the perceptual approaches. It is already clear that there are numerous points of contact between the ecological, the perceptual and the roles–rules strategies, which augur well for the eventual merger and integration of the research methodologies they represent.

There is thus a deep underlying affinity between many of the methods discussed under these four headings. It is notable, and perhaps inevitable, that nearly all of the methods considered rely on some form of perceptual-judgemental procedure by judges, or by participants in an interaction, for their sources of raw data. In a very important and inevitable way, Allport's dictum embodied in the "Why not ask them" exhortation reigns supreme. In the "new" social psychology, if there is to be one, reports by conscious and intelligent social actors as to how they perceive their environment and what they see as their reasons for different actions are the inevitable raw data we have to deal with. This does not mean, however, as Harre and Secord seem to imply, that we are restricted to the subjective analysis of open-ended and unquantifiable accounts. Rather, the whole gamut of social psychological techniques developed for the analysis of exactly such self-report data can potentially be applied to the study of social episodes. Only a small range of such techniques have been implemented in the study of social episodes so far. For example, the sophisticated models developed for the study of information integration strategies (Anderson, 1968) could be readily adapted to the study of social episodes. Which components of an episode are crucial in determining an observer's perception? Of the many "episode definition" cues available, how important are separate information cues, and how are these integrated into a coherent picture identifying the episode as being of one particular kind? A beginning has already been made on the study of issues such as these (Chapter 8). The number of other methods and techniques routinely used in social psychology for the analysis of self-report data is extremely large, and the prospects for adapting such techniques to the study of social episodes look promising. Rather than being restricted to analysing open-ended accounts in an intuitive fashion as implied by Harre and Secord's proposals, we should, on the contrary, be encouraged by these early successes to use and implement the whole range of psychological methodologies for the study of social episodes.

Some of these methods deserve particular mention. The different multidimensional scaling strategies appear to be tailor-made for exactly the kind of research task that the study of social episodes poses. Social episodes are extremely complex perceptual objects; very little is known, a priori, about the kinds of judgemental dimensions appropriate to their perception, and even less about the cognitive distinctions used by judges. MDS does not require any of this preliminary information: it is an emergent technique, with a simple and meaningful judgemental task, which results in a reliable, geometric representation of the perceptual space for social episodes. The applications of these methods to different tasks in the study of social episodes seem to be on the increase. The internal structure of episodes, perceptions of moves or behaviours within a defined episode context, or the perceptions of different categories of actors within different episode contexts are but a few of the areas where MDS techniques can be fruitfully applied.

6

Ecological Aspects of Social Episodes

Human social interaction is always situated interaction, in the sense that it takes place within well-defined physical settings. Even apparent exceptions to this rule, such as interaction carried out through audio or visual communication channels not necessarily located within a single behaviour setting, are unequivocably dependent on, and are influenced by, the physical characteristics of the communication channel, which in a broader sense, can be regarded as part of the ecological environment of the interaction.

Since the physical environment is thus so pervasively tied to human interaction, the possibility that regularities in social interaction can in some way be related to regular features of the physical environment was recognized fairly early. Behaviourist theories in particular were the first to suggest a broad correspondence between physical environmental variables, and the behaviours occurring within such environments. Although the emphasis on atomistic environment-behaviour chains, and the neglect of symbolic processes in interaction has rendered behaviourist theories of little use in the study of naturalistic social behaviour, this basic environmentalist approach survived in a radically altered form.

Rather than studying the effects of atomistic environmental variables on atomistic responses, the impact of the total, global environment on global behaviour patterns can be brought into the centre of the analysis. It is important to note that by adopting this perspective, we are no longer only concerned with physical environments in the strict sense. Such environments are impregnated with social meaning by virtue of the accumulated behaviour precedents which occurred within that setting. Complex environments thus affect social behaviour in two distinct ways. Firstly, in a purely physical sense, the restrictive or enabling physical characteristics of the environment make the performance of some actions possible, and others impossible. Such fairly obvious physical restrictions are of interest to architects and others involved in the planning of physical environments, as well as to environmental psychologists. For example, environmental variables such as propinquity, seating arrangements, size and flexibility of the interactive setting etc. clearly define the possibilities and the limits of social episodes.

The other effect of physical environments on behaviour is much more complex, and is symbolic rather than physical in character. Physical environments can and do function as symbols, or signifiers, representing a subset of social rules, conventions and expectations which are in force in a given behaviour setting. Studies by Price (Price, 1974; Price and Bouffard, 1974) mentioned earlier demonstrate this generic symbolic function of environments: different kinds of behaviours are appropriate on a bus, in a theatre or on the street. These differences are not rooted in the purely physical restrictions embodied in these environments, but are social conventions, which are merely symbolized by the physical behaviour setting. This dual effect of physical environments on social behaviour is reflected in Barker's (1968) definition of ecological psychology as "concerned with both molecular and molar behaviour, and with both the psychological environment (the life-space in Kurt Lewin's terms; the world as a particular person perceives and is otherwise affected by it) and with the ecological environment (the objective, pre-perceptual context of behaviour; the real-life settings within which people behave)" (p. 1). The ecological approach to the study of social episodes thus represents a unique fusion of two distinct psychological traditions: the external variable approach first perfected by behaviourists, and the study of the symbolic meanings of physical settings, as suggested, for example, by Lewin's field theory, and symbolic interactionism.

Since social episodes are situated interaction sequences, the methods and techniques of environmental analysis are directly relevant to our objective of studying social episodes empirically. The aim of this chapter is to draw upon this work in order to illustrate how it can be applied to the study of social episodes. There are several lines of research which have a bearing on our conceptualization of social episodes, and these will be discussed in turn.

The foremost contribution of ecological research is the development of a number of techniques for constructing empirical taxonomies of social episodes, social environments or even larger institutions.

From previous chapters it should be clear that the classification of social episodes and situations has not yet proceeded very far: typically, interest in individual differences and the sampling of subjects was not matched by equal interest in situations. The growing need for empirical taxonomies of situational and episodic characteristics is increasingly recognized by a whole range of researchers today.

The ecological approach to situational taxonomies recognizes the unique interdependence between behaviour settings and social behaviours.

Ecological taxonomies

The task *par excellence* of ecological psychology is description and categorization. In contrast to traditional, experimental psychology, the ecological approach aims to study and describe the frequency, conditions and consequences of behaviours as they naturally occur in physical settings (Proshansky *et al.*, 1970). The first problem encountered in this task is again the problem of unitization: what should be regarded as a unit of behaviour-in-environment? Barker and Wright (1955) in their pioneering study proposed behaviour settings as such a unit: behaviour settings are "stable, extra-individual units with great coercive power over the behaviour that occurs within them" (Barker, 1968, p. 17). The standing pattern of behaviour occurring within a particular milieu is a "discrete behaviour entity with unequivocal temporal-spatial coordinates . . . it is an extra-individual phenomenon; it has unique characteristics that persist when the participants change" (Barker, 1968, p. 18). As this definition suggests, Barker's understanding of the behaviour setting and its "standing patterns" of behaviour, and our approach to social episodes are remarkably similar. Both refer to stereotypical, culture-specific sequences of behaviour with a consensually understood rule-structure. The differences are mainly in emphasis: Barker regards the behaviour setting as the most important and accessible subject for analysis, while the present definition focuses more on the global characteristics of an episode as cognitively represented by individuals. His definition includes non-social, that is, solitary episodes, whereas we are mainly interested in interactive episodes. This distinction is a subtle one, since even non-social episodes are governed by social conventions. Finally, behaviour settings are behaviour-milieu synomorphs — that is, the behaviour patterns must be

uniquely anchored to particular space-time loci. The same requirement does not apply to social episodes, which may occur in different
locations, at different times, as long as such episodes are perceived and
interpreted as globally equivalent. Having thus defined the unit of
analysis, the first task of ecological psychology is to classify different
behaviour settings. The first step is a behaviour setting survey, the
listing of all possible physical settings within a cultural milieu. From
the list so constructed, non-behaviour settings (i.e. behaviour patterns
which are not synomorphous with a setting) are eliminated, followed
by the identification and elimination of overlapping settings in terms
of a series of criteria (see Chapter 5). The most complete survey and
taxonomy of behaviour settings was carried out in a small town in
Kansas, Midwest, in 1963–64. Over this period, 884 behaviour settings
were identified in the town. Some of these (175) were recurrent weekday behaviour settings, such as streets and sidewalks, coin-operated
laundry, school classes and playgrounds, and basketball games. Others
were unique and rarely occurring settings, such as veterans meetings,
household auction sales, etc. On any given day, one could chart the
process as behaviour settings become operational from the morning
onwards, and as they cease being accessible at given times (e.g. stores,
cafes closing). The accessible behaviour environment of Midwest thus
fluctuates from hour to hour, and from day to day. Saturdays and
Sundays represent only about one-half and one-third of the normal
weekday behaviour settings respectively. The 884 distinct behaviour
settings identified occurred 53 376 times over the year. About one third
of the 884 settings occur only once a year (e.g. American Legion
Memorial Day Service, Farm Bureau Board Picnic) whereas about 3%
of the settings occur nearly every day. Another characteristic of behaviour settings is their duration: some are continuously available
(e.g. street), others operate only for a few hours every year. The 884
behaviour settings identified during the year can be further reduced to
198 "genotypes", that is behaviour settings with non-interchangeable
programmes. For example, there are many behaviour settings involving the game of basketball (elementary school, high school, out-of-
town games etc.), which are all expressions of the same genotype, i.e.
basket-ball game, involving a unique pattern of behaviours. These 198
genotypical behaviour settings do in fact represent a good part of the
culture of the town: a "person familiar with Midwestern American
culture is informed by the genotype list and the data on the extent of

the behaviour possibilities within Midwest . . . For students of comparative cultures, the list and appendix provide data for investigating the relative diversity of towns in other cultures. For example, the town of Yoredale (population 1300) in Yorkshire, England had 213 behaviour setting genotypes in 1963–64, and Svelvik in Norway had 134 genotypes in 1960–61" (Barker, 1968, pp. 116-117). These behaviour setting genotypes are in effect classes of behaviour settings, and can be regarded as taxonomic categories of behaviour-in-environment units. The taxonomic criterion used is not some perceived attribute of the behaviour settings, as used for example in perceptual taxonomies of social episodes, but objective characteristics, such as the frequency, duration and occurrence of different behaviour settings, and the interchangeability of the behaviour patterns. Barker's work in Midwest and Yoredale is to date the most comprehensive effort to construct representative ecologically-based taxonomies of social behaviour. These behaviour setting genotypes are again surprisingly similar to our definition of social episodes. By concentrating on the ecological aspect of the interactions, rather than on the behaviour patterns embodied in different episodes, Barker's work is complementary to the more recent emphasis on the study of perceptions of social episodes. The dual nature of behaviour settings implicit in Barker's conception i.e. that behaviour settings are both physical and social entities, also provides a point of contact with social psychology.

Perhaps the most important difference between a social psychological approach and Barker's ecological psychology is that social psychologists would be interested in the subjective interpretations, meanings and perceptions that individuals attach to behaviour settings, whereas for Barker, only the external, observable similarities in behaviour are of interest. Thus, behaviour in a drug store is highly ritualized, and nearly everybody in that setting will behave in a predictable fashion, whether they are buying medicine for a friend, or procuring poison for an enemy (Barker, 1968, p. 29). From Barker's analysis, we do not know who is confident and who is anxious about the simple act of buying drugs in a drug store, how this simple episode fits into the interaction repertoire of different individuals, or which aspects of the drug store performance are problematic for which people.

Barker's approach has been influential in stimulating new interest in behaviour settings. Bechtel (1970, 1972) studied the behaviour settings in underprivileged urban areas and public housing developments, and compared these settings with small-town environments. Behaviour setting surveys were also carried out by Wright (1970), Wicker (1968, 1972), and others.

The approach adopted by Barker differs from most other studies of urban environments in its strong reliance on social and cultural norms as symbolized by behaviour settings to explain behaviour. This taxonomy of behaviour settings is of heuristic value, but difficult to generalize to other cultural milieux. After Barker, ecological psychology has developed in two directions. On the one hand, the "social psychological" approach has become increasingly interested in how people react to and perceive different environments. On the other hand, research evolved in a direction which placed growing emphasis on the characteristics of different environments *per se*, to the relative neglect of the subjective reactions people have to different ecological milieux. It will not be possible to provide even a superficial review of the many different branches of environmental psychology here. Instead, we shall consider the work of researchers who were most directly interested in the ecological aspects of interactive behaviour, in order to discover how their analyses may be helpful in our quest for an empirical approach to the study of social episodes.

The perceived environment

A different branch of environmental psychology may be traced to the pioneering work of Murray (1938), who first proposed that individual needs and environmental press may be considered as a single interactive system. While Murray's influence has been considerably greater in personality theory than in environmental psychology, there were some attempts to further develop and operationalize Murray's concept of environmental "press" (Stern *et al.*, 1956). In particular, studies of the institutional atmosphere or perceived climate of large-scale institutions such as universities represent an implementation of this programme (Pace and Stern, 1958).

The distinction between macro- and micro-environments may be a useful one here, the former including factors such as landscape, streets and whole institutions, and the latter environments such as a room, the equipment of a room, or a shop (Magnusson, 1974). Laumann and House (1970), for example, found that socio-economic status and traditional v. modern style are the two dimensions along which most living rooms can be distinguished. Canter and his co-workers (Canter and Lee, 1974; Canter, *et al*., 1974; Wools and Canter, 1970) in a series of studies explored the relationship between the person and the environment. In a study of judgements of people and their rooms it was found that there is a correlation between judgements of the individuals and their rooms in terms of an evaluative and a potency dimension, but not in terms of the activity dimension. This study suggests the possibility that a taxonomic system based on connotative dimensions may be equally applicable to the description of individuals and behaviour settings simultaneously. In other studies, observational and interview techniques were used to establish the relevant attributes of environments such as hospital wards to different categories of users.

One step removed from concern with the ecological environment only, but still firmly in the ecological tradition, are a series of studies by Moos and his co-workers, who attempted to construct a taxonomic system applicable to the systematic description of institutionalized environments (Moos, 1968, 1970, 1974a,b; Moos and Houts, 1968; Insel and Moos, 1974). Their studies encompassed eight diverse types of institutions, such as psychiatric wards, university residences, and correctional institutions. Conceptually, these studies tended to emphasize the subjective features of environments: "one might infer a general principle to the effect that the way one perceives his surroundings or environment influences the way one will behave in that environment" (Insel and Moos, 1974, p. 179). The common dimensions emerging from studies of these diverse institutionalized environments were identified as belonging to three distinct categories: (a) relationship dimensions, such as involvement, affiliation and cohesion; (b) personal development dimensions, such as autonomy, and intellectualism; and (c) system maintenance and change dimensions. The problem with taxonomies of this kind, based on ratings of rather unspecified and gross institutional environments, is that they may no longer have an immediate relevance to behaviour. It seems possible that the behaviour setting approach of Barker based on the analysis of behaviours in clearly specified micro-environments is not readily generalizable to the study of large-scale, complex environments.

Taxonomic studies of large-scale institutions and organizations account for a substantial part of the research, but are only of limited interest here, due to their remoteness from natural, everyday sequences of behaviour. A programme aimed at assessing industrial and educational environments was carried out by Stern and others (Pace and Stern, 1958; Stern, 1970; Stern *et al*., 1956), using Murray's need-press concept as a foundation. Factor-analysed scores from instruments such as the College and University Environment Scales (CUES) yielded five attribute dimensions which may serve as the basis of a taxonomy: practicality, community, awareness, propriety and scholarship. The Stern taxonomies are clearly descriptions of the beta-press, the sort of characteristics which are relevant to the subjective evaluation of an environment.

Other researchers, such as Astin (1962), Astin and Holland (1961), Rock *et al*., (1972), and Hopfner and Klein (1970) compared college environments in terms of objective information, available from records. The emerging attribute dimensions, such as affluence, size, masculinity, homogeneity of teaching and technical bias (Astin, 1962), or Graduate Record Examination scores, budget and selectivity (Rock *et al*., 1972) have only very remote behavioural implications. The difference between these factors and the factors obtained by Stern are an excellent illustration of the differences between the objective and the subjective approach to environmental assessment. While both taxonomies are of obvious heuristic value, it is likely that Stern's dimensions are more directly relevant to behaviour in these environments than are Astin's objective categories. (For a detailed review of the research on organizational climates, see James and Jones (1974) or Payne and Pugh (1976).)

Ecologically oriented taxonomies of situations have thus shown a two-directional development since Barker's pioneering conceptualization of the "behaviour setting". On the one hand, more elementary and reduced physical environments have been categorized, yielding taxonomic dimensions mainly reflecting restrictiveness, amenity value and the self-expressive roles of such simple ecological environments. The other line of research, classifying larger scale, mostly institutional environments has evolved in a direction which no longer has direct behavioural relevance. Studies continuing in Barker's tradition, such as Moos's assessment of psychiatric wards, appear most promising. It is noteworthy that these studies are mostly concerned with the subjective effects of the environment, or beta-press, and the socio-cultural norms embedded in the physical setting. We may regard these taxonomies as ecological only in the loosest sense. They are also far removed from interaction episodes, although the general characteristics and social atmosphere of institutions is probably significantly related to the quality of social episodes occurring within their walls.

Ecological variables and interaction episodes

As distinct from Barker's descriptive-analytic approach to the study of ecological aspects of interaction episodes, there also exists a more controlled, social psychological line of research which manipulates ecological variables in order to evaluate their effect on interaction processes. Alternatively, global interaction process variables may be controlled in order to analyse their effect on the subject's use and management of the ecological environment.

A series of studies by Altman and his co-workers (Altman, 1968; Altman and Lett, 1970; Altman and Haythorn, 1965) relied on such a technique to assess the effects of environmental variables on social interaction. Rather than asking the question "What regularities are there in behaviour in different environments?", as Barker did, they were interested in the way environmental and social variables interact. While environments undoubtedly have inherent facilitative and inhibitory effects on behaviour, individuals also use and shape the environment to manage and define interpersonal relationships. Thus, social actors are "not only affected by the environment, but also act upon it. Active use of the environment in the management of interpersonal relationships may be anticipatory or reactive, i.e. prearranging or prestructuring of the environment to create certain interaction settings v. use of the environment in reaction to developing events" (Altman, 1968, p. 4).

Pairs of men compatible or incompatible on four social need characteristics were used in a series of social isolation studies, and their management and use of the environment as a function of the social characteristics of the dyads was studied (Altman and Haythorn, 1965, 1967a,b; Haythorn and Altman, 1967). For example, when both men had a high need for dominance, exclusive territoriality was soon established, while a high level of interaction, often competitive, was maintained. In another study, the availability of privacy, the expected length of isolation, and the degree of stimulation from the outside world were the independent variables. Groups which were successful in completing the eight-day isolation displayed greater territoriality and more intense social interaction in the early stages of the experiment, while those who withdrew from the experiment prematurely showed low territoriality and interaction early on, and greatly increased territoriality and interaction just before they decided to abort the experiment. It appears that successful adaptation to the isolation situation involves an early accommodation between the partners, an important part of which is the satisfactory management of the environment and establishment of territorial boundaries.

Indeed, space and territory are intricately tied to human interaction episodes. There is considerable evidence for the highly important effect of simple proximity on social interaction. People who are spatially "close" are also more likely to develop close social relations (Festinger *et al.*, 1950). More recently, Baum and Valins (1973) compared the social interaction patterns of student dormitories having the traditional "corridor" arrangement, with dormitories where clusters of bedrooms shared joint living room and bathroom facilities, in a family-like living arrangement. This second design means not only closer proximity between individuals, but also a higher frequency of "chance" encounters between them. Not surprisingly, a more intimate, friendly and cohesive interaction milieu developed under these conditions. Physical proximity is one of the few extensively studied ecological variables which has been reliably tied to changes in social interaction patterns.

Whereas proximity typically refers to enduring, often architecturally determined, physical relations, the more volatile and changing variety of this ecological variable, personal distance, is no less important in the management of social episodes. Proxemics, the study of how personal space is used (Hall, 1959; Sommer, 1969), has contributed significantly to our understanding of the dynamics of interaction episodes. Perhaps the most interesting feature of personal space is that as an ecological variable, it is rigidly codified by different cultures. Not only have different cultures different ideas about what is the "proper" distance for a particular interaction episode (Hall, 1966; Little, 1968; Sommer, 1969), but distances thought to be appropriate are further broken down in terms of the status, sex, race, and age of the interactants. In the United States at least, lower-class people stand closer than middle-class people (Aiello and Jones, 1971), and black schoolchildren apparently prefer a closer interactive distance than do white schoolchildren (Jones and Aiello, 1973). In Western cultures, women tend to stand closer than men (Liebman, 1970), irrespective of the sex of their interaction partner. So far, most research into proxemics has sought to analyse differences in spacing as a function of cultural or individual variables. Clearly, there is another equally important variable that determines the codification of appropriate personal distances: the social episode enacted. Formal, restrictive social episodes call for greater interpersonal distances than informal, friendly ones (Hall, 1966; Argyle, 1969). It is not only true that particular social episodes call for a particular social distance, however; changes in personal spacing may signal the intended redefinition of the episode itself. It may well be that proxemics play an important, yet subtle role in the complex process of negotiations that precedes a mutually accepted definition of an interaction episode. The intricate, dynamic relationship between interaction episodes and ecological variables is only beginning to be explored. Although space is the most general such ecological dimension, only the first uncertain steps have been taken to study the spatial dimension in natural interaction episodes. It was recently shown, for example, that cues such as interpersonal distance and seating arrangement have a significant effect on how observers define an interaction episode (Forgas, 1978a). Other ecological variables, such as lighting (very important, for example, in the symbolic definition of heterosexual episodes!), temperature, and architectural features are also likely to be closely involved in the definition of episodes. One particular category of ecological objects, often referred to as "environmental props", are distinguished by being necessary for the enactment of particular episodes.

Environmental props and social episodes

In the approaches outlined so far, the characteristic relationship between global environments and global interaction episodes was the focus of attention. Drug stores, public transport buses or residential treatment institutions are global environments in the sense that the totality of the physical setting determines the nature of the social interactions possible within that setting. Similarly, proximity or personal space are global ecological dimensions.

Once we deviate from this global view, and begin to pay attention to particular components of the physical environment which encapsulates social life, it becomes obvious that certain objects, furnishings or physical components of the environment have a disproportionally important role in the definition and regulation of the interaction episodes occurring within that milieu. Such objects are commonly referred to as "environmental props"; although an unambiguous definition of what this term denotes has yet to emerge. Environmental props can be characterized by the fact that their presence or availability is an essential prerequisite to the performance of particular episodes. In a slightly different sense, environmental props can be regarded as crucial symbolic (rather than actual) components of interaction episodes, insofar as their presence or absence will have a fundamental effect on the symbolic difinition of the episodes, even if the props are not themselves essential elements of the action.

Games involving physical props are examples of the first kind of social episode. The necessity of having a chess table for playing chess, or a cricket bat for playing cricket are often-quoted examples illustrating the taken-for-granted, yet crucial role environmental props play in social behaviour (Argyle, 1976). More interesting, and less obvious is the subtle symbolism embodied in objects such as aggressive weapons (Berkowitz and Le Page, 1967), various audio and video-recording devices, or objects serving to identify the social role of the individuals displaying them, such as white coats, badges and labels. Props such as these may be incidental to the carrying out of the interaction itself, but are crucial in determining the meaning of that interaction episode. We often use such props in an intuitive, *ad hoc* manner. A good example is Milgram's (1974) well-known study of obedience, showing that many subjects are prepared to administer apparently lethal electric shocks when ordered to do so by the experimenter. In one condition, the experiment was carried out at a university campus, the experimenters wore white coats, resulting in the unambiguous definition of the episode as a respectable scientific experiment. By changing the behaviour setting to a downtown office and doing away with the symbolic paraphernalia of scientific respectability, Milgram was in effect relying on environmental props to bring about a redefinition of the episode.

There are relatively few physical objects which embody such strong and clearly understood symbolic meanings that they are sufficiently potent to define interaction episodes merely by their presence or absence. More typically, a whole constellation of environmental props is present, supporting and refining the overall meaning of the episode. Such symbolism is most clearly observable in architectural spaces specifically designed for carrying out ritualistic social interactions. For example, the spatial division, positioning and orientation of different parts of a church, the orientation of seats in different areas and the different decorations in specific spaces explicitly define symbolic territories, and support social distinction between the attendants, as well as represent spiritual distinctions (Joiner, 1971). Similarly, architectural spaces such as courtrooms "provide a further example of this kind of socio-spatial relationship. An empty courtroom conveys a great deal of information about the structure and underlying attitudes of British legal proceedings" (Joiner, 1971, p. 11). Further, the environmental props assembled in a courtroom clearly regulate and define the social interaction episode that may be performed in such a setting.

The positioning of environmental props such as furniture, chairs, coat-rack etc., in areas such as offices can be effectively used to communicate a desired definition of the social episode by the occupant of that office. The apportioning of private and public spaces by the skilful positioning of desks and chairs, the allocation of client chairs in a face-to-face or a side-by-side position, the visual orientation of the occupant of the desk as indicated by the mobility and positioning of his chair relative to clients' chairs, the relationship between the main entrance door and the occupant's position are all more or less subtle environmental cues and props signalling desired episode definitions to clients perusing that office. The display of objects communicating the status, position, interest and background of the occupant, such as diplomas, pictures, posters, and suchlike further strengthen the power of the occupant of the office to successfully define social episodes occurring within his territory.

To date no systematic study of such environmental props has been undertaken. We know about their importance mainly from the anthropologically-flavoured studies of microsociologists such as Goffman. In principle, it should be possible to empirically determine the symbolic importance of environmental props, by systematically controlling their absence or presence in interaction episodes, and by assessing the resulting changes in the definition and enactment of the episode. Such a procedure would perhaps be analogous to Garfinkel's rule-breaking studies, with the difference that physical objects, rather than behaviour routines are interfered with. Perhaps one day the communicative function of evironmental props in social episodes will be as active a research area as the study of, say, non-verbal communication signals is today.

The ecological study of interaction episodes has also been important in a special field of psychology: clinical psychology. Perhaps because clinical environments and hospitals are particularly heavily laden with symbolic meaning, as Goffman in his analysis of asylums showed (1970), the empirical study of such environments has been an increasingly active research area in recent years.

The ecological approach in clinical psychology

In a historical perspective, interest in physical and social environments as determinants of mental illness, or at least the specific behavioural symptoms of hospitalized patients, is not radically new. In a sense, Pinel's enlightened reformation of the physical and social environments of asylums in the 18th century, and the resulting radical behavioural changes in patients is still the most impressive demonstration of ecological effects on behaviour. While the pendulum swung back to mainly intrapsychic explanations of mental illness in the nineteenth and twentieth centuries, the period since the war has seen the rebirth of environmentalist theories of psychopathology. Specifically, the psychiatric hospital as a physical and social environment has received growing attention. Stanton and Schwartz in 1954 argued that the origins of many psychiatric symptoms can be located in the social environments the patients are confronted with in the hospital. Symptoms such as dissociation, manic excitement or incontinence were found by these authors to be related to such social environmental variables as staff disagreement as to how to manage a patient, lack of social support available to patients, and lack of opportunities for self-fulfilling activities. In an early and relatively little known work, Roger Barker (Barker *et al.*, 1953) used a Lewinian field-theoretical model to analyse the relationship between behavioural reactions to physical disability and handicap. In many interesting cases studies and examples they showed that an intricate relationship exists between the pathological behaviours of disabled persons and the physical and social variables in their "psychological field". These episodic factors are often subtle, informal and not immediately obvious to the casual observer. Psychiatric wards as "total" environments are particularly potent sources of ecological effects on behaviour. Sociological analyses of such pervasive social environments did not originate with Goffman, as is often thought. Caudill (1958) studied psychiatric hospitals as mini-societies, and his case-studies show in intricate detail how behaviours construed as "symptoms" are in fact often explainable as adaptive reactions to specific features of the hospital environment. Perhaps the most dramatic demonstration of such environmental effects of the patients' behaviour is to be found in Stotland and Kobler's (1965) study of a mental hospital. In this work, they present convincing arguments suggesting that a suicide epidemic which took place in a hospital could be plausibly explained in terms of changes in staff attitudes, morale and related changes in expectations of patient improvement, which in turn were caused by administrative changes in the financial and bureaucratic structure of the hospital.

The intricate social environment of mental hospitals has been most influentially analysed by Goffman (1961), using a social anthropological approach. His description of the many rituals and symbols used to maintain the two caste staff-inmate social structure of mental hospitals has precipitated some contemporary reforms. These studies provide the background to more recent work on the ecology of clinical settings, such as Moos's work on psychiatric environments. He has proposed a unique fusion of clinical and social ecological interests: this "social ecological approach" is loosely defined by him as the "multidisciplinary study of the impacts of physical and social environments on human beings" (1974, p. vii). Perhaps the most important word in this definition is "impact", signifying Moos's interest in the effects of the environment on the individual, and the relatively weak emphasis on the individual–environment (or person–situation) interaction.

The work is particularly interesting and relevant here because of its clinical psychological bent. As Moos, and many others before him, observed, it is very difficult to predict a patient's behaviour in settings other than the clinician's office. Moreover, traditional conceptions of personality in trait terms were of little help to clinicians. The turn to situational and environmental factors in the search for understanding and prediction was thus motivated by very much the same factors in clinical psychology as in personality theory and social psychology: a growing dissatisfaction with purely intrapsychic explanations of human behaviour. Moos was not the first to realize that the settings and milieux provided by psychiatric hospitals and community-based programmes for treating behaviour disorders have a profound effect on the behaviour of both the clients and the therapists. The research developed by Moos was innovative to the extent that it applied quantitative empirical techniques to the study and assessment of treatment environments, in a fashion which made the day-to-day functioning of the institutions studied indirectly measurable.

Since the evidence is overwhelmingly in favour of social-environmental effects on patient behaviour, the next task is obviously the construction of reliable and valid techniques for assessing treatment environments. The major instruments developed by Moos and his co-workers to evaluate treatment environments are the Ward Atmosphere Scale (WAS) and the Community-oriented Programs Environment Scale (COPES). These scales contain a number of true–false items which are organized into several subscales. These subscales fall into three distinct categories, which are identified by the authors as:

(a) Relationship dimensions (Involvement, Support and Spontaneity subscales),

(b) Personal Development or Treatment Program dimensions (Autonomy, Practical Orientation, Personal Problem Orientation and Anger and Aggression subscales), and

(c) System Maintenance and Change dimensions (Order and Organization, Staff Control and Program Clarity subscales).

These scales have now been administered to a large number of hospitals as well as community treatment programmes both in the United States and Britain. Results show that a very wide range of treatment environments can be identified using this instrument. It was also found that staff, on the whole, tended to present a more positive picture of hospital treatment environments than did patients, a finding indirectly supporting Goffman's thesis concerning the "two castes" social structure of psychiatric hospitals. Differences between staff and patients were much less marked for community-based treatment programmes. There were also some interesting cross-cultural differences between British and American hospitals, reflecting the attitude of *laissez-faire*, in British institutions, towards their patients.

The main use of these scales is clearly as objective classificatory instruments of treatment programmes. Yet the variables they measure also have a direct bearing on the kinds of social interactions that may occur within these environments, and in that sense, they are also measures of inclusive interactive "episodes". By measuring the objective characteristics of treatment programmes, we can also find out something about the quality of social relationships within those programmes. Social episodes, as elements of the subcultural milieu of the institutions studied, incorporate exactly the kinds of expectations and restrictions which Moos's instruments seek to measure. This is perhaps most clearly demonstrated in the case studies of treatment programmes presented by Moos (1974), where these instruments were used as tools for evaluating the kind of social environment presented by the programmes, and as a means whereby that milieu could be effectively changed.

The ecology of interaction episodes also plays an important role in another branch of clinical psychology: social skills therapy. Social skills therapy in essence seeks to develop skills in patients which enable them to perform effectively in the differently situated interaction episodes available in their milieu. The training itself involves modelling, role-playing, video-taped feedback, social reinforcement and transfer learning through "home-work assignments" as the basic tools for learning new skills (Goldstein *et al.*, 1976; Trower *et al.*, 1978). At each stage of the learning process, clients need to understand how ecological settings function as signifiers for social rule systems. Knowing how to engage in friendly conversation is by itself not enough: the client also has to know that such an episode is more likely to be compatible with some settings (e.g. pubs) than with others (e.g. lifts). The effective understanding and use of environmental props is another aspect of social skills. Social skills training programmes, despite their growing popularity in recent years, are still largely based on an intra-individual "skill" model (Argyle, 1969), to the relative neglect of situational and ecological factors in interaction, which are only taken into account on an *ad hoc* basis. One of the most important practical contributions of the study of social episodes is in the area of social skills therapy, and this will be argued in some detail in Chapter 9. Knowing how to decode, use and manipulate ecological cues in the interpretation and definition of social episodes is a major part of effective social skills; by studying social episodes empirically, we should come to understand better the parameters of this skill.

Summary and conclusions

In this chapter we sought to identify the relevance of the environmental dimension to the study of social interaction episodes. In many ways, the concerns of environmental psychology and some recent approaches to social psychology intersect: physical environments affect interpersonal behaviour, and in turn, behaviour settings are created and given meaning to by the interaction episodes enacted within their confines (Craik, 1973; Ittelson *et al.*, 1974). We may define the ecological component of interaction episodes in purely physical, objective terms, or we may include the total environment in this term, including the norms, traditions and cultural codes embodied by that environment. This latter approach, which we may perhaps label "ecological symbolism", is in keeping with Lewin's (1951) understanding of the psychological field, and has stimulated such influential research projects as Barker's (1968) work on behaviour settings. It is in this second, broader sense of the term that environments play an important part in the regulation and enactment of social episodes.

Perhaps the most important contribution of the ecological approach to social episodes is in the area of classification. Given the daunting complexity of interaction episodes, their physical setting offers one obvious criterion for a taxonomic system. This idea has been most successfully developed by Barker, and today, a whole range of ecologically based taxonomies of interactions, situations, institutions and behaviour settings exist. As well as offering taxonomic criteria, ecological variables also help to mould and shape interaction episodes. Physical proximity over long periods of time predisposes towards friendlier and more intimate interactions, and similarly, proximity is a signal of intimacy and friendliness in short-term, everyday interactions. Even more fascinating is the role of environmental props, physical objects imbued with symbolic episode-defining powers. The role of such props is most clearly visible in formal ceremonies (e.g. wedding rings, maces, gowns), but there are many less exalted examples of everyday episodes being defined by environmental props. We may take Harre and Secord's (1972) suggestions seriously in this respect: the analysis of formal episodes may indeed provide a model for understanding the symbolic role of physical props in everyday, enigmatic episodes.

We have also seen that ecological variables play an important part in clinical psychology, where the coercive power of behaviour settings is perhaps most ubiquitous, except perhaps for educational and corrective institutions. It is not surprising therefore that psychiatric wards belong to the most intensively studied behaviour settings. More recently, psychotherapies fashioned in terms of the educational rather than the medical model of mental illness, such as social skills training, have focused attention on the cognitive and social skills involved in the deciphering and manipulation of ecological aspects of interaction episodes.

These diverse areas of correspondence between ecological psychology and the study of social episodes offer promise for the future development of the study of social episodes. Each one of the areas discussed in this chapter suggests further issues for research. Behaviour setting taxonomies, as first developed by Barker, could be further refined by taking perceptual, as well as ecological variables into account (see Chapters 7 and 8). It may be that within each of the behaviour setting genotypes identified by Barker, we may find further subclasses of social episodes, differentiated in terms of their perceived restrictiveness, intimacy or anxiety-arousing potential. The use of our physical surroundings for managing interaction episodes is another promising area of research, which should lend itself to the controlled experimental methodology, once the basic dimensions of such behaviours have been adequately described. The methods and topics of such ecological analyses in many ways parallel those used in the perception of social episodes. Before we could attempt a final integration of this research, therefore, it will be necessary to look at the promises and achievements of research into the perception of social episodes. This is the task of the next two chapters.

7

The Perception of Social Episodes

Although the ecological approach to the study of social episodes is perhaps the oldest established method, as the previous chapter indicates, it is in the study of perceptions of social episodes and situations that the most significant advances have been made in recent years. This is not particularly surprising, since perceptual methodologies are more readily available and generalizable to the study of social situations than are other techniques. The aim of this chapter is to present some of the most recent approaches to the study of the perception of social episodes. In the next chapter, some of the factors affecting episode perception will be considered, and in Chapter 9, some applications of the perceptual approach in clinical and social psychology will be suggested.

However, before concentrating on present research and future prospects, it might be salutary to review the past briefly. There are several relevant studies which can be considered as antecedents of the current interest in social episodes. Of course, many of these studies did not define their task as studying the perception of social episodes, *per se*. Rather, they were carried out in order to obtain information about a social psychological problem only marginally related to situations or episodes. Thus, the well-known studies by Endler and his co-workers into the characteristics of anxiety-arousing situations were more concerned with anxiety than with situations. Nevertheless, they were among the first to apply empirical techniques to the study of perceptions of situations.

Situation perception, a term first coined by Cattell (1963), defines the scope and direction of this line of research. Endler and Magnusson (1974) argue that "situation perception can be regarded as legitimate a research field as for example person perception. The traditional methods, rating scales, questionnaires, the semantic differential technique, etc. that are used for data collection in person perception can also be applied in studies of situation perception . . . In our opinion, research in this field of situation perception is one of the most urgent and also one of the most promising tasks for psychology" (p. 16, 21).

Situation perception

The earliest such studies thus asked subjects to indicate their anticipated reactions to different situations rather than their perceptions of
the situations *per se*. Such a self-report inventory of elicited reactions
was constructed to study different anxiety reactions to anxiety-evoking
situations. Endler *et al.* (1962) pioneered the S–R Inventory of Anxiousness, a questionnaire which has been at the centre of a series of
investigations over the years. The inventory in effect asks respondents
how they would react to specific situations (e.g. you are going to meet
a new date) in terms of a number of response alternatives (e.g. mouth
gets dry, butterflies, etc.). The inventory contains 11 such situations
and 14 possible response modes, some of them descriptions of feelings
or internal states rather than operant behaviours.

In this study, as well as in numerous follow-up investigations (Endler and Hunt, 1966, 1968, 1969; Endler, 1974, 1975) such self-reported
responses were elicited in response to these 11 hypothetical anxiety
arousing situations. While these studies were mainly concerned with
quantifying the proportion of variance in responses attributable to the
situation and the individual, the data clearly contain information
which reflects the way subjects perceive these situations. The method
of three-mode factor-analysis suggested by Tucker (1964), was applied
to the data of Endler *et al.* (1962) by Levin (1965). The response factors
were (a) general distress, (b) exhilaration, and (c) autonomic responses. Situation factors included the following general dimensions:
(a) interpersonal stress situations (e.g. interview, competition, speaking before audience), (b) physical danger (e.g. in the woods at night,
etc.) and (c) unknown situations (e.g. starting on a long trip, etc.).
These dimensions appear to have some validity and they are also
reconcilable with previously proposed theories of anxiety (cf. Spielberger, 1966, 1972, 1975). More importantly, however, this study
showed that perceptions of stereotypical situations can in fact be studied by empirical methods. Naturally, these first studies left a lot to be
desired in terms of how much they tell us about the characteristics of
social episodes. The sample of situations was extremely small, the
situations were not representative of any particular social milieu, and
judgements were obviously affected by the range of alternatives offered
in the inventory.

A more satisfactory situation rating scale was developed by Sussman (in Mausner, 1966) asking subjects to "Imagine that you are in the following situation. Indicate your feelings of confidence in the situation described . . .". The situational dimensions emerging from this scale, such as subjective self-confidence and intimacy, are quite similiar to dimensions emerging from more recent studies. Katz (1964) reports the development of a content-analytic method for the study of inter-personal behaviour. This procedure involves the extraction of typical "critical interactions" from written materials, and their subsequent analysis in terms of motivational organizing principles. This procedure was a preliminary step to the development of Triandis's (1972) "be-haviour differential" and "role differential" scales, which have stimu-lated considerable research in this area. The concept of "subjective culture" (Triandis and Vassiliou, 1967) was proposed as a summary term to describe such consensual cultural expectations about social situations.

A slightly different line of research, which has some affinity with Triandis's work (1972) on subjective culture, placed primary emphasis on the perception of different roles and interpersonal relationships rather than on interaction episodes as such. Marwell and Hage (1970) analysed perceptions of 100 role relationships on 16 scales, using factor-analysis for the reduction of dimensionality. Argyle and Little (1972) asked polytechnic students to indicate how their behaviour would vary versus 12 hypothetical others. This study suggested that characteristics such as casual–constrained, warm–cold, domi-nance–submission, and self-confidence–lack of self-confidence might be some of the relevant dimensions. Werdelin (1975) asked a large sample of boys and girls to fill out a 39-item response inventory for a range of social situations, such as school work, public behaviour etc. The four factors which emerged discriminated situations in terms of the following constructs: (a) lack of self-confidence, (b) restlessness, (c) unbalanced temper and mood variations, and (d) anxieties and worries. It appears that subjective self-confidence in different situa-tions is a major dimension along which social episodes are generally discriminated.

Not surprisingly, however, anxiety-arousing situations held more fascination than any other type of situation for researchers. In a similar vein to Endler's studies, Ekehammar et al. (1974) asked students to report their responses to 17 anxiety-arousing situations, and found that such responses generally fall within two categories: psychic anxiety and somatic responses to anxiety. More interesting, however, is the factor-analysis of situations used as stimuli in this study, which yielded three main factors. Anxiety-arousing situations were found to fall into one of three categories: (a) threat of punishment (e.g. caught pilfering); (b) anticipation of pain (e.g. waiting at the dentist), and (c) inanimate fear situations (e.g. in the woods at night). These categories are comparable to Levin's (1965) dimensions, and again demonstrate the feasibility of using scaling methods to study the perception of complex social objects, such as global situations. Significantly the studies of anxiety-arousing situations and episodes have yielded a surprisingly coherent set of differentiating dimensions, which holds out promise that a manageable and meaningful descriptive system can be devised for the perception of other kinds of situations and episodes as well.

In one of his many studies concerned with situational effects on behaviour, Moos (1968) asked psychiatric patients and staff to complete rating scales indicating their feelings in different situations, some social and some solitary (e.g. group therapy session, getting up in the morning etc.). Eleven such situations were evaluated on 33 adjective pairs comprising the Setting Response Inventory (SRI). A factor analysis of responses revealed five factors which distinguished these situations from each other:

(a) trusting, approving, useful v. distrusting, suspicious and useless, or *evaluative* dimension;

(b) outgoing, extroverted, independent v. shy, introverted, dependent, or a *self-confidence* dimension;

(c) secure, sure, strong v. insecure, unsure, weak, or a *potency* dimension;

(d) involved, attentive, energetic v. uninvolved, inattentive, tired, or an *involvement* dimension;

(e) sociable, friendly, peaceful v. unsociable, unfriendly, angry, or a *friendliness* dimension.

While in this study again only a fairly restricted domain of situations was studied, the results are highly interesting. They suggest that judges perceive social settings or episodes not in terms of the physical, objective characteristics of the situation, but rather, in terms of subjective, connotative dimensions. As we shall see, this essentially subjective, interpretive reaction to situations will emerge as a central feature of perceptual studies of social episodes. These findings also strongly support the stand adopted by writers such as W. I. Thomas and the symbolic interactionists who maintain that it is the subjective, assimilated situation which determines social behaviour, and not the objective, external situation.

While in the studies considered so far perceptual dimensions of situations were only a by-product, in 1971 Magnusson published a study specifically aiming at the development of a technique for studying situation perception. He argues that "concerning the study of situational variation, we find ourselves at the same stage as that concerning the study of individual differences at the initial development period of differential psychology. It is probable that the task of determining individual dimensions was at that time regarded as being as full of difficulties as we now regard the task of attacking the dimensionality of situations" (p. 852). Magnusson (1971) regards situations as cognitive rather than physical entities, and consequently the task of research is to adequately represent the psychological dimensions differentiating these cognitive objects. The study consists of a factor-analysis of the similarity ratings of 36 intuitively selected situations. This procedure yielded five main factors, which are labelled as follows:

> (a) positivity, or situations which are seen as rewarding, e.g. receive praise, listen to an interesting lecture;
> (b) negativity, or experiences of failure, e.g. fail an exam, cannot answer a simple question;
> (c) passivity, or waiting and passing time, e.g. rest during a break, wait for others;
> (d) social interactive, or unstructured activity with other students, e.g. discuss politics, carry out joint group task;
> (e) individual activity, e.g. do homework, sit for an exam, etc.

These factors were also found to be relatively stable over time, indicating that the cognitive representation of situations is a relatively slow-changing process. In a follow-up study, Magnusson and Ekehammar (1973), using the same situations as stimuli, found comparable taxonomic dimensions. The problem with both of these studies is threefold: firstly, they made no attempt at a representative sampling of situations, a crucial question if the construction of an empirical taxonomy is attempted. Secondly, very small numbers of subjects were used, which makes generalization even within a well-defined subculture such as Stockholm University students problematic. Finally, the use of similarity ratings followed by factor-analysis allows only the *ad hoc* intuitive interpretation of factors. There is no reliable way the underlying effective differentiating dimensions could be disentangled, let alone labelled, on the basis of these data alone. The use of more sophisticated techniques for the reduction of dimensionality, such as multidimensional scaling (MDS), and more than one data collection method would have allowed the construction of a more valid taxonomy. The studies described later in this chapter were designed to overcome some of these problems.

Within the same paradigm, Ekehammar and Magnusson (1973) studied 20 stressful situations, using similarity ratings and factor-analysis, and obtained two situational factors, threat of pain and ego-threat. While these dimensions correspond fairly well with other taxonomies of stressful situations discussed above, the same objections as were made about the Magnusson (1971) and Magnusson and Ekehammar (1973) studies may also apply here.

More recently, Golding (1975) has given short descriptions of inter-active situations to 123 subjects. Twenty-nine such situation vignettes were rated. The aim of this study was to establish that person by situation interactions "occur because individuals reacting to putatively the same objective interpersonal situation construe the meaningfulness of situations differently" (p. 34). He reports that individuals construe these situations differently in terms of their personal style, and different conceptual "types" of individuals place different weights on such situational dimensions as friendliness, dominance, sociability, cooperation, etc. This study points to the interesting possibility that situation perception itself may show intra-individual consistency. It seems possible that one day different individual situation-perception styles may be identified. Just as we are now in a position to represent implicit theories of personality (Rosenberg and Sedlak, 1972), implicit theories of situations may also be analysed. The potential role of such studies in clinical psychology and social skills therapy will be discussed later.

With this study, the review of the "prehistory" of scaling perceptions of social episodes is completed. The rest of this chapter is devoted to the consideration of a series of three of our studies which have explicitly sought to investigate perceptions of social episodes. It may be concluded at this point that the transition from studying other phenomena to studying social situations *per se* was a gradual one, accomplished in several steps. Situations, initially incidental to the study of causes of anxiety, have slowly emerged as worthwhile objects of investigation in their own right. During this process, it became established that perceptions of situations and episodes can be studied using the same techniques which have been successfully applied to the study of person perception, for example. The study of situation perception could be regarded as just as legitimate a research area as the study of person perception, or the perception of stereotypes. This recognition has been anticipated by others, for example Cattell (1963), who appears to have been the first one to use the term situation perception.

It is noteworthy that all the perceptual studies of situations outlined here, collected by different researchers in different countries with different subject and situation samples, share certain important characteristics. Firstly, all managed to obtain a manageable number of intuitively meaningful dimensions and categories, which in the case of anxiety-arousing situations, fitted well with existing theories. Secondly, dimensions and categories tend to reflect affective and emotional rather than objective and cognitive situational characteristics—in other words, the connotative rather than the denotative meaning of situations was salient to subjects. And finally, there appears to be an emerging consensus that descriptive dimensions such as subjective self-confidence, intimacy and constraint may have a fairly universal relevance to describing perceptions of episodes.

Subcultural differences in episode perception

Social episodes are units of interaction which by definition exist within a cultural milieu. The term episode space may be used to describe the perceived patterned relationship between different kinds of social encounters within a cultural environment. At the same time episodes are also cognitive units which embody "models of behaviour" in the minds of individual members of a culture. Throughout this book, we have attempted to chart the background to such a conceptualization of social episodes, and to suggest empirical methods for their study. Our task in deriving a meaningful taxonomy of episodes is thus to explicate subjectively perceived differences between episodes composing the episode space. The first objective in the study of perceptions of social episodes is thus a quasi-anthropological one: the quantification of differences in episode perception between members of different subcultural groups. This was the major aim of the study to be presented here (Forgas, 1976a).

A perceptual taxonomy of episodes has important advantages when contrasted with some more traditional approaches, such as *a priori* category systems (Sells, 1963; Sherif and Sherif, 1969), classificatory systems developed in terms of need concepts (Rotter, 1954), and in terms of single response variables, such as anxiety (Ekehammar *et al.*, 1974), or solutions to paperwork problems (Frederiksen, 1972). These approaches are either too atomistic in their reliance on single responses as criteria, or else are unsuited to the explication of the cultural content of episodes.

It was the aim of the present study to show that the scaling of individual perceptions of social episodes can be accomplished in such a way that the resulting taxonomy reflects a degree of consensual agreement in a given subculture. A non-metric multidimensional scaling (MDS) procedure appears most appropriate for such a task because it allows data collection methods that make the complex cognitive comparisons intrinsically meaningful, without the imposition of external constructs by the experimenter. "Each subject determines which aspect of the stimulus . . . he will judge" (Jones and Young, 1973, p. 109). The interpretation of the episode space may also be accomplished empirically, by fitting separately scaled hypothesis dimensions to the multidimensional episode space (Rosenberg and Sedlak, 1972).

However, if subjects' perceptions of the episodes are in terms of a finite number of discrete categories rather than in terms of gradual changes along different continua, the MDS solution will at best only approximate the actual cognitive representation of the episode space (Torgerson, 1965). By applying an alternative procedure more sensitive to categorical structures, such as cluster analysis, to the same set of data (Jones and Ashmore, 1973), the adequacy of the two representations can be compared.

Finally, the culture specificity of episodes as defined here offers the possibility of some potentially interesting comparisons between subcultures. Are the cognitive maps of episodes structurally different in different subcultures? Do the same episodes occupy similar or different structural positions in different subgroups? If there are structural differences, could these be related to the objective circumstances of the different groups? In order to provide at least some initial insight into problems such as these, it was decided to carry out the present investigation in two substantially different subcultural samples simultaneously.

In summary, the present study had three objectives: (a) to explore the possibility of constructing an empirical taxonomy of social episodes based on individuals' perception of them; (b) to compare the effectiveness of dimensional and categorical representations of the same data using MDS and cluster analysis; and (c) to contrast differences between different subcultural groups in their representations of social episodes.

METHOD

The two subcultural groups studied were married, middle-class housewives living in the Oxford area, England, and undergraduate students at the University of Oxford. The selection of a representative range of social episodes was crucial for the study. Rather than using a selection of sundry *ad hoc* situations chosen on an intuitive basis, as in most previous studies, a special pilot study was run. A preliminary sample of subjects from each population group was given a questionnaire which asked them to give detailed accounts of their social interactions during the past 24 hours in the form of a diary, and to list their typical interactions which did not occur during this period. The 25 most frequently nominated and typical social situations were used as stimulus episodes (Table 1).

Similarity judgements of these episodes were obtained in the form of a categorization task, asking judges from each subculture to sort the episodes into homogeneous groups, "on the basis of their similarity. You may consider any aspect of the episodes in deciding whether they are similar or not". The number of times any two episodes were put into the same category provided the raw data from which an index of psychological relatedness, taking direct as well as indirect co-occurrence into account, was calculated (Forgas, 1976a, p. 201). This index was used as input to a non-metric multidimensional scaling analysis (TORSCA 9), and to a hierarchical clustering analysis.

In addition to the categorization task, subjects were also asked to rate the episodes on a number of bipolar scales. These judgements were later used to help with the interpretation of the episode space.

TABLE 1
The 25 most frequently mentioned social episodes used as stimuli for each subsample

Housewives	Students
1. Having a short chat with the house delivery man	1. Having morning coffee with the people in the department
2. Playing with your children	2. Having a drink with some friends in a pub
3. Your husband rings up from work to discuss something	3. Discussing an essay during a tutorial
4. Having a short chat with the shop assistant while shopping	4. Meeting an acquaintance while checking your pigeonhole for mail in college
5. Having dinner with your family	5. Going out for a walk with a friend
6. Shopping on Saturday morning with your husband at the supermarket	6. Shopping on Saturday morning with a friend at the supermarket
7. Attending a wedding ceremony	7. Acting as a subject in a psychology experiment
8. Having a drink with some friends in the pub	8. Going to the pictures with some friends
9. Washing up dishes after dinner with family help	9. Having a short chat with the shop assistant while shopping
10. Chatting over morning coffee with some friends	10. Getting acquainted with a new person during dinner in hall
11. Reading and talking in bed before going to sleep	11. Going to JCR meetings
12. Chatting with an acquaintance who unexpectedly gave you a lift	12. Chatting with an acquaintance before a lecture begins
13. Watching TV with your family after dinner	13. Discussing psychology topics with friends
14. Having a short chat with an acquaintance whom you unexpectedly met on the street	14. Meeting new people at a sherry party in college
15. Going to the pictures with some friends	15. Visiting your doctor
16. Discussing the events of the day with your husband in the evening	16. Chatting with an acquaintance who unexpectedly gave you a lift
17. Talking to other customers while queueing in a shop	17. Visiting a friend in his college room
18. Talking to a neighbour who called to borrow some household equipment	18. Going to see a play at the theatre with friends
19. Having guests for dinner	19. Going to the bank
20. Visiting a friend in hospital	20. Having an intimate conversation with your boy/girlfriend
21. Chatting with others while waiting for your washing in the coin laundry	21. Having a short chat with an acquaintance whom you unexpectedly met on the street
22. Talking to a neighbour through the backyard fence	22. Chatting with others while waiting for your washing in the coin laundry
23. Playing chess	23. Attending a wedding ceremony
24. Going to the bank	24. Watching TV with some friends
25. Visiting your doctor	25. Playing chess

Source: Forgas, 1976, p. 202.

DIMENSIONALITY

In deciding the optimum number of MDS dimensions, two main criteria can be used: (a) the minimum number of dimensions with a satisfactory level of fit ("stress") can be selected, and (b) the potential interpretability of the different solutions, as indicated by the correlations between bipolar hypothesis scales and MDS spaces may be taken into account (Table 2).

The results showed that a two-dimensional representation of social episodes was optimal for housewives, while a slightly more complex three-dimensional episode space best represented the episode domain of students.

INTERPRETATION

These representations were interpreted with the help of the bipolar scales, by fitting a line corresponding to each bipolar scale to the multidimensional episode space, using the ratio of the regression weights of the MDS axes as the slope of a line through the origin (Rosenberg and Sedlak, 1972), with significant and approximately orthogonal scales used as interpretive frameworks. The perceived episode domains, as represented by MDS, are shown in Figs. 1 and 2.

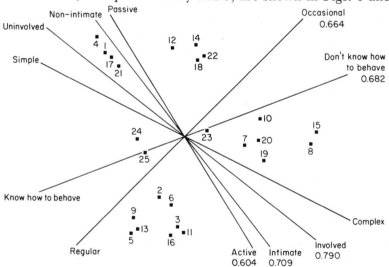

Fig. 1. The two-dimensional configuration of 25 episodes with six significant hypothesis scales fitted.

TABLE 2

Multiple correlation coefficients between hypothesis scales and each of five multidimensional configurations for both subsamples

Scale	Housewives					Students				
	1	2	3	4	5	1	2	3	4	5
Involved–uninvolved	0·702ᴵ	0·790ᴵ	0·835ᴵ	0·834ᴵ	0·856ᴵ	0·338	0·395	0·667ᴵ	0·551	0·789ᴵ
Simple–complex	0·463	0·586ᴵ	0·609	0·726ᴵ	0·757ᴵ	0·059	0·488ᴵ	0·575	0·522	0·708ᴵ
Active–passive	0·600ᴵ	0·604ᴵ	0·624ᴵ	0·632	0·718ᴵ	0·095	0·252	0·549	0·393	0·518
Pleasant–unpleasant	0·272	0·336	0·607	0·579	0·538	0·314	0·682ᴵ	0·761ᴵ	0·764ᴵ	0·791ᴵ
Intimate–nonintimate	0·698ᴵ	0·709ᴵ	0·764ᴵ	0·780ᴵ	0·819ᴵ	0·349	0·623ᴵ	0·801ᴵ	0·803ᴵ	0·829ᴵ
Very much at ease–very ill at ease	0·449	0·486	0·597	0·635	0·618	0·428	0·747ᴵ	0·725ᴵ	0·867ᴵ	0·879ᴵ
I know how to behave–don't know	0·389	0·682ᴵ	0·709ᴵ	0·743ᴵ	0·813ᴵ	0·394	0·570ᴵ	0·616ᴵ	0·662ᴵ	0·680ᴵ
Friendly–unfriendly	0·554ᴵ	0·621ᴵ	0·658ᴵ	0·738ᴵ	0·737ᴵ	0·540ᴵ	0·760ᴵ	0·864ᴵ	0·873ᴵ	0·880ᴵ
Occasional–regular	0·597ᴵ	0·664ᴵ	0·685ᴵ	0·700ᴵ	0·693ᴵ	0·094	0·432	0·446	0·628	0·641
Organized–disorganized	0·569ᴵ	0·629ᴵ	0·805ᴵ	0·825ᴵ	0·830ᴵ	0·238	0·465	0·562	0·618	0·620
Cooperative–competitive	0·315	0·371	0·388	0·614	0·837ᴵ	0·293	0·550	0·538	0·596	0·569
Formal–informal	0·175	0·179	0·542	0·617ᴵ	0·789ᴵ	0·364	0·850ᴵ	0·877ᴵ	0·925ᴵ	0·929ᴵ
Stress	13%	4·5%	2·8%	1·8%	1·5%	23%	10·5%	6·2%	3·8%	2·6%

ᴵ $P < ·001$. Source: Forgas, 1976, p. 203.

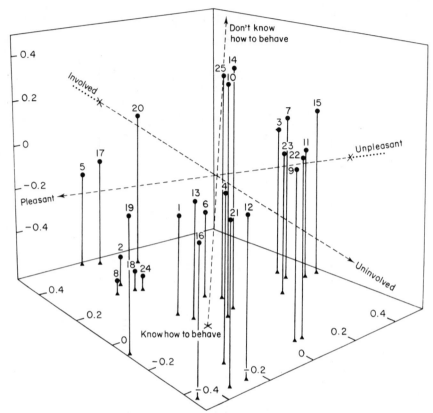

Fig. 2. The three-dimensional representation of 25 episodes with three hypothesis scales fitted.

The interpretive bipolar scales fitted to the episode space are also shown.

The episode space for housewives appears to be interpretable in terms of two general attribute clusters: the perceived intimacy, involvement and friendliness of episodes is the first such dimension, and the subjective self-confidence or competence of the actors, related to the frequency and regularity of the episodes is the second one. For students the perceived episode space is adequately defined by three, approximately orthogonal property dimensions: involvement, pleasantness and know how to behave (i.e. subjective self-confidence).

Results and discussion

The overall results indicate that by using the present techniques, a psychologically meaningful and statistically satisfactory representation of the cognitive organization of different social episodes can be achieved. The main attributes of social episodes emerging from this study, involvement or intimacy and subjective self-confidence, are promising as criteria for a classificatory system. Similar attributes were found to be relevant not only in person perception (Rosenberg *et. al.*, 1968) but also in some other studies of social situations (Pervin, 1976; Wish, 1975).

These representations can be related to the particular social milieu and experiences of the judges. For housewives, episodes seen as non-intimate (e.g. Item 4: chatting with the shop assistant) are superficial, routine encounters with relative strangers in the course of performing daily chores. On the other hand, more intimate and involved episodes are clearly differentiated into regular interactions performed with confidence mostly with family members (e.g. Item 5: having dinner with the family), and activities regarded with far less self-confidence mostly social functions or entertainments (e.g. Items 8 and 15). It is remarkable that the alternative represented by self-confident but non-intimate interactions, so characteristic of institutionalized working environments, is almost completely absent. Clearly, the social environment of housewives provides few encounters of this type.

The representation of the episode structure of students was three-dimensional. It seems an intriguing possibility to account for the extra dimension either in terms of the greater cognitive complexity of students or in terms of their wider and more varied stimulus field.

The involvement dimension mainly differentiates encounters with friends and acquaintances on the basis of the duration and intimacy of the episode. The evaluative (pleasant–unpleasant) dimension seems to reflect the degree of situational constraint implied by different episodes (Price and Bouffard, 1974), with open and uncontrolled interactions seen as pleasant (e.g. Items 19, 16, and 5), and controlled and restrictive activities, such as tutorials, acting as a subject in an experiment, and attending formal meetings, being negatively evaluated.

The function of the self-confidence ("know how to behave") dimension in differentiating episodes is interesting because it relates to previous work on anxiety responses to different situations (Bryant and

Trower, 1974; Ekehammar and Magnusson, 1973). Episodes involving prolonged interaction with strangers (i.e. the "getting acquainted" process) elicit the highest level of apprehension (Items 10, 14, and 25), thus supporting Bryant and Trower's (1974) finding with a similar sample and showing that substantial numbers of students find episodes of this kind rather difficult to cope with.

Students seem to regard episodes involving entertainments and socializing with friends with great self-confidence (Items 2, 8, 18, and 24), in strong contrast to housewives, who viewed nearly identical episodes with a lack of self-confidence. The very different subjective definition of these interactions, involving nearly indistinguishable activities and objective characteristics, suggests that a classification of episodes in terms of objective factors may not tap the psychologically meaningful differences. While "socializing with friends" for students is a natural, self-selected entertainment, for housewives it may be a more formal, organized affair, with an element of self-presentation and potential loss of face (Goffman, 1955).

Thus, both dimensional representations provide a picture of the episode space which is (a) readily interpretable and meaningful, (b) appears to be sensitive to the cultural differences between the samples, and (c) tends to differentiate episodes primarily in terms of their perceived subjective, connotative rather than denotative, characteristics. It was surprising to note that the activities which make up an episode, the physical aspects of the environment, and other objective factors were of little consequence in determining this structure.

In addition to MDS, these data were also subjected to a categorical analysis.

The two hierarchical clustering configurations shown in Fig. 3 provide some important additional cues to the interpretation of the episode space.

For housewives, the three large primary categories, which could be labelled as "casual," "family," and "social," divide into subclusters in terms of the relationship to the interaction partner. Thus, family episodes can be differentiated by whether they involve the husband (Items 3, 11, and 16) or the whole family (Items 2, 5, 6, 9, and 13). Casual encounters can involve strangers (Items 1, 4, 17, and 21) and friends and neighbours (Items 12, 14, 18, and 22). It appears that the underlying dimensions of involvement and self-confidence closely match the relationship to the interaction partner.

For students, the primary division of episodes is in terms of the categories of people they involve: friends, acquaintances, strangers, people in their official capacity. When compared with the categorical structure of episodes for housewives, a reversal of the importance of

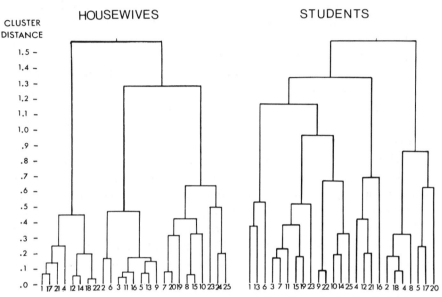

Fig. 3. Results of the hierarchical clustering analysis of 25 episodes for each of two subsamples.

differentiating criteria is apparent. Housewives differentiate their social episodes primarily in terms of which area of their lives they relate to (family, social, or casual), and the interaction partner is only a secondary criterion, whereas for students their relationship to people they encounter is of primary importance, and further subdivision is apparently in terms of intimacy, self-confidence, area of life, and so on.

This study was thus successful in showing that important subcultural differences exist in the perception of social episodes and that such differences can be quantified and empirically related to the social background and milieu of the judges. It was also found that the dimensional representation of the episode space was adequate, and included nearly all the information that was obtained from the categorical analysis of the same data. It may be concluded that since the construction of dimensional models is always possible, and since such models apparently include all the information that is contained in categorical representations, it is reasonable to adopt as a working assumption that social episodes are in fact perceived in terms of a finite number of attributes in multidimensional space. This study has also contributed to our understanding of cognitive dimensions relevant to episode perception. The present results, as well as results from previous studies strongly suggest that a classificatory system in terms of a limited number of perceived connotative attributes may be the most promising. Subjects perceived episodes not in terms of their objective characteristics, but rather, in terms of how they, as participating individuals, felt about them.

A demonstration of quantitative differences in episode perception across subcultures also supports theories such as symbolic interactionism which maintain that episodes and situations are social products. The two subcultures studied here, although their behaviour environment in the objective sense was similar, and they moved through many of the same behaviour settings during their daily routines, had nevertheless very different cognitive representations of the episodes which take place within those settings. While subcultural differences in episode perception are thus predicted by some influential theories, it is not certain that similar differences would also exist among groups within the same subculture. This is the issue to be explored in the next section.

Group differences in episode perception

Cognitive representations of social episodes are created and continually changed in the course of social interaction (Chapters 3 and 4). As the previous study has shown, different subcultures tend to develop diverging perceptions of their episode domains. It would be interesting to see whether more volatile, *ad hoc* cultural units, such as small groups, also have a tendency to develop different representations of social episodes, even when their members come from the same subcultural background. By looking at smaller cultural entities such as groups, it also becomes possible to study the effects of specific variables on episode perception, such as group cohesion, task success, and frequency and intensity of interaction. The present study sought to evaluate a central prediction of symbolic interactionist theory, that symbolic representations of interactions episodes are a function of the characteristics of the primary group in which they arise (Cooley, 1966; Blumer, 1969; Mead, 1956). In particular, a cohesive and intensive group should have a more differentiated and better integrated episode domain which is perceived with a greater degree of consensus than would be the case with a loosely structured and heterogenous group.

The development of group norms and group cultures in small primary groups, such as sports teams, is a much studied field in social psychology. Not only do "norms frequently originate and reside in the functional group" but "groups may provide the individual with a frame of reference for perceiving their world" (Hollander and Hunt, 1971, p. 414). One particularly relevant research tradition is the study of reference groups (Hyman, 1942; Hyman and Singer, 1968; Merton, 1957). Small, cohesive groups with a regular pattern of intra-group interaction and in competition with similar groups are most likely to develop a strong sense of group identity, and a corresponding group culture (Cartwright and Zander, 1968; Sherif and Sherif, 1969). To the extent that natural groups have different milieus, interaction styles and climates, their perception of social episodes should also be different.

Although the idea that the perception of social reality is the product of group experience is thus a common one (Cooley, 1966; Festinger, 1950; Newcomb, 1950), investigations showing the effects of group membership on social perception are relatively rare; studies demonstrating such effects in naturalistic settings are even more difficult to find. One recent study demonstrating the development of appropriate cognitive structures as a result of group socialization is Friendly and Glucksberg's (1970) analysis of the use of subcultural lexicons. These authors studied the acquisition of group-specific jargon terms in individuals new to the group and those already well socialized into it, using an MDS procedure. They conclude that "The initial hypothesis that MDS would reflect changes in semantic structure as a function of group membership has been amply confirmed." (p. 64).

Could such differences also be found in the cognitive representation of social episodes? Do primary groups perceive social episodes in a way which is different from judgements of other, comparable groups, and also differs from judgements of the same episodes by the relevant subculture? In terms of the definition and operationalization of social episodes advanced here, any social unit with a common interactive experience may be expected to have developed a shared concept of stereotypical episodes as part of its culture. Functioning sports teams, which typically engage in a wide range of competitive, task-oriented, as well as purely social episodes, and which have a relatively stable membership, are thus ideally suited to the investigation of group milieux.

In the present study differences in episode perception between two intact groups (sports teams) were evaluated. These two groups were matched for size, longevity, subcultural background, age, sex, intelligence and the socio-economic background of their members, but were substantially different in terms of their group milieu and interaction style. While one group was an intensive social unit with a regular and broad pattern of group interaction, the second group was more fragmented, with a more erratic and restricted range of interactions. Based on symbolic interactionist theory, the following differences between the episode domains of these two groups were expected.

DIFFERENTIATION

The more intensive group, having acquired a broader and more detailed interactive experience, should have a more complex and differentiated cognitive representation of its social episodes.

INTEGRATION

The more intensive group may be expected to have not only a more differentiated, but also a better integrated episode domain. For example, task-related (playing sport) and purely socio-emotional episodes should not be significantly separated, since group members interact with equal frequency in both kinds of episodes. In the less intensive group, where members interact primarily in the context of performing the group task (playing sport), but less frequently in purely social episodes, we may expect a significant separation between these two kinds of episodes in the episode space. (Clearly, other indices of episode integration may be more appropriate to other kinds of groups.)

CONSENSUS

Since members may also be expected to have a more thorough experience of the episodes in the more intensive group, there should also be greater similarity, or consensus among them in how they perceive the group's episode space.

In summary, then, it was expected that the more cohesive and homogenous group should have developed an episode domain which is better *differentiated*, more *integrated*, and is perceived with a greater degree of *consensus* than is the case in a less intensive group.

The two groups

According to reports by informants from both teams, the two groups were substantially different in their cohesiveness, homogeneity, fragmentation and interactive styles. Team 1 consisted mainly of players of comparable ability, who were highly motivated to achieve the best possible results for their team. As a consequence, this team engaged in a regular routine of shared training sessions. Team members also regularly interacted with each other in other, not directly rugby-related episodes. According to reports by members, a stable and well-recognized pattern of relationships was also characteristic of this team. In summary, Team 1 was a unified and highly cohesive unit, with uniformly recognized and respected leaders, and a regular pattern of training and other social events in which team members participated.

Team 2, in contrast, consisted of members of widely differing ability. In this team there were several members who had played rugby in the University First and Second teams, and were thus much more experienced players than the rest. As a result, the existence of four or five "stars" contributed to a fairly loose multi-centred social structure, without much cohesion or group identification. The primary loyalties of the most experienced players lay outside the team. This team did much less shared training, and there was less common social activity amongst team members. It may be noted that although this team was better endowed with experienced players, Team 1 performed about equally well in the inter-college rugby competition, thanks to its greater motivation and cohesion.

Quantitative indices

In order to substantiate these subjectively reported differences between the teams, quantitative data were also collected. Members in each team were asked to rate each other on 12 bipolar scales, which were based on adjectives suggested by members themselves as best differentiating between individuals. On the basis of these bipolar ratings, a series of dissimilarity matrices were calculated, and were used as input to a multi-dimensional scaling analysis of the group structure (Jones and Young, 1973; Forgas, 1979a).

The best fitting sociometric space was three-dimensional for Team 1, and two-dimensional for Team 2, accounting for 54% and 52% of the variance respectively. For Team 1, characteristics such as friendliness and likability were relatively more important in defining the sociometric structure, while in Team 2, aggressiveness and extroversion were more salient. Both the complexity and the attributes defining these sociometric representations thus confirmed the differences between the teams as suggested by members' descriptions.

In order to objectively evaluate the reported greater fragmentation of Team 2, a multiple discriminant analysis was carried out (Dixon, 1973) evaluating the differences between the centroids of the "stars" and other members in the group's sociometric space. "Stars" and others were found to be significantly differentiated in the group space Team 2, ($D^2=9.27$; d.f.$=2$; $P<0.01$), whereas no such clearly differentiated subgroup could be identified in Team 1, once again confirming subjective reports to that effect.

It was concluded that the two teams were indeed different in terms of sociometric structure as well as interaction style, but similar with respect to most other variables.

Selection of social episodes

In order to be able to compare structural differences between the episode domains of the teams, it was necessary to select a sample of social episodes which were equally relevant to both teams. This sample was derived as a result of a semi-formal elicitation procedure conducted with the help of one member from each team. On the basis of informal conversations with other team members, two contact members compiled a list of salient and typical social encounters which were generally thought to be characteristic of the usual interaction patterns of the team. On the basis of these lists, a joint list containing the most important episodes for both teams was constructed. This list was informally validated within each of the teams, insofar as the contact members took the lists back to the teams, and solicited comments on possible omissions /repetitions/misunderstandings, etc. While this pro-cedure might appear rather informal, it was adopted since (a) the two teams were fairly small and accessible, (b) meaningful comments were easily obtained from team members, and (c) a more rigid paper-and-pencil pilot study to elicit social episodes would have pre-empted much of the enthusiasm and interest in the main study. In fact the episode lists suggested by the two teams were surprisingly similar, and were readily merged into a final list of 18 episodes which were used as stimuli (Table 3).

TABLE 3

List of the 18 social episodes used as stimuli in both rugby teams

1. Having a short chat with an acquaintance whom you unexpectedly met on the street	10. Having a drink with some friends in a pub
2. Going to the pictures with some friends	11. Discussing tactics in the changing room before a game
3. Discussing an essay during a tutorial	12. Having a meal in hall
4. Meeting new people at a sherry party in college	13. Having a drink in the JCR bar after a game
5. Playing a rugby match	14. Going to a party
6. Visiting a friend in his college room	15. Having an intimate conversation with your girlfriend
7. Talking in the changing room after winning a game	16. Chatting with an acquaintance before a lecture
8. Talking in the changing room after losing a game	17. Travelling to an away match with team friends
9. Having morning coffee in the JCR with friends	18. Participating in a training session

Selection of bipolar scales

In order to ensure the inclusion of subject-, object- and situation-relevant scales in the questionnaire (Beach and Wertheimer, 1961; Fuchs and Schäfer, 1972), an informal validation procedure was fol-lowed. Twelve bipolar scales used in the previous study (Forgas, 1976a), supplemented by further dimensions derived from the litera-ture (Magnusson, 1971; Pervin, 1976; Wish et al., 1976) were shown to members of the teams, who were asked to comment on their rel-evance to the episodes. On the basis of this feedback, 10 bipolar scales were selected, and members were asked to rate each of the 18 episodes on these scales.

Analysis

Carroll and Chang's (1970) Individual Differences Multidimensional Scaling (INDSCAL) program was used. In principle, INDSCAL locates the best fitting orthogonal dimensions describing the stimuli, by identifying the axes which judges rely on most heavily. Thus, the output configuration is defined by unique and directly interpretable stimulus axes, which should "correspond to meaningful psychological dimensions in a very strong sense" (Carroll and Chang, 1970, p. 285), while differences between individuals or subject sub-groups can also be readily evaluated.

In order to provide suitable input to INDSCAL, judgements of episodes were first converted into dissimilarity measures (Chapter 5). Using this formula, for each subject and for each bipolar scale a dissimilarity matrix was constructed, resulting in 25 such matrices for each team (15 respondent matrices and 10 scale matrices).

Results and discussion

For Team 1, the three-dimensional representation appeared optimal. The addition of a fourth dimension resulted in only a minimal increase in the variance accounted for, while the two-dimensional solution accounted for 10% less variance. For Team 2, a two-dimensional episode space appeared best suited, which accounted for 16% more variance than one dimension, while a third dimension yielded only a 5% improvement in this figure. Three dimensions for Team 1, and two dimensions for Team 2 thus appeared to be both necessary and sufficient to adequately represent their respective episode spaces. Although the determination of optimal dimensionality in MDS analyses is not based on objective criteria alone, in the present case there is strong indication that the episode space of Team 1 was indeed more complex and better differentiated than the episode space of Team 2, thus supporting the first hypothesis.

The episode spaces for the two teams, showing in effect how a hypothetical "average" team member would cognitively represent the team's episodes, are shown in Figs 4 and 5.

In Team 1, the first dimension was closely related to bipolar scales such as cooperative–competitive (0·756) and friendly–unfriendly (0·746). This dimension differentiated friendly and sociable interactions, such as chatting with a friend, or going out together, from more hostile and competitive episodes, such as discussions after a lost game, or the rugby match itself, and was labelled *friendliness*. The second dimension, related to the intimate–non-intimate (0·701), formal–informal (0·689) and at ease–ill at ease (0·681) scales, tended to separate formal and more anxiety-arousing situations, such as tutorials or sherry parties, from intimate and informal encounters such as meetings with girlfriends, or going to a pub. This dimension was accordingly labelled *intimacy*. The third dimension was marked by the self-explanatory active-passive scale, and was labelled *activity*.

For Team 2, the first dimension was clearly related to the at ease (0·746), pleasant (0·685) and involved (0·675) scales. This dimension was interpreted as a general *evaluative* dimension, differentiating between liked and enjoyable activities (girlfriend; pub; rugby match) and disliked or unpleasant situations (sherry party; tutorial; after lost

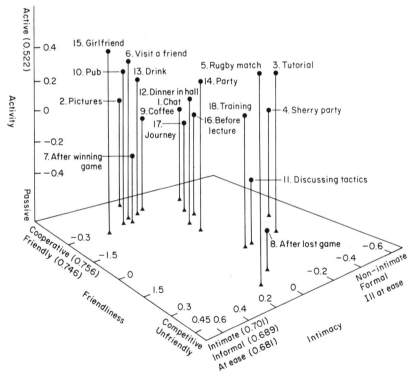

Fig. 4. The three-dimensional episode space for Team 1, showing the bipolar scales used in labelling the INDSCAL dimensions.

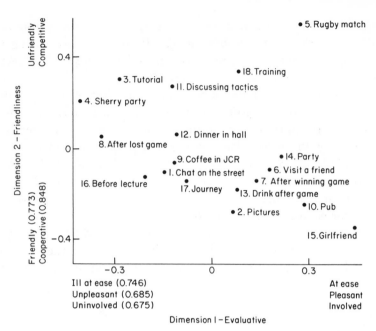

Fig. 5. The two-dimensional episode space for Team 2, showing the bipolar scales used in labelling the INDSCAL dimensions.

game). The second dimension for this team was again marked by the cooperation (0·847) and friendliness (0·773) scales, differentiating episodes in terms of *friendliness*, similar to the first dimension for Team 1.

The differences between the episode spaces again appear to reflect the different group milieux of the two teams. Friendliness and cooperation are seen as relatively more salient aspects of episodes in Team 1 than in Team 2. The intimacy dimension of Team 1's episodes has no similar counterpart in Team 2. The overall *evaluative* dimension in Team 2 may be indicative of a more critical and detached cognitive representation of social episodes in this more fragmented and heterogenous team. However, caution should be exercised in interpreting these differences, since the labelling of the INDSCAL dimensions was not unequivocally based on objective criteria.

How are individual episodes positioned in the episode spaces? Both teams differentiate between superficial, casual encounters (chatting on the street, before a lecture, on a journey) and the more involved social activities, such as going to a pub, visiting friends, going to the pictures, etc. Sherry parties are seen rather negatively in both teams (!), and the rugby match itself is a social occasion well separated from other episodes for both teams. These episode spaces are in some ways similar to the representation of social episodes derived from a more general student sample in the previous study, insofar as the same kinds of cognitive distinctions tend to be made. However, there are also some interesting differences between the two teams. Playing rugby is seen as an extremely competitive but positively evaluated activity in Team 2, while the same episode is judged to be less extreme on both dimensions by Team 1. Training is a more competitive activity in Team 2 than in Team 1, while discussion in the changing room after a lost game is seen as a more negative episode by Team 1 than by Team 2. These differences make some intuitive sense in terms of what has been said about the characteristics of the teams before. The fact that these differences appear to be more marked for rugby-related episodes tends to confirm the expectations formulated earlier.

According to the integration hypothesis, it was expected that task-related and purely social episodes would be better integrated in the episode space of Team 1 than Team 2, reflecting the more regular interactive experience of Team 1 outside rugby-related activities.

In the first instance those episodes relating to playing rugby or being a member of a rugby team were identified (Nos 5, 7, 8, 11, 13, 17, 18 in Table 1). The differences between the perception of rugby and non-rugby episodes were evaluated by a multiple discriminant analysis (Dixon, 1973), in which the differences between the centroids of the coordinates of these two clusters of episodes were tested. This test in effect evaluates whether the differences in the episode space between the average "rugby" and "non-rugby" episode are significant. The results of this analysis for each of the teams are shown in Table 4. This analysis shows that in the more heterogenous, fragmented and less cohesive Team 2, rugby-related episodes were perceived as significantly separated from other, non-rugby related episodes in the episode space. In the more cohesive and homogenous Team 1, there were no significant differences between the centroids of rugby and non-rugby episodes. These differences support the integration hypothesis: relatively less frequent interaction as a group outside the directly rugby-related events explains why in Team 2 rugby-related episodes seem to occupy a special place. In Team 1, with more frequent and regular group interaction, rugby-related episodes were not significantly differentiated as a cluster in the episode space.

TABLE 4

Multiple discriminant analyses of the positions of rugby and non-rugby episodes in the episode space of each of two teams

	Mean scores			Discriminant function coefficients			Categorized as		Mahalanobis D^{2}[1]	Significance
	Dim.1	Dim.2	Dim.3	Dim.1	Dim.2	Dim.3	1	2		
Team 1:										
1. Rugby episodes (N=7)	0·008	0·108	−0·052	0·787	2·247	−0·822	4	3		
2. Non-rugby episodes (N=11)	0·006	−0·070	0·048	−0·299	−1·392	0·599	4	7	1·180	NS
Team 2:										
1. Rugby episodes (N=7)	0·154	−0·993	—	4·011	1·336	—	4	3		
2. Non-rugby episodes (N=11)	−0·098	0·002	—	−2·549	−0·849	—	3	8	7·006	0·05

[1]The value of Mahalanobis D^{2} can be used as a Chi-square to test the hypothesis that the mean coordinates were the same for these two groups of episodes on 2 or 3 dimensions (Dixon, 1973).

It was also expected that in the more cohesive Team 1, members would perceive their social episodes with a greater degree of consensus than in Team 2. In addition to constructing a geometric representation of the episode space, INDSCAL also contains as its output a so-called subject space. In this space, individual subjects are located along the dimensions of the stimulus space, and their position is determined by the extent to which they relied on one of the INDSCAL stimulus dimensions in their judgements. These subject coordinates, or subject dimension weights, thus numerically indicate relative differences in cognitive style between individual judges. According to the consensus hypothesis, there should be less divergence in the subjects weights of Team 1 than Team 2.

This was evaluated by comparing the dispersion of group members in the subject space of each team (distance between an individual subject's position and the group centroid). For the group with the greater consensus, the variance of subject positions in the subject space should be less than in the less cohesive team. An F-test of the variances indicated that in fact there was significantly greater agreement in the representation of the episode space by members of Team 1, than in Team 2 ($F=4\cdot89$; d.f.$=14,14$; $P<0\cdot01$), thus supporting the consensus hypothesis.

These results, then, show that in the more heterogenous Team 2 there was significantly more disagreement in the way episodes were perceived than in Team 1. It may be that differences in the way "stars" and others perceived the episodes of Team 2 may partially account for this finding. This possibility was evaluated by comparing the subject weights of "stars" and other team members using a multiple discriminant analysis. Results showed that "stars" and others indeed judged social episodes significantly differently in this team ($D^2=7\cdot89$; d.f.$=2$; $P<0\cdot025$;. In particular, "stars" found the evaluative dimensions relatively more salient in their judgments of episodes than did other team members.

Conclusions

The general expectation that cognitive representations of social episodes would reflect characteristics of the group milieux in which they arise has thus been confirmed. Although the teams were similar in terms of most criteria, and were equally familiar with the episodes studied, their different interaction patterns were strongly reflected in how they distinguished among social episodes. The more cohesive and integrated Team 1 generated an episode space which was better differentiated, more integrated and perceived with a greater degree of consensus than was the case for Team 2.

How can we explain the differences in episode differentiation, integration and consensus between the two teams? It may be assumed that these differences reflect the differential socialising influences of the teams. Thus, among "the more subtle but important features of an increased degree of socialisation is the capacity to differentiate—to make finer distinctions in the relevant cognitive material" (Tannenbaum and McLeod, 1967, p. 34). Cognitive representations of the social world and social interaction are inseparably tied together (Mead, 1934; Cooley, 1966). Just as implicit theories of personality reflect an individual's interactive experience (Rosenberg and Sedlak, 1972), implicit theories of social episodes are expressions of the sedimentation of accumulated interactive practice (Schutz, 1970).

In general terms, the demonstration of such differences by empirical methods has implications for the study of how representations of the social world are acquired. In recent years, the *Zeitgeist* of social psychology has been increasingly cognitive, descriptive and focused on real-life interaction processes. The present findings clearly show that social cognition can be empirically related to the interactive milieu of the individuals studied.

Individual differences in episode perception

The studies discussed so far have demonstrated not only the possibility of studying perceptions of global episodes by empirical means, but have also showed that such perceptions reflect the subtle subcultural and group differences between respondents. The present study focused on how individual differences influence the perception of social episodes (Forgas, 1978a).

The range of variables which might affect the way an individual comes to see the social episodes occurring within his environment can be very wide. Perhaps the most interesting such group of variables are those which pertain to differences between individuals in regard to their social position, role and status within their groups. The symbolic interactionist approach, to which the present conceptualization of social episodes is closely related, also postulates that internal representations of cultural objects, such as social episodes, are influenced not only by the cultural milieu, but also by individual differences in assimilating and interpreting the culture. Symbolic interactionists (Blumer, 1969; Cooley, 1966; Mead, 1934) have consistently emphasized the importance of primary groups in influencing social perception. Such groups are "primary in several senses, but chiefly in that they are fundamental in forming the social nature and ideals of the individual" (Cooley, 1972, p. 301). Indeed, the process of interaction between the group and the individual and the effect of the social group on the experience and conduct of the individual member is at the heart of the theory (cf. Mead, 1956, p. 115). In the course of social interaction, experiences of interaction episodes are symbolized and internalized, and emerge as symbolic expectations that regulate future social interaction: we normally act by an individually internalized definition of the episode (Goffman, 1974). To the extent that individuals who occupy different positions in their group are exposed to different kinds of interactions, their perception of social episodes should also differ. The aim of this study was to demonstrate a significant relationship between two social structural variables (a member's formal status, and his sociometric position), and two social perception variables (his perception of the group and its social episodes) in an intact academic group.

The method adopted for demonstrating such a relationship was a fusion of symbolic interactionist approaches and multivariate statistical techniques. Theorists such as Blumer (1969) have always maintained that human group activity should be studied through the eyes and the experience of the participants. This proposition will be taken seriously here. Thus, this investigation is an attempt to represent the social episodes and structure of an intact group by quantitative descriptive techniques, using the group members' knowledge and understanding of their own social environment as the raw data.

In effect, an individual's cognitive representation of (a) other group members and (b) relevant social episodes will be the main objects of study. These representations can be thought of as constituting cognitive domains, consisting of "phenomenal objects which a person treats as functionally equivalent, and the attributes by which he comprehends these objects" (Scott, 1969, p. 262). It was expected that individual group members who differed in terms of their position in the group and in terms of their formal status, would have different representations of these two cognitive domains.

The method used to represent the episode space of the group was similar to that used in the previous studies, based on an MDS analysis of judgements of episodes.

The representation of a group's social structure can be achieved in several ways. Traditional sociometric techniques (Moreno, 1951; Bales, 1970; Clark, 1953) are based on the interpersonal preference choices of partners, usually in terms of preselected criteria, which at best represent only a small part of the complex web of relationships within the group. Jones and Young (1973) managed to substantially improve on this technique, by using a multidimensional scaling analysis of perceived group structure. According to them, every member of the group has an internal representation of all other members relative to each other and himself: "individuals in the social environment are perceived and responded to as multidimensional stimuli" (Jones and Young, 1973, p. 119). This method yielded a realistic and stable multidimensional representation of the group in geometric space. Davison and Jones (1976) successfully used a similar conceptualization of group structure to predict interpersonal attraction in an intact group. This approach was also adopted here.

The other sociometric variable to be considered here, formal status, can be defined (Linton, 1945, p. 77) as the position of an individual in the prestige system of his society. In the academic group studied here, status was readily established in terms of formal role categories, such as "faculty," "research students," and "other staff."

An *a priori* relationship between social position and social perception is difficult to predict without an intimate knowledge of the group. However, certain kinds of relationships are suggested by our theoretical framework. For example, an individual who is perceived as dominant and highly competent by the group may be more sensitive to shortcomings in others and therefore may be more evaluative and critical in his judgements of peers than are submissive individuals. These individuals may also be more selective and evaluative in their perception of social episodes, without being concerned with the anxiety-evoking potential of these episodes. In contrast, individuals who occupy low status positions in the group, or are otherwise negatively evaluated, may find its social episodes more difficult and restrictive and may be more sensitive to anxiety-evoking aspects of social episodes in their judgements. Each such relationship assumes that an individual's symbolic representation of the group and its episodes is a function of his unique interactive experience within the group, and that this experience in turn depends on his social position.

In summary, the aims of this study were to represent empirically (a) the social structure and (b) the social episodes of an intact academic group and to evaluate the relationship between these two variables. Formal status sub-groups such as faculty, students, and staff were expected to differ in their perception of the group and in their cognitive representation of its social episodes. Moreover a group member's sociometric position in the group was also expected to be related to his perception of the group and to his representation of the group's social episodes.

Method

GENERAL BACKGROUND

The group studied consisted of 16 members of a large psychology department at a British University, and included faculty members, postdoctoral researchers, visiting academics on sabbatical leave (faculty), research students of various standing (students), and research assistants and secretarial staff (staff). Each member had a permanent office in a clearly demarcated group area. Group members knew each other and interacted regularly for at least six months prior to the study both inside and outside the department. The group, according to most of its members, was an intensive and cohesive social unit that represented more than just a working environment. Before conducting the study, the cooperation of group members was obtained informally and the objectives and procedure of the study were outlined. All but one group member were willing to cooperate.

The study was carried out in two stages about three weeks apart. In the first stage, information about the social structure of the group was obtained, while in the second stage its social episodes were studied.

STAGE I—SOCIAL STRUCTURE

As a first step, the perceived sociometric structure of the group was established. Group members were asked to rate each other for perceived similarity, and these data were analysed by an INDSCAL procedure (Chapter 5). In addition to direct similarity ratings, group members also rated each other on a number of bipolar scales, selected as "relevant to describing members of the group" in the course of a separate study (Forgas *et. al.*, 1979a): The scales used are shown in Fig. 6. The resulting three-dimensional configuration was interpreted with the help of separately scaled bipolar property dimensions, yielding the following three attribute dimensions: *sociability* or friendliness, *creativity* and task and intellectual *competence*. These attributes are clearly relevant to an individual's perceived position in an academic group. Although these characteristics are quite similar to those emerging from other studies, it would be futile to seek an exact correspondence. It is more likely that "dimensions, though possibly related across groups in some abstract sense, reflect psychological factors peculiar to the particular group studied" (Davison and Jones, 1976, p. 607). The

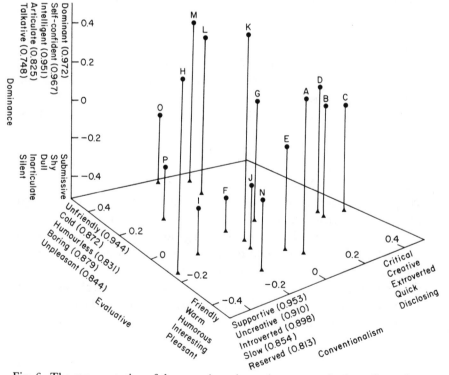

Fig. 6. The representation of the group's sociometric structure in three dimensions, showing the bipolar scales used in labelling the INDSCAL dimensions. (A−E = faculty members; F−M = research students; N−P =staff.)

perceived structure of the group, as it would be seen by a hypothetical "average" member is shown in Fig. 6.

It is interesting that neither status, nor political persuasion were salient dimensions along which group members could be descriminated, as found, for example, by Jones and Young (1973) in an American academic group. It is probable that status differences were more subtle and politics less important in this group than in the group studied by them. In particular, an additional multiple discriminant analysis indicated that the three formal status sub-groups, faculty, staff and students were significantly differentiated when all three-dimensions of the INDSCAL sociometric structure are considered in conjunction (Table 6). However, differences between members of these sub-groups in their perception of the sociometric structure failed to reach significance. Thus, there appeared to be considerable agreement and unanimity in the cognitive representations faculty, staff and students had of the group. This was somewhat unexpected, and may again indicate that the crude subdivision of the group into faculty, staff and students may not have tapped the most salient status differences among members. Sociometric position may offer a more sensitive measure of individual differences, which is more likely to be related to an individual's perception of the group.

SOCIOMETRIC POSITION AND THE PERCEPTION OF THE GROUP

The relationship between an individual's sociometric position in the group (his stimulus coordinates) and his style of judging the group (his subject weights) was analysed by a canonical correlation analysis of these two vector variables. Two significant canonical factors ($R_{c1}=0.789$; $R_{c2}=0.421$) accounted for most of the variance between these two sets of variables. In particular, the *competence* dimension in the group structure and the *sociability* dimension in the subject space were found to be related ($r=0.71$, $P<0.01$). Individuals seen as highly competent and dominant apparently relied more on the sociability dimension in their judgements of others than did persons seen as incompetent and submissive. Since our competence dimension also reflects dominance and intelligence (Fig. 6), it is perhaps not surprising that dominant individuals are more evaluative and critical in their judgements of others. Social competence in particular is an important component of this dimension (self-confidence, articulateness, talkativeness), while social skills are strongly reflected in the sociability dimension (interesting, humorous, pleasant). It may be that persons who are themselves socially competent tend to weight social skills higher in differentiating among others than do persons who are low in social competence.

The second significant canonical factor indicated a relationship between an individual's position on the *creativity* dimension and his reliance on this same dimension to evaluate others ($r = -0.68, P < 0.01$). Individuals seen as uncreative found this dimension of low salience, while creative group members relied more on this dimension in their judgements. Since our creativity dimension also strongly reflected interpersonal style (extroversion, being critical, and disclosing), this result also shows that disclosing and extroverted group members found similar characteristics salient in others. Those who were seen as introverted, reserved, etc., perhaps not surprisingly, relied less on this dimension.

The preceding analyses therefore support the existence of a relationship between social position and perception: although formal status was not related to the perception of the group, sociometric position significantly affected a member's perception of the group.

STAGE II—SOCIAL EPISODES

Having thus established a reliable and quantitative representation of the perceived sociometric structure of the group, the next task was to represent the perception of social episodes by the group as a whole, and by each individual member separately.

The episodes to be studied were selected on the basis of a series of informal discussions with group members, who were asked to list all the typical and characteristic interaction situations which occurred within the group. Participant observation of group activities helped to validate the episodes so derived. The most commonly mentioned 17 episodes shown in Table 5 were used as stimuli. Judgments of these episodes were obtained in the form of ratings on bipolar scales, which were subsequently converted into dissimilarity matrices using the procedure outlined in Chapter 5. The rating scales themselves were specially constructed to be situation, object and subject-relevant (Beach and Wertheimer, 1961), and included the following adjective pairs: cooperative–competitive; formal–informal; ill at ease in this

TABLE 5
List of the 17 social episodes used as stimuli in the study

1. Discussing your work/research with another member of the group	10. Having lunch and chatting at lunchtime in somebody's office
2. Monday morning informal group meetings at coffee	11. Being a guest at your supervisor's house for drinks
3. Closed research seminars with only group members present	12. Going on a picnic with the group
	13. Having coffee break on the concourse
4. Going out with group members to have lunch at somebody's college	14. At a dinner party at one of the group member's house
5. Having a meeting/supervision with your supervisor	15. Going to the general office to get/arrange something
6. Assisting to run a laboratory class	16. At a party at somebody else's house
7. Reunion meetings or seminars with old members of the group	17. Going to the Graduate Club for lunch with some members of the group
8. Going to the pub on Friday night after a seminar	
9. Giving tutorials to undergraduates	

Source: Forgas, 1978a, p. 438.

situation—not ill at ease; socio-emotional—task oriented; intimate—non-intimate; simple—complex; involved—uninvolved; tense—relaxed; flexible—rigid; pleasant—unpleasant; interesting—boring. (Similar dimensions were reported by Forgas (1976a), Magnusson (1971), and Wish (1975) in their studies of episode perception.)

These data were again analysed by the INDSCAL method. The social interaction episodes of this group could be best represented in terms of four perceptual dimensions. The fourth dimension accounted for a 10% increase in the variance over three dimensions, while a fifth dimension contributed only an additional 4%. The four-dimensional solution, accounting for 62% of the variance, was thus both sufficient and necessary to represent these social episodes adequately.

This episode space, shown in Fig. 7, essentially represents how a hypothetical "average" group member could see the characteristic interactions of the group and the attributes differentiating them. The first dimension, *anxiety*, differentiated self-confident and relaxed encounters (e.g. going to the pub and at a party) from more formal and threatening ones (e.g. meeting with supervisor, running a class). This dimension was closely related to bipolar scales, such as tense—relaxed, at ease—ill at ease, and formal—informal (Fig. 7). The second dimension, *involvement*, reflected the judges' perception of the perceived intensity or superficiality of the episodes, separating simple, uninvolved encounters (e.g. morning coffee) from complex, involved episodes (e.g. discussing work, seminars). The third dimension was *evaluative*, differentiating between pleasant and interesting social occasions, such as parties, and boring and unpleasant episodes, such as arranging things

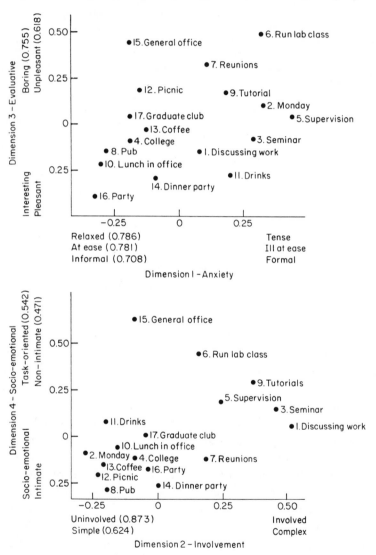

Fig. 7. The representation of the group's social episodes in four dimensions, showing the bipolar scales used to label the INDSCAL dimensions.

at the general office, or running a lab class (!). The fourth dimension separated *socio-emotional* and intimate kinds of episodes from task-orientated and non-intimate situations. These four attribute dimensions are quite similar to those found in some previous studies, and further strengthen the impression that the classification of social episodes in terms of a small number of connotative attribute dimensions is a feasible task. It appears that groups from widely differing social environments (American, Swedish, and English students, English housewives and academics) nevertheless tend to perceive social episodes in terms of a limited number of connotative attribute dimensions, such as self-confidence or anxiety, involvement, intimacy, friendliness, and evaluation. Any subcultural differences between the groups studied seem most likely to affect (a) the number of dimensions necessary to represent the episode space and (b) the relative importance attached to similar dimensions by different groups.

Despite these similarities between the present study and its predecessors, the subculture and even group-specificity of these implicit cognitive dimensions cannot be overlooked. For example, the perceptual dimensions used by a group of housewives and students (Forgas, 1976a) and the present group reflect their different social milieux. Thus, the representation of the present group is more complex (four as against three and two dimensions for students and housewives, respectively). The *anxiety* dimension was more important to this group, perhaps reflecting the more competitive atmosphere of an academic environment. The differentiation of episodes in terms of task-orientation, a dimension not used by the other groups, is again characteristic of a permanent working environment. Important features of the social environment are thus once again directly reflected in the perception of the episode space. Beyond the intrinsic interest of representing the hypothetical average individual's view of the group's interactions, which in the present case closely reflects the characteristics of a functioning academic group, the main interest of this study was the evaluation of individual differences in such perceptions.

Do faculty, staff and students have a different way of perceiving the same sample of episodes? In terms of the characteristics of the INDSCAL model, such differences would be revealed in the dimension weights for individual judges, which in effect indicate the relative salience, or importance of a particular attribute of episodes to a particular individual. A multiple discriminant analysis of subject weights

TABLE 6

Differences between formal status sub-groups in terms of (a) their sociometric position in the group, (b) their perception of the group, and (c) their perception of the group's social episodes

Formal status groups	(Multiple discriminant analysis) Mean dimension weights				Classified as			Significance
	Dim. 1	Dim. 2	Dim. 3	Dim. 4	Faculty	Students	Staff	
(a) Position in the group								
	Evaluative	Conventionalism	Dominance					
1. Faculty (N=5)	-0.161	0.272	0.048	—	5	0	0	$D^2 = 40.49$
2. Research students (N=8)	0.037	-0.099	0.039	—	0	6	2	d.f. = 6
3. Staff (N=3)	0.169	-0.147	-0.186	—	0	1	2	$P < 0.001$
(b) Perception of the group								
	Evaluation	Conventionalism	Dominance					
1. Faculty (N=5)	0.491	0.246	0.232	—	4	0	1	
2. Research students (N=6)	0.370	0.371	0.334	—	0	4	2	NS
3. Staff (N=3)	0.341	0.389	0.363	—	0	1	2	
(c) Perception of social episodes								
	Anxiety	Involvement	Evaluative	Task orient				
1. Faculty (N=5)	0.153	0.376	0.258	0.184	4	1	0	$D^2 = 26.83$
2. Research students (N=7)	0.252	0.293	0.185	0.344	0	6	1	d.f. = 8
3. Staff (N=3)	0.414	0.258	0.268	0.129	0	1	2	$P < 0.01$

Source: Forgas, 1978, p. 441.

for members of these three status sub-groups showed that significant differences in perceptual style existed between faculty, staff and students (Table 6). It was found that faculty members placed more emphasis on the involvement dimension in their judgements of episodes; students differentiated between episodes mainly in terms of the socio-emotional v. task-oriented dimension, while other staff members relied most on the anxiety dimension in their perception of episodes (Fig. 8). These differences can perhaps be best explained in terms of the different social experiences of these status subgroups. Anxiety was a salient attribute for staff, but not for faculty, reflecting probably the different social skills and experiences of these two groups. Faculty were most likely to be engaged in formal, but non-involving episodes, and involvement was thus an important dimension for them. Students were more sensitive to the work or purely social character of interaction situations, which is again a distinction which could be expected to be functionally salient to this group (Tajfel, 1969).

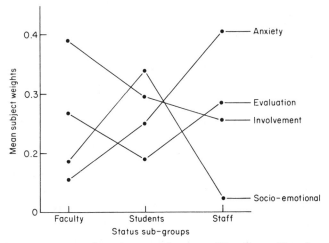

Fig. 8. Differences between formal status sub-groups (Faculty, staff, students) in their perception of social episodes: mean dimensions weights for each status sub-group on each of four episode dimensions.

Since individuals belonging to different status categories were thus found to perceive social episodes differently, the next question was to find out whether informal differences, that is, an individual's position in the perceived sociometric structure of the group, were also related to episode perception. Are episodes perceived differently by sociable as against unsociable, creative as against uncreative, or competent as against incompetent individuals—in other words, individuals who occupy different positions on the attribute dimensions which define the sociometric structure of the group (Fig. 6)?

To explore the relationship between an individual's sociometric position in the perceived group structure and his perception of social episodes, a canonical correlation analysis of the judges' coordinates on the INDSCAL dimensions of the group structure and their subject weights on the episode dimensions was performed. This analysis indicated an overall significant relationship between these two groups of variables (R_{c1} =0·922; R_{c2} =0·517), thus suggesting that sociometric position and episode perception were indeed related. Specifically, group members seen as unsociable relied more on the *anxiety* (r = −0·669, P <0·01) and *evaluative* (r = −0·562) dimensions in their judgements of episodes than did group members judged to be sociable. For competent group members, the *anxiety* (r = −0·687, P <0·01) and *socio-emotional* (r = −0·519, P <0·05) episode dimensions were of little importance, and the *evaluative* (r =0·525, P <0·05) episode dimension was more salient, than for group members who were not seen as competent. Position on the *creativity* dimension in the group was not directly related to episode perception. Thus, group members who are seen as friendly, warm, humorous, interesting, and pleasant, in other words, sociable (Fig. 6), tend not to discriminate between social episodes in terms of whether they are tense or relaxed, ill at ease or not, formal or informal, pleasant or unpleasant, and interesting or uninteresting (*anxiety* and *evaluative* dimensions Fig. 7). In other words, persons seen as sociable are presumably also more socially skilled, and therefore less concerned with the anxiety or evaluative attributes in their perception of social episodes. Conversely, individuals judged to be unsociable by the group (i.e. cold, unfriendly, etc.) are likely to have experienced more negative outcomes in their interactions with others, and are therefore more sensitized to the anxiety and unpleasantness of the social episodes in which they participate.

Persons perceived as high in social and task competence (dominant, self-confident, intelligent, articulate, and talkative—the *competence* dimension in Fig. 7) are more critical and tend to differentiate between social episodes in terms of evaluation (pleasantness). This same group of people also tended to use more evaluative criteria in their judgements of other group members. On the other hand, individuals perceived as highly competent did not rely on the anxiety and socio-emotional dimensions in their judgements of social episodes.

These findings are not only intuitively satisfying, but also confirm the general predictions of symbolic interactionist theory. In the course of their everyday contacts with other group members, individuals create an impression, or social persona, in others, and this is reflected in how others perceive them in the multi-dimensional group structure. In the course of the same interactions, however, they also symbolize their own experiences, and this is reflected in the dimensions they find salient in their cognitive representations of social episodes. The demonstration of a quantitative relationship between these two sets of variables thus suggests that one source of individual differences in episode perception is the differential social and interactive experience of the judges.

The present study was thus successful in empirically demonstrating a relationship between an individual's formal and informal position in his immediate group on the one hand, and his perception of the group and its episodes on the other. Symbolic interactionists have always maintained that in order to understand social behaviour, we must take into consideration an individual's internal symbolic representation of the relevant social situation and its requirements. These symbolic representations of situations, in turn, were thought to arise out of the collective cultural experience of the group and the position of the individual within it. The empirical demonstration of exactly such a connection in the present study, albeit in a limited context, is clearly congruent with the postulates of this theory.

However, there are many other individual variables which could be worthy of investigation. Considering that this area of research is extremely new, one can only hint at the possibilities, without being able to cite empirical evidence. Demographic variables, such as age, sex, socio-economic status, education or income can all be relevant in differentiating between individuals in terms of how they perceive social episodes. Personality characteristics and attitudes are another group of potentially important variables. In a recently completed study, Forgas et al. (1979b) studied the perception of violent episodes in a student sample. Amongst other things, it was found that the judges' age, sex and social attitudes were significantly related to the way they perceived aggressive incidents. The present study can thus be regarded as a pointer towards the new kind of research that becomes possible once an empirical quantification of how social episodes are perceived is realized. The numerous variables which affect episode perception can now be investigated and this is the topic of the next chapter.

Summary

Of the four research strategies applicable to the study of social episodes (Chapter 5), research on the perception of social episodes has been the most active in recent years. Numerous investigators, some of whom were not directly interested in social episodes, have shown that the empirical representation of how routine interactions are cognitively represented is quite possible. It is also remarkable that the techniques used to achieve this were quite similiar, multidimensional scaling being one of the most suitable such methods. The third important conclusion which can be drawn on the basis of this research is that the cognitive representation of social episodes strongly reflects an individual's feelings about, and affective reactions to an interaction, and not necessarily the objective features of the episode. As we have seen earlier, both in psychology (Chapter 3) and in sociology (Chapter 4) such subjective definitions of situations are increasingly accepted on conceptual grounds. It is notable that empirical research has now supported this approach.

Contrary to some earlier apprehensions it was found that the number of social episodes of which people have a direct knowledge is quite manageable. Even more surprising is the recurrent finding that a few connotative attribute dimensions, such as social anxiety, intimacy, involvement and task-orientation tend to emerge as the common dimensions differentiating episodes in widely differing samples. Studies to be discussed in the next chapter further confirm this impression, suggesting that the most salient features of episodes may well be described by their location parameters along a few such dimensions.

New research, summarized in the last sections of this chapter, has also established that the cognitive representation of episode domains is highly sensitive to subcultural, group, and individual differences. The exploration of the variables which have an effect on episode perception is the next task, and some early work in this area will be considered in the next chapter.

8

Elements of Episode Perception

Having demonstrated that the empirical representation of episode domains is not only feasible, but that such representations reliably reflect subcultural, group and individual differences, this chapter will look at some of the factors which influence such representations. In a sense, the studies discussed in the previous chapter have already shown the importance of generic social and cultural factors, and the individual's interactive experience to the cognitive representation of social episodes. The present chapter seeks to further elaborate some of those variables which have an influence on episode perception.

Episodes, as symbolic representations of routine interaction sequences, are made up of a multiplicity of information cues. Idiosyncratic differences between perceivers, the overall constraint embedded in episodes, the role relationship between the interaction partners, the physical environment, as well as non-verbal behaviour are all cues which may affect episode perception. Since the study of situations and episodes is a new field, we do not as yet have any systematic model of the variables which play a role in episode perception. The material to be covered in this chapter inevitably suffers from too little integration. But each of the studies to be considered here has contributed to our understanding of the complex factors which ultimately influence our internal representation of social episodes.

First of all, factors inherent in the perceiver himself need to be considered—we have all developed more or less idiosyncratic ways of viewing the world and our interactions within it. Just as our implicit theories of personality influence how we see other people (Rosenberg and Sedlak, 1972), it is likely that individuals develop implicit theories of social episodes. Pervin's work on the perception of social situations is a nice illustration of how such idiosyncratic differences can be analysed and related to the perceiver's life circumstances.

Idiographic studies of episode perception

Pervin was amongst the chief contributors to the controversy in personality theory regarding personological as against situational factors
in behaviour. He has consistently taken an interactionist stance, and
has argued for a conception of the situation or environment as perceived by the actor (Pervin, 1968). He has also strongly espoused
Brunswik's (1956) compelling, and yet generally disregarded arguments for a "representative design" in psychological research—a design which would place just as much emphasis on sampling a representative range of the individual's normal life environment as on sampling
subjects. The study of perceptions of social situations was an inevitable
corollary to such an approach. As Pervin pointed out, "we know little
about the dimensions people use to perceive and organise situations or
about the process of person–situation interaction" (1976, p. 465). The
approach adopted by him to accomplish such a task differs in one
significant way from similar approaches: he chose to study individuals
rather than cultural groups. He argued that "the personality of each
individual could be understood in terms of the patterns and stability
of change in feelings and behaviours in relation to a defined group of
situations . . . this approach might serve as the basis for the future
development of a taxonomy of situations and behaviours in situations"
(1975b, p. 1).

The subjects studied were thus treated as unique individuals, rather
than as representatives of specified groups. The methodology employed required subjects, firstly, to list a number of situations characteristic of their everyday life. In the second step, they were asked to
describe each situation in terms of adjectives or traits, to indicate how
they *feel* in each one of the situations, and to describe their *behaviours*
in each situation. As a result of these four steps, four lists for each
subject were generated: situations, situation characteristics, feelings in
situations and behaviours in situations. In the final step, subjects were
asked to indicate the applicability of each of the above categories to
each of the situations listed. These data were analysed individually for
each subject, by means of a series of factor-analyses of the situations,
based on the different categories of data collected about them.

The results of this study were quite unexpected. Firstly, it was found
that the number of situations listed by each subject was fairly similar,
falling between 23 and 29. These situations were clustered into four or

five homogeneous categories, such as Home–Family, Friends–Peers, Relaxation–Recreation, Work, School, Alone. While these categories appear to reflect the objective characteristics of the situations, closer scrutiny of individual perceptual patterns indicated that a subject's subjective reaction to different situations was in fact very important. For one subject, the situations were discriminated along the following dimensions: warm, supportive v. cold, rejecting; tense, threatening v. relaxed, calm; interesting, stimulating v. dull, boring; constraining v. free (Pervin, 1975a, p. 18). Descriptions of situations in particular were heavily weighted towards affective components: "What is striking is the extent to which situations are described in terms of affects (e.g. threatening, warm, interesting, dull, tense, calm, rejecting) and organized in terms of similarity of affects aroused by them" (Pervin, 1976, p. 471). This conclusion has been reached by many other studies, and it strongly suggests that affective reactions, in terms of connotative rather than denotative characteristics, underlie the perception of social episodes and situations (Osgood et al., 1957; Mehrabrian and Russell, 1974). However, the most striking aspect of Pervin's study is that it focuses on idiosyncratic differences rather than communalities in episode perception. We all too often disregard unique individuals for the sake of studying abstract, general processes of social behaviour (Chapter 2). Of the few studies of social episodes carried out so far, Pervin's work is the only one relying on idiographic rather than nomothetic methods. It is for this reason that his work was presented at the beginning of this chapter. Whatever general factors in episode perception will be demonstrated by later studies, the perceiving individual is the prime creator of his world of social episodes, and as such, the most important "variable" in episode perception. Perhaps a closer look at the episodes which were important for one of Pervin's subjects may better illustrate the potential of this method (Table 1). An inspection of this table indicates not only that it was possible to determine empirically the clustering of the life situations by a particular individual, but also that the grouping of the situations, the terms used to describe them, and the behaviours performed in them reflect the unique individual experiences of the person studied. The further development of such idiographic methods, using more sophisticated analytic techniques, appears most promising in its clinical applications. Since the number of social episodes experienced and listed by any individual is quite manageable, and since such episodes are discriminated mainly

TABLE 1

Two examples of Pervin's (1976) analyses of situation perception

(a) Illustrative results from the factor analysis of Jennifer's ratings of situation characteristics ($n=64$), feelings ($n=62$), and behaviours ($n=59$) for 23 situations

Factor (% variance)	Illustrative situations	Situation traits	Feelings	Behaviours
Home—Volatile (35%)	mother blows up at me honest with parents about leaving mother refuses gift someone else comes home upset	emotional, angry, volatile, excitable	angry, pressured, involved, insecure, unhappy	sensitive, concerned, caring, suppressed, confused, not compulsive
School Work—Pressure to Perform (18%)	have to participate in class have to perform at work do the job wrong at work in a strange place	demanding, threatening, pressuring, awkward, challenging, embarrassing, unconcerned	self-conscious, challenged, vulnerable, awkward, pressured, anxious	self-conscious, controlled, ambitious, determined, compulsive, cool, responsible, diligent, non-rebellious
Friends, Alone (6%)	with friend—no problem with friend—problem alone	emotional, gentle, friendly, generous	caring, concerned, comfortable, melancholy, sad	concerned, caring, emotional, involved, insightful, responsive
Uncertain (5%)	come home from Philadelphia in a crowd taking the bus to class want to leave to go to Philadelphia in a strange place	ambiguous, non-defined uncertain, unconcerned, ignoring	bottled-up, melancholy, sad, lonely, frustrated, confused	preoccupied, detached, quiet, self-conscious, controlled, cool, introverted

Factor (% variance)	Illustrative situations	Situation traits	Feelings	Behaviours
Home–Family (35%)	talking with parents eating dinner with wife visiting my in-laws talking with wife	warm, caring, friendly, relaxed, inviting	affectionate, warm, secure, caring	caring, warm, affectionate, easygoing, emotional, pleasant, warm, open
Work–School (18%)	talking with patients at the clinic having lunch with patients and staff tutoring kids with problems participating in staff seminar seminar at school	thought-provoking, interesting, challenging, stimulating	challenged, curious, actualizing, interested, fascinated	curious, extroverted, warm, friendly, questioning
Private Recreation (8%)	reading for pleasure going to museum in New York shopping in New York	diverse, stimulating, enjoyable, spontaneous, fun	excited, pleasure-seeking, without a care in the world, stimulated, uninhibited	relaxed, intelligent, elated, awed, curious
Tension (5%)	driving alone in bad weather arguing with my wife talking with patients who are acting out	frustrating, threatening, intense, tense, anxiety-producing	nervous, tense, anxious, under pressure, displeased, depressed	frustrated, anxious, angry, emotional
Friends and Public Reaction (3%)	drinking in Mike's Bar joking with friend Pete relaxing in Jack's apartment talking with friends in the snack bar at school drinking in a New York bar	innocuous, tolerant, permissive, pleasant	friendly, easygoing, exhibitionistic, bored	flashy, extroverted, friendly, sociable, exhibitionistic

Source: Pervin, 1976, pp. 467–468.

in terms of subjective, affective reactions, it is possible that such attribute dimensions of social situations may contain important diagnostic information about an individual's life circumstances, social relations, and history of social interactions. Pervin himself maintains that "it seems likely that most of the situations encountered by an individual could be conveniently classified into one of a relatively small number of categories" (1975b, p. 8). Furthermore, those categories are likely to be variable across individuals, although perhaps still reflecting a finite cultural repertoire of episodes available. If we want to understand why a particular individual differentiates among social episodes in the way he does, we should begin by looking at his unique life environment, by sampling his "representative" situations. The most important factors affecting episode perception are likely to reside in the perceiving individual. Much work remains to be done—in particular, the relationship between episode perception styles and other personality variables needs to be explored (Chapter 9).

Having briefly looked at the perceiver, factors affecting episode perception which are external to the individual will be considered. The restrictiveness of social episodes is perhaps the most pervasive such variable.

Perceived constraint of social episodes

An important global variable which commonly influences episode perception is the social constraint embedded in different episodes. Price's work has already been mentioned in previous chapters. The main thrust of this research is towards discovering the restrictiveness of different kinds of situations, based on subjects' ratings of the appropriateness of a number of behaviours in a range of situations. Some situations are such that only a very few, or perhaps only one, behaviour was seen as appropriate in them (Price and Bouffard, 1974). On the other hand, other situations are compatible with a very wide range of behaviours. By summarizing the appropriateness ratings of all the behaviours studied over a particular situation, it is possible to calculate an index of constraint or restrictiveness. This is an interesting construct, since there is quite a bit of evidence already indicating that one of the main properties of social situations and episodes is the extent to which they are seen as anxiety-evoking. The constraint implied by a particular situational definition can in turn be expected to be related to such anxiety reactions. Even more important, however, is the fact that several of the new approaches to the study of social episodes discussed here place particular emphasis on the study of social rules and rule systems as the key to understanding social behaviour. The constraint index calculated by Price and Bouffard (1974) is probably related to the extent to which social rules and conventions are present in a particular social situation. Thus, according to their results, situations which are private are the least governed by social rules. Sitting at home in one's own bedroom is compatible with an extremely wide range of permissible behaviours, limited perhaps only by physical and physiological, but not social restraints. In public situations, on the other hand, there is always some element of social convention and restraint present. For example, riding in a bus or walking on the street are still fairly loosely-defined activities, yet there are many things which one could do at home but would not be allowed to do in these situations. At the far extreme we find highly formalized and ritualized social situations, such as dinner parties, ceremonies such as weddings, or explicitly regulated games. Such situations are characterized by a very high degree of conventional regulation. Price and Bouffard's (1974) approach, although not primarily concerned with the kinds of issues outlined above, offers a feasible methodology for quantifying and operationalizing such variables.

Clearly, the perceptual approach is not the only feasible one to be used in studying constraint. One could seek to construct a constraint index by establishing the extent of rule restraint in different situations by other, empirical methods; this could be the intentional breakage of rules, the performance of a standardized set of behaviours in a range of situations and the observance of the proportion of them which is considered rule-breaking, and so on. There is some scope for further developing the unidimensional constraint index proposed by Price and Bouffard (1974) into a more sophisticated, multidimensional measure, which could take into account several aspects of restrictiveness.

In a subsequent study, Price (1974) further elaborated on his initial method, by seeking to find out whether "subsets or classes of behaviours can be discovered which are uniquely appropriate in certain subsets or classes of situations" (1974, p. 569). This is indeed a very interesting problem, since it entails not only the classification of situations, but also the classification of behaviours. This latter task is a particularly difficult one, especially if one considers that the perceived

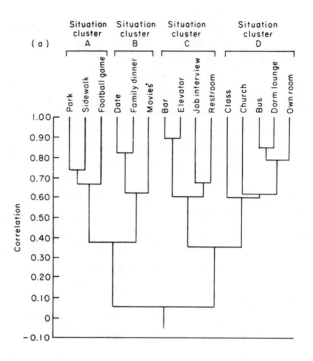

(a)

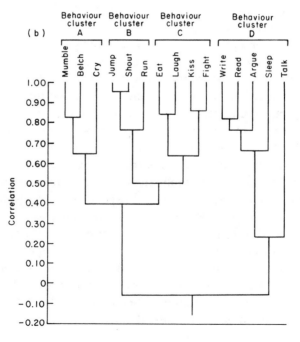

(b)

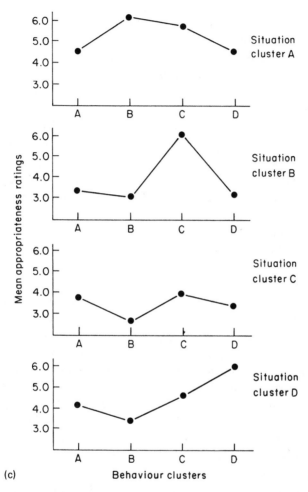

Fig. 1. Results of the cluster-analysis of (a) situations and (b) behaviours, and an analysis of the relationship between clusters of behaviours and different clusters of situations.

(a) Dendogram of the cluster-analysis of situations.
(b) Dendogram of the cluster-analysis of behaviours.
(c) Cluster profiles of situation clusters plotted in terms of behaviour clusters.
Source: Price, 1974.

relationship between behaviours is inevitably context or situation dependent. The method used was essentially similar to that developed in the previous study. Fifty-two students were asked to rate on a scale from 0–9 the appropriateness of 15 behaviours (run, talk, kiss, shout, belch, etc.) in each of 15 situations (e.g. in church, on a date, on a bus, etc.). The 15 behaviours and 15 situations were selected from self-report activity diaries kept by a pilot sample of 15 students. The results were analysed by a cluster-analytic procedure, resulting in four behaviour clusters and four situation clusters. Next, the mean appropriateness ratings of each of the four clusters of behaviours in each of the four clusters of situations were calculated. (For the dendrogram of situation and behaviour clusters, see Fig. 1.) The results presented in the figure above clearly show that clusters of behaviours were found to be uniquely appropriate in particular clusters of situations. For example, behaviours such as eat, laugh, kiss and fight are most appropriate in intimate-friendly situations, such as date, family dinner or at the movies; on the other hand, in superficial or formal public situations (bar, elevator, job interview, restroom) nearly all behaviour clusters are reasonably appropriate, but none highly appropriate. Thus it appears that some kinds of situations may not be marked by any unique group of behaviours. Obviously, Price's study does not in itself provide conclusive evidence for any of these relationships. The general approach, however, appears to be highly promising. Price tends to interpret his findings primarily in terms of the person v. situation issue, suggesting that "at least a portion of the variance associated with the behaviour × situation interactions in these studies reflect lawful relationships between certain classes of situations and the behaviours either demanded or prohibited by those situations" (p. 581). The taxonomy of situations obtained in this study is based on perceptions of the appropriateness of behaviours, and not on judgements of the situations *per se*; it is all the more interesting that the kind of situation clusters constructed were highly similar to taxonomic categories derived in other studies. Despite the small scale and lack of generalizability of these results, they are important because they demonstrate the feasibility of a uniform taxonomy of episodes and situations, and offer a quantitative method whereby constraint, or the presence of rules in a situation can be established. It may well be that constraint, or restrictiveness, will emerge as one of the most important objective characteristics of social situations which affects our perception of them.

Role relationships and episode perception

There is a lot of similarity between the concept of roles, embodying sets of expected behaviours from occupiers of given social positions, and the concept of social episodes which refer to accepted scripts of interaction in specified situations. Terms such as role expectations, role performance, role conflict and role interpretation, developed in role theory, have their exact counterparts in the analysis of social episodes (Chapter 1). Beyond this similarity, the most important difference is that episodes are more inclusive units than roles, indeed particular role relationships have an important function in defining an episode and influencing our perception of it. A casual conversation between shopkeeper and customer or husband and wife are entirely different episodes. If one wants to analyse the variables which affect episode perception, the role relationship between the interactants is clearly one of the most important factors to be considered. Perceptions of role relationships have not been extensively studied in social psychology, except for the recent work by Myron Wish and his co-workers at the Bell Laboratories. The project sought to measure and quantify the human element in communication, people's perceptions of the relationship between different categories of communicators (e.g. supervisor–employee), and their conceptualization of the situational context in which communication occurs. Both of these objectives are relevant to our present interest in social episodes: the perception of the role relationship between the participants in a social episode is clearly a crucial component of the definition of that episode.

The main contribution of the research programme is methodological. The studies carried out by Wish and his associates were among the first to use multidimensional scaling (MDS) techniques for the analysis of perceptions of such complex cognitive objects as role relationships or communication episodes.

A study of perceptions of interpersonal relationships (in effect, stereotypical role-relationship labels) was carried out by Wish et al. (1976). In this study, college students were asked to judge the overall perceived similarity between interpersonal relations, such as husband–wife, parent and teenager, lawyer and client, supervisor and employee, taking into account the ways such partners "typically think and feel about each other, act and react towards each other, and talk and listen to each other". This procedure allowed subjects to indicate any implicitly perceived differences between the relationship labels, one of the major advantages of the MDS method. These similarity matrices were analysed by the INDSCAL procedure, described in previous chapters, and the stimulus axes were interpreted with the help of independently scaled bipolar dimensions. Four dimensions were found to underlie perceptions of interpersonal relations. The first dimension differentiated competitive and hostile relations (e.g. political opponents) from cooperative and friendly relations. The second dimension separated relations where power is equally shared (e.g. siblings) from relations where power was unequal (teacher and pupil).

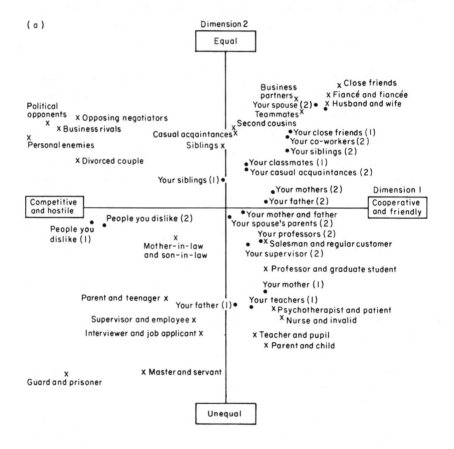

x Denotes a typical dyadic relation between the designated individuals.

• Denotes a relation between the subject and the designated individual.
  The subject's childhood relations are indicated by a (1), while the
  subject's current relations are indicated by a (2).

Task-related and formal relations (interviewer and job applicant) and familial relations (parent and child) were defined by the third dimension, while the fourth dimension reflected the perceived intensity of different role relationships (e.g. husband and wife against casual acquaintances) (Fig. 2).

These perceptual dimensions are not unlike the episode perception dimensions found in several other studies, suggesting that the personal relationships inherent in different episode definition labels are an important component of the overall perception of that episode. An interesting aspect of this study was that differences between different

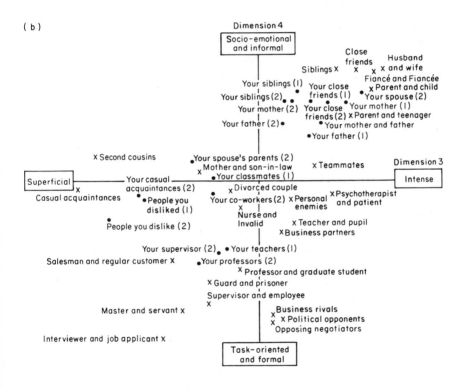

X Denotes a typical dyadic relation between the designated individuals.

● Denotes a relation between the subject and the designated individual.
The subject's childhood relations are indicated by a (I), while the
subject s current relations are indicated by a (2).

Fig. 2. The four-dimensional INDSCAL solution for 25 "typical" and 25 "own" role relations. (a) Dimensions 1 v. 2 (b) Dimensions 3 v. 4 Source: Wish *et al.*, 1976.

groups of judges, in terms of the salience they attributed to different stimulus dimensions, were also evaluated. While these differences were fairly predictable (e.g. left-oriented students and students doing arts courses attributed more importance to the equal–unequal dimension than right-wingers and students studying marketing), the method of analysis, using subject weights calculated by INDSCAL, points to the general applicability of this strategy for studying individual differences in episode perception.

In a related study, perceptions of complete communication episodes rather than dyadic relations only, were studied (Wish, 1975c). This study is particularly interesting from our point of view, since it sought to assess the relative importance of two episode definition cues: the relationship between the interactants, and the definition of the situation context, on judgements of complete episodes made up of factorial combinations of these cues. Eight situational contexts (e.g. attempting to work out a compromise, talking at a large social gathering, discussing controversial social issues, etc.) were combined with 16 dyadic relation labels (e.g. husband and wife, etc.) resulting in 128 complete episode labels. Eight of the dyadic relations referred to stereotypical role relations, and eight relation labels involved the subject as one of the interactants (e.g. you and your spouse, your best friend, your enemy, etc.). Judges were asked to rate each of the composite episode descriptions on 14 *ad hoc* bipolar scales, such as cooperative–competitive, friendly–hostile, etc. The similarity matrices required as input to MDS were derived from these bipolar scale ratings indirectly, using the root-mean-square differences between all subjects' judgements of two stimuli on a given scale as an index of similarity (see discussion and formula in Chapter 5).

The interpretation of the five-dimensional representation of these combined episode labels was based on the dimension weights for individual bipolar scales. The first dimension again separated cooperative and friendly episodes from competitive and unfriendly ones (e.g. you and your spouse pooling knowledge to solve problem v. bitter enemies blaming each other for a serious error). The second dimension differentiates intense episodes (e.g. husband and wife blaming one another for serious error) from superficial ones, such as casual acquaintances having a brief exchange. Equal and symmetric episodes (you and your spouse talking at a social gathering) and unequal and asymmetric episodes (master and servant working together, with one directing the other) were differentiated by the third dimension, equality. The fourth dimension was labelled formal v. informal, and finally, the fifth dimension differentiated task-oriented episodes from non-task-oriented ones.

These dimensions are quite compatible with those found in the first study. However, the most interesting feature of the present study was that the relative contribution of the two episode definition cues (interpersonal relationship, and situational context) to the positioning of combined episode labels on each of the five INDSCAL dimensions were also analysed, using an ingenious application of the analysis of variance technique. Thus, the eight situation contexts and 16 interpersonal relations can be regarded as the two independent variables (factors), and the coordinates of the episodes on each of the five INDSCAL dimensions as the dependent variables. (In order to obtain an estimate of the error variance, replications of the values in each cell were obtained by running a series of separate INDSCAL analyses for sub-groups of judges.) The relative contribution, in terms of variance accounted for, of the two variables included in each episode vignette relationship and situational context, is shown in Table 2. As the results summarized in Table 2 clearly show, certain characteristics of an episode, such as task-orientation, cooperation and intensity are mainly dependent on the situation context, while equality and formality are mainly defined by the relationship between the partners. It is interesting that when one of the interactants involved in the episode is the judge himself, he will judge equality and formality as more dependent on the relationship than when the interactants are others, described by abstract role categories. The interaction between relationship and situational cues was also significant in most cases, although accounting for a much smaller percentage of the variance. The interaction of these two cues is nicely illustrated by the positioning of individual episode labels. For example, on the cooperative–competitive dimension, a husband and wife dyad was seen as more strongly cooperative when the situation requires cooperation, and more strongly competitive when the situation demands competition, than casual acquaintances.

This study is thus particularly worthy of attention, not only because of the ingenious use of sophisticated data-analytic techniques, but also because of the substantive findings it reports. The dimensions defining the episode space are meaningful and enable us to quantify important characteristics of the episodes. The relative weights of relationship cues and situational cues in episode perception are also interesting, although with different groups of judges and different kinds of episodes, quite different findings may be obtained (see next study by Forgas, 1978, unpublished data).

TABLE 2

The contribution of the interpersonal relationship and the situation context to perceptions of communication episodes—analyses of variance (role relations)

Effects	Variance accounted for	SS	d.f.	MS	F
Dim. 1: "Cooperative and Friendly v. Competitive and Hostile"					
Relations	35·6%	45·62	7	6·517	81·76
Situations	60·6%	77·58	7	11·082	139·05
Rel. × Sit.	3·1%	3·90	49	0·080	5·78
Error	0·7%	0·87	63	0·014	
Dim. 2: "Intense v. Superficial"					
Relations	23·5%	30·13	7	4·305	74×·61
Situations	73·4%	93·89	7	13·413	232·46
Rel. × Sit.	2·2%	2·83	49	0·058	3·05
Error	0·9%	1·19	63	0·019	
Dim. 3: "Equal and Symmetric v. Unequal and Asymmetric"					
Relations	72·7%	93·01	7	13·287	113·96
Situations	22·0%	28·13	7	4·018	34·46
Rel. × Sit.	4·5%	5·71	49	0·117	7·29
Error	0·8%	1·01	63	0·016	
Dim. 4: "Informal v. Formal"				•	
Relations	88·4%	113·10	7	16·160	418·65
Situations	4·3%	5·55	7	0·793	20·54
Rel. × Sit.	5·3%	6·82	49	0·139	3·61
Error	1·9%	2·43	63	0·039	
Dim. 5: "Task Oriented v. Non-task Oriented"					
Relations	5·8%	7·46	7	1·066	10·54
Situations	89·3%	114·28	7	16·325	161·47
Rel. × Sit.	3·9%	4·96	49	0·101	5·11
Error	1·0%	1·25	63	0·020	

0·01 Significance level for main effects is approximately 3·03.
0·01 Significance level for interaction is approximately 1·88.
Source: Wish, 1975c, p. 76.

The interaction partner and situational cues in episode perception

The main limitation of Wish's study was that it did not attempt to evaluate perceptions of a sample of episodes which would be representative of the interactive experience of any particular group. Since the main thrust of Wish's investigation is towards the discovery of the "human element" in communication episodes, and not the study of social episodes *per se*, this is perhaps not surprising.

In this section we shall consider a study which sought to extend and generalize Wish's findings, using a similar methodology, but a more representative sample of stimuli and two independent subject groups, representing different subcultural environments (Forgas, 1978, unpublished data). The question to be examined is: how important are the identity of the partner and the nature of the interaction respectively in determining the perception of episodes.

The method adopted was to select a number of different types of interaction partners with whom the subjects had interacted regularly, and a number of situation contexts in which these interactions occurred. By factorially combining different interaction partners with different situations, the respective effects of these two components of the episode on subject's perceptions could be evaluated.

The categories of interaction partners were selected in such a way that they represented a wide range of different people who were familiar to subjects, and with whom they had interacted in a number of different situational contexts. Seven such categories for each of two subcultural groups, housewives and students, were constructed, based on self-report data:

(1) family and close relatives;
(2) immediate circle of friends;
(3) friend(s) of the opposite sex;
(4) children with whom you are acquainted;
(5) casual acquaintances;
(6) students in your college (for students)/neighbours (for housewives);
(7) professional people (doctors, lawyers, or university dons for students).

The selection of situation contexts was partially based on evidence from Wish's (1975c) earlier study, and from Forgas's (1976a) study, as well as on open-ended responses from the subject groups. These situation contexts had to be well known and commonly experienced by the subjects, and at the same time, be quite different in their characteristics and requirements. Four such situation contexts were selected, which varied in terms of two central characteristics: involvement v. superficiality, and socio-emotional v. task-orientation. As we saw earlier, these are important aspects of social situations, according to the evidence of several studies. The four situation contexts were thus:

(1) Chatting casually on the street (superficial–socio-emotional);
(2) Discussing some minor problem (superficial–task-oriented);
(3) Having an intimate conversation at home or at a party (involved–socio-emotional); and
(4) Working closely together on a project or activity (involved–task-oriented).

The seven different kinds of interaction partners and these four situation context labels were combined to create 28 complete social episode descriptions, for example, "Chatting casually on the street with a member of your family or a close relative", and "Discussing some minor problem with a casual acquaintance". The 28 episodes were rated by two separate groups of judges, housewives and students, on 36 bipolar scales.

The analysis of these data consisted of the following steps: (a) the construction of a multidimensional representation of the 28 episodes for each of the respondent groups (housewives and students) separately, and the interpretation of these multidimensional spaces; (b) the analysis of variance of the position of composite episodes in this multidimensional space, as a function of the two independent variables, actor and episode context. For both the housewives and the students sample, a three-dimensional representation of the 28 episodes appeared optimal. For both of these subject groups, the three attribute dimensions differentiating episodes were similar, and reflected the extent to which judges perceived episodes as *involving*, their relative *self-confidence* in the different episodes, and the *task-oriented* against socio-emotional nature of the episode. These dimensions are similar to those derived by Wish (1975), Forgas (1976a, 1978dc) and others, and again suggest the rather uniform relevance of characteristics such as involvement, self-confidence and task-orientation to judgements of social episodes. The absence of subcultural differences on this occasion possibly reflects the fact that the episodes were *ad hoc*, selected in terms of *a priori* criteria, and not on the basis of representative sampling.

The position of any one episode in this episode space can be regarded as a function of two factors, interaction partner and situation context. A multivariate analysis of variance showed that in effect both of these variables had a highly significant overall effect on how the episodes were perceived. However, of greater interest here is the respective contribution of these two cues to the perception of social episodes on each of the three INDSCAL dimensions. This was accomplished by a series of univariate analyses of variance, which are summarized in Table 3.

This table shows that on the first dimension, perceived involvement, the identity of the partner accounted for a far higher percentage of the variance than did situational cues. It seems that for both housewives and students, involvement in an episode is primarily a function of the partner. Self-confidence in an episode apparently also depends on the identity of the partner, but the contribution of the situation context is much more important here. Finally, task orientation against socio-emotional orientation of an episode, perhaps not surprisingly, depends on situational cues, although the identity of the interaction partner is still important.

These results are somewhat different from Wish's (1975c) findings, in which the two independent variables and their interactions accounted for more than 98% of the variance on each of his five dimensions. It may well be that the importance attributed to different cues in perceptions of social episodes varies with the subculture studied. This appears to be contradicted, however, by the rather similar reaction of the two subcultural groups, housewives and students, studied here.

Perhaps the most general finding emerging from this study is that the category of the interaction partner is a consistently important cue in determining perceptions of social episodes. In the negotiation of everyday episodes, when a potential participant seeks to form an accurate perception of the proposed episode, the information most frequently asked for is the category to which the interaction partner(s) belong. The common questions when episodes are negotiated: "Who is going to be there?" and "Who with?" confirm this fact. The present study offers some empirical evidence for the relative importance of such cues in the perception and negotiation of different kinds of encounters.

TABLE 3
Analyses of variance of judgements of composite episodes, evaluating the contribution of (a) the interaction partner and (b) the situation context to position in the INDSCAL stimulus space

Effects	Variance accounted for	Sum of squares	Degrees of freedom	Mean squares	F value	Sig.
I. Housewives						
Dimension 1: Involvement						
A. Interaction partner	63·6%	3·22	6	0·538	292·62	0·001
B. Situation context	10·9%	0·58	3	0·192	104·76	0·001
A × B	19·9%	0·99	18	0·055	29·90	0·001
Error	2·6%	0·21	112	0·002		
Dimension 2: Self-confidence						
A. Interaction partner	56·9%	2·79	6	0·465	58·15	0·001
B. Situation context	18·8%	0·92	3	0·306	36·32	0·001
A × B	5·1%	0·25	18	0·014	1·67	0·1
Error	19·2%	0·94	112	0·008		
Dimension 3: Task orientation						
A Interaction partner	25·3%	1·28	6	0·213	13·13	0·001
B. Situation context	29·5%	1·47	3	0·490	29·68	0·001
A × B	9·0%	0·45	18	0·025	1·50	0·1
Error	35·7%	1·78	112	0·016		
II. Students						
Dimension 1: Involvement						
A. Interaction partner	74·4%	3·69	6	6·617	385·77	0·001
B. Situation context	9·4%	0·47	3	0·158	98·88	0·001
A × B	12·9%	0·64	18	0·036	22·23	0·001
Error	3·3%	0·18	112	0·002		
Dimension 2: Self-confidence						
A. Interaction partner	59·3%	2·96	6	0·493	61·62	0·001
B. Situation context	14·8%	0·74	3	0·246	31·14	0·001
A × B	8·0%	0·40	18	0·022	2·78	0·005
Error	17·8%	0·89	112	0·008		
Dimension 3: Task orientation						
A. Interaction partner	16·9%	0·83	6	0·138	5·52	0·001
B. Situation context	21·8%	1·07	3	0·356	14·24	0·001
A×B	3·8%	0·19	18	0·010	0·40	NS
Error	57·3%	2·81	112	0·025		

Environmental and behavioural cues

The complex relationship between social behaviour and physical behaviour settings has already been reviewed in Chapter 6. The concept
of behaviour settings, first introduced by Barker (Barker, 1968; Barker
and Wright, 1955), implies that particular environments are associated
with typical, recurring social behaviour patterns. From the definition
of its setting, much of the ongoing behaviour can be predicted without
any further information about the aims, motivations or personalities
of the social actors (Stern *et al.*, 1956).

The symbolic value of environments in social behaviour has been
most explicitly recognized by researchers working within the symbolic
interactionist paradigm. Bennett and Bennett (1970) write for
example:

> All social interaction is affected by the physical container within which
> it occurs. The various elements of the container establish a world of
> meaning through the arrangement of nonverbal symbolism. For this
> reason, the common practice in the social sciences of focussing on
> behaviour without reference to the physical setting would seem to ignore
> an important dimension of the total picture of interaction. (p. 190)

The intricate relationship between physical behaviour settings and
social behaviour in a medical setting was elegantly analysed by Ball
(1970), and "regions" play an important part in many of Goffman's
(1959, 1963) penetrating analyses of public and private behaviour. In
this sense, behaviour settings are not mere physical environments;
rather, they are well understood symbolic codes representing social
norms and expectations about appropriate and inappropriate
behaviours.

In social psychology only the most cursory attempts have been made
to deal with the environmental dimension in interactive behaviour and
social perception. The present study (Forgas and Brown, 1977) was
mainly concerned with the role which physical environments play in
defining interaction episodes for observers. By asking subjects to judge
slides of different interactions superimposed on different behaviour
settings, the contribution of the behaviour setting to judgements of the
encounters can be evaluated. That behaviour settings have such a
definitional function in social perception follows not only from Barker's
(1965, 1968), Moos's (1973, 1974) and others' understanding of the
concept, but also from accumulating evidence suggesting the culturally

coded, stereotypical nature of many social encounters (Forgas, 1976a, 1978a; Triandis, 1972).

In contrast with previous studies, in which abstract labels were used to describe social episodes, in this study photos of different behaviour settings and different interactants were used to represent social episodes. A visual representation was chosen, because the cues to be studied, behaviour setting and interactive behaviour, are intrinsically more suited to a visual medium.

Four interacting dyads were instructed to enact a series of different levels of interaction intimacy, and these interactive poses were photographed. Similarly, a series of photos were taken of a wide range of behaviour settings, from open street markets to theatre lobbies. Both series of photos were pre-judged by a pilot sample, and on the basis of these judgements, behaviour setting and behavioural cues were matched on six bipolar scales (warm/cold; simple/complex; pleasant/unpleasant; passive/active; intimate/non-intimate; tense/relaxed). Finally, the different interaction scenes and behaviour settings were factorially combined by superimposing the dyads on the behaviour settings. Slides of these combined interaction episodes were rated by subjects on the same six bipolar scales as were used in the pilot study.

These data were analysed with the help of a MANOVA, followed by individual analyses of variance for each of the rating scales. Overall, both behaviour setting and non-verbal behaviour cues had a significant effect on judgements, and the interaction of these two variables was also significant. In particular, the episode was judged to be more "warm" and "relaxed" when it occurred in the more intimate physical environment. Correspondingly, behavioural cues between the interactants affected judgements on four scales. The episode was seen as more "warm", "intimate", "pleasant" and "relaxed" when the models displayed more intimate non-verbal cues. Most interestingly, however, the interaction of these two cues was highly significant. The nature of this interaction is clearly represented in Fig. 3. As Fig. 3 shows, a behaviour setting which was judged to be comparatively warm, intimate, pleasant and relaxed served to accentuate interpersonal behaviours within this setting. On the other hand, setting 2, judged to be more cold, unintimate, unpleasant and tense, appeared to attenuate behavioural cues in this setting, irrespective of whether interpersonal intimacy or lack of intimacy is expressed. From the evidence of this analysis it thus appears that behaviour settings affect observer judgements of social episodes by providing information which increases or decreases the salience of the observed interpersonal behaviours.

The two behaviour settings used in this study may have influenced observer judgements of the "intimate" and "non-intimate" interac-

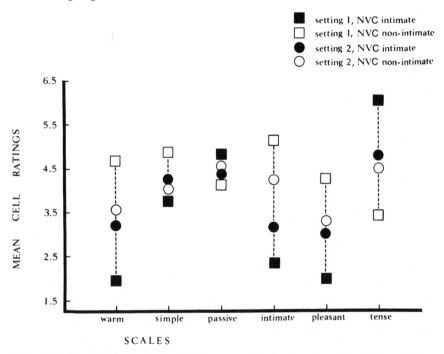

Fig. 3. A graphical analysis of the interaction of behavioural and behaviour setting cues in the perception of social episodes: mean cell ratings on the six rating scales.

tions occurring within them in two different ways. Firstly, environments exude a certain atmosphere, which may be referred to as the connotative meaning of behaviour settings for observers. Alternatively, in the sense Barker (1963) used the term, behaviour settings have social meanings in being the coded representations of social norms. Considering the relatively reduced stimulus situation represented by slides of interacting couples, and the use of connotative rather than denotative scales for the measurement of responses, it seems likely that the perceived atmosphere rather than the symbolic meaning of the settings was important. It is likely, however, that in many everyday situations, social perception is often based on such connotative impressions.

On the whole, the present results suggest that environmental cues play an important and non-obvious role in the perception of social episodes. While a more extensive range of matched stimuli is needed before generalizations could be made, the findings are encouraging. Further studies of the effects of environmental characteristics on social perception, using more realistic stimulus materials, and more sophisticated measurement methodologies, would be required to more accurately assess the role of physical environmental cues in the perception of social episodes.

Episode definition and the perception of realistic interactions

In the last two studies it was shown that cues such as the behaviour setting, and the identity of the interaction partner as well as the nature of the interaction play an important and quantifiable role in affecting the perception of social episodes.

In everyday social life, we frequently find ourselves in the situation of witnessing an interaction between two people we know. Under these circumstances a hypothetical definition of the observed episode, determined by the known relationship between the interactants and other observable situational cues will automatically arise in our minds. If we then continue to observe that interaction, the behaviours of the partners will automatically be evaluated against the standard defined by our definition of the episode in terms of the cues available to us. In a nutshell, the study to be described here (Forgas, 1978b) takes this paradigmatic situation as its starting point, and seeks to discover the importance of such implicit expectations in judgements of actual interactions.

Existing studies concerned with the perception of social encounters have generally failed to take observers' expectations of episodes as an explicit variable into account. Several studies indicate, however, that social interaction, and non-verbal aspects of social interaction in particular, are not only regulated by implicit social norms, but that these norms are often defined in terms of the relationship between the interactants. As early as 1944 Heider and Simmell demonstrated that subjects were able to make consistent judgements about social relationships even with such extremely reduced non-verbal stimuli as moving, interacting geometric figures. Similar results were reported by Shor (1957) and Marek (1963). In a more recent study Thayer and Schiff

(1973) showed that judgements of the length of relationship between two stimulus characters were directly related to the duration and reciprocity of gaze between them. While these studies show that social relationships can be inferred from non-verbal behaviour, Little (1965) demonstrated the complement of this effect: for different classes of relationships and in different cultures, consistently different levels of non-verbal behaviours, such as proximity, are seen as appropriate.

In a related line of research, it was demonstrated that intimacy levels in social encounters are maintained within fairly strictly defined equilibria (Argyle and Dean, 1965; Patterson, 1973). This in turn implies the necessary existence of a shared cultural concept of what is "appropriate" behaviour for a given episode, as defined by a relationship and a given behaviour setting.

Indeed it is surprising that while in real life the appropriateness of social behaviour is most frequently evaluated in terms of the definition of the episode, the effects of this variable on the perception of actual performances were not explored earlier. By combining different episode definitions and actual performances the relative weights of each of these information sources can be assessed. This study was thus designed to assess the importance of episode definition cues on (a) judgements of an observed encounter, (b) judgements of the relationship between the interactants, and (c) the perception of the stimulus persons as individuals.

The method employed in this study relied on a further extension of the methods used in the previous experiment. Rather than photographs, videotaped interaction sequences were used as stimuli. Couples were instructed to enact sequences of intimate, involved, and non-intimate, superficial interactions in a behaviour setting which defined the episode as a conversation between a male and a female during morning coffee time. All judges were familiar with the setting and the general episode. In addition to this information, judges were provided with a selective written definition of the episode, which identified the interactants either as a married couple, or as two people who had just met recently. The definition of the global episode, and corresponding expectations, were thus manipulated in such a way that either an intimate, or a non-intimate interaction was expected. The videotaped interaction episode was in fact either intimate or non-intimate, and these two kinds of expectations and two kinds of interactions were combined in a factorial design. Subjects were asked to indicate their perception of the episode and the participants on a series of bipolar scales, as well as in open-ended responses.

The results indicated, firstly, that as expected, behavioural cues were on the whole more important in determining judgements than were episode definition cues, although episode definition cues significantly affected judgements on at least some of the scales. (This analysis was based on multivariate and univariate analyses of variance, and the calculation of Frijda's (1969) Average Relative Shift measures). Surprisingly, however, and contrary to cue integration processes in other areas of social perception, the importance of episode definition cues increased rather than decreased when observed behaviour and expectations were incongruous. This suggests that cultural expectations embodied in the definition of the episode have an unexpectedly salient effect on judgements of realistic encounters, particularly when such encounters are contrary to expectations (Fig. 4).

In addition to judgements of the encounter as a whole, subjects were also asked to make judgements about the interactants as individuals. The analysis of these data, again by means of analysis of variance

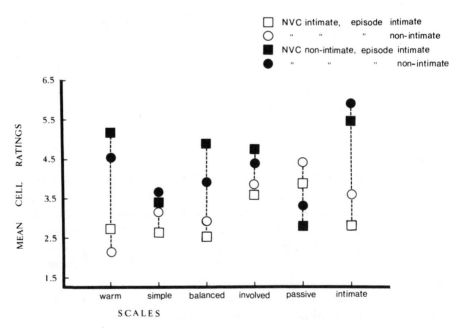

Fig. 4. A graphical summary of cell means by scales for every combination of behavioural and episode definition cues. Source: Forgas, 1978b.

techniques, showed that in an episode defined as non-intimate, involving a couple just getting acquainted, males are seen as significantly more insecure, nervous and dislikable than in an episode defined as intimate, involving a very well-known other. Judgements of the female actor were affected by the episode definition in a much more evaluative way: when thought to be acting in an intimate episode, the female actor was seen as significantly more likable and as behaving significantly more appropriately than in a non-intimate episode. These results probably reflect the cultural stereotype of males and females. Males are expected to be the initiators of intimacy, and are seen as insecure and nervous in an episode which is by definition not intimate (a "getting acquainted" episode). In contrast, the female role implies warmth and intimacy, and behaviour in a non-intimate episode may thus be seen as inappropriate (Fig. 5).

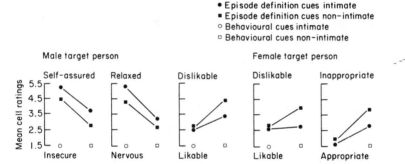

Fig. 5. The effects of episode definition and behavioural cues on person perception judgements, on selected bipolar scales where episode definition cues reached significance (cell means).

The present findings help to shed some light on the way observers evaluate social interaction episodes as a whole, and on how different components of what they see and what they expect to see affect their judgements. While the limited sample of episodes and stimulus couples does not warrant generalizations, the findings are nevertheless encouraging in several respects.

It appears that when behaviour is congruent with the definition of the episode, behaviour cues dominate perception. Together with studies of non-verbal expression (Frijda, 1969; Watson, 1972) these results suggest that in the absence of cue conflict, perceived *in situ* behaviour is the most important single source of information, even when complex and realistic social stimuli are used.

In a sense, it is more interesting to see what happens when actual behaviour violates the definition of the encounter. To what extent will preconceptions about the encounter and the relationship between the individuals be revised? It seems from the present study that behaviour cue dominance decreases when the episode definition is violated, contrary to numerous previous findings showing the extreme resilience of behavioural cues to any modification (Heider, 1958, p. 54; Miller, 1976; Schneider and Miller, 1975). Cognitive expectations about an interaction episode are apparently much more resistant to such discounting. Instead, behaviours conflicting with the definition of the episode appeared to interact with episode definition cues. Thus, intimate behaviour by strangers and non-intimate behaviour by a married couple were judged more extremely than interactions congruent with the definition of the episode.

The effects of the episode context on person perception judgements

The problem to be considered here is an important aspect of episode perception. Most of the studies in this chapter were concerned with the effects of components of social episodes as cues on the perception of the global episode. In the present section whole social episodes will be conceptualized as single cues, which in turn are expected to influence the perception of other categories of social stimuli, such as persons. Since episodes are by definition important units of social life and experience within a defined milieu, the perception of people, and whole groups should also be affected by the context provided by the particular social episode. Only a few studies of person perception have come close to demonstrating something like a situational effect on judgements, and none have studied the effects of the relevant episodic context on person perception.

It is characteristic of this area of research that the effects of episodic factors on person perception were only investigated when the situational manipulation was thought of as a representation of some other, preconceived independent variable. There is little evidence in the person perception literature which would indicate that researchers have attributed any intrinsic importance to the episode or situation in which person perception occurs, other than as a carrier of manipulations of independent variables. This approach, as was suggested in

Chapter 2, is characteristic of many studies in social psychology: in search of controlling and manipulating variables, the natural context in which social behaviour and perception occurs is ignored: "It is the potentially vital context effects which are typically excluded from many controlled studies of interpersonal judgement" (Warr and Knapper, 1968, p. 356–7).

In a study by Argyle *et al.* (1977, unpublished data) an attempt was made to establish that the episode in which the target person is judged is of some importance in determining judgements. The method adopted to show this involved the judgement of a number of different categories of individuals personally known to the judges (family, friends, etc.) in the context of four different episodes, on a number of bipolar scales.

In the first instance, results were analysed by a multivariate analysis of variance technique, which showed that judgements were significantly affected by the episode context, the target person, as well as the subcultural background of the judges. Next, a series of multidimensional scaling analyses were carried out in order to represent the perceived differences between the target person judged in each of the four social episodes which provided the context for judgements. It was again found that the perceived differences between the target individuals were seen as significantly different in different episodes. Moreover, a factor analysis of the use of the judgemental dimensions in each of the episodes also demonstrated that different clusters of personality characteristics were seen as relevant to describing the target persons in different episodes. Thus, bipolar scales reflecting the social skills and evaluation of an individual were salient when the episode was socio-emotional in orientation, or represented a significant degree of involvement between the partners. In contrast, scales reflecting social status were salient in superficial task oriented episodes, and scales representing competence were used most frequently to describe individuals in involved, task-oriented situations. This study suggested that just as individuals rely on a limited number of dimensions to describe others (Dornbusch *et al.*, 1965, Rosenberg and Sedlak, 1972), there are only a few characteristics which are relevant to differentiating between people in a given episode. The episode context thus had an important effect on the perception of people, even when the target persons were well-known to the judges. The personality characteristics used to describe these individuals were also episode-specific, fluctuating with the requirements of the social situation. This study showed that the episode context is a crucial, and often neglected factor in social perception.

In another study, Forgas *et al.* (1979a) attempted to demonstrate episodic differences in interpersonal judgements in a much more enduring and intimate social unit, a functioning academic group. The object of this study was to evaluate the tentative conclusions drawn from the previous study in a functioning, ongoing social environment: how important a role do episodes play in affecting the interpersonal perceptions of group members in an intact group, and how is their representation of the group as a whole influenced by the particular episode being enacted?

It was expected that well-defined social episodes within an intact group have a far-reaching function in organizing the social experience and perceptions of the members: group members' perception of each other, as well as the perceived structure of the group and the attribute dimensions used to describe it are not invariant, but should fluctuate with the episode specified.

The way group members perceive each other and the attribute dimensions they use to represent the group may be said to constitute the effective social structure of the group. (This approach to social structure was already used in a study by Forgas (1978a), described in Chapter 7). In those terms, the group as perceived by its members is analogous to a cognitive domain (Scott, 1969), and the representation of its structure requires the uncovering of implicitly perceived differences between group members (Jones and Young, 1973). Although this approach to the study of social structure is an extremely useful one, like all other approaches, including Moreno's (1951) sociometric technique, it is based on the assumption that perceived social structure is relatively permanent. In contrast, the central argument of the present study was that perceived group structure can be expected to be more complex in some situations than in others, and the attribute dimensions relevant to differentiating the group would also depend on the requirements of the episode.

Accordingly, it was expected that both the number and the identity of the attribute dimensions defining the perceived structure of the group would be episode-specific. Further, formal status differences between faculty, students and staff should be differentially relevant in different episodes. Finally, members belonging to these different status categories were also expected to display systematic differences in their reactions to the different episode contexts.

The overall approach in this study was to derive a representation of the group as seen by its members in each of four episodes. Four episodes from the wide range of commonly occurring encounters were selected, which included both work and non-work, superficial and intensive episodes. The four episodes were the following:

(1) Having a drink together in the pub on a Friday night, after the regular weekly seminars ("pub"),

(2) Having morning coffee with other group members in the department ("morning coffee"),

(3) Being a guest at a faculty member's house for drinks ("party"), and

(4) Participating in one of the group research seminars ("seminar").

Group members were asked to rate each other in each of these four typical episodes on 10 bipolar scales, which were selected from a larger pool in a pilot study by the judges themselves. (Some of these scales were found to be relevant to every episode, others applied only to one or two episodes.) These data were analysed by a series of four INDS-CAL analyses, reconstructing in effect the perceived structure of the group in each of the four episodes.

In the first two episodes, pub and morning coffee, two dimensions were optimal for representing the group, while in the second two episodes (party and seminar) three dimensions were required, suggesting the greater differentiation of the group in the party and seminar episodes. In the pub episode, interpersonal *evaluation* in the sense of being an enjoyable companion, and *extroversion* were the two attribute dimensions differentiating between group members. In the morning coffee episode a more intellectual *evaluative* dimension and a *self-confidence* dimension were found to differentiate group members best. In the third social episode, being a guest at a party given by a faculty member, *self-confidence*, interpersonal *warmth* and *ingratiation* (!) were seen as the salient traits differentiating the group, while in the fourth episode, a research seminar, *dominance*, *creativity* and *supportiveness* were the most important attributes.

The first two episodes, pub and morning coffee, are obviously fairly regular, easy-going and simple interactions, social rather than task-oriented in character. Accordingly, a simpler two-dimensional representation was sufficient to reflect the perceived differences between group members. The major dimension in both episodes was evaluative, although interpersonal qualities and skills (talkativeness, humour, friendliness) were more important in the pub, while during morning coffee intellectual skills also played a part (talkativeness, being interesting, pleasant and quick). It appears that morning coffee, an episode occurring in a "formal" behaviour setting, the department, called for slightly different personal qualities. The other dimensions also reflect this: in the pub a straightforward extroversion dimension was seen as relevant, while at morning coffee, self-confidence was more important.

In the second two episodes not only more complex representations were necessary (three as against two dimensions), but the identity of the dimensions was also more episode specific. Thus, ingratiation at a party at a faculty member's house was a highly specific attribute dimension used to differentiate between group members. In the research seminar episode, seen by many group members as a highly competitive, intellectually demanding situation involving a fair amount of exposure to criticism, self-confidence, creativity and supportiveness were, understandably, the salient dimensions.

Are formal status differences between faculty, students and staff equally salient in each of these episodes? One may expect that status difference between, say, faculty and students should be more marked at a research seminar and at a faculty member's party, than in a neutral, essentially social setting, such as a pub. This was evaluated by a series of multiple discriminant analyses, evaluating the significance of the differences between the positions of these three status groups in the perceived group space in each of four episodes. Status differences were seen as most marked in the seminar episode, followed by the "party" episode, whereas status sub-groups were not seen as significantly different in the pub and morning coffee episodes. These results clearly suggest that even such socially ascribed and formalized personal attributes as status are not cross-situationally invariant: some episodes magnify status differences, and others tend to decrease them, contrary to some common assumptions in social psychology.

Would members of these different formal status groups, as judges, react differently to the episode contexts presented? This was evaluated by four multiple discriminant analyses of the judges' subject weights, which indicate the relative salience of each of the INDSCAL dimensions to each individual judge: there was greatest agreement across status groups in the judgement of the group in the pub episode. In the research seminar episode, students, most likely to be exposed to criticism, found the third dimension, supportiveness, a more salient attribute than did other status groups. In the morning coffee episode, the evaluative dimension was relatively more salient to faculty and staff, while the self-confidence dimension was more relevant to students in their judgements of the group. Differences in judgements were most marked in the party episode: while self-confidence was seen as most salient overall, first-year research students also emphasized warmth, and both faculty and staff found ingratiation a salient dimension (Fig. 6).

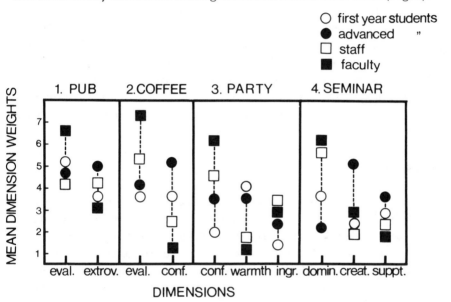

Fig. 6. Differences between the four *a priori* status groups in their perception of the group in each of four episodes. Source: Forgas *et al.*, 1979a.

This study was thus successful in showing that interpersonal judgements even within a permanent and well-established group are strongly affected by the nature of the social episode providing the context. Both the complexity of the judgements, and the attribute dimensions used were episode-specific.

It is interesting to compare these dimensions, derived within the context of specified episodes, with comparable dimensions constructed without the specification of the episode context. Jones and Young (1973) found that political persuasion, research interests and status were the three dimensions best describing the academic group they studied—further, these dimensions were found to be rather stable over time, and were not affected by minor changes in group membership. All three dimensions reported by these authors refer to rather abstract, enduring, permanent characteristics of the members as individuals. They do not describe personal characteristics directly relevant to everyday functioning and behaviour within the group. The same point can be made about Davison and Jones's (1976) comparable study. It appears that interpersonal judgements made in a contextual vacuum will be qualitatively different from judgements based on experience in a specified episode. If these differences could be reliably replicated in a wider population, it would strongly suggest that the lack of predictive validity of some research in social perception may be at least partly due to the investigators' failure to specify the relevant episode context. In other words, the level of abstraction at which these studies tended to operate appears to be too far removed from the everyday complexity of such judgements. The specification of the episode context may well be the most important factor ignored.

Summary

In this chapter we have considered a rather heterogeneous collection of studies bound together by a shared interest in factors which influence episode perception. As research into the way in which episodes are cognitively represented is perhaps the most active area today, there is some hope that the gaps will eventually be filled, and a comprehensive model of how cognitive representation of episodes are constructed will emerge.

Any such model would have to include the characteristics of the individual judge, reflecting his biographic experiences and motivations. While Pervin's analysis offers a viable methodology for studying unique individuals' episode spaces, a more comprehensive theoretical model is also needed. Phenomenologist theorists, such as Schutz, have a lot to say about the processes whereby an individual's knowledge of his life-world is accumulated (Chapter 4). Perhaps a fusion of such phenomenologist models with sophisticated statistical descriptive techniques may further stimulate research in this area.

The extent to which episodes are constrained by rules is another important element in episode perception, as Price's studies have suggested. As the concept of rules is receiving increasing attention in social psychology (Collett, 1977), it seems likely that Price's index of constraint defined in terms of limitations placed on behaviours may be further elaborated into a multidimensional measure, reflecting restrictiveness, sanctions, rule consensus and other elements of constraint in episodes more specific than those studied by Price.

Role relationships between the participants are no doubt among the most important determinants of episode perception, as are behaviour setting cues. The effects of such cues on the cognitive representation of global episodes could be further evaluated, using techniques developed in the study of information integration strategies in person perception (Anderson, 1974). The studies discussed in this chapter merely introduce this possibility.

In the second part of the chapter the focus shifted somewhat from concentrating on the elements influencing episode perception to a study of how episodes themselves function as cues affecting our judgements of observed interactions, and other people. This latter point is a most important one. Social psychology, like personality theory has traditionally accepted the assumption of intrapsychic consistency, that is, that social behaviour and perception are relatively stable across situations and episodes (Argyle and Little, 1972; Mischel, 1968; Ball, 1970). Our perceptions of other people, or whole groups were assumed to be stable, irrespective of the episode context. The studies presented here throw some doubt on this assumption. However, there is no reason why the episode, which in previous studies was shown to be a readily quantifiable unit (Chapter 7), should not be explicitly taken into account in studies of social behaviour and perception. Another possibility for research would be to concentrate on the attributes and traits of people which are made most salient in particular episodes. Such situation-specific personal attributes or "situated identities" have played an important role in microsociological analyses of social behaviour. Using methods similar to those outlined in the last study of this chapter (Forgas et al., 1979a) empirical analyses of such situated identities may become possible.

Despite their exploratory nature then, these studies are suggestive of numerous research topics which will ultimately contribute to our understanding of how social episodes are cognitively represented. Having surveyed these diverse approaches to the study of social episode, in the next chapter some of the practical applications of research on social episodes will be considered.

9

Some Applications of Episodes in Personality Theory, Clinical Psychology and Social Psychology

We have seen how the concept of social episodes is rooted in psychological and sociological theory (Chapters 3 and 4) and what sorts of techniques are applicable to their empirical study (Chapters 5, 6, 7 and 8). Having demonstrated the feasibility of these techniques, the potential uses of studies of social episodes needs to be considered. Such applications extend far beyond the boundaries of social psychology. To the extent that interactionism, the study of cognitive structures and emphasis on everyday behaviour is the current *Zeiteist* in psychology, cognitive representations of social episodes may be of wider interest.

The purpose of this chapter is to describe some of the possible applications of the study of social episodes in three areas of psychology where interest in such situational entities has been greatest in recent years, in personality theory, clinical and social psychology.

Episodes and situations in personality theory

It is in personality theory, with its long history of attempts to produce a predictive theory of behaviour first in typological, and later in trait terms, that awareness of the importance of situational factors has been most acute in recent years. This interest is reflected in the increasing number of papers explicitly concerned with the person v. situation problem. Is behaviour to be explained in terms of enduring characteristics residing within individuals, as personality theorists have long assumed (personologism), or are different situations the major source of variance in behaviour (situationalism)? (See Endler and Magnusson, 1976, for a comprehensive collection of the relevant papers.)

PERSONOLOGICAL APPROACHES

The task of personality theory and research is perhaps the most daunting in psychology, since it is in this area that we face most directly the need to predict the behaviour of individuals, with all the complexity that this implies. The earliest attempts to give a personological explanation of behaviour were based on *typologies*. Typologies of individuals go back to antiquity, and Hippocrates' four basic types of temperament (choleric, melancholic, sanguine and phlegmatic) have shown an extraordinary staying power, if not in psychology, then at least in popular usage. No less popular are Kretschmer's (1926) attempts to relate psychological disorders to body build (e.g. "pyknic" and "asthenic" types), and the later extension of this typology to normals. His theory was developed by Sheldon (1949), who proposed three body-build based types (endomorphic, mesomorphic, ectomorphic). These biologically based typologies of personality, although manifestly speculative in their origins, have profoundly affected popular thinking. Perhaps only one typology was more successful in this respect, Jung's (1923) introverted and extroverted categories. These attempts to account for the rich variety of individual behaviour in terms of typologies proved largely unsuccessful. It is arguable, however, that the failure of the typological approach was attributable to the naïveté of the methods used for defining types, rather than to the inherent falsity of the underlying principle of the existence of "human types". The continuing use of typological terms in everyday, commonsense situations suggests that typological approaches to personality may have some role to play, if only to explain everyday "naïve" psychology.

Dynamic, motivational models of personality constitute the second main theoretical stream. These theories assume that deep-seated, and often unconscious motivations and impulses are the most important determinants of personality. Such impulses are not directly ascertainable, and can only be discovered through the study and interpretation of observable surface behaviours, which are the "symptoms" revealing the hidden mainsprings of personality. Dynamic theories have also included models of the structure, development and topography of personality (Freud, 1959). Until the recent advent of behaviourism in clinical psychology, dynamic theories were important as integrative models in an otherwise increasingly eclectic discipline. Their influence on academic psychology has been much more limited, however, due to the serious difficulties associated with the quantification of the variables included in dynamic models of personality.

With the failure of type-theories in personality, and the limited appeal of dynamic models, trait-theories have become dominant, and have remained so for the past 50 years. As Mischel (1973) suggests, "During the last 50 years, when basic concepts were changing rapidly in most fields of psychology, the most fundamental assumptions about the nature of personality seem to have been retained with few substantial modifications" (p. 152). The central assumptions of these trait-based approaches to personality are that "personality comprises broad underlying dispositions which pervasively influence the individual's behaviour across many situations and lead to consistency in his behaviour . . . These dispositions are not directly observed, but are inferred from behavioural signs . . ." (p. 153). As a consequence of this orientation "personality research has been a quest for such underlying broad dimensions", leading to the development of "hundreds of tests designed to infer dispositions and almost none to measure situations" (Mischel, 1973, p. 153).

THE ASSUMPTION OF CROSS-SITUATIONAL CONSISTENCY

The central assumption of trait theories of personality, cross-situational consistency, came under fire fairly early on, but without much impact on personality theorists until quite recently. In a widely ignored article published in the *American Journal of Sociology*, Reinhardt (1937) was one of the first to point out the shortcomings of this model: "The reliability of predictions as to future behaviour . . . when based solely upon a personality classification derived from individual reactions in a clearly defined type of situation depends not upon the constancy of individual purpose alone . . . but also upon the continuance or recurrence of the same type of situation" (p. 492). More important from the point of the current person v. situation controversy was the gradual accumulation of evidence suggesting that the personal consistency model underlying trait theories is only valid in certain circumscribed situations. Thus self-ratings of traits on paper-and-pencil instruments, the very stuff of personality tests, are fairly consistent over time. Similarly, other behaviours may also be consistent as long as the situation is more or less exactly replicated. Finally, personality traits with a strong intellectual component were shown to have a reasonably high cross-situational consistency, which may be interpreted as the reflection of the well-known "g" factor in different tasks requiring intellectual problem solving. What the studies have not shown, however, is that pure personality traits can predict behaviour across different situations. Although the evaluation of this emerging empirical evidence began more than a decade ago (Fiske, 1961; Vernon, 1964; Peterson, 1968), the person v. situation issue has only developed into a full-blown controversy in the early seventies. Some of the empirical evidence substantiating the situationist point of view has already been discussed earlier, and will not be repeated here.

The current controversy was strongly stimulated by Mischel's (1968, 1969) arguments. He reviewed a broad spectrum of empirical studies and concluded that both trait and state theories are based on the assumption of intrapsychic consistency in behaviour, an assumption which is clearly not supported by the evidence. As a replacement, he offers social behaviour theory, which "seeks the determinants of behaviour in the conditions that covary with the occurrence, maintenance, and change of behaviour . . . social behaviour theory seeks order and regularity in the form of general rules which relate environmental changes to behaviour changes" (1968, pp. 149–150). This formulation implicitly emphasizes the importance of physical, external, environmental forces on shaping behaviour, and has a strong flavour of the old S–R formulations. This approach, which has, perhaps unjustly, been labelled "situationism", was no doubt strongly influenced by the current *Zeitgeist* in psychology with its strong reliance on positivistic methodology, and the patent success of pragmatic behaviour therapies in clinical psychology, formerly a client-branch of personality theory.

Mischel's arguments have been criticized on numerous accounts. The most important of these is that he appears to ignore cognitive mediating factors in the determination of behaviour, and he also seems to deny the role of individual differences, in favour of assigning a causal determinant status to situations. Thus, Alker (1972) sought to defend the trait model by arguing that cross-situational consistency is not a necessary assumption for trait theories. He argued that personality variables remain a major source of variance in behaviour, and criticized the studies showing situational differences on methodological grounds (the samples were too homogeneous, disturbed rather than normal people were used, etc.). Bem (1972a) and later Endler (1973) have taken issue with Alker's propositions, defending Mischel's position in its most important aspects Bowers (1973) has also criticized Mischel's alleged "situationism", but his critique was oriented more towards the perceived extremity of Mischel's S–R formulations, and not against the substance of his thesis. Thus, he suggested that "situationism has gone too far in the direction of rejecting the role of organismic or intrapsychic determinants of behaviour . . . It is my argument that both the trait and the situationist positions are inaccurate and misleading and that a position stressing the interaction of the person and the situation is both conceptually satisfying and empirically warranted" (p. 307).

Much of this controversy has been superseded by Mischel's later, much more moderate and more cognitively oriented conceptualization of the issue. He distances himself from a purely situationist position:

> Evidence for the lack of utility of inferring hypothesised global trait dispositions from behavioural signs should not be misread as an argument for the greater importance of situations than persons (Mischel, 1973, p. 259).

Instead, he suggests that the individual's previous social learning history may contribute to his idiosyncratic perception and interpretation of given situations, resulting in idiosyncratic behaviour in terms of the meaning the situation has for the individual. Thus, it "becomes important to assess the effective stimuli, or 'stimuli as coded', which regulate his responses in particular contexts. These stimuli as coded should not be confused with the totality of objective physical events" (pp. 259–260). Aside from the S–R terminology, this position comes surprisingly close to what phenomenologists have said all along: the perceived, subjective, phenomenological situation, and not the objective situation is the most important determinant of behaviour. The "cognitive transformations" an individual employs in interpreting a situation are the foci of interest: "Assessing the acquired meaning of stimuli is the core of social behaviour assessment" (Mischel, 1968, p. 190). Mischel (1973) goes some way towards developing his cognitive social learning model of personality. He proposes that instead of traits, person variables such as cognitive construction competencies, encoding strategies and personal constructs, behaviour-outcome and stimulus-outcome expectancies in particular situations, subjective stimulus values and self-regulatory systems and plans should be studied. This may well be feasible and even profitable in one-to-one clinical settings, where individual learning therapies may be constructed on the basis of an investigation of such cognitive, individual variables. But it is also clear that this method is drastically different from the nomothetically-oriented mainstream of psychological research, and its implications are more far-reaching than the sedate S–R terminology would suggest. For Mischel's (1973) cognitive social learning approach to personality appears to be, in everything but terminology, a recipe for idiographic, subjective and interpretative analysis of unique meanings and construals of unique individuals of the situations they encounter.

What does this rather drastic shift in personality theory imply for social psychology? Social psychology, like most other branches of psychology has for long operated on an implicit personal consistency assumption. Individuals were assumed to perceive each other, conform to social pressure, or hold attitudes in a fairly steady, constant and consistent fashion. Situational differences in such social behaviours were never subjected to study, except when situational variations were conceived as manipulations of some independent variable. The changing emphasis in personality theory should thus have profound implications for social psychology, and more will be said about this later.

Mischel's cognitive social learning theory is significant in another respect. It represents perhaps the farthest departure of learning theorists into the realm of the subjective, cognitive world. As the reviews of psychology and sociology in the previous two chapters showed, this seems to be very much in keeping with the *Zeitgeist* of social science today. In proposing to place the study of social episodes, and social episodes as perceived and interpreted by the actor in particular into the focus of social psychological research, we are receiving support from a most unexpected quarter: social learning theory.

INTERACTIONISM

Mischel's softened approach to the person–situation issue signified the apparent resolution of this controversy, and the growing acceptance of interactionist models of personality (alas, not much empirical research in this vein has been forthcoming yet). In his excellent review of the evolution of the interactionist point of view in psychology, Ekehammar (1974) concludes: "with respect to personality it seems reasonable to state that the conceptions have converged and are converging towards an interactionist conceptualization, with a simultaneous emphasis on the person's psychological representation and construction of his environment. For the earlier situationists, for example, this trend is reflected by the gradual conceptual change of Mischel's social behaviourism . . . Thus, if interactionism is not the *Zeitgeist* of today's personality psychology, it will probably be that of tomorrow's" (p. 1045).

Just as Mischel and his critics have arrived at an interactionist and psychological conceptualization of the situation built on an essentially behaviouristic foundation, Pervin (1968, 1975c) has reached back to the phenomenologist tradition of Lewin and Murray to arrive at a similar conclusion. In his review of relevant research and theories, he has considered both the physical v. psychological environment issue, and the methodological problems of interactionist research. Pervin conceptualizes the situation and the organism as parts of a single field, in continuous interaction with each other, a position similar to that adopted by Lewin. In his review of research on the effects of individual and situational factors on performance and satisfaction, Pervin (1968) has pointed to the inadequacy of purely intrapsychic, trait-based theories. On the other hand, he also realized the limitations of purely situational approaches, and unlike Mischel (1968), he did not advocate a situational model. As he asserted, "In one way or another, the history of psychology reflects systems based upon an exaggerated emphasis on the individual or the environment—McDougall (1908) and Ross (1908), psychoanalysis and S–R theory, introspection and behaviourism, need theory v. role theory . . . There is now sufficient literature to indicate that these are useless controversies since there is either truth in both points of view or in neither" (Pervin, 1968, p. 56). Instead of concentrating either on the individual, or on the situation, psychology should finally place primary emphasis on their unique inter-relationship: "for each individual there are environments (interpersonal and noninterpersonal) which more or less match the characteristics of his personality. A 'match' or 'best fit' of individual to environment is viewed as expressing itself in high performance, satisfaction, and little stress in the system, whereas a 'lack of fit' is viewed as resulting in decreased performance, dissatisfaction and stress of the system" (Pervin, 1968, p. 56). Pervin's idea of the individual–environment system as a unit of analysis is strongly reminiscent of Lewin's conception of the "life space", and similar interactionist formulations by Angyal (1941), Murphy (1947), Murray (1938) and Helson (1964), which were considered earlier.

As far as research methodology is concerned, Pervin appears to be firmly advocating Brunswik's "representative design", or the study of representative samples of life situations for a small number of subjects, as the most appropriate strategy (Chapter 8).

EPISODES AND PERSONALITY

Thus it appears that the recent acute concern with episodic and situational effects on behaviour in personality has brought about a marked shift in theory towards interactionism, and in methodology towards studies of features of situations and episodes, to complement existing work on personality variables. Perhaps the main result of the person–situation controversy has been the gradual recognition that unless we conceptualize, operationalize and quantify situational variables, the current predictive validity of much of the research in personality, as well as in social psychology cannot be further improved upon. Yet the number of studies taking situational factors explicitly into account is still negligible, mainly because the task of studying situations often appears so daunting. The problem of how situational taxonomies could be constructed is gradually gaining a central place in personality research (Frederiksen, 1972). The study of social episodes in general, and the empirical techniques suggested in Chapters 5, 6, 7 and 8 in particular offer a viable solution for studying situations. If the future of personality theory is interactionism, the development of quantitative measures of episodes are essential to it. By combining measures of individuals (on personality tests) and measures of social episodes (on implicit cognitive dimensions), a much better prediction and explanation of actual behaviour can be achieved, than if we were to rely on only one of these measures.

The first area of application of the study of social episodes in personality research is thus the construction of episode taxonomies. In many ways, this process parallels the early development of personality research itself. At that time, the basic problem was to find a limited number of attribute dimensions, or personality traits, which would be suitable to describe the infinite variety of individual differences between people. Similarly, the task of research on situations is to construct a limited number of situation attribute dimensions along which most situations and episodes could be located.

Ultimately, measures of personality and measures of episodes may be joined in an interactive formula predicting behaviour. This would be a fulfilment of Lewin's original ideas embodied in his well-known $B = f(P, E)$ equation. Paradoxically, the measurement of B, or behaviour, may be the greatest remaining obstacle to this achievement: we have no commonly accepted behaviour taxonomies nor agreed methods for quantifying behaviour beyond the *ad hoc* requirements of particular experiments.

Using judgements of people and judgements of situations as measures of P (person) and E (environment) respectively, we are also exposed to a possible tautology, insofar as measures of the situation will not be independent of the personal characteristics of the judges. To the extent that judgements of situations and episodes are consensual (and according to the evidence, they are), we may regard such measures as independent of individual personological variables. In summary, then, taxonomies of social episodes offer a promising contribution to extending the validity of personality research by allowing the quantification of situations in interactive models of behaviour.

The second area of relevance is much more in keeping with traditional personality research. Mischel (1973) suggested that instead of person variables, such cognitive habits as situation construction competencies, subjective expectations and plans in various situations should be studied. These are in fact standard, habitual ways for an individual to view and interpret his life episodes. By studying episode perception in unique individuals, using idiographic methods rather than cultural representation nomothetically, we come close to fulfilling Mischel's (1973) suggestions. In other words, episode perception competencies can be construed as analogous to personality traits. The complexity, differentiation, and sensitivity that an individual achieves in his cognitive construal of episodes is an important personality attribute, not previously studied in personality research. The methods proposed here for the study of social episodes offer a possible approach to assessing such construction competencies. In particular, the research originated by Pervin (1976) and Forgas (1978a), reviewed in Chapter 7 and Chapter 8, appears interesting in that respect.

By looking at such general episode perception skills, we not only gain an impression of an individual's cognitive processes. We also obtain a model of the judge's phenomenological lifespace, his subjective construal of important and meaningful interaction routines in his current experience. This may be particularly important in clinical, diagnostic contexts, and will be considered in more detail later.

Another point of contact between personality research and the study of social episodes is offered by the surprising similarity between personality variables and attributes of social episodes. It seems that many personality traits can be located in a two-dimensional, extroversion–introversion and neuroticism framework (Eysenck and Eysenck, 1964). As it turns out (Chapters 7 and 8), episode dimensions bear a surprising resemblance to such a framework. Self-confidence or social anxiety is perhaps the most commonly reported episode characteristic. This attribute may be regarded as the situational counterpart of the personality dimension of neuroticism or anxiety. Eysenck's second personality dimension, introversion–extroversion can be construed as the personality equivalent of the commonly found involvement or intimacy dimension in social episodes. These apparent similarities are only partially explained by the fact that both sets of attributes are based on individual judgements.

These similarities between personality traits and episode attributes suggest at least the possibility that personological and situational variables may be located within a joint dimensional framework. Such a model would go one step beyond interactionism, approaching the organic relationship between situational "press" and personal "need" forces suggested by Murray.

It appears, thus, that the contemporary extension of personality research to take into account interactive, person–situation processes calls for a conceptualization of behaviour episodes, and for a technique of quantifying them. Both of these objectives are well served by the study of social episodes as developed here.

Episodes in clinical psychology

Personality theory and clinical psychology were always closely related, the latter often being seen as the "applied" branch of the former. Theories of personality, from Freud to Rogers, were often rooted in clinical experience and vice versa, academic theories often gave birth to clinical practices. How did the person–situation controversy affect clinical psychology?

Until the recent advent of the different behaviour therapies, clinical psychology was nearly exclusively dominated by theories which relied on the assumed cross-situation consistency of individual behaviour for their explanations of illness. The multitude of tests, inventories, scales and other paper-and-pencil instruments have but one thing in common: they seek to measure enduring, relatively unchanging aspects of an individual's personality. The medical model of mental illness itself, which is so dominant in our conceptualizations of psychopathology, relies on assumed intrapsychic dysfunctions in the individual for its diagnosis and therapy of mental disorders. The enduring dominance of personological theories in clinical psychology had several important consequences. Firstly, it tended to de-emphasize the importance of situational, interpersonal or environmental variables in the genesis of mental illness. Secondly, treatments were oriented towards correcting enduring dysfunctions, and not towards improving the capacity to cope in specific kinds of situations, which was often all that was needed.

SITUATIONAL THERAPIES

The revolution brought about by behaviour therapies, social skills training programmes, and the different cognitive and symbolic self-reinforcement therapies can hardly be over-estimated. Clinical psychology, together with personality theory, was one of the last bastions in psychology to hold out against the increasing dominance of situational theories. As we have seen, social learning theorists such as Mischel contributed more than their fair share to the ferment in personality theory, although in the process their ideas might have changed more than those of their original opponents. There is no such single identifiable personality who is responsible for the introduction of situationism (i.e. behaviour therapies) in clinical psychology. Rather, we can speak of an initially slow, and currently rapidly accelerating process whereby the clinical psychological profession is becoming gradually convinced of the utility of the situational (behaviour therapy) approach. The main difference between traditional and behavioural therapies is that the behaviour therapist views disturbed behaviour as a situational, rather than a personological problem. He addresses himself to the task of correcting responses in specific situational contexts, using situational variables in the course of his manipulation of "reinforcement contingencies". Notions of enduring internal causes of maladaptive behaviour, be they biochemical, physiological or psychodynamic, are only of peripheral interest to him. Although there is often no more connection between behaviour therapies and learning theory than adherence to a shared, and often empty, S–R terminology, it has been customary to use learning theories as a reference point in describing behaviour therapies. The term "situational therapy" would be a much more appropriate and correct description of these approaches. Studies of social situations and social episodes have an important role to play in this branch of clinical psychology.

Corresponding to the two major learning theoretical paradigms in psychology, we can distinguish between classical conditioning and operant conditioning behaviour therapies.

Perhaps the most widely used classical conditioning technique is counterconditioning, which includes such techniques as reciprocal inhibition, desensitization and aversive conditioning. The usefulness of these methods rests on a conceptualization of neuroses as simply persistent maladaptive learned habits, which are typically associated with persistent anxiety. Wolpe (1958, 1969) suggested that the association between anxiety and the stimuli eliciting anxiety can be weakened by the introduction of a competing and pleasant stimulus. For example, muscle relaxation and the associated feeling of well-being are incompatible with the anxiety response of physical and mental tension normally elicited. In a more general sense, the creation of a situation or episode which calls for responses other than the typical anxiety response lies at the heart of the theory. It is noteworthy that for this situational treatment to be effective, it must be perceived by the patient in an appropriate way—in other words, the situation which is being manipulated is the patient's private, subjective situation and not the external, objective situation.

Assertiveness training is another well-known method. The rationale for its use is that if the patient concentrates on self-expression, control and self-assertion in otherwise anxiety-evoking situations, this preoccupation will be incompatible with the habitual anxiety response—in addition, a presumably socially adaptive response style is also being acquired.

Behaviour therapies based on classical conditioning typically also involve the assessment of the patients' perception of the different anxiety-arousing situations—the construction, as it were, of a subjective anxiety hierarchy. This is a preliminary step to systematic desensitization training which involves the gradual association of pleasant sensations with previously anxiety-arousing situations. As in counterconditioning, the "positive", or pleasant stimulus is provided by relaxation training, and patients are asked to associate this relaxed state with increasingly anxiety-arousing situations. Desensitization training continues until the patient is able to experience all situations without the previous anxiety response.

A further therapeutic technique is aversive conditioning, used for the elimination of undesirable responses. This technique has been most frequently used with alcoholics, homosexuals and drug addicts, and involves the administration of aversive stimuli (shocks, pain, social disapproval) as soon as the undesired response is emitted. It is this technique which is most heavily fraught with ethical problems, since the response to be eliminated is no longer anxiety, but can be any other kind of socially disapproved behaviour, for example, expressions of homosexual affection and arousal.

It is noteworthy that the units of diagnosis and therapy used here are once again situations or episodes—whole, meaningful sequences of interactive behaviour and experience which the patient perceives as anxiety-evoking. Since behaviour therapies are typically based on individual treatment, the therapist customarily relies on the patient's self-report in identifying or operationalizing episodes or situations. Clearly such an unsystematic approach to diagnosing and manipulating perceptions of complex episodes may be fraught with difficulty. Patients' reports are subject to numerous biases, such as social desirability, primary or secondary gain in labelling some episodes as "difficult", or simply lack of knowledge or conscious awareness of the real sources of anxiety in complex situations. The uncritical reliance on unchecked self-report data on reactions to episodes is indeed striking in situational therapies. Idiographic studies of a client's cognitive episode domains, as described in Chapter 8, offer a reliable method for assessing individual episode hierarchies.

BEHAVIOUR MODIFICATION

In contrast to these behaviour therapies rooted in the classical conditioning paradigm, the different techniques going under the name of "behaviour modification" take operant conditioning models as their starting point. The aim of these therapies is to eliminate inappropriate or maladaptive modes of behaviour by systematically manipulating their consequences, or their "reinforcement contingencies", to use Skinner's terminology. Behaviour modification programmes are based on the initial identification of the frequency of the target behaviour to be changed, as well as on an analysis of all the possible environmental variables which may reinforce or control the target behaviour. The initial and most successful application of these techniques took place in strictly restricted environments, such as the "total institution" (Goffman, 1963) represented by the psychiatric ward. Many patient management problems, as well as diverse manifestations of disturbed behaviours could be controlled by the skilful manipulation of reinforcements. The introduction of "token economies" in psychiatric wards is the best example of attempts to institute uniform systems of reinforcements.

In contrast with behaviour therapies based on the classical conditioning model, behaviour modification is not based on the client's subjective understanding of the situation or the episode he finds himself in. The conceptualization of behaviour modification therapies is much more atomistic, seeking to identify given behaviours and relevant reinforcements without regard to the situational context. Instead of seeking to alter the patient's cognitive understanding of the episode and his own role in it, behaviour modification concentrates on his elementary behaviours only. This leads us to one of the potential problems of this approach: the acquisition of appropriate responses, or the elimination of inappropriate ones typically takes place in a restricted, atypical environment and social context. For these changes to be effective, it is of central importance that the newly acquired responses should be generalized to other, dissimilar kinds of situations and episodes. This is of little significance for permanently hospitalized patients, where behaviour modification is used simply as a tool for ward management, but is crucial in the large majority of cases, where the aim of the therapy is the ultimate reintegration of the client into society. By neglecting the situational or episodic context it is easy to lose sight of the problem of response generalization, an all-important criterion for the ultimate success of the therapy. The importance of having a reliable representation of a client's episode structure thus arises in a different form in behaviour modification therapies. The therapist needs to know the normal interaction routine of the client in order to design the therapeutic situation in such a way that it should be easily generalizable to real-life episodes.

SOCIAL SKILLS THERAPY

A most interesting extension of the different behaviour therapies rests on the application of social learning (as against S–R theoretical) principles in therapy. Concepts such as imitation, modelling and vicarious reinforcement can be successfully applied in clinical practice (Bandura, 1969). Perhaps the most significant offspring of these efforts is the spreading popularity of the different social skills training therapies.

Social skills training therapy has a double parentage. On the one hand, it can be related to the different learning therapies, and as such, it is primarily an application of the social learning model to the acquisition of a wide range of interactive skills, using modelling, role-playing, social reinforcement and response generalization as the main stages in the training (Goldstein et al., 1976).

There is a second background to social skills training, however, which can be found in social psychology. The experimental study and analysis of different verbal and non-verbal communication skills in social psychology has eventually led to the emergence of a set of standards or norms describing the "normal" pattern of occurrence of such subtle communicative behaviours as eye-contact, spacing, or paralinguistic cues (Argyle and Kendon, 1967). It was but a short step from this research to the observation that in many clinical patients the performance of these routine interactive behaviours is defective, and to the proposal of a "skills" model of social behaviour. According to this conceptualization, advanced primarily by Argyle (1969), social skills can be understood as any other motor or performance skills. Deficiencies in social skills are presumably due to inadequate learning experiences, and the remedy lies in the rehearsal of the desired behaviours until the necessary level of skill is achieved (Trower et al., 1978).

Social skills training has become one of the most popular branches of situational therapies, and is currently widely applied both in the treatment of psychiatric patients, in order to facilitate their re-integration into the community (Goldstein et al., 1976), and in the training of otherwise normal clients, such as students, who experience specific difficulties in their interpersonal relations, and where these difficulties can be related to their deficiencies in social skills (Bryant and Trower, 1974). In contrast to the extremely widespread use of these techniques, the ultimate clinical evaluation of the method is yet to emerge.

The techniques used in social skills training include a fairly eclectic set of procedures, which are all based on heightening the client's awareness of his existing social performance, and the teaching of improved skills. The more learning theoretically oriented therapies use four basic processes: the first step is the acquisition of the desired skill through modelling, with the model being presented on video or audio tape. The second step is the performance of the desired skill by the learner himself, via role playing, followed by the provision of social reinforcement or approval by the trainer. The fourth, and perhaps most crucial stage in the therapy is transfer learning, or the practice and implementation of the acquired skill in a wide range of situations. This is normally done by "homework", or the practice performance of the skill by the trainee in the course of his normal everyday routine.

Structured learning therapy (Goldstein *et al.*, 1976), as described above, pays relatively little attention to individual differences in the perception and interpretation of situations and episodes, and tends to asssume that there are a set of uniform and essential skills necessary for successful "community living". These skills are in effect always embedded in typical episodes, which strongly reflect the mores and habits of a given cultural milieu at a given point in time. Thus, the skill episodes used to illustrate essential social performances by Goldstein *et al.*, (1976), taking the American culture as standard, may sound absurd in other cultures. The point is that definitions of what is a socially skilled performance are not universal, but are relative to (a) the culture in which the skill is to be performed, and (b) within that culture, the particular social episode which is to be successfully performed. The learning therapeutical approach tends to devote less than adequate attention to these factors.

The second school of social skills training relies on a much more intensive, and more client-centred approach for its effectiveness. The process is described in some detail by Trower *et al.* (1978). The first step in this therapy is the establishment of the existing level of skill, and the identification of the individual's areas of difficulty in social performance. Training proceeds from the simple to the more complex skills, and is characterized by the use of a wide range of eclectic techniques going well beyond the learning processes used in structured learning therapy. The client's subjective understanding of his difficulties is always sought, and is actively encouraged during therapy. Video-tape feedback is frequently used to confront the client with his previous performance, and to provide him with feedback to facilitate further learning. Such cognitive feedback procedures are used to complement usual social reinforcement techniques. Skills are conceptualized not simply as complex motor performances, but the correct identification of the requirements of the situation—a complex cognitive task—is also taught. This brand of social skills training is thus more thorough, more client-centred and more cognitively oriented than are simple learning therapies.

It nevertheless shares an important shortcoming with all forms of social skills training. Namely, that social skill is conceptualized as an intra-psychic, cross-situational quality, something which resides in the individual, and is generalizable across different interaction situations and episodes. This assumption can be wildly inaccurate. Even the most "unskilled" people perform successfully in certain situations, with certain other partners. Most people who would be held skilled can recall several situations or episodes where their performance is less than adequate. For example, in a "normal" population of students, an extremely high percentage may report difficulties in situations such as going to a party, making contact with a member of the opposite sex, etc. (Bryant and Trower, 1974). What is missing from the skills model is thus an appreciation of the essential episode specificity of social skills. Even though typical situations are used as the vehicle for social skills training, at no point is the client's perception and understanding of the requirements of social episodes studied, nor are his perceptions of particularly difficult situations assessed. In diagnosing social skills deficiencies, we look for behavioural inadequacies to the complete exclusion of situational contingencies. Yet it seems likely that social skills deficiences are at least partly attributable to a failure to adequately represent the nature and requirements of interaction episodes. Indeed, in a study currently underway we have found that skilled and unskilled subjects have significantly different representations of social episodes (Forgas and Gilligan, 1979, unpublished data). Just as in personality theory the quantification and measurement of situational variables has become one of the most important tasks for research, in social skills training we are facing the same problem. The development of quantitative diagnostic methods for assessing social episodes and situations as experienced by a client is a pressing need. A related problem is the need for objective information about the characteristics of typical social episodes within a culture, not as perceived by the client, but as defined by the "normal" majority. At the moment, a trainer's intuitive knowledge as to what constitutes adequate and skilled performance, for example, at a dinner party or at a job interview, constitutes the criterion for the skill to be achieved. Obviously, the scope for errors, misunderstandings, and simply incorrect assessment of episodes by the trainer is extremely wide. One of the purposes of this book is to demonstrate that the objective study of social episodes is not only feasible today, but that it is the only avenue open to us if we want to extend the scope of psychological enquiry. The potential of this method in social skills therapy is perhaps greater than in any other applied branch of psychology. By representing the stereotypical "correct" interaction episode within a subcultural milieu, we can construct an objective yardstick whereby skilled performance can be evaluated.

In summary, the recent advent of behaviour therapies in clinical psychology can be construed as signalling the end of the dominance of personological theories in this discipline, and the gradual emergence of first situational, and ultimately, interactionist theories. Many of the behaviour therapies discussed rely explicitly on a situational or episodic formulation of behaviour, and indeed, take the client's perception and cognitive representation of the episode as an important variable in therapy. However, situations and episodes are always invoked intuitively, in the absence of any quantified or objective information about their characteristics. This is most obvious in social skills training, where the client's adoption of socially approved modes of performance in specific episodes is the ultimate aim. Neither the client's perception of the relevant episode, nor the existing consensual definition of what constitutes "skilled" performance in that episode are studied empirically. The contribution of the approach advocated here is that of providing a suitable framework, and appropriate methodologies for representing social episodes objectively, as seen by members of a specific subcultural group, or by a given individual member of that group.

Social episodes and social psychology

It is perhaps surprising that social psychology, the natural domain, as it were, for the study of social episodes, has paid little attention to episodic or situational concepts to date. This is at least partly explained by the discipline's preoccupation with the esoteric and unrepresentative episode typically created in the laboratory.

Although problems of external validity continued to haunt social psychological experiments, and the unrepresentative situations created in such classic experiments as Asch's (1952) studies of conformity, Milgram's (1974) studies of obedience, or the risky shift studies (Pruitt, 1971) were often criticized, the laboratory "episode" continued to be in the forefront of social psychological research. More recently, the reorientation taking place in personality theory, and the realization that the laboratory episode has its own cultural definition (Rosenthal, 1966; Wuebben *et al.*, 1974) led to the emergence of the present concern with social episodes and situations as meaningful objects of study.

EPISODIC DIFFERENCES IN SOCIAL BEHAVIOUR

Social psychologists, like personality theorists and clinical psychologists, tended to operate on the basis of the intrapsychic consistency assumption, at least until recently (Argyle and Little, 1972). Social behaviour, the perception of others, attitudes and values, prejudice or the reactions of groups were implicitly assumed to be cross-situationally invariant. Yet evidence to the contrary has been available for decades. La Piere's (1934) classic study of differences in racial discrimination under different situational conditions is but one well-known example. It is not that social psychologists denied the importance of episodic differences in behaviour; rather, in their quest for cross-situational regularities, they have ignored the obvious situation specificity of many social acts.

It is in demonstrating the untenability of the cross-situational consistency assumption that the study of social episodes has important implications for social psychology. Even such enduring characteristics as perceptions of each other by members of an established social group are in fact dependent on the episode context, as we have seen in Chapter 8. In effect, the culturally-defined episode context is one of the most salient and common variables social psychologists have to deal with. Different episodes call for different personality characteristics, behaviours and attitudes.

Although social psychologists showed little interest in the study of representative situations, as Brunswik (1956) proposed, they have been conspicuously successful in using systematic research designs to discover the characteristics of selected, *ad hoc* situations and episodes. In a general sense, most social psychological experiments can be construed as attempts to discover the parameters of a particular episode. Experimenters tend to think of such parameters as independent variables—yet in effect what they are manipulating is mostly their subjects' perception of the episode confronting them. The need for subtle and not so subtle deception strategies to distract the subjects' natural episode perception competencies is ample evidence for this (Kelman, 1967; Mixon, 1974). From this perspective, the main body of social psychological research may be seen as the amassment of information about an extremely large number of episodes, without much information about the dimensions along which these episodes can be related to each other. Results of such empirical studies can be described generally according to the formula "In episode X, persons of category Y will behave in the following manner . . .", the ubiquitous format for summarizing studies in introductory textbooks. It is notable that the description of the episode itself is usually given in objective terms (e.g. "when confronted by discrepant judgements by a majority of others" for the Asch conformity episode), yet for any real explanation of the resulting behaviour, it is immediately necessary to take into account the subject's subjective representation or interpretation of the episode confronting him. This is exactly what Deutsch and Gerard (1955) did in their analysis of components of the Asch conformity experiment.

Much of social psychological theorizing is of this kind, in essence, seeking to construct models of cognitive episode construction and interpretation processes. The popular homeostatic theories of Newcomb (1950), Festinger (1957) and others, attribution theory, self-perception theory (Bem, 1972b), the theory of psychological reactance (Brehm,1966), or information integration theory (Anderson, 1974) all describe episode interpretation processes in specified kinds of situations. Such theories in effect construct a model of the relationship between an objective situation, and the internal episode to which social actors react.

We can see then, that despite their apparent lack of interest, social psychologists do little else than study social episodes. What they have not done is to study social episodes representatively, attempting to clearly relate episodes to each other, and thereby ensuring the greater generalizability of the results of their studies. The lack of accumulation of knowledge of ever greater generality in social psychology is not necessarily due to the historicity of social science data (Gergen, 1973). More likely it can be attributed to the fact that researchers are habitually trained to focus on the intra-episodic intricacies between independent and dependent variables, thus losing from sight between-episode relationships.

In assessing the external validity of social psychological experiments we are commonly relying on the intuitive evaluation of the manipulated experimental episode as being representative of a class of real-life episodes. It would clearly be advantageous to have some quantitative evidence to back up such estimates. The techniques for assessing perceptions of social episodes described here (Chapter 5) offer just such a possibility. For example, if we could quantify an experimental episode, such as the Asch-type conformity situation, as high on the social anxiety and low on the involvement dimension this would provide empirical guidelines as to the type of real-life episodes in which the findings can be expected to hold. In contrast, conformity in low anxiety, high involvement episodes may imply a completely different episode interpretation process on the part of the subjects. The suggested distinction between normative and informal social pressures in conformity episodes reflects just such a difference in episode perception on the part of the subjects (Deutsch and Gerard,1955).

In summary, then, our social behaviour is at least as much determined by fluctuations in episode requirements as by personally consistent behaviour dispositions. Social psychology has been, to a large extent, the study of contrived episodes thought to be representative of some class of real-life episodes. It is a logical and necessary development that the sampling of episodes should be placed on a more systematic footing. The description and categorization of social episodes based on an individual's cognitive representation of them offers a feasible technique with which to accomplish such a task.

SOCIAL PSYCHOLOGICAL APPROACHES TO EPISODES

There were several attempts in social psychology to come to grips with the obvious episodic nature of social behaviour. For the most part, these attempts tended to remain on the level of speculative analysis.

Originally, in accordance with the external stimulus approach of Chein (1954) and Gibson (1959), and in keeping with the tenets of learning theory, Rotter (1954, 1955), Sherif and Sherif (1956; 1963) and others tended to stress the role of the objective social environment in affecting behaviour. Others, for example Sells (1963) and Arnault (1963) suggested hypothetical taxonomic systems for describing situational variables, and research on organizational environments may be construed as an implementation of part of this programme (Astin, 1972; Pace and Stern, 1958).

The other main stream of interest in episodes is more directly rooted in the cognitive, phenomenological tradition of Lewin (1951), Koffka (1935), Murray (1951), and Asch (1952). Episodes or situations are internal, cognitive representations of environmental objects according to this approach; terms such as "phenomenal field" (Snygg, 1941), "life space" (Lewin, 1951), "behavioural world" (Herbst, 1970) or Merleau-Ponty's (1962) perceived situation all refer to such cognitive representations of external situations.

Some researchers went further, and offered explicit operationalizations of social episodes. Watson and Potter (1962), for example, in one of the earliest attempts to define a unit of interaction, claim that their objective "in constructing a new unit for the analysis of interaction was to create a unit which could focus upon an interpersonal system rather than an individual" (p. 24). Their definition of such a unit, an episode, is as follows:

> episode is to denote an analytically derived unit of interaction defined in terms of a unitary role system, a single focus of attention, and only one relationship expressed by axis partners towards that which is the focus of attention . . . Our image of the episode is much like Newcomb's (1953) of the A–B–X system . . . A to B re X (p. 254).

This definition, building on pre-existing models of interaction, suffers from the shortcoming that it is only applicable to simple and atomistic units. The invocation of the relevance of role and rule systems is similar to Argyle's (1976) more recent approach, and suggests that Watson and Potter's (1962) definition also entails a strong cultural element, even though this is not explicitly emphasized.

The most productive approaches to social episodes have concentrated on the cultural, consensual element in different interaction sequences. In one such programme, social episodes were used as the central units to understand and analyse cultural differences in interaction.

In their research programme concerned with facilitating cross-cultural communication, Triandis and his co-workers have used the concept of stereotypical episodes as their main conceptual unit (Triandis, 1972; Triandis et al., 1968). This approach had its precursor in Flanagan's (1954) interest in the "critical incident". "By an incident is meant any observable human activity that is sufficiently complete in itself to permit inferences and predictions to be made about the person performing the act" (Fiedler *et al.*, 1970, p. 2). This definition is closely related to Barker and Wright's (1955) earlier definition of behaviour settings as symbolic embodiments of cultural expectations of interaction episodes.

Based on the notion of subjective culture, Triandis and his co-workers argued that training in cross-cultural communication must involve an assimilation of the subjective culture of the group to be approached. They developed a series of instruments, called the culture assimilator, which in essence contained the brief description of a series of typical episodes, characteristic of the culture, which students were asked to interpret or analyse. The trainee would eventually assimilate the correct cultural meaning of the different episodes. This method is of great interest, since it represents one of the few attempts to use social episodes as objects of empirical research. The use of typical social episodes as the main carriers of knowledge of a culture is noteworthy, and is congruent with the definition of social episodes proposed here. Using the techniques outlined earlier (Chapters 5, 7 and 8), cultural perceptions of stereotypical episodes could be quantitatively represented, instead of the free-response or intuitive accounts predominantly used to date.

In another research programme, Scheflen (1964, 1971) studied patterns of social interaction, mostly in psychiatric ward environments. He suggested a taxonomic system of behavioural units, in which the largest unit, a "presentation", is strongly reminiscent of an episode in the dramaturgical sense. Scheflen's approach to the study of these presentations or episodes was essentially clinical and interpretative. He describes a sequence of events as they occur within the group, and offers his own interpretation of the meanings of these events, following Goffman's methodology. Since he applied this kind of analysis to a fairly restricted range of episodes only, and his analyses are more detailed and intensive than Goffman's, Scheflen's work shows greater affinity with social psychological research. He is also consistently interested in more subtle channels of interpersonal communication, such as non-verbal behaviour. In contrast to most other researchers interested in episodes, Scheflen pays relatively little attention to the cultural content of his episodes; his main interest is the intra-psychic motivations, intentions and strategies of the actors within the framework of restricted episodes, such as a clinical interview.

One interesting approach to the study of episodes is Bjerg's (1968) work on the analysis of complex human interactions, such as conversations. "Our concepts have to be such that they can take account of total social events" he writes (p. 206). His approach is generally applicable to analyses of both verbal and non-verbal aspects of social interaction, and is a good example of the practical application of the kind of methodology proposed by Harre and Secord (1972).

Bjerg introduces the concept of "agon" to denote the context, the framework within which interaction takes place: "our task is to get to know the timetables, the rules, the handicaps, the actual moves and messages of each agon" (p. 209). Within these frames, agons, or interaction settings in the wider sense, the events of the interaction can be analysed as a flow of messages, as an exchange of goods, or as the alternating sequence of moves. Bjerg explicitly states that such frames or agons must be of a "quite general nature . . . constituting shared contexts for interaction within a given group or culture" (p. 212). His empirical work has led to the listing of a number of recurring "agons", and some main elementary types of moves that can be made within an agon (e.g. demand–offer–give–yield–withhold, etc.).

This approach incorporates several conceptual refinements. Perhaps most important is the distinction made between the two components of an episode, the setting, frame or "agon", incorporating some aspects of the purpose, outcome and social definition of the episode, and the moves, referring to both the idiosyncratic behaviours of the actors, and to regularities in the within-episode sequencing of acts. Secondly, the explication of the three alternative ways of analysing interaction as exchanges of messages, goods or moves (communication, exchange theory and game-theory approach respectively) seems a promising clarification. The distinction between "agons" and moves within agons is similar to the distinction between the social expectations and definitions attached to behaviour (e.g. role expectation) and the actual behaviour within this framework (e.g. role performance) (Merton, 1957), or the distinction between episode expectations and episode performance suggested in Chapter 1.

An exhaustive treatment of episodes as useful analytical concepts in social psychology is offered by Harre and Secord (1972), as mentioned earlier. They define episodes as "any sequence of happenings in which human beings engage which has some principle of unity. Episodes have a beginning and an end which can usually be identified" (p. 10), and later "any natural division of social life is an episode" (p. 147).

These authors present a strong criticism of the positivist, variable-manipulating type of experimental social psychology, and argue for an anthropomorphic, realistic conception, in which men are seen as conscious social actors. This approach is clearly related to the dramaturgical model mentioned earlier: "Social behaviour is mostly consciously self-monitored rule following . . . /whereby/ people present themselves under what they take to be suitable personas" (Harre and Secord, p. 147). Unfortunately, the approach, and the definition of episodes offered, are probably too unspecific to be readily adopted in empirical research.

Another area in social psychology where our current approach to the study of social episodes may be readily adopted is in the area of applied research. Existing studies, as well as further work proposed here have so far concentrated on the study of episode domains which were in some sense representative of the life environment of the judges. There are, however, several categories of social interaction episodes which are of applied interest, and thus warrant special scrutiny. Encounters involving aggression and violence, or encounters involving heterosexual relationships are two important examples.

Interactions involving aggression or violence are of obvious heuristic as well as practical interest, yet we know very little about the kinds of distinctions people make between different occurrences of violence. Perceived severity or seriousness of violent acts is the only dimension so far studied, and there is already considerable evidence indicating that such a unidimensional representation does not do justice to the complex and subtle distinctions normally made between different aggressive episodes. In a recent study, we have tried to discover the kinds of distinctions people naturally make between aggressive episodes which they have personally experienced themselves (Forgas *et al.*, 1979b). A representative sample of aggressive episodes was obtained from a pilot study, where subjects were asked to list as many aggressive incidents personally experienced by themselves as possible. In the second stage of the study, the similarities between the most frequently mentioned such episodes were derived, and used as input to an MDS analysis. Results showed that a complex, four-dimensional episode space was necessary to represent the intuitively perceived differences between aggressive incidents. The ubiquitous "seriousness" dimension was only indirectly represented in this episode space. Instead, judges tended to differentiate aggressive incidents in terms of

(a) their probability of occurrence, (b) justifiability, (c) the presence or absence of provocation and emotional arousal, and (d) the extent to which the incident was under control and was likely to be punished (Fig. 1).

It thus appears that naturally occurring aggressive episodes are perceived and experienced in a multidimensional psychological domain. Contrary to popular belief as well as implicit legal assumptions, perceived severity is not the most important attribute of aggressive incidents. Insofar as the legal system seeks to reflect popular perceptions of aggressive acts, methods such as the ones described here may be applicable to the empirical representation of such complex perceptions. Since individuals engaged in law enforcement typically have some degree of latitude in interpreting and labelling some behaviours as criminal, the perceptual distinctions used by them are of particular importance and could also be studied using the present methods. The implementation of these methods in large-scale studies could provide important information not only about changes in popular perceptions of aggression and crime, but also about the perceptual differences between individuals who are involved in the legal process, whether they are judges, offenders, jury members, policemen or victims.

Aggressive episodes are of course not the only applied domain where the study of social episodes may be of importance. Other episode categories, for example, heterosexual encounters, may also be studied by these methods, and we are currently engaged in some research in this area. Social psychological research into applied areas may thus be another important domain which could benefit from the study of social episodes.

There are then a number of precedents for studying social episodes in social psychology, as well as a number of contemporary research programmes seeking to place the study of social episodes on an empirical basis. Social psychological techniques, particularly methods developed in areas of research into social perception processes, should be readily applicable to the study of social episodes. The discipline of social psychology, uniquely poised between sociology and psychology, is the ideal domain for such research. Social psychologists, in one way or another, have always researched stereotypical social episodes. A clearer understanding of the real importance of episodic variations in social behaviour, and the integration of the various isolated research projects mentioned here should contribute to the rapid expansion of

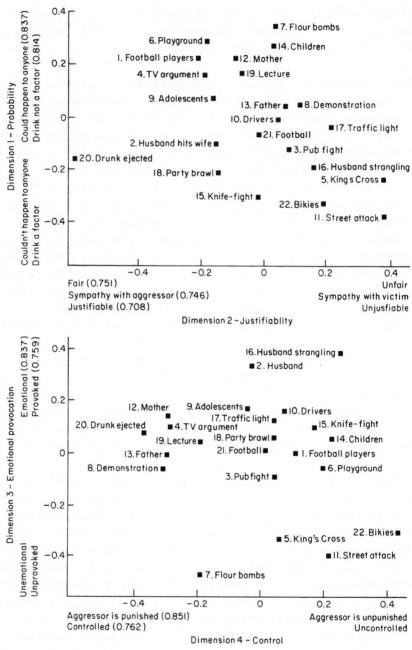

Fig. 1. The four-dimensional representation of 22 aggressive episodes showing the bipolar dimensions used to label the INDSCAL axes. (See also Forgas *et al.*, 1979b.)

the study of social episodes as an important area in social psychology.

Summary and conclusions

The current *Zeitgeist* of psychology is moving towards more cognitive, interactive and realistic models of human social behaviour. Traditional theories, assuming either the primacy of intrapsychic dispositions (personologism), or emphasizing the role of environmental variables (situationism) are being replaced by models seeking to represent the interaction between these factors. This change is affecting three areas in particular: personality theory, clinical psychology and social psychology, and it is in these areas that the study of social episodes has most significant implications. Personality theory in particular acted as a catalyst in this process. The commonly recognized shortcomings of intra-psychic "trait" theories have been most succinctly summarized by Mischel's (1968, 1969) social behaviour theory, suggesting the importance of situations as well as individuals as determinants of behaviour.

In this theory the physical, objective situation was emphasized, which has exposed Mischel to charges of not recognizing the interactive, cognitively mediated nature of situational effects on behaviour (Bowers, 1973). Mischel's argument that "it is essential to study the behaviours of a given person as a function of the conditions in which they occur" (1968, p. 296), has elicited a great deal of criticism. It has been suggested, for example, that situation-specificity is more apparent than real, since frequently people create their own situations (Wachtel, 1973b). In Mischel's more recent (1973) "cognitive social learning" theory, the emphasis has shifted to studying situations and episodes as they are cognitively constructed by individuals. Such a strategy should have widespread implications for other branches of psychology, such as clinical psychology (Trower *et al.*, 1978), and social psychology (Argyle and Little, 1972).

Clinical psychology is also undergoing rapid changes prompted by the growing impact of behaviour therapies on the one hand, and phenomenological-*Gestalt* theories on the other, resulting in an emerging flexibility and eclecticism in the discipline (Garfield and Kurtz, 1976). A cognitive-learning perspective, representing the merger of these "internalist" and "situationist" approaches is a recent development. "On the one hand, this hybrid recognizes the important role of private events and intrapersonal factors in adjustment, and on the other, it emphasizes the role of environmental variables in influencing personal phenomenology and performance" (Mahoney, 1977, p. 7). This approach is the clinical equivalent of Mischel's "cognitive social learning theory", and like the latter, it calls for methods for studying how individuals cognitively represent the life situations in which they move. Our approach to the study of social episodes is directly relevant to this objective. One of the most pressing tasks facing a cognitive-learning perspective in clinical psychology is "the development of more reliable methods for assessing cognitive phenomena" (Mahoney, 1977, p. 10), and it is in this area that the techniques described here have a contribution to make.

In summary, then, it is considered that research on cognitive representations of social episodes is the most rapidly developing field in the study of naturalistic interaction routines. The future prospects for joining these conceptual trends in personality and clinical psychology with the techniques already available for analysing episode perception appear excellent. We could do little more than hint at the numerous possibilities in this chapter. The next few years will no doubt see a striking increase in research into social episodes in these most directly affected branches of psychology.

10

Social Episodes: Summary, Conclusion and Implications

The central aim of this book was to demonstrate that concepts such as social episode can be adequately operationalized and studied using available quantitative empirical methods.

The objectives of this final chapter in particular are three-fold:

(a) to recapitulate the main arguments that precipitated the current interest in social episodes;

(b) to critically assess the research on social episodes that has been carried out so far;

(c) to consider the implications and future prospects of this branch of social psychology.

The argument for a study of social episodes

The study of social episodes is the result of the joint influence of a number of conceptual developments which have taken place in social psychology in recent years. The *Zeitgeist* of the discipline may be characterized by a number of major trends, such as the growing influence of cognitive theories (Carroll and Payne, 2976), an increasing interest in situational and episodic regularities in behaviour, and an emerging methodological ecclecticism. The growing awareness of sociological research and theories, as well as inroads made by linguistic, structuralist and anthropological thought have also significantly contributed to these developments. In other words, the traditional model of social psychology as a predominantly laboratory and experimental science is being replaced by the notion that any approach that yields useful and replicable data is acceptable. Clearly, the study of social episodes described here benefited from each one of these trends.

The concept of episodes itself, referring to cognitive representations of culturally coded interaction sequences, is rooted in major theoretical schools both in psychology and in sociology. In psychology, the S–R theoretical conceptualization of the situation as a more complex stimulus configuration gave way to the cognitive phenomenological view, defining situations in terms of how social actors perceive and cognitively represent them. Similarly, in sociology concern with "situational analysis" can be traced back to the work of Max Weber, and was explicitly proposed by W. I. Thomas, Florian Znaniecki, Willard Waller, Whorff and members of the symbolic interactionist school. The surprising similarities between the conceptualization of the situation or the episodes offered by psychologists such as Koffka, Lewin, Murray, Brunswik and more recently Mischel, Pervin and Ekehammar, and sociologists such as Thomas, Mead, Cooley, Schutz, Goffman and Garfinkel have gone unrecognized for too long. The study of social episodes may be seen as capitalizing on this dual heritage, by freely borrowing from both the psychological and the sociological traditions. Such similarities between psychological and sociological social psychology notwithstanding, it should also be clear that as far as research methodology is concerned, this book advocates psychological techniques in preference to sociological ones. The reason for this lies in the implicit belief in the need for objective, quantifiable data when such complex social objects as social episodes are studied, and the greater accumulated expertise and sophistication of psychologists in dealing with these kinds of data.

In Chapters 3 and 4 we have reviewed in some detail both the psychological and the sociological heritage of the study of social episodes. Rather than going over the same ground here, it may be advantageous to draw together the streams of development which are common to both disciplines, and which have contributed most to our approach to the study of social episodes.

Cognitivism

Both human psychology, and contemporary sociological schools share a growing emphasis on internal, cognitive structures and processes as the most promising explanatory concepts of social behaviour. Just as behaviourism has focused on observable behaviours as the proper topic for psychology, cognitivism may be seen as an increasingly coherent credo which emphasizes the need to study cognitive processes and structures in order to understand behaviour. This tendency is particularly visible in psychology. Mischel's (1973) cognitive social learning approach to personality is an excellent example of a theory which is phenomenological in its orientation, suggesting the primacy of internal cognitive representations over external stimuli, while still apparently adhering to a learning theoretical terminology. Exactly the same sentiments are echoed in clinical psychology, where the cognitive learning trend has been amply documented in recent years (cf. Mahoney, 1974). These recent developments, although it is rarely acknowledged explicitly, represent a direct continuation of the cognitive-phenomenological tradition of Lewin, Heider and Murray in psychology. Thus, Murray suggested that "situations are susceptible to classification in terms of the different kinds of effects which they exert (or may exert) on the subject, that is, in terms of their significance to his well-being" (1951, p. 459). The same orientation is echoed in Bowers' more recent suggestion that "the situation is a function of the observer, in the sense that the observer's cognitive schemas filter and organize the environment in a fashion that makes it impossible ever to completely separate the environment from the person observing it" (1973, p. 328). Similarly, social episodes are useful explanatory concepts insofar as individuals have shared cognitive representations of them, and such representations are related to their behaviour in such episodes.

Cognitivism in social psychology can be further subdivided into two sub-areas: structuralist and functionalist cognitive approaches. Functionalist cognitive theories have been around for much longer, and it is remarkable that the genealogy of most such theories may be traced to the writings of one man: Fritz Heider. His interest in "naive psychology", and the processes whereby phenomenal causality is assigned by social actors is directly or indirectly responsible for some of our most influential theories today. Heider's cognitive balance principle, elaborated by Newcomb and Osgood, and reincarnated in Festinger's cognitive dissonance theory, has recently stimulated such new theories as Brehm's theory of psychological reactance and Bem's theory of self-attribution. Another line of theories traces its origins to Heider's interest in the way attributions of phenomenal causality are made, and through the work of Jones and Davis, is indirectly responsible for the spreading influence of attribution theories. Yet another line of cognitive functionalist research, the study of information integration strategies as developed by Anderson, is also indebted to Heider's speculations about interpersonal perception. In one way or another, modern social psychology is characterized by the dominance of cognitive theories which in effect are functionalist in orientation, seeking to construct models of how cognitive processes are related to social behaviour. What is remarkable is that most of these theories have Heider's "naive psychology" as their ancestry, yet both in their terminology and in their professed aims, many of them pay homage to the external variable approach of S–R formulations (cf. Bem, 1972a).

As a recent addition to functionalist cognitivism, and largely stimulated by structuralist anthropology and linquistics, social psychologists have also become increasingly interested in studying cognitive structures. Characteristically, they have brought their sophisticated psychological techniques to bear on this task, and have achieved some remarkable successes. Studies of the structure of beliefs (Bem, 1970a) as well as the cognitive structure of values (Rokeach, 1973) represent applications of the cognitive structuralist approach in social psychology. W. Scott's research on the structure of natural cognitions, and his more recent work on the structural properties of natural groups is also an excellent example of a psychological application of structuralist strategy (Scott, 1967, 1978). Attempts to transfer linguistic methods directly to psychological research are also common, although no major findings employing this strategy have emerged as yet.

The study of social episodes, particularly the perceptual strategy emphasized here, may be seen as incorporating both the functionalist and the structuralist approaches. Its aim is the construction of empirical models, in order to analyse differences in the cognitive representation of social episodes by subjects. The techniques used are psychological, but the underlying rationale is to represent domains of *social* cognition. Once such a representation is achieved, the next task is to understand how cognitive representations of episodes are related to behaviour. This enterprise is functionalist in orientation, and follows in the footsteps of such phenomenologist theorists as Heider, Lewin, Kelly and others.

The cognitivist trend is also evident in sociology, but it is less explicitly associable with specific theories. Mead's symbolic interactionism, and Schutz's phenomenological theory are the two most important root sources of recent cognitive approaches. Both symbolic interactionism, and phenomenological sociology rely heavily on internal, cognitive processes for their explanations of social action. Symbolic interactionism in particular has explicit predictions about the role of cognitive mediating variables in social behaviour, which have not been evaluated to date, mainly due to the lack of available empirical methods. According to symbolic interactionism, cognitive representations of the social world arise in the course of social interaction, and a shared culture, as well as the socialized individual, are the products of this process. Different interaction experiences should thus result in different cognitive structures. The studies described in Chapters 7 and 8 demonstrate that such predictions of this most influential theory can in fact be empirically tested. These theories are functionalist in orientation, and offer a potentially rich source of empirical hypotheses about social episodes. With the advent of new statistical techniques, such long-neglected cognitive theories as symbolic interactionism should finally occupy their rightful place in empirical social psychological research.

The study of social episodes is thus characterized by a heavy emphasis on cognitive variables. Both social psychology and sociology show a growing tendency to rely on internal cognitive theories, and this is reflected in the conceptualization of social episodes adopted here. The study of cognitive representations of social episodes is already an important research area, while sociological theories such as symbolic interactionism offer a rich variety of hypotheses about the development and functioning of such cognitive representations in regulating behaviour.

Situationism

The second major trend both in psychology and in sociology is the interest in situational, as against intrapsychic, regularities in behaviour. Changes in behaviour as a function of different situations or episodes hold a new fascination for psychologists as well as microsociologists, who have traditionally operated within the framework of the "intrapsychic consistency" assumption (Ball, 1972). Although situations or episodes as worthwhile objects of research are a relatively recent phenomenon, the behavioural sciences have always used situation manipulations in their research. W. I. Thomas, a sociologist, recognized this in 1927, when he pointed out that "The situational method is the one in use by the experimental physiologist and psychologist who prepare situations, introduce the subject into the situation, observe the behaviour reactions, change the situation, and observe the changes in the reactions" (Thomas, 1966, p. 155). Despite this realization, it took another 40 years before any systematic study of situations and episodes was undertaken.

One of the hallmarks of psychological social psychology is its concentration on the individual, and its attempt to explain social behaviour in terms of individual, rather than episodic or situational characteristics. The belief in stable intra-organismic constructs such as "traits", "motives" and "dispositions" as ultimate explanations of behaviour has characterized not only personality research, but social psychology as well. As reservations about the utility of the trait approach (Peterson, 1965; Vernon, 1964) have developed into a serious challenge during the last decade, with suggestions for a radically different situational (Mischel, 1968) or interactionist (Bowers, 1973) orientation, it has become clear that "the implications for other areas of psychology where trait models have been used should receive serious attention" (Argyle and Little, 1972, p. 1). If situations and episodes are as important co-determinants of social behaviour as most of the present studies seem to suggest, then the development of methods capable of evaluating situational and episodic attributes is of great importance. The methods for the assessment of the perceived features of episodes proposed here have a role to play in that task.

The definition of what exactly a situation or an episode should mean is a major problem. Early learning theorists, in the tradition of British associationist philosophers such as Mills were in no doubt that situations are simply aggregates of simpler, elementary stimuli. The untenability of this assumption was recognized very early, and Tolman's concept of "cognitive maps" heralded the emergence of a new, holistic and cognitive conceptualization of the situation. Secondly, the social rather than physical nature of situations was recognized, particularly by theorists working within the cognitive, phenomenological paradigm. Finally, the subjective, perceived rather than the objectively measurable situation was recognized as the most promising conceptualization if the reliable prediction of behaviour is desired. The concept of social episodes embodies each one of these theoretical developments. The main interest of the present work is thus in holistic rather than atomistic, social rather than physical, potential rather than actual, and subjective (perceived) rather than objective (physical) situations (Chapter 3). Social episodes thus refer to relatively complex cognitive representations of interactions, which at the same time constitute part of the local culture, have a potential normative influence on behaviour, and whose meaning is subjective, that is, it can only be discerned through the study of individuals familiar with those situations. This definition of social episodes has a lot in common with some other approaches. Thus, Altman (1968) suggested that "situation definition is a subjective analysis of what a situation calls for and its demands, and an internalised plan of behaviour (but not necessarily of an aware nature)" (p. 25). Similarly, conceptualizations by Pervin (1975), Magnusson, (1971), Bjerg (1968), Watson and Potter (1962), Goffman (1963), Scheflen (1965) and Wish (1975) of related concepts also tend to emphasize the internal, cognitive nature of situations.

The main thrust of situational research has been towards the discovery and construction of situational taxonomies. Just as the concept of situations itself has undergone profound changes over the past few decades, attempts to construct situational taxonomies have shown a similar change. Early attempts to construct situational taxonomies in purely objective terms (Sells, 1963; Arnault, 1963) gave way to more subjective, perceptually oriented taxonomies. Thus, the most important features of situations and episodes are not necessarily those which can be reliably and objectively measured. Rather, consistencies in individuals' reactions to them offer a more meaningful set of criteria for classifying situations. In particular, affective, emotional reactions to situations, or the connotative meaning of situations (Osgood *et al.*, 1956) have emerged as the most useful taxonomic criteria. Recently, Mehrabian and Russell (1975) have further elaborated on this theme, suggesting that "human judgements of diverse samples of stimuli can be characterized in terms of three dimensions: evaluation, activity, and potency. We have termed the corresponding emotional responses pleasure, arousal and dominance" (p. 28). What is remarkable about this proto-taxonomy is that it corresponds closely to the cognitive dimensions which were found to characterize the cognitive representation of social episodes. In particular, evaluation in terms of being interesting and pleasant, and in terms of social anxiety and anticipated difficulty are the most commonly found episode dimensions. Thus it appears that human reactions to, and cognitive representations of such complex socio-cultural stimuli as social episodes may be described in terms of a limited number of connotative attribute dimensions.

Situationalism has also been a growing movement in sociology, especially in microsociological theories. As we have seen in Chapter 4, W. I. Thomas's situational analysis, and Mead's interest in symbolic interaction have continued to exert an influence. The interest of microsociologists such as Goffman and Garfinkel in the definition, negotiation and enactment of interaction episodes sprang from this same historical tradition. The cultural definition of social episodes, or situation definition in Thomas's terms, is the very essence of social life: "As long as definitions of situations remain constant and common we may anticipate orderly behaviour reactions. When rival definitions arise . . . we may anticipate social disorganisation and personal demoralisation" (1966, p. 166).

Thus we have seen that situationalism, that is, an interest in and the study of situational regularities in social behaviour, is very much in the forefront of both psychological and sociological thinking at the moment. The concept of situation underlying this interest is radically different from earlier, physicalistic conceptualizations. The "situation" or episode that has a potential to influence social behaviour is the cognitive episode, the one that exists in the cognitive representations individual social actors have about the regularities of behaviour expected in their cultural milieu. The study of social episodes has thus emerged as a result of these dual forces of influence in recent years: cognitivism and situationalism. Such conceptual changes would have been insufficient however, to result in a distinct empirical line of research. Social psychology, a discipline which happens to lie on the crossroads of these changes had to become more open to methodological eclecticism if the full potential of these conceptual developments was to be realized. The growing openness to new ideas in social psychology, following the dissensions of the past decade, is the third trend which contributed to the emerging study of social episodes.

Changes in social psychology

The numerous criticisms and internal turmoil in social psychology over the past decade was the third force which stimulated the study of social episodes, and provided the main impetus for writing this book. The apparently irreconcilable gap between hard-nosed experimental psychologists and advocates of the new breed of interpretative, descriptive social psychology (Harre, 1977), at the cost of some oversimplification, may be seen as the latest reincarnation of the age-old conflict between empiricism and rationalism, the search for causes as against the search for reasons, the conflict between prediction and explanation (Bruner, 1976). Whatever the theoretical merits of these opposing views, in practice the reconciliation of the two methodologies implied is not only possible, but desirable. It is possible to study cognitive representations of complex social phenomena by quantitative, empirical methods. This book is then, in a sense, the outcome of the clash between these two orientations. It should be clear that the road chosen does not belong firmly to either camp. The study of social episodes represents a bridge between hard-nosed empirical methodology, and interest in complex, natural examples of social behaviour which is very much in the phenomenological-interpretative tradition.

The periodic interruption of "normal science" (Kuhn, 1962), such as the one brought about by internal dissension in social psychology in the seventies, offers unique opportunities for synthesis, and for the mapping out of new directions. It should be clear that this book is not one of the messianic genre, common in recent years, which after a devastating criticism of the discipline seeks to introduce some radically new approach or methodology. Rather, the aim was to summarize and synthesize the main points raised by the many critics, and to suggest a modification of the methods and concerns of social psychology in the light of what is valid and reasonable within the criticisms. It was argued that the most influential critics do in fact share a number of crucial points, and that these can be adequately answered by a social psychology which concentrates on naturalistic social behaviour within given social episodes, and which makes use of some of the most recent analytic techniques available for the descriptive study of such complex units of behaviour.

To what extent does a study of social episodes overcome recent criticisms of social psychology (Chapter 2)? Firstly, we should perhaps consider the most general issue, that of the possibility of a Kuhnian "paradigmatic shift". If we have a paradigm in social psychology—and it is doubtful that we do—it could only be described as a most general belief in quantification and the need to rely on replicable, and in that sense, objective, data. Right through the brief history of social psychology there have always been numerous techniques and methods which could satisfy these criteria, without being "experimental" in the contemporary sense. Some of the most influential and ingenious studies were born of such eclecticism: Sherif's summer camp studies (Sherif et al., 1961), Festinger et al's, (1950) studies of a housing estate, or even Lewin's (1948) work on group dynamics show none of the restrictive marks of experimental orthodoxy. In that sense, the study of social episodes is just another branch in an eclectic discipline, which has always defied the imposition of a strict paradigm. Harre's insistence that a profound paradigmatic shift, replacing a mechanistic and positivistic paradigm with a humanistic and anthropomorphic one must take place before social psychology can reach its full potential, is too dramatic a scenario. The mechanistic model has never been universally accepted; and some of its greatest detractors have managed to make classic empirical contributions to social psychology. Solomon Asch, the initiator of many classical research topics, is an excellent example. While insisting on the unity of human experience as the only proper topic for social psychology, he nevertheless managed to fuse this interest with a sophisticated quantitative methodology. He argued that "Those who dream of objectivistic social psychology fail to realise that such a program can be pursued only if the data of experience are taken into account openly. We are today far from able to describe the most obvious and most significant social acts except in the language of direct experience" (Asch, 1972, p. 18). Just as Asch's *Gestalt* psychology can be comfortably accommodated within the allegedly restrictive paradigm of experimental social psychology, the study of social episodes will also find its place. The kind of radical reorientation advocated by Harre, and hinted at by McGuire (1973) is not really a necessary prerequisite for such an accommodation.

This is not to say that the changes which are taking place are not important for the future of social psychology. But such changes are evolutionary rather than revolutionary, and are organically rooted in the historical development of the discipline. In Chapters 3 and 4 it was suggested that even such an apparent neologism as "social episode" has in fact a deep historical anchorage, both in psychology and in sociology.

Having thus disposed of the possibility of a paradigmatic shift, we should attempt to assess the extent to which the study of social episodes will live up to the criteria set by recent critics of social psychology. It certainly represents a deviation from an experimental and atomistic approach, insofar as it places complex, integrated human behaviours and perceptions into the focus of analysis. It is phenomenological rather than physicalistic in orientation, since a social actor's cognitive representation of an episode, and not the objective features of the episode are studied. On the issue of description versus prediction, discussed in some detail in Chapter 2, the study of episodes incorporates both as different stages in the research process (Chapters 7 and 8). The creative, hypothesis-generating phase of research has only just begun, and inevitably, studies of social episodes have tended to be descriptive rather than predictive to date. This does not mean that in time, the critical, hypothesis-testing phase of research will not be of equal importance. Indeed, some of the studies described here in Chapters 7 and 8 have already pointed the way towards the possibility of evaluating hypotheses about social episodes. A greater balance between description and prediction, between the creative and critical phases of research is one trend that most critics would see as desirable. I hope such a balance will be achieved with the study of social episodes.

The status of the subject in social psychological research is another modal topic in contemporary social psychology. Apart from ethical considerations the main problem relates to the kind of information that we wish to obtain from subjects. Are they to be regarded as mere reactors to the elaborate experimental episodes we devise, or should they be considered equal partners in the scientific enterprise, as informants and helpers in understanding the regularities in social behaviour. In the first role their intelligence and ingenuity in devising explanations is a potential threat, in the second role it is an asset we cannot do without. Role playing, the collection of open-ended accounts or argument based on the model of the legal system are some of the variants for co-opting the subject as an equal participant in research. The study of social episodes has much affinity with these methods. Due to the nature of the subject matter, we need to study our informants' cognitive representations of social reality. Their cooperation and insight is helpful in getting an accurate picture, and there is no need to subvert their episode construction capabilities by deception. This does not mean that controlled experimental studies of social episodes are not on occasion appropriate. The study of perceptions of naturalistic encounters as a function of episode definition cues described in Chapter 8 is an example of such an experimental approach. On the whole, however, the study of social episodes is an area which by and large is exempt from the most damaging criticisms of experimental techniques of subject manipulation.

In summary, then, we have seen that the study of social episodes does in fact satisfy some of the major concerns raised by recent critics about social psychological methods, without departing from the major accepted paradigm of the discipline. It merely seeks to reach back to everyday social behaviour and experience, much in the tradition of Lewin, Murray, Brunswik and Asch. "Every field of enquiry must begin with the phenomena that everyday experience reveals, and with the distinctions it contains . . . it is necessary to add that a psychology based on phenomenal data alone must remain incomplete . . . We need . . . an objective psychology that will account for the structure of experience" (Asch, 1972, p. 19). This is the very task that the study of social episodes has addressed itself to.

Major findings

Cognitivism, situationism and recent changes in social psychology were identified as the main sources that encouraged recent interest in social episodes. As these trends have gained importance over the past few years, empirical studies of social episodes have also become more and more numerous. We have considered a large number of such studies on these pages, many of them designed by us with the specific objective of evaluating different aspects of the perception of episodes. What are the main results of these efforts to date?

Perhaps the most fundamental finding is that despite the apparently very large number of episodes which exist and their seeming complexity, judges have no difficulty in identifying interaction units with an impressive degree of consensual validation. Even more interesting is the fact that the number of such episodes occurring in the life routine of any one individual or a group are nowhere near as numerous as commonly assumed. In fact, nearly all studies considered here were based on the analysis of 15–30 social episodes, which were found to be quite representative of a social milieu or the daily routine of an individual. Even Barker's exhaustive surveys of behaviour settings suggest that in such large-scale environments as whole towns no more than about 200 behaviour setting genotypes can be identified. Pervin's (1976) subjects could not list more than about two dozen episodes in a completely open-ended questionnaire, and the daily interactions of such small groups as academic units or sports teams may be adequately represented by less than 20 episodes (Forgas, 1978a, 1979a). Indeed, it was found difficult to elicit a much greater number even with intensive questioning.

The second major finding is that individuals indeed have a fairly stable and clear cognitive representation of the episodes practised in their environment, and that such representations can be easily quantified and explicated. Such models of cognitive representations of social episodes are reliable insofar as similar structures were found to emerge irrespective of the particular data collection procedure used, and the representations were fairly stable over time (Chapter 7).

Such multidimensional representations of the cognitive space for social episodes are the foundation on which further research rests. The first application of such models is in the construction of taxonomies of social episodes for particular social milieux, groups or even individuals. We have repeatedly seen throughout this discussion that the quantification of complex situations and episodes, preferably in terms of how individuals perceive and react to them, is sorely needed in such diverse areas as personality research and clinical and social psychology. Episode taxonomies in effect quantify such complex interaction situations within a common coordinate framework. Thus, the identification of the attributes underlying the cognitive representation of social episodes is one of the major achievements of this line of research. Dimensions such as social anxiety and self-confidence, involvement or intensity, intimacy and friendliness and evaluation have repeatedly emerged from several studies, suggesting that a few connotative attribute dimensions are potentially sufficient to describe a very wide range of episodes. This research parallels earlier efforts in personality research, and recent studies of implicit theories of personality (Rosenberg and Sedlak, 1972). Just as the infinite range of individual personalities may be adequately described in terms of a small number of attribute dimensions, the infinite variety of social episodes can be equally adequately characterized in terms of a small number of attribute dimensions reflecting in effect individuals' reactions to such episodes. The three studies described in Chapter 7 demonstrate that such empirical representations of episode domains do in fact reflect the particular characteristics of the subcultures, groups, or individuals who practise these episodes. The possibility of constructing sensitive and quantifiable models of episode spaces offers the prospect of experimental studies of the factors affecting episode perception.

We have seen in Chapter 8 that there are a number of important variables which affect episode perception. Idiosyncratic individual characteristics, the role constraint of different episodes, the role relationship between the interactants and the physical environment or behaviour setting are the most important such cues so far demonstrated. It was also shown that social episodes themselves have a highly salient effect on other kinds of social perception judgements. Even interpersonal judgements within a well-established group, where members have known each other for some time and have interacted regularly in a broad range of episodes, are significantly influenced by the episode context. Thus, contrary to the assumption of individual consistency implicit in most studies of social perception, judgements of other people can be shown to fluctuate as a function of the episode context. Since in everyday life all social judgements are performed within the context of some episode, the specification of the parameters of such episodes is clearly an important future task.

Most of these findings are the outcome of research into the perception of social episodes, in effect the application of social perception methodology to the study of social episodes. Although this strategy appears the most fruitful one to date, other strategies have also yielded interesting results. The ecological approach of Barker in particular has been influential in helping to delimit the range of interactive settings that exist, and in constructing ecologically based taxonomies of behaviour routines. The structuralist approach has also yielded some important insights, demonstrating that at least some interactive behaviours may be shown to be subject to implicit rules of structure and sequencing (Clarke, 1976). The roles–rules model is in fact substantially related to the perceptual strategy. In studying social behaviour, "we should treat social interaction as a social product, and then try to discern in the people involved in the interaction the template or representation of this structure that led to this product" (Harre, 1977, p. 287). This was in fact the main objective of our studies of cognitive representations of social episodes. Harre's ethogenic approach (Harre, 1976, 1977; Marsh et al., 1978) to the study of social episodes, although similar in interest, is substantially different in its methods, choosing to concentrate on the interpretive analysis of subjective accounts as its main source of data. Objectors to this approach point to the lack of objectivity in the techniques used, and to exaggerated claims of universal relevance (Schlenker, 1977). Ethogenic studies "lack the control, precision and intersubjective reliability of experiments. A reader is often at the mercy of the researcher, trusting that subjective interpretations of ongoing events are reasonably accurate" (Schlenker, 1977, p. 325). Argyle and his research group at Oxford are also engaged in a series of studies of social situations employing the roles-rules strategy, with the essential difference that their methods are based on social psychological techniques rather than on microsociological analyses (Argyle *et al.*, 1979).

Empirical research on social episodes has thus already resulted in a number of highly interesting and relevant findings, and if one takes into account the number of research programmes currently in progress in this area, it seems assured that future results will be no less interesting. Some of the most promising areas for future research will be briefly considered later, while in the next section the major implications of the current approach to the study of social episodes will be discussed.

Implications

The central objective of this book was to present a first summary of an approach towards the study of natural interaction units, and to establish the feasibility of quantitative representations of such episodes. To the extent that interest in the study of social episodes and situations is on the increase in several areas of psychology, the approach outlined here should have direct implications for such areas. In addition, insofar as the present conceptualization of social episodes is directly based on some theories which were previously thought to be too ambiguous to be incorporated into social psychological research, the study of social episodes should also have some implications for the future status of such theories.

Symbolic interactionism in particular is closely related to the present approach to social episodes. The quantitative demonstration that the perception of social episodes is not only subculture-specific but that it is also the function of the particular interactive experience of the group or the individual (Chapter 7) supports one of the main propositions of symbolic interactionism. Insofar as the present methods and conceptualization of episodes allow the empirical evaluation of such hypotheses, symbolic interactionist theory should be of growing importance in guiding our research. Other, less comprehensively developed theories such as Goffman's dramaturgical model, Garfinkel's ethnomethodology or Harre's ethogenic strategy may similarly benefit from the possibilities outlined here for studying social episodes empirically. The relationship between such theories and the study of social episodes is a symbiotic one—many of our concepts and arguments were borrowed from these theories and now our methods and techniques may perhaps contribute to the further development of these theories by encouraging empirical research.

The implications of the study of social episodes for specific areas of social-, personality-, and clinical psychology are even more important, and have been treated in some detail in Chapter 9.

Perhaps the most pervasive implication emerging from this book is that social episodes and situations cannot be regarded as simply carriers of *ad hoc* devised manipulations of independent variables as was often the case to date. The present findings also strongly support the arguments posed by Rosenthal (1966), Wuebben *et al.* (1974), and others regarding the special nature of the episode of the psychology experiment. The basic stance of much of social psychology, assuming that episodes or situations are epiphenomenal to investigations of social behaviour and perception, cannot be maintained: instead, episodes and situations should be regarded as valid areas of investigation in their own right.

In most studies in social psychology, the detailed description and specification of the background and characteristics of the subjects is an obvious requirement, since it delimits the generality and, sometimes, the validity of the findings. Yet descriptions of the relevant social context or episode, and its requirements are hardly ever given in published articles. Just as the characteristics of the subjects define the population of individuals for whom the findings can be expected to hold, the characteristics of the experimental situation delimit the generality of the findings across different situations. As Rosenthal (1966) and others point out, the population of comparable relevant situations is often restricted to experimental episodes. Since methods of quantifying and describing situational variables are increasingly available, including the procedures outlined here, the specification of the perception of the experimental episode in objective terms should be a natural requirement. If the connotative dimensions underlying the perception of social episodes can be shown to be few, and fairly general (as these studies indicate they may well be), then the description of experimental episodes in standard terms, such as high, medium or low position on dimensions such as involvement, anxiety, self-confidence or task-orientation should become possible.

Research and theory in personality have also been "dominated by the trait model, which presumes latent predispositions that manifest themselves in terms of response consistencies across different situations" (Endler and Magnusson, 1976, p. xi). In the last 15 years, increasing numbers of researchers have questioned the validity of the trait model, and demands for studies of situational characteristics have been growing at an even faster rate (Frederiksen, 1972; Endler and Magnusson, 1974). Yet very few studies have emerged, and "there has been no *systematic* attempt to study situations *psychologically*" (Endler, 1975, p. 15). The dominant view emerging from the person v. situation controversy appears to be a sophisticated interactionism (Ekehammar, 1974; Bowers, 1973; Mischel, 1973), assuming the mutual interdependence of situational and personality factors in determining behaviour.

While numerous well-developed and sophisticated measures of personality variables are already available, measures of situations, particularly situations as perceived by the actors, are missing. The studies presented here provide a feasible approach to the quantification and measurement of situational and episode characteristics. Ultimately, the availability of quantified data on persons, situations and behaviours-in-situation should make it possible to exactly represent the interactions of personological and situation variables in producing behaviour. The present investigations may be helpful by offering a consistent operationalization of episodes, and a methodology for their study.

A further implication of these results for personality theory derives from the view that people not only perceive and react to, but actively construe situations and episodes (Wachtel, 1973a,b; Mischel, 1973). In this sense, style of episode perception can be conceptualized as analogous to a personality trait; there is an element of individual consistency in how episodes are perceived. In this sense, the present techniques are applicable to the assessment of the complexity, differentiation and quality of episode perception as an individual variable. Mischel (1973) also makes this point: "For many purposes, it is valuable to assess the quality and range of the cognitive constructions and behavioural enactments of which the individual is capable" (p. 266). The study of episode perception as a person-specific variable would complement the study of episodes as cultural units, and may open up a new perspective in an area where empirical research is at the moment non-existent. The eventual classification of individuals in terms of their episode perception strategies into high or low involvement or high or low self-confidence groups would be of obvious heuristic, as well as empirical value.

A related area for which the present results have implications is clinical psychology. With patients diagnosed as social phobics, social inadequates or even schizophrenics, behavioural therapies such as social skills training therapy have been found to be extremely useful (Bryant et al., 1978). This model assumes that the lack of social skills is attributable to inadequate socialization experiences, but it does not distinguish between simple lack of skills in the technical sense, and the inadequate perceptions and cognitive representations of social situations. This distinction may be crucial, since some patients may have adequate skills, but lack experience and sensitivity in their judgements of different social episodes. Some preliminary studies carried out by us recently have shown that socially skilled and unskilled individuals indeed have significantly different cognitive representations of social episodes (Forgas and Gilligan, 1979, unpublished data). Using the techniques presented here to evaluate an individual's perception and internal representation of social episodes, a useful diagnostic tool may be developed, which may help to identify social episodes in which the greatest difficulty is experienced, just as the repertory grid technique is used to identify areas of problematic interpersonal relations.

In summary, the methods of assessing the perception of social episodes demonstrated here have important implications for those areas of social, clinical and personality psychology where the lack of techniques for the quantification of situational variables has most hindered research: in the field of person–situation interaction research, and in the assessment of individual competencies in episode perception, both in clinical and in normal subjects.

Some future prospects

We have only managed to chart the beginnings of the study of social episodes as a scientific enterprise here. Numerous prospective avenues of research are opened up by the present approach, which is in effect a combination of quantitative empirical methodology and a conceptualization of social episodes as cognitive representations of interactions. Based on the studies presented here, a number of promising research projects may be envisaged, primarily studies using the perceptual strategy. Some of these projects are an extension of the work already carried out, others seek to implement the techniques advocated here in new areas of practical interest. We are currently engaged in active research in several of the areas to be mentioned below.

THE GENERALITY OF THE DIMENSIONS UNDERLYING EPISODE PERCEPTION

In most of the studies carried out so far two or three generally similar attribute dimensions emerged as underlying the perception of episodes. The possibility that a finite number of connotative dimensions would underlie judgements of social episodes by widely differing subcultural groups appears a promising prospect. The establishment of such a general framework for judgements would essentially require the further extension of the present studies in widely differing subcultural milieux. With a broadening circle of studies, the validity of a basic connotative dimensional framework for the measurement of social episodes could ultimately be established.

IDIOGRAPHIC STUDY OF PERCEPTIONS OF SOCIAL EPISODES

The work outlined here was mainly concerned with studies of social episodes characteristic of large social units (subcultural milieux, social groups). It is possible to apply the perceptual strategy to an intensive study of how the social episodes which constitute the "life environment" of selected individuals are cognitively represented. This is in line with Brunswik's (1956) arguments for "representative design" in psychology, and follows the preliminary work by Pervin (1976), who used factor-analytic methods to study perceptions of social episodes. The method to be used could be based on an intensive sampling of social episodes or situations which are recurrently experienced by an individual, using a diary technique or some other open-ended procedure, and a quantitative analysis of the distinctions made between such episodes to represent the complexity of the cognitive representations, and the attributes which an individual sees as the most important differentiating features between episodes. New multidimensional scaling techniques, such as Young and Cliff's (1972) ISIS (Interactive Scaling with Individual Subjects) would appear to be particularly applicable to such a task. Ultimately, if a standard technique for assessing an individual's perception and cognitive representation of his significant episodes could be developed, this would also have important uses as a diagnostic technique in clinical psychology.

DEVELOPMENTAL STUDY OF EPISODE PERCEPTION

Just as judgements of moral dilemmas or perceptions of personal relationships have been shown to become more differentiated and sophisticated with age and maturation (Piaget, 1962; Kohlberg, 1966, 1969), we may expect that the complexity and sophistication of a child in dealing with the social episodes in his environment should also increase. The acquisition of a capacity to make subtle and complex distinctions between social episodes is an important aspect of adult social competence. The perceptual strategy in particular can be readily applied to children, since simple categorization judgements alone can provide necessary data for MDS analysis. Numerous interesting hypotheses could be examined; for example, it could be expected that perhaps an undifferentiated "evaluative" dimension underlying the perception of episodes in young children should be gradually differentiated into dimensions such as involvement, self-confidence or task-orientation, which were found in adults in the present study. Differences in episode construction competencies between children at different stages of cognitive development (Piaget, 1952) may also be evaluated using the perceptual strategy.

INTERCULTURAL COMMUNICATION IN SOCIAL EPISODES

An important requirement for successful assimilation to a host culture is for the newcomer to understand clearly and to handle effectively the new culture's definition of different interaction situations (Schutz, 1970). The culture assimilator developed by Triandis (1972) trains individuals to perceive correctly and to learn to conform to the requirements of critical episodes. Similarly, the term "situational ethnicity" refers to the observation that different situations or episodes determine which of a person's ethnic or communal identities is appropriate in an episode (Paden, 1967). A logical extension of existing work on the culture assimilator technique, and on cognitive anthropology is the quantitative study of such cultural and ethnic differences in the cognitive representation of social episodes. Such investigations may be designed with a view to identifying episodes where differences between the perception of different ethnic groups are most marked, and then to study such episodes intensively, to pinpoint the moves and actions most likely to cause confusion and disruption. The results of these studies might be applicable to a culture training programme that emphasizes differences between migrant and native cultures in their execution of social episodes.

STUDIES OF SPECIFIC EPISODE DOMAINS

Existing studies, as well as the studies proposed, have concentrated on the study of episode domains which were in some sense representative of the life environment of the subjects. There are, however, several categories of social interaction episodes which warrant special scrutiny. Episode domains involving violence, and heterosexual encounters are two obvious categories of interaction the study of which is both of practical and of heuristic interest.

THE PERCEPTION OF VIOLENT EPISODES

Interactions involving aggression or violence have received more interest from social scientists than just about any other field, yet we know very little about the kinds of cognitive distinctions people normally make between different instances of naturally occurring and personally experienced violence. The perceived severity of violent acts is the only dimension studied, and the results indicate that such a unidimensional representation does not do justice to the complex and subtle distinctions commonly made between different categories of violence (Forgas *et al.*, 1979b; Sherman and Dowdle, 1972). Future studies may use multidimensional scaling techniques to analyse the distinctions made between a representative sample of commonly experienced violent situations by judges directly acquainted with those episodes. It may also be of interest to analyse the differences that exist in the cognitive representation of violent episodes among such sub-groups in the criminal justice system as policemen, magistrates, defendants, and victims.

THE PERCEPTION OF SEXUAL EPISODES

Episodes involving heterosexual pairs, particularly in the early stages of the acquaintance process, are more clearly regulated by subtle and not so subtle conventions than are most other kinds of interaction (Cagnon, 1976). Cultural and individual differences in the perception of these episodes account for a large percentage of the self-reported social skills deficiencies of students and young people in general (Argyle and Little, 1972; Bryant and Trower, 1974). Future research may seek to represent commonly occurring heterosexual interaction situations, and to analyse the cognitive representation and expectations attached to those situations by individuals of different sex, age and ethnic background. The aim of such studies could be to identify the episodes which are most ambiguous and difficult to negotiate, and to pinpoint the different existing interpretations of such episodes. Social anthropologists such as Margaret Mead have done some pioneering work in this area. There is no reason why the quantitative methodology of social psychology could not be brought to bear on this problem.

EPISODE CONTEXT AND STEREOTYPING

Research on the perception of national and racial stereotypes, perhaps more so than any other area of social perception, has relied on the assumption of individual consistency. The whole concept of prejudice is based on the assumption that discrimination of races or nations is carried by the individual alone, but not by the situation or episode. Although some of the earliest studies (LaPiere, 1934) have strongly suggested the importance of the situational context in stereotyping, this lead was not followed up. The present techniques provide a promising approach to the study of the effects of the episode context on judgements of stereotypes. The delimitation of those episodes conducive to stereotyping, and those which are not, should also be of ultimate practical importance.

The projects considered above all seek to study global episodes as their unit of analysis. There is also the possibility of studying the internal rules, sequences and behaviours within particular episodes. Both the structuralist and the roles–rules research strategies (Chapter 5) imply such an approach. These techniques concentrate on the internal structure of particular social episodes, rather than the perceived differences between episodes. Such an approach is based on an identification of significant and meaningful units or moves within a specified episode, and the discovery of important transition points that have the potential for altering, or redefining the outcome of the episode. Existing research on social skills (Argyle and Kendon, 1972), as well as on the sequential nature of natural conversations (Clarke, 1977) and other social behaviours (Kendon et al., 1975) suggests that the capacity to perceive and use such transition points accurately is an essential aspect of skilled social performance. Work by Dickman (1963), Barker (1968) and Newtson and Engquist (1976) has shown that the stream of behaviour can be successfully and reliably divided into single meaningful moves, which judges from a specified cultural environment can easily identify. New research might involve an intensive analysis of episodes found to be important to particular individuals, or groups, including problem episodes reported by social skills clients, or ambiguous components of heterosexual episodes. The methods to be used may be based on the video-recording of an episode and the presentation of this record to judges. The questions which can be explored may focus on:

(a) the recognized sequential structure of the episode;
(b) the identification of important transition points in the action;
(c) an analysis of the range of choices or alternatives available to actors at each transition point;
(d) the range of interpretations which can be applied to each move or action in the light of the previous history of the interaction.

These data could be analysed by multivariate statistical methods resulting in a schematic representation of the internal structure of the episodes so studied.

THE EFFECTS OF CUE CHANGE IN THE REDEFINITION OF AN EPISODE

The present investigations were only concerned with the effects cues such as the behaviour setting or the relationship between the actors as given in the definiton of the episode. Such episode definiton cues can often change while the interaction is actually in progress. Thus, the encounter may shift to a new physical location (change in behaviour setting cues), or new actors may join in (change in the relationship cues). In everyday interaction, the redefinition of an episode as a result of cue changes is often ritualized: to leave the dining room and go to the lounge at a dinner party, or the arrival of the last guest, result in a more or less subtle redefinition of the encounter. The effects of such cue changes on episode perception could be studied by using either (a) verbal descriptions to analyse reactions to abstract, disembodied episodes, or (b) filmed or videotaped interaction sequences with consciously manipulated episode cue changes. Both of these strategies are likely to yield interesting insights into cultural and individual differences in social perception, and the factors affecting naturalistic social interaction in particular.

With the development of more and more sophisticated mathematical models of cue integration processes in other areas of social perception (Anderon, 1968b, 1971, 1974; Kaplan, 1971a,b; Wyer, 1970), the extension of these techniques to the study of episode perception is an obvious possibility. Since the definition and identification of social episodes is clearly a function of the interaction of multiple cue sources, these mathematical techniques would be particularly applicable here.

Summary

The purpose of this chapter was to draw together the several lines of argument upon which the study of social episodes is based, and to outline the major findings, implications and prospects of this area of research in social psychology. As we have seen, after the concentrated criticisms of the early seventies, the current *Zeitgeist* of social psychology may be characterized by a growing eclecticism and tolerance towards new approaches and techniques. The growing impact of cognitivist theories, and conceptualizations of social behaviour emphasizing situational rather than personological regularities are the other two major sources of influence which have precipitated the study of social episodes. Finally, it may be noted that the concept of social episodes, as well as the changes described above are equally characteristic of microsociological and social psychological theory. Social episodes as an area of study may thus be seen as bridging the gap between sociological and psychological social psychology, a joining of forces often recommended but rarely accomplished to date.

The second major feature emphasized here was the use of quantitative methods for studying social episodes, many of which were recently developed for the study of social perception phenomena. Multidimensional scaling techniques played a particularly important part in the studies discussed here. The accumulated results have shown that the quantitative representation of how social episodes are cognitively represented by different subcultures, groups or individuals is

indeed a feasible task, and that such representations reliably and sensitively reflect the characteristics of such environments. We have also seen that several of the factors affecting episode perception, such as role relationships or the behaviour setting are equally accessible to empirical study.

The implications of this approach for such often neglected cognitive social psychological theories as symbolic interactionism were discussed. The possibility of quantifying episodes also has important implications for many areas of social psychological research, particularly studies of social perception phenomena.

Social episodes as a term denoting stereotypical units of interaction within specified cultural milieux, of which individuals have a shared cognitive representation provides the foundation for these studies. Other conceptualizations of interaction units are also possible (Argyle *et al.*, 1979) and may lead to significant new developments in this area of social psychology. By providing a first summary and review of this branch of research, it is hoped that further efforts to study natural interactions empirically will be encouraged.

Bibliography

Abelson, R. P. (1962). Situational variables in personality research. *In* "Measurement in Personality and Cognition". (S. Messick and J. Ross, Eds), Wiley, New York.

Abelson, R. P. (1976). Script processing in attitude formation and decision making. *In* "Cognition and Social Behaviour." (J. Carroll and J. Payne, Eds), Lawrence E. Erlbaum, Hillsdale, New Jersey.

Aiello, J. R. and Jones, S. E. (1971). Field study of the proxemic behaviour of young school children in three subcultural groups. *Journal of Personality and Social Psychology*, **19**, 351–356.

Alker, H. A. (1972). Is personality situationally specific or intra-psychically consistent? *Journal of Personality*, **40**, 1–16.

Allport, F. H. (1924). *Social psychology*. Houghton-Mifflin, Boston.

Altman, I. (1968). Ecological aspects of interpersonal functioning. Paper presented at the Symposium on "The Use of Space by Animals and Humans", American Association for the Advancement of Science, Dallas, Texas.

Altman, I. and Haythorn, W. W. (1965). Interpersonal exchange in isolation. *Sociometry*, **23**, 4, 411–426.

Altman, I. and Haythorn, W. W. (1967a). The ecology of isolated groups. *Behavioural Science*, **12**, 169–182.

Altman, I. and Haythorn, W. W. (1967b). Effects of social isolation and group composition on performance. *Human Relations*, **20**, 4, 313–340.

Altman, I. and Lett, I. (1967). *A model of the ecology of interpersonal relationships*. Naval Medical Research Institute, Bethesda, Maryland.

Altman, I. and Lett, E. E. (1970). The ecology of interpersonal relationships: a classification system and conceptual model. *In* "Social and Psychological Factors in Stress." (J. B. McGrath, Ed), Holt, Rinehart and Winston, New York.

Anderson, N. H. (1968). A simple model for information integration. *In* "Theories of Cognitive Consistency: A sourcebook." (R. P. Abelson, E. Aronson, W. J. McGuire, T. M. Newcomb, M. J. Rosenberg and P. H. Tannenbaum, Eds), Rand McNally, Chicago.

Anderson, N. H. (1971). Integration theory and attitude change. *Psychological Review*, **78**, 171–206.

Anderson, N. H. (1974). Cognitive algebra: Integration theory applied to social attribution. *In* "Advances in Experimental Social Psychology," Vol. 7. (I. Berkowitz, Ed), Academic Press, New York and London.

Angyal, A. (1941). "Foundations for a Science of Personality." Harvard University Press, Cambridge, Mass.

Argyle, M. (1969). "Social Interaction." Methuen, London.

Argyle, M. (1975). Predictive and generative rules models of P × S interaction. Paper presented at the Symposium of Interactional Psychology, Stockholm, June 1975.

Argyle, M. (1976). Personality and social behaviour. *In* "Personality". (R. Harre, Ed), Blackwell, Oxford.

Argyle, M. and Dean, J. (1965). Eye contact, distance and affiliation. *Sociometry*, **28**, 289–304.

Argyle, M. and Kendon, A. (1967). The experimental analysis of social performance. *In* "Advances in Experimental Social Psychology", Vol. 3. (L. Berkowitz, Ed), Academic Press, New York and London.

Argyle, M. and Little, B. R. (1972). Do personality traits apply to social behavior? *Journal for the Theory of Social Behavior*, **2**, 1–35.

Argyle, M., Alkema, F., and Gilmour, R. (1970a). The communication of friendly and hostile attitudes by verbal and non-verbal signals. *European Journal of Social Psychology*, **3**, 385–402.

Argyle, M., Salter, V., Nicholson, H., Williams, M., and Burgess, P. (1970b). The communication of friendly and superior attitudes by verbal and non-verbal signals. *British Journal of Social and Clinical Psychology*, **9**, 222–231.

Argyle, M., Trower, P., and Bryant, B. (1974). Explorations in the treatment of personality disorders and neuroses by social skills training. *British Journal of Medical Psychology*, **47**, 63–72.

Argyle, M. Forgas, J. P. and Ginsburg, G. P. (1977). Are personality traits a function of the situation? (Oxford University unpublished.)

Argyle, M., Furnham, A., and Graham, S. (1979). "Social situations." Methuen, London. (In preparation.)

Armistead, N. "Reconstructing social psychology." Penguin, Harmondsworth, Middx.

Arnault, M. D. (1963). The specification of a "social" stimulus. *In* "Stimulus Determinants of Behavior". (S. B. Sells, Ed), Ronald, New York.

Aronson, E., and Carlsmith, J. M. (1969). Experimentation in social psychology. *In* "Handbook of Social Psychology", Vol. 2, 2nd Ed. (Lindzey, G., and Aronson, E., (Eds), Addison-Wesley, Reading, Mass.

Asch, S. E. (1946). Forming impressions of personality. *Journal of Social Psychology*, **41**, 258–290.

Asch, S. E. (1952). "Social Psychology." Prentice-Hall, New York.

Asch, S. E. (1972). The data of social psychology. *In* "Current Perspectives in Social Psychology". (E. Hollander and R. Hunt, Eds), Oxford University Press, Oxford and New York.

Astin, A. W. (1962). An empirical characterisation of higher educational institutions. *Journal of Educational Psychology*, 224–235.

Astin, A. W. (1972). "Manual for the Inventory of College Activities." National Computer Systems, Minneapolis, Minn.

Astin, A. W. and Holland, J. L. (1961). The environmental assessment technique: A way to measure college environments. *Journal of Educational Psychology*, **52**, 308–316.

Austin, J. L. (1962). "How to do things with words." Clarendon Press, Oxford.

Avant, I. L. and Helson, H. (1973). Theories of perception. *In* "Handbook of General Psychology". (B. B. Wolman, Ed), Prentice-Hall, Englewood Cliffs, New Jersey.

Baker, R. F. and Young, F. (1975). A note on the empirical evaluation of the ISIS procedure. *Psychometrika*, **40**, 413–414.

Bales, R. F. (1970). "Personality and Interpersonal Behaviour." Holt, Rinehart and Winston, New York.

Ball, D. W. (1970). An abortion clinic ethnography. *In* "Social Psychology Through Symbolic Interaction". (G. P. Stone and H. E. Farbermann, Eds), Ginn-Blaisdell, London.

Ball, D.W. (1972). The definition of the situation: some theoretical and methodological consequences of taking W. I. Thomas seriously. *Journal of the Theory of Social Behavior*, **2**, 1, 61–83.

Bandura, A. (1969). "Principles of Behaviour Modification." Holt, Rinehart and Winston, New York.

Barker, R. G. (1960). Ecology and motivation. *In* Nebraska Symposium on Motivation, (M. R. Jones, Ed), 1–49. University of Nebraska Press, Lincoln, Nebraska.

Barker, R. G. (Ed), (1963). "The Stream of Behavior." Appleton-Century-Crofts, New York.

Barker, R. G. (1965). Explorations in ecological psychology. *American Psychologist*, **20**, 971–14.

Barker, R. G. (1968). "Ecological Psychology." Stanford University Press, Stanford.

Barker, R. G. and Schoggen, P. (1973). "Qualities of Community Life." Jossey-Bass, San Francisco.

Barker, R. G. and Wright, H. F. (1955). "Midwest and its Children." Row, Peterson, Evanston, Illinois.

Barker, R. G., Meyerson and Gonicki. (1953). "Adjustment to Physical Handicap and Illness." Social Science Research Council, New York.

Baum, A. and Valins, S. (1973). Residential environments, group size and crowding. Proceedings of the APA, 81st Annual Convention, 211–212.

Beach, L. and Wertheimer, M. (1961). A free-response approach to the study of person cognition. *Journal of Abnormal and Social Psychology*, **62**, 367–374.

Bechtel, R. B. (1970). A behavioural comparison of urban and small town environment. *In* EDRA Two: Proceedings, 2nd Annual Environment Design Research Association Conference. (J. Archer and L. Esser, Eds), Carnegie-Mellon University, Pittsburgh.

Bechtel, R. B. (1972). The public housing environment: a few surprises. *In* "Environmental Design: Research and Practice". (W. J. Mitchell, Ed), University of California Press, Los Angeles.

Bem, D. S. (1972a). Constructing cross-situational consistencies in behaviour: Some thoughts on Alker's critique of Mischel. *Journal of Personality*, **40**, 17–26.

Bem, D. S. (1972b). Self-perception theory. *In* "Advances in Experimental Social Psychology", Vol. 6. (L. Berkowitz, Ed), Academic Press, New York and London.

Bennett, D. J. and Bennett, J. D. (1970). Making the scene. *In* "Social Psychology through Symbolic Interaction." (G. P. Stone and H. A. Farberman, Eds), Ginn-Blaisdell, Waltham, Mass.

Berger, P. and Luckman, T. (1967). "The Social Construction of Reality." Allen Lane, London.

Berkowitz, L. (1975). "A Survey of Social Psychology." The Dryden Press, Hinsdale, Illinois.

Berkowitz, L. (1976). Theoretical and research approaches in experimental social psychology. *In* "Contemporary Scientific Psychology". (A. R. Gilgen, Ed), Academic Press, New York and London.

Berkowitz, L. and Le Page, A. (1967). Weapons as aggression eliciting stimuli. *Journal of Personality and Social Psychology*, **7**, 202–207.

Bierskolt, R. (1969). Introduction. *In* "On Humouristic Sociology". (F. Znaniecki, Ed), University of Chicago Press, Chicago.

Bieri, J. (1971). Cognitive structures in personality. *In* "Personality Theory and Information Processing". (H. M. Schroder and P. Suedfeld, Eds), Ronald Press, New York.

Bishop, D. W. and Witt, P. A. (1970). Sources of behavioral variance during leisure time. *Journal of Personality and Social Psychology*, **16**, 352–360.

Bjerg, K. (1968). Interplay-analysis. *Acta Psychologica*, **28**, 201–245.

Blake, R. R. (1958). The other person in the situation. *In* "Person Perception and Interpersonal Behavior". (R. Tagiuri and L. Petrullo, Eds), Stanford University Press, Stanford.

Blau, P. M. (1964). "Exchange and Power in Social Life." John Wiley, New York.

Blumer, R. (1969). "Symbolic Interactionism." Prentice-Hall, Englewood Cliffs.

Bowers, K. S. (1973). Situationism in psychology: An analysis and a critique. *Psychological Review*, **80**, 307–336.

Brehm, J. W. (1966). "A Theory of Psychological Reactance." Academic Press, New York and London.

Brittan, A. (1973). "Meanings and Situations." Routledge and Kegan Paul, Boston.

Bruner, J. (1976). Psychological theories and the image of man. Herbert Spencer Lecture, University of Oxford.

Bruner, J. S., Shapiro, D. and Tagiuri, R. (1958). The meaning of traits in isolation and in combination. *In* "Person Perception and Interpersonal Behaviour". (R. Tagiuri and L. Petrullo, Eds), Stanford University Press, Stanford.

Brunswik, E. (1950). The conceptual framework of psychology. *International Encyclopedia of Unified Science*, **1**, 10. University of Chicago Press, Chicago.

Brunswik, E. (1955). Representative design and probabilistic theory in a functional psychology. *Psychological Review*, **62**, 193–217.

Brunswik, E. (1956). "Perception and the Representative Design of Psychological Experiments." University of California Press, Berkeley, California.

Bryant, B. and Trower, P. (1974). Social difficulty in a student population. *British Journal of Educational Psychology*, **44**, 13–21.

Burton, R. V. (1963). Generality of honesty reconsidered. *Psychological Review*, **70**, 481–499.

Campbell, D. (1974). Kurt Lewin Award Address, Society for the Psychological Study of Social Issues, New Orleans. (Mimeo.)

Canter, D. and Lee, T. (1974). "Psychology and the Built Environment." The Architectural Press, Tonbridge.

Canter, D., West, S. and Wools, R. (1974). Judgments of people and their rooms. *British Journal of Social and Clinical Psychology*, **13**, 113–118.

Carlson, R. (1971). Where is the person in personality research? *Psychological Bulletin*, **75**, 203–219.

Carroll, D. J. and Chang, J. J. (1970). Analysis of individual differences in multidimensional scaling via N-way generalisation of 'Eckart-Young' decomposition. *Psychometrika*, **35**, 283–319.

Carroll, J. S. and Payne, J. W. (Eds) (1976). "Cognition and Social Behaviour". Lawrence Erlbaum Assoc., Hillsdale, New Jersey.

Cartwright, D. and Zander, E. (Eds) (1968). "Group Dynamics." (3rd Ed) Harper and Row, New York.

Cattell, R. B. (1963). Personality, role, mood, and situation-perception: A unifying theory of modulators. *Psychological Review*, **70**, 1–18.

Caudill, W. (1958). "The Psychiatric Hospital as a Small Society." Harvard University Press, Cambridge, Mass.

Chein, I. (1954). The environment as a determinant of behaviour. *Journal of Social Psychology*, **39**, 115–127.

Chomsky, N. (1965). "Aspects of the Theory of Syntax." Mouton, The Hague.

Christie, R. (1965). Some implications of research trends in social psychology. *In* "Perspectives in Social Psychology". (O. Klineberg and R. Christie, Eds), Holt, Rinehart and Winston, New York.

Cicourel, A. V. (1964). "Method and Measurement in Sociology." The Free Press, New York.

Cicourel, A. V. (1974). "Cognitive Sociology: Language and Reasoning in Social Interaction." The Free Press, New York.

Clark, R. H. (1973). Analysing the group structure of combat rifle squads. *American Psychologist*, **8**, 333.

Clarke, D. D. (1976). The use and recognition of sequential structure in dialogue. *British Journal of Social and Clinical Psychology*, **14**, 333–339.

Clarke, D. D. (1977). Rules and sequences in conversation. *In* "Social Rules and Social Behaviour". (P. Collett, Ed), Blackwell, Oxford.

Cline, M. G. (1957). The influence of social context on the perception of faces. *Journal of Personality*, **25**, 142–158.

Coleman, J. S. (1968). Review symposium of Harold Garfinkel's "Studies in Ethnomethodology". *American Sociological Review*, **33**, 126–130.

Collett, P. (Ed), (1977). "Social Rules and Social Behaviour." Blackwell, Oxford.

Cook, M. (1973). "Interpersonal Perception." Penguin, Harmondsworth.

Cooley, C. H. (1966). "Social Process." Southern Illinois University Press, Carbondale.

Cooley, C. H. (1972). Primary groups. *In* "Classic Contributions to Social Psychology". (E. Hollander and R. G. Hunt, Eds), Oxford University Press, Oxford and New York.

Cottrell, S. J. (1970). Some neglected problems in social psychology. *In* "Social Psychology through Symbolic Interaction". (G. P. Stone and H. A. Farberman, Eds), Ginn-Blaisdell, Waltham, Mass.

Craik, K. H. (1971). The assessment of places. *In* "Advances in Psychological Assessment". (P. McReynolds, Ed), pp. 40–62. Science and Behaviour Books, Palo Alto, California.

Craik, K. H. (1973). Environmental psychology. *Annual Review of Psychology*, **24**, 403–422.

Cronbach, L. J. (1957). The two disciplines of scientific psychology. *American Psychologist*, **12**, 671–684.

Cronbach, L. J. (1975). Beyond the two disciplines of scientific psychology. *American Psychologist*, **30**, 116–127.

Cronbach, L. J. and Gleser, G. C. (1953). Assessing similarity between profiles. *Psychological Bulletin*, **50**, 456–473.

Davison, M. L. and Jones, L. E. (1976). A similarity-attraction model for predicting sociometric choice from perceived group structure. *Journal of Personality and Social Psychology*, **33**, 601–612.

de Saussure, F. A. (1974). *Course of General Linguistics*. (trans. Wade Baskm). Collins, London.

Desmonde, W. H. (1970). The position of George Herbert Mead. *In* "Social Psychology through Symbolic Interaction". (G. P. Stone and H. E. Farberman, Eds), Ginn-Blaisdell, London.

Deutsch, M. and Gerard, H. (1955). A study of normative and informational social influences on individual judgement. *Journal of Abnormal and Social Psychology*, **51**, 629–636.

DeWaele, J. P. and Harre, R. (1974). The personality of individuals. *In* "Personality". (R. Harre, Ed), Blackwell, Oxford.

Dickman, H. R. (1963). The perception of behavioural units. *In* "The Stream of Behaviour". (R. C. Barker, Ed), Appleton-Century-Crofts, New York.

Dixon, W. J. (Ed), (1973). BMD: Biomedical Computer Programs. University of California Press, Berkeley.

Dornbusch, S. M., Hastorf, A. H., Richardson, S. A., Muzzy, R. E. and Vreeland, R. S. (1965). The perceiver and the perceived: their relative influence on the categories of interpersonal cognition. *Journal of Personality and Social Psychology*, **1**, 434–440.

Douglas, J. D. (Ed). (1970). "The Relevance of Sociology." Appleton-Century-Crofts, New York.

Douglas, J. D. (Ed). (1973). "Understanding Everyday Life." Routledge and Kegan Paul, London.

Durkeim, E. (1938). "The Rules of Sociological Method." University Press, Chicago.

Ekehammar, B. (1974). Interactionism in personality from a historical perspective. *Psychological Bulletin*, **81**, 1026–1048.

Ekehammar, B. and Magnusson, D. (1973). A method to study stressful situations. *Journal of Personality and Social Psychology*, **27**, 176–179.

Ekehammar, B., Magnusson, D. and Ricklander, L. (1974). An interactionist approach to the study of anxiety. *Scandinavian Journal of Psychology*, **15**, 4–14.

Elms, A. C. (1975). The crisis of confidence in social psychology. *American Psychologist*, **30**, 967–976.

Elnas, A. C. (1975). The crisis of confidence in social psychology. *American Psychologist*, **30**, 967–976.

Endler, N. S. (1973). The person versus the situation—a pseudo issue? A response to Alker. *Journal of Personality*, **41**, 287–303.

Endler, N. S. (1974). A person-situation interaction model for anxiety. *In* "Stress and Anxiety in Modern Life". (C. D. Spielberger and I. G. Sarason, Eds), V. H. Winston, Washington, D.C.

Endler, N. S. (1975). The case for person-situation interactions. *Canadian Psychological Review*, **16**, 12–21.

Endler, N. S. and Hunt, J. McV. (1966). Sources of behavioral variance as measured by the S–R Inventory of Anxiousness. *Psychological Bulletin*, **65**, 336–346.

Endler, N. S. and Hunt, J. McV. (1968). S–R Inventories of Hostility and comparisons of the proportions of variance from persons, responses, and situations for hostility and anxiousness. *Journal of Personality and Social Psychology*, **9**, 309–315.

Endler, N. S. and Hunt, J. McV. (1969). Generalisability of contributions from sources of variance in the S–R Inventories of Anxiousness. *Journal of Personality*, **37**, 1–24.

Endler, N. S. and Magnusson, D. (1974). Interactionism, trait psychology, and situationism. Reports from the Psychological Laboratories, University of Stockholm, No. 418, 1974.

Endler, N. S. and Magnusson, D. (Eds), (1976). "Interaction Psychology and Personality." John Wiley, New York.

Endler, N. S., Hunt, J. McV. and Rosenstein, A. J. (1962). An S–R Inventory of Anxiousness. *Psychological Monographs*, No. 17, **76**.

Eysenck, H. S. and Eysenck, S. B. G. (1964). "Manual of the Eysenck Personality Inventory." University of London Press, London.

Farber, I. E. (1964). A framework for the study of personality as a behavioral science. *In* "Personality Change". (P. Worchel and D. Byrne, Eds), Wiley, New York.

Fernandez, R. (1977). "The 'I', the 'Me' and 'You'." Praeger, New York.

Festinger, L. (1950). Informal social communication. *Psychological Review*, **57**, 271–282.

Festinger, L. (1957). "A Theory of Cognitive Dissonance." Row, Peterson, Evanston, Illinois.

Festinger, L., Schachter, S. and Back, K. (1950). "Social Pressures in Informal Groups: A Study of a Housing Community." Harper, New York.

Fiedler, F. E., Mitchell, T. R. and Triandis, H. C. (1970). "The culture assimilator: an approach to cross-cultural training." University of Washington, Department of Psychology, Technical Report 70–5.

Fishbein, M. and Ajzen, A. (1975). "Belief, Attitudes, Intention and Behaviour." Addison-Wesley, Massachusetts.

Fiske, D. W. (1961). The inherent variability of behaviour. In "Functions of Varied Experience". (D. Fiske and S. Maddi, Eds), Dorsey Press, Homewood, Illinois.

Flanagan, J. C. (1954). The critical incident technique. Psychological Bulletin, 51, 327–358.

Forgas, J. P. (1976a). The perception of social episodes: categorical and dimensional representations in two different social milieus. Journal of Personality and Social Psychology, 33, 199–209.

Forgas, J. P. (1976b). Reactions to national stereotypes in four European countries: an unobtrusive study. Journal of Social Psychology, 99, 37–42.

Forgas, J. P. (1977). Polarization and moderation of person perception judgements as a function of group interaction style. European Journal of Social Psychology, 7, 175–187.

Forgas, J. P. (1978a). Social episodes and social structure in an academic setting: the social environment of an intact group. Journal of Experimental Social Psychology, 14, 434–448.

Forgas, J. P. (1978b). The effects of behavioural and cultural expectation cues on the perception of social episodes. European Journal of Social Psychology, 8, 203–213.

Forgas, J. P. (1978c). The effects of the interaction partner and the situation context on the perception of social episodes. (University of New South Wales unpublished.)

Forgas, J. P. (1979a). Multidimensional scaling: a discovery method in social psychology. In "Emerging Strategies in Social Psychology". (G. P. Ginsburg, Ed), Wiley, London.

Forgas, J. P. (1979b). Social episodes and group milieu: a phenomenological analysis. The Journal of Social Psychology (in press).

Forgas, J. P. and Brown, L. B. (1977). Environmental and behavioural cues in the perception of social encounters. American Journal of Psychology, 90, 635–644.

Forgas, J. P. and Brown, L. B. (1978). The effects of race on observer judgements of nonverbal communications. Journal of Social Psychology 104, 243–251.

Forgas, J. P., Kagan, C. M. and Frey, D. (1977). The cognitive representation of political personalities: a cross-cultural comparison. International Journal of Psychology, 12, 19–30.

Forgas, J. P. and Dobosz, B. (1979). The perception of heterosexual relationship prototypes. (University of New South Wales unpublished.)

Forgas, J. P., Argyle, M. and Ginsburg, G. P. (1979a). Social episodes and person perception: the fluctuating structure of an academic group. The Journal of Social Psychology (in press).

Forgas, J. P., Brown, L. B. and Menyhart, J. (1979b). Dimension of aggression: the perception of aggressive episodes. British Journal of Social and Clinical Psychology (in press).

Forgas, J. P., Brown, L. B. and Menyhart, J. (1979c). Some determinants of the perception of political leaders: a multidimensional scaling approach. Australian Journal of Psychology (in press).

Forward, J., Canter, R. and Kirsch, N. (1976). Role-enactment and deception methodologies: Alternative paradigms? American Psychologist, August, 1976.

Frederiksen, N. (1972). Toward a taxonomy of situations. *American Psychologist*, **27**, 114–123.

Frederiksen, N., Jensen, O., Beaton, A. E. and Bloxom, B. (1973). *Prediction of Organisational Behaviour*. Pergamon, New York.

Freedman, J. L. (1969). Role playing: psychology by consensus. *Journal of Personality and Social Psychology*, **13**, 107–114.

Freud, S. (1959). *Collected Papers*. Vols. I–V. Basic Books, New York.

Frey, J. and Newtson, D. (1973). Differential attribution in an unequal power situation: biased inference or biased input? Proceedings, 81st Annual Convention, A.P.A., **8**, 125–126.

Friendly, M. L. and Glucksberg, S. (1970). On the description of subcultural lexicons: A multidimensional approach. *Journal of Personality and Social Psychology*, **14**, 55–65.

Frijda, N. H. (1969). Recognition of emotion. *In* "Advances in Experimental Social Psychology", Vol. 4. (L. Berkowitz, Ed), Academic Press, New York and London.

Fuchs, A. and Schäfer, B. (1972). Kriterien und Techniken der Merkmalselektion bei der Konstruktion eines Eindrücksdifferentials. *Archive für Psychologie*, **124**, 282.

Gagnon, J. H. (1976). "Human Sexualities." Scott, Foresman and Co., Glenview, Illinois.

Garfield, S. L. and Kurtz, R. (1976). Clinical psychologists in the 1970's. *American Psychologist*, **31**, 1–9.

Garfinkel, H. (1967). "Studies in Ethnomethodology." Prentice-Hall, Englewood Cliffs, New Jersey.

Garfinkel, H. (1975). The origins of the term "ethnomethodology" (1968). *In* "Ethnomethodology". (R. Turner, Ed), Penguin, Harmondsworth.

Garfinkel, H. and Sacks, H. (1970). On formal structures of practical actions. *In* "Theoretical Sociology". (J. L. McKinney and E. A. Tiryakiar, Eds), Appleton-Century-Crofts, New York.

Gergen, K. J. (1973). Social psychology as history. *Journal of Personality and Social Psychology*, **26**, 309–326.

Gibson, J. J. (1959). Perception as a function of stimulation. *In* "Psychology: A Study of a Science". pp. 456–501. (S. Koch, Ed), McGraw-Hill, New York.

Gibson, J. J. (1960). The concept of the stimulus in psychology. *American Psychologist*, **15**, 694–703.

Ginsburg, G. P. (1979). "Emerging Strategies in Social Psychology." Wiley, London.

Girard, R. A. and Cliff, N. (1976). A Monte Carlo evaluation of interactive multidimensional scaling. *Psychometrika*, **41**, 43–64.

Glass, R. (1968). Urban sociology in Great Britain. *In* "Readings in Sociology". (R. E. Pahl, Ed), Pergamon Press, London.

Goffman, E. (1955). On face-work: an analysis of ritual elements in social interaction. *Psychiatry*, **18**, 213–231.

Goffman, E. (1959). "The Presentation of Self in Everyday Life." Doubleday, Garden City, New York.

Goffman, E. (1961). "Encounters." Bobbs-Merrill, Indianapolis.

Goffman, E. (1963). "Behaviour in Public Places." The Free Press, Glencoe.

Goffman, E. (1964). "Stigma." Prentice-Hall, Englewood Cliffs, New Jersey.

Goffman, E. (1967). "Interaction Ritual." Anchor Books, Garden City, New York.

Goffman, E. (1970). "Asylums." Penguin, Harmondsworth.

Goffman, E. (1971). "Relations in Public." Basic Books, New York.

Goffman, E. (1972). "Strategic Interaction." Ballantine Books, New York.

Goffman, E. (1974). "Frame Analysis." Penguin, Harmondsworth.

Golding, L. (1975). Flies in the ointment: Methodological problems in the analysis of percent of variance due to persons and situations. *Psychological Bulletin*, **82** (2), 278–288.

Goldstein, A., Sprafkin, R. P. and Gershaw, N. J. (1976). *Skill Training for Community Living: Applying Structured Learning Therapy*. Pergamon Press, New York.

Gump, P. V., (1971). The behavior setting: A promising unit for environmental designers. *Landscape Architecture*, **61**, 130–134.

Guthrie, E. R. (1940). Association and the law of effect. *Psychological Review*, **47**, 127–148.

Guthrie, E. R. (1952). "The Psychology of Learning" (revised edition). Harper and Bros., New York.

Hall, E. T. (1959). "The Silent Language." Doubleday, Garden City, New York.

Hall, E. T. (1966). "The Hidden Dimension." Doubleday, Garden City, New York.

Harre, R. (1970). Foreword, *In* "The Sociology of the Absurd". (S. M. Lyman and M. B. Scott), Appleton-Century-Crofts, New York.

Harre, R. (1974). The conditions for a social psychology of childhood. *In* "The Integration of a Child into a Social World". (R. Richards, Ed), Cambridge University Press, Cambridge.

Harre, R. (Ed), (1976). "Personality." Blackwell, Oxford.

Harre, R. (1977). The ethogenic approach: theory and practice. *In* "Advances in Experimental Social Psychology". Vol. 10, (L. Berkowitz, Ed), 783–314.

Harre, R. and De Wade, J. P. (1976). The ritual for incorporation of a stranger. *In* "Life Sentences". (R. Harre, Ed), Wiley, New York.

Harre, R. and Secord, P. F. (1972). "The Explanation of Social Behaviour." Basil Blackwell, Oxford.

Hartshorne, H. and May, M. A. (1928). "Studies in the Nature of Character: Studies in Deceit." Macmillan, New York.

Hastorf, A., Schneider, D. J. and Polefka, J. (1970). "Person Perception." Addison-Wesley, Reading, Mass.

Haythorn, W. and Altman, I. (1967). Personality factors in isolated environments. *In* "Psychological Stress". (M. Appley and R. Turnbull, Eds), Appleton-Century-Crofts, New York.

Hebb, D. O. (1974). What psychology is about. *American Psychologist*, **29**, 71–79.

Heider, F. (1958). "The Psychology of Interpersonal Relations." Wiley, New York.

Heider, F. and Simmel, M. (1944). A study of apparent behaviour. *The American Journal of Psychology*, **57**, 243–259.

Helson, H. (1959). Adaptation-level theory. *In* "Psychology: A Study of a Science", Vol. I. (S. Koch, Ed), McGraw-Hill, New York.

Helson, H. (1964). "Adaptation-level Theory: An Experimental and Systematic Approach to Behaviour." Harper and Row, New York.

Herbst, P. G. (1970). "Behavioural Worlds: The Study of Single Cases." Tavistock, London.

Higbee, K. L. and Wells, M. G. (1972). Some research trends in social psychology during the 1960's. *American Psychologist*, **27**, 963–966.

Hilgard, E. and Bower, G. H. (1966). "Theories of Learning." (3rd Ed). Appleton-Century-Crofts, New York.

Hillery, G. A. (1955). Definitions of community: areas of agreement. *Rural Sociology*, **20**, 121–130.

Hinde, P. A. (Ed), (1970). "Animal Behaviour: A Synthesis of Ethology and Comparative Psychology." (2nd Ed). McGraw-Hill, New York.

Hollander, E. P. and Hunt, R. G. (Eds), (1971). "Current Perspectives in Social Psychology", (3rd Ed). Oxford University Press, New York.

Homans, G. L. (1958). Human behaviour as exchange. *American Journal of Sociology*, **63**, 597–606.

Homans, G. L. (1961). "Social Behaviour: Its Elementary Forms." Routledge and Kegan Paul, London.

Homans, G. L. (1964). Bringing men back in. *American Sociological Review*, **29**, 809–818.

Homans, G. L. (1967). "The Nature of Social Science." Harcourt Brace Jovanovich, New York.

Hopfner, R. and Klein, S. P. (1970). "Elementary School Evaluation Kit." University of California, Los Angeles.

Hull, C. L. (1943). "Principles of Behaviour." Appleton-Century-Crofts, New York.

Hull, C. L. (1951). "Essentials of Behaviour." Yale University Press, New Haven.

Hyman, H. H. (1942). The psychology of status. *Archives of Psychology*, No. 269.

Hyman, H. H. and Singer, E. (Eds), (1968). "Readings in Reference Group Theory and Research." Free Press, New York.

Hymes, D. (1967). Models of the interaction of languages and social setting. *Journal of Social Issues*, **23**, 8–28.

Insel, P. M. and Moos, R. H. (1974). Psychological environments: expanding the scope of human ecology. *American Psychologist*, **29**, 179–188.

Israel, J. and Tajfel, H. (Eds), (1972), "The Context of Social Psychology: A Critical Assessment." Academic Press, London and New York.

Ittelson, W. H. (Ed), (1973). "Environment and Cognition." Seminar Press, New York.

Ittelson, W., Proshansky, H., Rivlin, L. and Winkel, G. (1974). "An Introduction to Environmental Psychology." Holt, Rinehart and Winston, New York.

James, L. R. and Jones, A. P. (1974). Organisational climate: A review of theory and research. *Psychological Bulletin*, 1096–1112.

James, W. (1892). "Psychology: Briefer Course." Henry Holt and Co., New York.

Janis, I. L. and King, B. T. (1954). The influence of role playing on attitude change. *Journal of Abnormal and Social Psychology*, **49**, 211–218.

Jessor, R. (1956). Phenomenological personality theories and the data language of psychology. *Psychological Review*, **63**, 173–180.

Joiner, D. (1971). Social ritual and architectural space. *Journal of Architectural Research and Teaching*, **3**, 11–22.

Jones, E. E., Davis, K. E. and Gergen, K. J. (1961). Role playing variations and their informational value for person perception. *Journal of Abnormal Social Psychology*, **63**, 302–310.

Jones, L. E. and Young, F. W. (1973). Structure of a social environment: longitudinal individual differences scaling of an intact group. *Journal of Personality and Social Psychology*, **24**, 108–121.

Jones, R. A. and Ashmore, R. D. (1973). The structure of intergroup perception: categories and dimensions in views of ethnic groups and adjectives used in stereotype research. *Journal of Personality and Social Psychology*, **25**, 428–438.

Jones, R. A. and Rosenberg, S. (1974). Structural representations of naturalistic descriptions of personality. *Multivariate Behavioural Research*, **9**, 217–230.

Jones, S. E. and Aiello, J. R. (1973). Proxemic behaviour of black and white first-, third-, and fifth-grade children. *Journal of Personality and Social Psychology*, **25**, 21–27.

Jung, C. G. (1923). "Psychological Types." Harcourt, Brace, Jovanovich, New York.

Kando, T. M. (1977). "Social Interaction." The C. V. Mosby Co., St. Louis.

Kantor, J. R. (1924). "Principles of Psychology," Vol. 1. Principia Press, Bloomington.

Kantor, J. R. (1926). "Principles of Psychology," Vol. 2. Principia Press, Bloomington.

Kantor, J. R. (1969). "The Scientific Evolution of Psychology," Vol. 2. Principia Press, Chicago.

Kaplan, M. F. (1971a). Dispositional effects and weight of information in impression formation. *Journal of Personality and Social Psychology*, **18**, 279–284.

Kaplan, M. F. (1971b). The effect of judgmental dispositions in forming impressions of personality. *Canadian Journal of Behavioural Science*, **3**, 43–51.

Katz, E. W. (1964) "A Content-analytic Method for Studying Interpersonal Behaviour." University of Illinois Technical Report 19.

Kelly, G. A. (1955). "A Theory of Personality: The Psychology of Personal Constructs." Norton, New York.

Kelman, H. C. (1967). Human use of human subjects: the problem of deception in social psychological experiments. *Psychological Bulletin*, **67**, 1–11.

Kelman, H. C. (1972). The rights of the subject in social research: an analysis in terms of relative power and legitimacy. *American Psychologist*, **27**, 989–1016.

Kendon, A., Harris, R. M. and Ritchie, M. (Eds), (1975). "Organisation of Behaviour in Face-to-Face Interaction." Elsevier, Amsterdam.

Klausner, S. Z. (1971). "On Man and His Environment." Jossey-Bass, San Francisco.

Koestler, A. (1967). "The Ghost in the Machine." Macmillan, New York.

Koestler, A. and Smythies, J. R. (1969). "Beyond Reductionism: New Perspectives in the Life Sciences." Macmillan, New York.

Koffka, K. (1935). "Principles of Gestalt Psychology." Harcourt Brace Jovanovich, New York.

Kohlberg, L. (1966). A cognitive-developmental analysis of children's sex-role concepts and attitudes. *In* "The Development of Sex Differences". (E. E. Maccoby, Ed) Stanford University Press, Stanford.

Kohlberg, L. (1969). Stage and sequence: The cognitive-developmental approach to socialisation. *In* "Handbook of Socialisation Theory and Research". (D. A. Goslin, Ed) Rand McNally, Chicago.

Kolb, W. (1944). A critical evaluation of Mead's I and M concepts. *Social Forces*, March, 291–296.

Krause, M. S. (1970). Use of social situations for research purposes. *American Psychologist*, **25**, 748–753.

Kretschmer, E. (1926). "Physique and Character." Harcourt Brace Jovanovich, New York.

Kruskal, J. B. (1964a). Multidimensional scaling by optimizing goodness of fit to a non-metric hypothesis. *Psychometrika*, **29**, 1–27.

Kruskal, J. B. (1964b). Non-metric multidimensional scaling: A numerical method. *Psychometrika*, **29**, 115–129.

Kuhn, T. S. (1962). "The Structure of Scientific Revolutions." University of Chicago Press, Chicago.

Kuhn, M. H. (1970). Major trends in symbolic interaction theory in the past twenty-five years. *In* "Social Psychology through Symbolic Interaction". (G. P. Stone and H. E. Farberman, Eds) Ginn-Blaisdell, Waltham, Mass.

Lalljee, M. (1975). Cognitive aspects in the study of facial expressions of emotion. Mimeo, University of Oxford.

Lapiere, R. T. (1934). Attitudes v. actions. *Social Forces*, **13**, 230–237.

Laumann, E. O. and House, J. S. (1970). Living room styles and social attributes: the patterning of material artefacts in a modern urban community. *Sociological and Social Research*, **54**, 321–342.

Levin, J. (1965). Three-mode factor analysis. *Psychological Bulletin*, **64**, 442–452.

Levine, M. (1974). Scientific method and the adversary model. *American Psychologist*, **29**, 661–677.

Levinger, G. and Snoek, J. (1972). "Attraction in Relationship: A New Look at Interpersonal attraction." General Learning Press, Morristown, New Jersey.

Lewin, K. (1935). "A dynamic theory of personality. Selected Papers." McGraw-Hill, New York.

Lewin, K. (1936). "Principles of Topological Psychology." McGraw-Hill, New York.

Lewin, K. (1938). "The Conceptual Representation and the Measurement of Psychological Forces." Duke University Press, Durham, North Carolina.

Lewin, K. (1948). "Resolving Social Conflicts." Harper, New York.

Lewin, K. (1951). "Field Theory in Social Science. Selected Theoretical Papers." Harper, New York.

Liebman, M. (1970). The effects of sex and race norms on personal space. *Environmental Behaviour*, **2**, 208–246.

Lindesmith, A. R. and Strauss, A. L. (1956). "Social Psychology: The Revised Edition." Holt, Rinehart and Winston, New York.

Linton, R. (1945). "The Cultural Background of Personality." Appleton-Century-Crofts, New York.

Little, K. B. (1965). Personal space. *Journal of Experimental Social Psychology*, **1**, 237–247.

Little, K. B. (1968). Cultural variations in social schemata. *Journal of Personality and Social Psychology*, **10**, 1–7.

Lyman, S. M. and Scott, M. B. (1972). "The Sociology of the Absurd." Appleton-Century-Crofts, New York.

McDougall, W. (1908). "Introduction to Social Psychology." Methuen, London.

McGuire, W. J. (1967). Some impending reorientations in social psychology: Some thoughts provoked by Kenneth Ring. *Journal of Experimental and Social Psychology*, **3**, 124–134.

McGuire, W. J. (1973). The yin and the yang of progress in social psychology: seven koan. *Journal of Personality and Social Psychology*, **26**, 446–456.

Magnusson, D. (1971). An analysis of situational dimensions. *Perceptual and Motor Skills*, **32**, 851–867.

Magnusson, D. (1974). The person and the situation in the traditional measurement model. Reports from the Psychological Laboratories, University of Stockholm, 426.

Magnusson, D. and Ekehammar, B. (1973). An analysis of situational dimensions: a replication. *Multivariate Behavioural Research*, **8**, 331–339.

Magnusson, D. and Ekehammar, B. (1975). Anxiety profiles based on both situational and response factors. *Multivariate Behavioural Research*, **10**, 27–43.

Magnusson, D. and Heffler, B. (1969). The generality of behavioural data. III. Generalization as a function of the number of observational situations. *Multivariate Behavioural Research*, **4**, 29–42.

Magnusson, D., Gerzen, M. and Nyman, B. (1968). The generality of behavioral data. I. Generalization from observations on one occasion. *Multivariate Behavioural Research*, **3**, 295–320.

Mahoney, M. J. (1977). Reflections on the cognitive learning trend in psychotherapy. *American Psychologist*, 5–12.

Marek, J. (1963). Information, perception and social context I: Simple level of perceptual response. *Human Relations*, **16**, 209–231.

Marsh, P., Rosser, E. and Harre, R. (1978). *The Rules of Disorder*. Routledge and Kegan Paul, London.

Marwell, G. and Hage, J. (1970). The organization of role relationships: A systematic description. *American Sociological Review*, **35**, 884–900.

Mausner, B. (1966). Situational and personal factors in social interaction. Office of U.S. Naval Research, (mimeo).

Mead, G. H. (1934). "Mind, Self and Society." University of Chicago Press, Chicago.

Mead, G. H. (1956). "On Social Psychology." (A. Strauss, Ed), University of Chicago Press, Chicago.

Mehrabrian, A. (1972). "Nonverbal Communication." Aldine, Atherton, Chicago.

Mehrabrian, A. and Russell, J. A. (1974). "An Approach to Environmental Psychology." MIT Press, Cambridge, Mass.

Meltzer, B. N. and Petras, J. W. (1972). The Chicago and Iowa schools of symbolic interactionism. *In* "Symbolic Interaction". (S. G. Morris and B. N. Meltzer, Eds), Allyn and Bacon, Boston.

Mennell, S. (1974). "Sociological Theory: Uses and Unities." Praeger Publishers, New York.

Merleau-Ponty, M. (1962). "The Phenomenology of Perception." Routledge and Kegan Paul, London.

Merton, R. K. (1957). "Social Theory and Social Structure" (revised edition). The Free Press, Glencoe.

Milgram, S. (1963). Behavioural study of obedience. *Journal of Abnormal and Social Psychology*, **67**, 371–378.

Milgram, S. (1974). "Obedience to Authority: An Experimental View." Tavistock, London.

Miller, A. G. (1972). Role-playing: An alternative to deception? A review of the evidence. *American Psychologist*, **27**, 623–636.

Miller, A. G. (1976). Constraint and target effects in the attribution of attitudes. *Journal of Experimental and Social Psychology*, **12**, 325–330.

Miller, D. R. (1963). The study of social relationships: Situation, identity, and social interaction. *In* "Psychology: A Study of a Science". (S. Koch, Ed), pp. 639–739. McGraw-Hill, New York.

Mischel, W. (1968). "Personality and Assessment." Wiley, New York.

Mischel, W. (1969). Continuity and change in personality. *American Psychologist*, **24**, 1012–1018.

Mischel, W. (1973). Toward a cognitive social learning reconceptualization of personality. *Psychological Review*, **80**, 252–283.

Mischel, W. (1975). Introduction. *In* "Interactionism in Personality". (Endler, N. S. and Magnusson, D., Eds), Academic Press, London and New York.

Mixon, D. (1972). Instead of deception. *Journal for the Theory of Social Behaviour*, **2**, 145–177.

Mixon, D. (1974). If you don't deceive, what can you do? *In* "Reconstructing Social Psychology". (N. Armistead, Ed), Penguin, Harmondsworth.

Moos, R. H. (1968). Situational analysis of a therapeutic community milieu. *Journal of Abnormal Psychology*, **73**, 49–61.

Moos, R. H. (1969). Sources of variance in responses to questionnaires and in behavior. *Journal of Abnormal Psychology*, **74**, 405–412.

Moos, R. H. (1970). Differential effects of psychiatric ward settings on patient change. *Journal of Nervous and Mental Disease*, **5**, 316–321.

Moos, R. H. (1972). Assessment of the psychosocial environment of community-oriented psychiatric treatment programs. *Journal of Abnormal Psychology*, **79**, 9–18.

Moos, R. H. (1973). Conceptualizations of human environments. *American Psychologist*, **28**, 652–665.

Moos, R. H. (1974). "Evaluating Treatment Environments: A Social Ecological Approach." Wiley, New York.

Moos, R. H. and Clemes, S. (1967). Multivariate study of the patient–therapist system. *Journal of Consulting Psychology*, **31**, 119–130.

Moos, R. H. and Daniels, D. (1967). Differential effects of ward settings on psychiatric staff. *Archives of General Psychiatry*, **17**, 75–83.

Moos, R. H. and Houts, P. S. (1968). Assessment of the social atmospheres of psychiatric wards. *Journal of Abnormal Psychology*, **73**, 595–604.

Moreno, J. L. (1951). "Sociometry: Experimental Method and the Science of Society." Beacon House, New York.

Morris, C. (1946). "Signs, Language and Behaviour". Prentice-Hall, London.

Moscovici, S. (1972). Society and theory in social psychology. *In* "The Context of Social Psychology: A Critical Assessment". (J. Israel and H. Tajfel, Eds), Academic Press, New York.

Moscovici, S. and Zavallloni, M. (1969). The group as a polariser of attitudes. *Journal of Personality and Social Psychology*, **12**, 125–135.

Mullins, N. C. (1973). *Theories and Theory Groups in Contemporary American Sociology*. Harper and Row, New York.

Murphy, G. (1947). "Personality: A Biosocial Approach to Origins and Structure." Harper, New York.

Murray, H. A. (1938). "Explorations in Personality." Oxford University Press, Oxford and New York.

Murray, H. A. (1951). Toward a classification of interaction. *In* "Toward a General Theory of Action". (T. Parsons and E. A. Shils, Eds), Harvard University Press, Cambridge, Mass.

Myers, A. and Myers, G. E. (1972). Discussion of papers on nonverbal communication. *Comparative Group Studies*, **3**, 487–496.

Nelson, E. A., Grinder, R. E. and Mutterer, M. L. (1969). Sources of variance in behavioural measures of honesty in temptation situations: methodological analyses. *Developmental Psychology*, **1**, 265–279.

Newcomb, T. M. (1943). "Personality and Social Change." Dryden, New York.

Newcomb, T. M. (1950). "Social Psychology." Holt, Rinehart and Winston, New York.

Newcomb, T. M. (1953). An approach to the study of communicative acts. *Psychological Review*, **60**, 393–404.

Newtson, D. (1973). Attribution and the unit of perception of ongoing behaviour. *Journal of Personality and Social Psychology*, **28**, 28–38.

Newtson, D. (1976). Foundations of attribution: the unit of perception of ongoing behaviour. *In* "New Directions in Attribution Research". (J. Harvey, W. Ickey and R. Kidd, Eds), Erlbaum, Hillsdale, New Jersey.

Newtson, D. (1976). Meaning in ongoing behaviour: the second derivative of movement. Paper presented at APA Symposium, Social Behaviour as a Process Over Time, Washington.

Newtson, D. and Engquist, G. (1976). The perceptual organisation of ongoing behaviour. *Journal of Experimental and Social Psychology*, **12**, 436–450.

Newtson, D., Engquist, G. and Bois. (1965). The objective basis of behaviour units. *Journal of Personality and Social Psychology*, **35**, 847–867.

Nisbet, R. (1965). "Emile Durkheim." Prentice-Hall, Englewood Cliffs, N.J.

Orne, M. T. (1962). On the social psychology of the psychological experiment: with particular reference to demand characteristics and their implications. *American Psychologist*, **17**, 776–783.

Osgood, C. E. and Suci, G. J. (1952). A measure of relation determined by both mean differences and profile information. *Psychological Bulletin*, **49**, 251–262.

Osgood, C. E., Suci, G. J. and Tannenbaum, P. H. (1957). *The Measurement of Meaning*. University of Illinois Press, Urbana.

Pace, C. R. (1968). The measurement of college environments. *In* "Organizational Climate: Explorations of a Concept". (R. Tagiuri and G. H. Litwin, Eds), Graduate School of Business Administration, Harvard University, Boston.

Pace, C. R. and Stern, G. G. (1958). An approach to the measurement of psychological characteristics of college environments. *Journal of Educational Psychology*, **49**, 269–277.

Paden, J. N. (1967). Situational ethnicity in urban Africa with special reference to the Hausa. Paper presented at the African Studies Association Meeting, New York.

Parsons, T. (1937). "The Structure of Social Action." McGraw-Hill, New York.

Parsons, T. (1951) "The Social System." Free Press, New York.

Patterson, M. L. (1973). Compensation in nonverbal immediacy behaviours: A review. *Sociometry*, **36**, 237–252.

Payne, R. L. and Pugh, D. S. (1976). Organisational structure and organisational climate. *In* "Handbook of Industrial and Organisational Psychology". (M. D. Dunnette, Ed), Rand-McNally, Chicago.

Pearce, W. B. (1976). The co-ordinated management of meaning: a rules-based theory of interpersonal communication. Mimeo, Department of Communication, University of Massachusetts.

Pervin, L. A. (1968). Performance and satisfaction as a function of individual environment fit. *Psychological Bulletin*, **69**, 56–68.

Pervin, L. A. (1975a). The representative design in person–situation research. Symposium on Interactional Psychology, Stockholm, June 1975.

Pervin, L. A. (1975b). A free-response description approach to the analysis of person–situation interaction. Educational Testing Service Research Bulletin, No. 22, Princeton, New Jersey.

Pervin, L. A. (1975c). Definitions, measurements and classifications of stimuli, situations and environments. Educational Testing Service Research Bulletin, No. 23, Princeton, New Jersey.

Pervin, L. A. (1976). A free-response description approach to the study of person–situation interaction. *Journal of Personality and Social Psychology*, **34**, 465–474.

Peterson, D. R. (1965). Scope and generality of verbally defined personality factors. *Psychological Review*, **72**, 48–59.

Peterson, D. R. (1968). "The Clinical Study of Social Behavior." Appleton-Century-Crofts, New York.

Piaget, J. (1952). "The Origins of Intelligence in Children." International University Press, New York.

Pollner, M. (1975). Sociological and common-sense models of the labelling process. *In* "Ethnomethodology". (R. Turner, Ed), Penguin, Harmondsworth.

Popper, K. (1959). "The Logic of Scientific Discovery." Basic Books, New York.

Popper, K. (1963). "Conjectures and Refutations." Routledge and Kegan Paul, London.

Popper, K. (1970). Normal science and its dangers. *In* "Criticism and the Growth of Knowledge". (Lakatos and Musgrove, Eds), Cambridge University Press, Cambridge.

Popper, K. (1972). "Objective Knowledge: An Evolutionary Approach." Clarendon, Oxford.

Postman, L. and Tolman, E. C. (1959). Brunswik's probabilistic functionalism. *In* "Psychology: The Study of a Science". (S. Koch, Ed), McGraw-Hill, New York.

Price, R. H. (1974). The taxonomic classification of behaviors and situations and the problem of behavior-environment congruence. *Human Relations*, **27**, 567–585.

Price, R. H. and Bouffard, D. L. (1974). Behavioral appropriateness and situational constraint as dimensions of social behavior. *Journal of Personality and Social Psychology*, **30**, 579–586.

Proshansky, H. M. (1976). Environmental psychology and the real world. *American Psychologist*, **31**, 303–310.

Proshansky, H. M., Ittelson, W. H. and Rivlin, L. G. (Eds). (1970). "Environmental Psychology: Man and his Physical Setting." Holt, Rinehart and Winston, New York.

Pruitt, D. (1971). Choice shifts in group discussion: an introductory review. *Journal of Personality and Social Psychology*, **20**, 339–366.

Quine, W. V. (1969). "Ontological Relativity." Columbia University Press, New York.

Raush, H. L. (1965). Interaction sequences. *Journal of Personality and Social Psychology*, **2**, 487–499.

Raush, H. L. (1972). Process and change. *Family Processes*, **11**, 275–298.

Raush, H. L., Dittman, A. T. and Taylor, T. J. (1959a). The interpersonal behavior of children in residential treatment. *Journal of Abnormal and Social Psychology*, **58**, 9–26.

Raush, H. L., Dittmann, A. T. and Taylor, T. J. (1959b). Person setting and change in social interaction. *Human Relations*, **12**, 361–378.

Raush, H. L., Farbman, I. and Llewellyn, L. G. (1960). Person, setting and change in social interaction: II. A normal control study. *Human Relations*, **13**, 305–333.

Reinhardt, J. M. (1937). Personality traits and the situation. *American Journal of Sociology*, **2**, 492–500.

Ring, K. (1967). Experimental social psychology: Some sober questions about some frivolous issues. *Journal of Experimental Social Psychology*, **3**, 113–123.

Robinson, P. (1972). "Language and Social Behaviour." Penguin, Harmondsworth.

Robinson, P. (1977). The rise of rule: Mode or node? *In* "Social Rules and Social Behaviour". (P. Collett, Ed), Blackwell, Oxford.

Rock, D. A., Baird, L. L. and Linn, R. L. (1972). Interaction between college effects and students' aptitudes. *American Educational Research Journal*, **9**, 110–121.

Rogers, C. R. (1951). "Client-Centered Therapy: Its Current Practice, Implications and Theory." Houghton Mifflin, Boston.

Rogers, C. R. (1959). A theory of therapy, personality and interpersonal relationships, as developed in the client-centered framework. *In* "Psychology: A Study of a Science". Vol. 3, pp. 184–256. (S. Koch, Ed), McGraw-Hill, New York.

Rokeach, M. (1973). "The Nature of Human Values." Free Press, New York.

Rosenberg, S. and Jones, R. A. (1972). A method for investigating and representing a person's implicit theory of personality: Theodore Dreiser's view of people. *Journal of Personality and Social Psychology*, **22**, 372–386.

Rosenberg, S. and Sedlak, A. (1972). Structural representations of implicit personality theory. *Advances in Experimental Social Psychology*, **6**, 235–297.

Rosenthal, R. (1966). "Experimenter Effects in Behavioural Research." Appleton-Century-Crofts, New York.

Rosenthal, R. and Rosnow, R. L. (Eds), (1969). "Artifact in Behavioural Research." Academic Press, New York and London.

Rosnow, R. L., Goodstadt, B. E., Suls, J. M. and Gitter, A. J. (1973). More on the social psychology of experiment: when compliance turns to self-defence. *Journal of Personality and Social Psychology*, **27**, 337–343.

Ross, E. A. (1908). "Social Psychology." McMillan, New York.

Rotter, J. B. (1954). "Social Learning and Clinical Psychology." Prentice-Hall, New York.

Rotter, J. B. (1955). The role of the psychological situation in determining the direction of human behavior. *In* "Nebraska Symposium on Motivation". pp. 345–368. (M. R. Jones, Ed), University of Nebraska Press, Lincoln, Nebraska.

Sakoda, J. M. (1952). Factor analysis of Oss situational tests. *Journal of Abnormal and Social Psychology*, **47**, 843–852.

Sandell, R. G. (1968). Effects of attitudinal and situational factors on reported choice behavior. *Journal of Marketing Research*, **5**, 405–408.

Sargent, S. S. (1965). Discussion of Gardner Murphy's paper. *In* "Perspectives in Social Psychology". (O. Klineberg and R. Ainslie, Eds), Holt, Rinehart and Winston, New York.

Scheflen, A. E. (1964). The significance of posture in communication systems. *Psychiatry*, **27**, 316–331.

Scheflen, A. E. (1971). Living space in an urban ghetto. *Family Process*, **10**, 429–450.

Scheflen, A. E. (1972). "Communicational Structure: Analysis of a Psychotherapy Transaction." Indiana University Press, Bloomington.

Schlenker, B. R. (1974). Social psychology and science. *Journal of Personality and Social Psychology*, **29**, 1–15.

Schlenker, B. R. (1977). On the ethogenic approach: etiquette and revolution. *In* "Advances in Experimental Social Psychology". (L. Berkowitz, Ed), **10**, 315–330.

Schneider, D. J. and Miller, R. S. (1975). The effects of enthusiasm and quality of arguments on attitude attribution. *Journal of Personality*, **43**, 693–708.

Schutz, A. (1970). "On Phenomenology and Social Relations." (H. R. Wagner, Ed), University of Chicago Press, Chicago.

Scott, W. A. (1969). Structure of natural cognitions. *Journal of Personality and Social Psychology*, **12**, 261–278.

Scott, W. A. (1962). Cognitive complexity and cognitive flexibility. *Sociometry*, **25**, 405–414.

Scott, W. A. (1963). Cognitive complexity and cognitive balance. *Sociometry*, **26**, 66–74.

Scott, W. A. (1978). Sociometric indices of group structure. *Australian Journal of Psychology*, **30**, 41–57.

Seligman, M. (1976). The generality of laws of learning. *Psychological Review*, **77**, 406–418.

Sells, S. B. (Ed). (1963). "Stimulus Determinants of Behaviour." Ronald, New York.

Sells, S. B. (1973). Prescriptions for a multivariate model in personality and psychological theory: ecological considerations. *In* "Multivariate Analysis and Psychological Theory". (J. P. Royce, Ed), Academic Press, London.

Sheldon, W. H. (1949). "Varieties of Delinquent Youth." Harper and Brothers, New York.

Sherif, M. (1935). A study of some social factors in perception. *Archives of Psychology*, **27**, 1–60.

Sherif, M. and Sherif, C. W. (1956). "An Outline of Social Psychology." Harper and Brothers, New York.

Sherif, M. and Sherif, C. W. (1963). Varieties of social stimulus situations. *In* "Stimulus Determinants of Behaviour". pp. 82–106. (S. B. Sells, Ed), Ronald, New York.

Sherif, M. and Sherif, C. W. (1969). "Social Psychology." Harper and Row, New York.

Sherif, M., Harvey, O. J., White, B. J., Hood, W. E. and Sherif, C. W. (1961). "Intergroup Conflict and Cooperation: The Robbers' Cave Experiment." University of Oklahoma Book Exchange, Norman, Oklahoma.

Sherman, R. C. and Dowdle, M. D. (1974). The perception of crime and punishment: a multidimensional scaling analysis. *Social Science Research*, **3**, 109–126.

Shor, R. E. (1957). Effect of preinformation upon human characteristics attributed to animated geometric figures. *Journal of Abnormal and Social Psychology*, **54**, 124–126.

Skinner, B. F. (1971). "Beyond Freedom and Dignity." Knopf, New York.

Smith, M. B. (1972). Is experimental social psychology advancing? *Journal of Experimental Social Psychology*, **8**, 86–96.

Snygg, D. (1941). The need for a phenomenological system of psychology. *Psychological Review*, **48**, 404–423.

Sommer, R. (1969). *Personal Space*. Prentice-Hall, Englewood Cliffs, New Jersey.

Spence, I. and Domoney, D. W. (1974). Incomplete designs for nonmetric multidimensional scaling. *Psychometrika*, **39**, 469–490.

Spence, I. and Ogilvie, J. (1973). A table of expected stress values for random rankings in nonmetric multidimensional scaling. *Multivariate Behavioural Research*, **8**, 511–517.

Spielberger, C. D. (1966). Theory and research on anxiety. *In* "Anxiety and Behavior". (C. D. Spielberger, Ed), Academic Press, New York and London.

Spielberger, C. D. (1972). Anxiety as an emotional state. *In* "Anxiety: Current Trends in Theory and Research", Vol. 1. (C. D. Spielberger, Ed), Academic Press, New York and London.

Spielberger, C. D. (1975). Implications of the state-trait conception for interactional psychology. Stockholm Conference on Interactional Psychology.

Stanton, A. and Schwartz, M. (1954). "The Mental Hospital: A Study of Institutional Participation in Psychiatric Illness and Treatment." Basic Books, New York.

Staples, L. M. and Robinson, W. P. (1973). Address forms used by members of a department store. *British Journal of Social and Clinical Psychology*.

Stern, G. G. (1970). "People in Context: Measuring Person-Environment Congruence in Education and Industry." Wiley, New York.

Stern, G. G., Stein, M. J. and Bloom, B. S. (1956). "Methods in Personality Assessment." Free Press, Glencoe, Ill.

Stone, G. P. and Farberman, H. E. (Eds). (1970). "Social Psychology Through Symbolic Interaction." Ginn-Blaisdell, Waltham, Mass.

Stotland, E. and Kobler, A. (1965). "Life and Death of a Mental Hospital." University of Washington Press, Seattle.

Stricker, L. J., Messick, S. and Jackson, D. N. (1967). Suspicion of deception: Implications for conformity research. *Journal of Personality and Social Psychology*, **5**, 379–389.

Swanson, G. E. (1968). Review symposium of Harold Garfinkel's "Studies in ethnomethodology." *American Sociological Review*, **33**, 122–124.

Tagiuri, R. (1968). Person perception. *In* "The Handbook of Social Psychology (2nd ed.) Vol. III. pp. 395–449. (G. Lindzey and E. Aronson, Eds), Addison-Wesley, Reading, Mass.

Tagiuri, R. and Petrullo, L. (Eds). (1958). "Person Perception and Interpersonal Behaviour." Stanford University Press, Stanford.

Tajfel, H. (1969). Social and cultural factors in perception. *In* "The Handbook of

Social Psychology", Vol. III, (2nd ed.) (G. Lindsey and E. Aronson, Eds), Addison-Wesley, Reading, Mass.

Tannenbaum, P. H. and McLeod, M. (1967). On the measurement of socialisation. *Public Opinion Quarterly*, **31**, 27–37.

Thayer, S. and Schiff, W. (1969). Stimulus factors in observer judgment of social interaction: facial expression and motion pattern. *The American Journal of Psychology*, **81**, 73–83.

Thayer, S. and Schiff, W. (1973). Observer Judgment of social interaction: eye control and relationship inference. *Journal of Personality and Social Psychology*, **30**, 110–114.

Thomas, W. I. (1923). "The Unadjusted Girl." Ginn, Boston.

Thomas, W. I. (1928a). "The Child in America." Knopf, New York.

Thomas, W. I. (1928b). Situational analysis: the behaviour pattern and the situation. *Reprinted in* "W. I. Thomas on Social Organisation and Social Personality." (M. Janowitz, Ed), University of Chicago Press, Chicago.

Tinbergen, N. (1965). "Social Behaviour in Animals." Methuen, London.

Tolman, E. C. (1935). Psychology versus immediate experience. *In* "Collected Papers in Psychology." University of California Press, Berkeley. (Reprinted from *Philosophy of Science*, **1935**, 356–380.)

Tolman, E. C. (1948). Cognitive maps in rats and men. *Psychological Review*, **55**, 189–208.

Tolman, E. C. (1949). The psychology of social learning. *Journal of Social Issues*, **5**, Supplement Series No. 3.

Torgerson, W. S. (1965). Multidimensional scaling of similarity. *Psychometrika*, **30**, 379–393.

Triandis, H. C. (1972). "The Analysis of Subjective Culture." Wiley-Interscience, New York.

Triandis, H. C. (1975). Social psychology and cultural analysis. *Journal for the Theory of Social Behaviour*, **5**, 81–106.

Triandis, H. C. and Vassiliou, V. (1967). "A comparative analysis of subjective culture." University of Illinois, Technical Report No. 55.

Triandis, H. C., Vassiliou, V. and Nassiaku, M. (1968). Three cross-cultural studies of subjective culture. *Journal of Personality and Social Psychology*, Monograph Supplement, **8**, (4), 2, 1–42.

Trower, P., Bryant, B. and Argyle, M. (1978). "Social Skills and Mental Health." Methuen, London.

Tuan, Y. F. (1972). Environmental psychology: A review. *Geographical Review*, **62**, (2), 1–12.

Tucker, L. R. (1964). The extension of factor analysis to three-dimensional matrices. *In* "Contributions to Mathematical Psychology". (N. Frederiksen and H. Gulliksen, Eds), Holt, Rinehart and Winston, New York.

Tucker, L. R. and Messick, J. (1963). An individual differences model for multidimensional scaling. *Psychometrika*, **28**, 333–367.

Tversky, A. (1977). Features of similarity. *Psychological Review*, **84**, 327–352.

Vernon, P. E. (1964). *Personality Assessment: A Critical Survey*. Wiley, New York.

Wachtel, P. (1973a). Psychodynamics, behavior therapy and the implacable experimenter: An inquiry into the consistency of personality. *Journal of Abnormal Psychology*, **82**, 324–334.

Wachtel, P. L. (1973b). On fact, hunch, and stereotype: A reply to Mischel. *Journal of Abnormal Psychology*, **82**, 537–540.

Wagner, H. R. (Ed). (1970). "Alfred Schutz on Phenomenology and Social Relations." University of Chicago Press, Chicago.

Wallace, P. E. C. (1968). Review symposium of Harold Garfinkel's "Studies in ethnomethodology." *American Sociological Review*, **33**, 124–126.

Waller, W. (1961). "The Sociology of Teaching." John Wiley and Sons, New York.

Warr, P. (1973a). Towards a more human psychology. *Bulletin of the British Psychological Society*, **26**, 1–8.

Warr, P. (1973b). Better working lives: A university psychologist's view. *Occupational Psychology*, **47**, 15–22.

Warr, P. (1977). Aided experiments in social psychology. *Bulletin of the British Psychological Society*, **30**, 2–8.

Warr, P. and Knapper, C. (1968). "The Perception of People and Events." John Wiley and Sons, London.

Watson, J. B. (1913). Psychology as the behaviourist views it. *Psychological Review*, **20**, 158–177.

Watson, J. B. (1919). "Psychology from the Standpoint of a Behaviourist." Lippincott, Philadelphia.

Watson, J. and Potter, R. J. (1962). An analytic unit for the study of interaction. *Human Relations*, **15**, 245–263.

Watson, S. G. (1972). Judgment of emotion from facial and contextual cue combinations. *Journal of Personality and Social Psychology*, **24**, 334–342.

Weber, M. (1947). "The Theory of Social and Economic Organisation." (A. M. Henderson and T. Parsons, trans.), (T. Parsons, Ed), Free Press, Glencoe, Ill.

Weber, M. (1968). "Economy and Society." Bedminster Press, New York.

Werdelin, I. (1975). "Factor analyses of an inventory of behaviour in social situations." Mimeo, Department of Educational and Psychological Research, School of Education, Malmö, Sweden.

Wicker, A. W. (1968). Undermanning, performances, and students' subjective experiences in behaviour settings of large and small high schools. *Journal of Personality and Social Psychology*, **10**, 255–261.

Wicker, A. W. (1972). Processes which mediate behaviour: environment congruence. *Behavioral Science*, **17**, 265–277.

Wish, M. (1974). "Role and personal expectations about interpersonal communication." Mimeo, The Bell Laboratories.

Wish, M. (1975). Subjects' expectations about their own interpersonal communication: a multidimensional approach. *Personality and Social Psychology Bulletin*, **1**, 11–20.

Wish, M. (1976). "Perceptions of interpersonal relations." Mimeo, The Bell Laboratories.

Wish, M., Deutsch, M. and Biener, L. (1970). Differences in conceptual structures of nations: An exploratory study. *Journal of Personality and Social Psychology*, **16**, 361–373.

Wish, M., Deutsch, M. and Kaplan, S. J. (1976). Perceived dimensions of interpersonal relations. *Journal of Personality and Social Psychology*, **33**, 409–420.

Wohlwill, J. and Carson, D. H. (Eds). (1972). "Environment and the Social Sciences: Perspectives and Applications." American Psychological Association, Washington, D.C.

Wolff, K. H. (1964). Definition of the situation. *In* "A Dictionary of the Social Sciences". (J. Gould and W. K. Kolb, Eds), The Free Press, New York.

Wools, R. and Canter, D. (1970). The effect of the meaning of buildings on behaviour. *Applied Ergonomics*, **1**, 144–150.

Wolpe, J. (1958). "Psychotherapy by Reciprocal Inhibition." Stanford University Press, Stanford.

Wolpe, J. (1969). "The Practice of Behaviour Therapy." Pergamon Press, New York.

Wright, H. F. (1970). "Children in the Smalltown and Largetown U.S.A.: A Summary of Studies in the Ecological Psychology of Community Size." University of Kansas, Lawrence.

Wuebben, P. L., Straits, B. C. and Schulman, G. I. (1974). "The Experiment as a Social Occasion." The Glendessary Press, Berkeley, California.

Wyer, R. S. (1970). Information redundancy, inconsistency and novelty and their role in impression formation. *Journal of Experimental Social Psychology*, **6**, 111–127.

Young, F. W. (1970). Nonmetric multidimensional scaling: recovery of metric information. *Psychometrika*, **35**, 455–473.

Young, F. W. and Cliff, N. (1972). Interactive scaling with individual subjects. *Psychometrika*, **37**, 385–415.

Young, F. W., Takane, Y. and Lewyckyi, P. (1978). Three notes on ALSCAL. *Psychometrika*, 1978 (in press).

Zimbardo, P. G. (1973). A Pirandellian Prison. *New York Times Sunday Magazine*, **April 8**, 38–60.

Znaniecki, F. (1969). "On Humanistic Sociology." University of Chicago Press, Chicago.

Subject Index